Zohar, Bereshith to Lekh Lekha

Or, Book of Light

Translated by

Nurho de Manhar

First published in 1900-14

Published by Left of Brain Books

Copyright © 2023 Left of Brain Books

ISBN 978-1-397-66988-9

First Edition

All rights reserved. No part of this publication may be reproduced, distributed, or transmitted in any form or by any means, including photocopying, recording, or other electronic or mechanical methods, without the prior written permission of the publisher, except in the case of brief quotations permitted by copyright law. Left of Brain Books is a division of Left Of Brain Onboarding Pty Ltd.

PUBLISHER'S PREFACE

About the Book

"This is the only extensive translation of a portion of the Zohar, the longest and one of the most important texts of the Kabbalah[..]

The Zohar is a Kabbalistic commentary on the Hebrew Bible. Long before the 'Bible Code,' Jewish scholars were attempting to wring deep meaning out of every syllable of the text of the Hebrew Bible, using numerology, gematria, and other techniques. Dozens of pages in this book are devoted to analyses of the hidden meaning behind first few letters of Genesis! This might seem ultra-pedantic; however, the Zohar makes the Biblical text come to life, brimming with mystical significance. Seemingly unimportant details and turns of phrase, which you may have read long ago and forgotten, lead to immense vistas of a mysterious world inside the world.

This is not a critical edition; written by a pseudonymous Theosophist, probably British, it is laced with out-of-place terminology such as 'Karma' and 'Planes.' It nevertheless lets you wade in the rip current of one of the most magical of the world's sacred texts, and leaves you gasping for air and wanting more."

(Quote from sacred-texts.com)

CONTENTS

PUBLISHER'S PREFACE
PREFACE 1
INTRODUCTION 31
    THE LILY.. 32
    THE OCCULT ORIGIN OF ALHIM 36
    THE MYSTICISM OF THE ALPHABET... 40
    THE INITIATION OF RABBI HIYA 44
    THE MYSTERIOUS STRANGER.. 49
    ABUNDANT GOODNESS 58
    EXPOSITION OF BIBLE MYSTERIES 61
    THE FOURTEEN PRECEPTS... 71
GENESIS 82
    CHAPTER I. 83
    CHAPTER II. 95
    CHAPTER III. 101
    CHAPTER IV. 110
    THE KING'S PALACES 119
    ON ISRAEL OR THE CHILDREN OF LIGHT 122
    THE PRAYER OF RABBI SIMEON 123
    PREVIOUS WORLDS AND RACES 125
    CHAPTER IX. 129
    SYMBOLISMS OF MAN 132
    THE STRANGE VISITOR 135
    SYMBOLISM OF THE DIVINE LIFE AND HUMAN DESTINY 138
    CHAPTER XIII. 144
    A KABBALISTIC SYMPOSIUM BY RABBI SIMEON'S STUDENTS 154
    CHAPTER XV. 157
    A SYMPOSIUM OF RABBI SIMEON'S STUDENTS 163
    THE DEVACHANIC OR HEAVENLY SPHERES...................................... 171
    HIGHER DEVACHANIC OR HEAVENLY SPHERES 177
    RABBI SIMEON'S DISCOURSE ON PRAYER... 182
    DEVACHANIC SPHERES AND MANSIONS 186
    CHAPTER XXI. 190
    CHAPTER XXII. 193
    CHAPTER XXIII. 195
    FURTHER KABBALISTIC EXPOSITIONS OF THE SIX DAYS OF CREATION 200
    CHAPTER XXV. 204

CHAPTER XXVI.	206
CHAPTER XXVII.	211
RABBI SIMEON'S ANALOGIES OF THE DIVINE LIFE IN MAN	215
CHAPTER XXIX.	217
THE TWO SERPENTS, ASTRAL FLUID AND THE ANIMAL NATURE	220
A FURTHER SYMPOSIUM OF RABBI SIMEON'S STUDENTS	223
CHAPTER XXXII.	229
TRADITIONS CONCERNING ADAM	233
MALE AND FEMALE CREATED HE THEM	235
THE ANTEDILUVIANS AND THEIR MAGICAL ARTS	236
CHAPTER XXXVI.	239
OF THE PATRIARCH HENOCH AND THE SIN OF THE ANTEDILUVIANS	240
THE DIVINE COMPASSION	242
CHAPTER XXXIX.	245
TRADITIONS CONCERNING NOAH	247
CHAPTER XLI.	250
CHAPTER XLII.	255
CHAPTER XLIII.	259
CHAPTER XLIV.	267
KABBALISTIC EXPLANATION OF THE FEAST OF TABERNACLES AND THE LOULAB	269
THE OCCULTISM OF SACRIFICES	271
A VEXATA QUESTIO IN BIBLICAL PHILOLOGY	274
KABBALISTIC EXPLANATION OF THE GOAT AZAZEL	276
RABBI SIMEON'S REFLECTIONS ON THE SUPREME AND ITS UNION WITH HUMAN SOULS	278
CHAPTER L.	280
THE OCCULT MEANING OF THE SIX HUNDRED YEARS OF NOAH'S LIFE	281
ADAM SITTING AT THE GATE OF THE GARDEN OF EDEN	283
REMARKS ON THE DESTROYING ANGEL AND THE ANTEDILUVIANS	285
KABBALISTIC REMARKS ON THE COVENANT OR UNION OF THE HIGHER AND LOWER SELF	287
VARIOUS KABBALISTIC EXPOSITIONS OF BIBLICAL TEXTS	289
THE DIVINE LEHAEROT ON EZECHIEL'S VISIONS	291
THE MYSTERY OF THE BOW IN THE CLOUD	293
RABBI JEHUDA'S DISCUSSION WITH THE MERCHANT, ON JACOB'S PILLAR	296
THE SYMBOLISM OF THE FOUNDATION STONE	298
RABBI SIMEON ON MYSTERIES AND THE HIGHER LIFE	301
SYMBOLISM OF THE COLORS OF THE BOW IN THE CLOUD	303
THE MYSTERY OF THE CURSING OF CANAAN BY NOAH	304
REMARKS ON PREDESTINATION	306
CHAPTER LXIV.	308
THE THAUMATURGICAL ERECTION OF SOLOMON'S TEMPLE	309
THE MYSTERY OF THE LOGOS	311
THE IDOLATRY OF THE POSTDILUVIANS	313
THE TOWER OF BABEL	315

A COMPARISON BETWEEN NOAH AND MOSES	317
WHY THE ANIMAL WAS DESTROYED BY THE DELUGE	321
THE GILGAL OR REVOLUTION ANIMARUM	325
AND EVERY LIVING SUBSTANCE WAS DESTROYED WHICH WAS UPON THE FACE OF THE GROUND. GEN. VII. 23	327
WHAT TWO RABBIS LEARNED FROM A YOUTH	330
CHAPTER LXXIV.	335
COMPARISON BETWEEN ADAM AND THE POSTDILUVIANS	337
RABBI SIMEON ON THE CLOSING OF THE SANCTUARY	338
THE OBJECT OF BUILDING THE TOWER OF BABEL	339
THE PRIMEVAL LANGUAGE AND THE BOOK OF ADAM	340
ON WORDS AND THE PHILOSOPHY OF SOUND	342
SECTION LEKH LEKHA OR THE CALL OF ABRAM	345
INTERLOCUTORY EXPLANATIONS	348
ABRAHAM'S FIRST STUDIES IN OCCULTISM	350
ABRAHAM'S INITIATION INTO THE LESSER MYSTERIES	355
ABRAHAM'S DESCENT INTO EGYPT FOR INITIATION INTO THE HIGHER MYSTERIES	358
CHAPTER LXXXV.	359
KABBALISTIC COSMOLOGY	362
KABBALISTIC PHILOSOPHY OF THE SOUL	366
ABRAHAM'S INITIATORY PROBATION	370
THE ESOTERIC EXPLANATION OF LOT'S PARTING FROM ABRAHAM	372
REMARKS ON THE SCHEKINA	374
RABBI ELEAZAR AND RABBI HEZEKIAH, AND THEIR NOCTURNAL STUDIES	377
RABBI JOSE ON THE SEVEN HEAVENS OR FIRMAMENTS	380
KABBALISTIC REMARKS ON MARRIAGE	382
ON THE STUDY OF THE SECRET DOCTRINE	383
RABBI ABBA'S VISIT AND WHAT OCCURRED	385
A FEAST OF THE CIRCUMCISION	388
CHAPTER XCVII.	391
CHAPTER XCVIII.	397
A FEAST OF CIRCUMCISION (CONTINUED)	402
CHAPTER C.	405
RABBI ABBA'S PUNISHMENT	407

PREFACE

AS a preliminary to the translation of the great Kabbalistic work, "The Sepher Zohar, or Book of Light," we purpose to sketch in brief outline the history of its origin, the nature and purpose of its doctrines and teachings, as also the great influence of its philosophy which is reflected in the writings of Albert the Great, Reuchlin, Raymond Lully, Boehmen, More the Platonist, Spinoza, Balzac, and many others whose names are famous in the annals of literature and learning. To the readers of the late Madame Blavatsky's works, "Isis Unveiled" and "The Secret Doctrine," this will doubtless prove acceptable and enable them to understand and comprehend those parts in which she has incorporated the philosophy respecting the Sephiroth and shown its close similarity in many of its aspects with Eastern teachings. There is scarcely a page in which some reference to it is not found, with Hebrew words, the explanation of which would have enhanced the value of the above works and added to the enjoyment and edification of theosophical students in general. To supply this desideratum it will be necessary to give details respecting Kabbalah of which the Zohar is justly considered to be the prolific fountain from which has flowed that stream of occult philosophy that has entered so largely as an element in the teachings of mystics of ancient and modern times.

The ancient Jews were not different from other nations in having occult schools and institutions in which secret doctrines were inculcated and imparted to neophytes, or the sons of the prophets, as they are termed in the Bible. These teachings were twofold in their nature and character, and denominated Beresith, or the science of the natural world; also Mercaba, which had relation to heavenly or spiritual science, and which was esteemed and regarded as most sacred and never to be revealed except to initiates, and then only orally, as amongst the ancient Druids. That which was received was termed "Kabbalah," a Hebrew word, signifying reception, or, rather, what is received and handed on to others in short aphorisms and mnemonical words, the meaning of which could only be deciphered and comprehended by those who had successfully passed through a long course of esoteric studies. For instance, A D M, or Adam, taught that the soul of Adam the first was incarnated in David the King and will eventually appear in the form of the Messiah. It is said that Kabbalah first originated after the expulsion of Adam from the Garden of Eden, and was communicated to him by the angel Raziel in order that he might be better able, through attending to its teachings, to regain his lost estate. The common tradition and most generally accepted is that Moses himself was the real author of Kabbalah, having received it during his residence of forty days and nights on Mount Sinai. After his descent therefrom he imparted it to Aaron, who in turn handed it on to his sons, through whom it was given to the seventy elders of the children of Israel and coadjutors of Moses in juridical government and polity. Through the judges, especially the prophet Samuel, it was delivered to David and Solomon, the latter becoming renowned throughout the East for his extensive and profound knowledge of Kabbalah, by which he was able to perform marvelous things and acquire control over all beings, demons, spirits of the air, fire and water, and make them his obedient and subservient ministers.

During the reigns of the various kings of Israel and Judah we gather that this Kabbalah was widely taught and studied in the schools or colleges of the prophets, presided over by hierophants, of whom Elijah and Elisha were remarkable examples, and distinguished not only by their loftiness of character, but also for their knowledge and manipulation of nature's occult forces and powers, by which they stand out boldly and prominently in Jewish history. These occult societies were generally distinguished by the wearing of some special badge or emblem indicative of the peculiar occultism of which they were the professed followers and adherents, such as a raven or hawk, eagle or dove, a lion, a wolf, an ox or a lamb. Their members, whenever sent out on any benevolent expedition or political mission, always went in couples, similar to the rule of custom in vogue at the present time with monks and nuns in the Roman Catholic community. From this fact we obtain a satisfactory and rational explanation of the extraordinary and miraculous feeding of Elijah by two ravens, who brought him in his place of retirement and concealment bread and meat for his daily sustenance. Instead of two birds noted for their thievish propensities, we see how two members of an occult school, who were perfectly acquainted with the whereabouts of Elijah, and so ministered to the bodily wants and necessities of their great hierophant. It is also related of Alexander the Great, on his entering into one of the chief cities of Egypt, that he was welcomed by twelve doves at the head of a large procession of the citizens, and who greeted his presence with some remarkable signs of congratulation, the strangeness of which vanishes and disappears when we recognize in these doves members of some occult institution held in veneration by the general populace, and thus qualified to be the exponents of their good wishes and feelings toward the conquering Alexander. The Babylonian captivity brought the Jews into immediate contact with Chaldean and Persian philosophy, which introduced a great change in their speculative ideas of the creation and divine government of the world, Chaldean magic and occult science became objects of deep interest and study, and ultimately resulted in the formation of new societies and sodalities, in which secret rites and ceremonies were performed and celebrated. All knowledge of their teachings was jealously guarded, and their members were bound by the most solemn oaths not to divulge or reveal them to the profane or common people. These esoteric schools abounded throughout the East, especially in parts of Arabia and adjacent countries.

And now we enter into the historic domain and gather from the pages of Philo Judaeus, a famed Jewish mystic and philosopher, who in his treatise on the advantages accruing from a contemplative life makes mention and reference to the Essenes and gives a somewhat full account of their methods and objects of study. They lived an ascetic life, and at stated intervals indulged in meditation after reading portions of sacred hooks or writings entrusted to them. At other times they assembled in solemn conclave for interchange of thoughts and ideas which had come to them in the seclusion and silence of their cells. "They spoke slowly and with deliberation," says Philo, "regarding eloquence not so much as clearness in expression of ideas. They frequently repeated themselves in order that their sayings might become engraved on the minds of their auditors. In the interpretation of Scripture they indulged greatly in the use of allegories, as the law appeared to them like a living being. The physical body was the letters and words; the soul was the invisible spirit hidden within them, a spirit by which the student, guided and led by reason, begins searching after those things which are of importance to him; discovering most wondrous and beautiful thoughts under the form that envelops them; rejecting mere outward symbols in order to lead the mind to the light and for the use and advantage of those who, with a little aid, are able to perceive truths and things invisible by means of and through things visible." They fully recognized that the spiritual world was no remote region in the universe, but was surrounding them and not very far away from them. For them there existed no broad deep gulf, no solid wall or partition between the natural and spiritual worlds, no insuperable and impenetrable barrier between them and the spirits of great and good men made perfect and who had once been teachers to nations. If differences there was between them, it was one of state and condition, and this they endeavored to mitigate and obviate by purity of life and thought, esteeming no self-denial too great, no sacrifice too transcendant or comparable to the enjoyment of spirit intercourse and instruction, resulting in the subjugation of their lower nature, and so clarifying their minds that they became luminous mirrors in which were reflected the secrets of the universe. This was their philosophy as expressed by an old Arabian sago. "When my soul," said he, "shall become in harmony with the divine life, then will it be a reflection of nature's great and secret truths."

Such is the general description of these occult schools or lodges widely prevalent in the East, and which continued to exist to the time of Rabbi Simeon ben Jochai, the great Kabbalist and reputed author of "The Zohar, or The Book of Light," whose name is held in reverence and esteem by all true students of occult philosophy. His biography, though short, is not uninteresting in its character and details. He lived and taught in the reign of Hadrian, the Roman Emperor, when the Jewish nation was subject to much hardship and persecution and their Rabbis or recognized teachers labored under grievous disabilities, being prohibited from giving instructions to their students, a restriction which Rabbi Simeon had the singular boldness and courage to ignore and disregard, and thus incurred the anger and displeasure of the Roman rulers. He had to flee for his life and conceal himself in an unknown and solitary abode. He had been holding a discussion in one of the synagogues with Jehuda ben Illai and Jose ben Halefta, two famous Rabbis, on the comparative character of Jewish and Roman manners. Jehuda commenced his discourse with an eloquent eulogium on the Romans as the greatest promoters of the material convenience and civilization of the people they governed, instancing their public works, architecture, and the patronage they gave to the useful arts. When Rabbi Jose's turn came to speak he exhibited the cautiousness which had given him the surname of "The Prudent," and observed an impressive silence. The discretion of his colleagues was, however, lost upon Simeon, whose animosity to the Romans for the harshness and cruelty exhibited toward his brethren vented itself in a fiery invective against the oppressors, which, becoming the topic of public conversation, aroused and excited the displeasure of the civil authorities. He, along with the above Rabbis, was summoned to appear before the magistrates. The silence of Rabbi Jose was deemed a sufficient ground for banishment to Sepphoris; Rabbi Jehuda was allowed to exercise the office of a preacher in the synagogue; but Rabbi Simeon was condemned to death, a sentence which he evaded and escaped by immediate and timely flight, accompanied by his son Eliezar. For several years he remained in seclusion and lived as a hermit in a cavern, engaged in the development of Kabbalistic science as embodied in the Book of Zohar. After the death of the Emperor Antoninus he left his place of concealment and reappeared as the founder of a school in Tekoa, a town in Palestine. About three hundred of his sayings are recorded in the Talmud. The whole of his life was absorbed and spent in the study of Kabbalah, in which science he was and still is regarded as one of its most eminent masters. He lived in a world of his own, in a region beyond the bounds of ordinary nature. Students and learned Rabbis from all parts flocked to him and enrolled themselves as members of his school, in which subjects of the highest philosophy were discussed. Instructions by great teachers, such as Moses, who in the Zohar is styled The Faithful Shepherd, and the great prophet Elijah, who in luminous and resplendent forms appeared in their midst, were imparted on matters and subjects of the most abstruse and occult character, and which were recorded in secret writing by students deputed and chosen for that object. There is an affecting account of his death given by one of his students in the "Idra Seta, or "Lesser Assembly," one of the appendices to the Zohar. As a teacher he had lived and as a teacher he died, surrounded by scholars who loved him dearly. "Mercy," he was saying, "hath ascended unto the Holy of Holies, for there Adonai hath commanded his blessing forevermore, even life everlasting." There was a sudden pause. His head fell slowly on his breast. Intently gazing upon him, they listened in deep silence for further words, but no words came from those lips that had been so eloquent in speech. They were his last words, and not inappropriate as a finale to a life like his. Suddenly a strange supernatural light surrounded the house. "At that moment," says Rabbi the Scribe, "I heard a voice, which said: 'Before thee are countless days of blessedness,' and then another, saying: 'He asked life of thee and thou gayest him the years of eternity.' Throughout all that day the flame continued around the house, and no man entered or went forth. I lay weeping and sobbing on the ground. At length the fire departed, and I perceived that the soul of him who was the Light of Israel had departed also. His corpse was reclining on the right side, and a smile was on his face. Eliezar, his son, took his hands and kissed them. We could find no utterance for our grief till tears began to flow. Three times his son fell down in speechless sorrow. At length the power of utterance came to him, and he cried, 'Father! Father!' As the funeral procession moved toward the grave a light revealed itself in the air, and a voice was heard exclaiming: 'Come! Gather yourselves together to the marriage feast of Simeon.'"

Ere entering upon the analysis of the Zohar and its con-tents, we would premise that the Kabbalists teach that the Divine Being has expressly committed his mysteries to certain chosen individuals, who in their turn handed down to others who proved themselves worthy recipients of them. These mysteries relating to man's spiritual existence and guidance are concealed in parts of the Holy Scriptures, the interpretation of which is the province of Kabbalah. To understand these mysteries the student will find it necessary to acquaint himself with the metaphysical principles as laid down in the earliest writings and documents of this science, as in later times professors of Kabbalah have incorporated with it many of their own ideas and philosophic doctrines culled from Greek and Arabian sources. Kabbalah as a constituted science or system of Theosophy is divided into two separate sections, The Theological and The practical; this dealing with the visible creation and termed Bernhik; that dealing with the spiritual world and the attributes and perfection of the Divine Being is denominated the Mercaba, or the chariot throne, with its attendant angels, as seen and described in the opening chapters of the Book of Ezekiel the Prophet.

The doctrines of Creation are succinctly outlined in the "Sepher Yitsira, or Book of Creation," the imputed author of which is said to be no less a personage than Abraham the Patriarch himself. As this work, with a translation of its contents, will form a subject of future consideration, we shall confine our remarks to the no less important Kabbalistic work, The Zohar.

In order that our readers may obtain a clearer idea of the philosophy of this strange and remarkably interesting book, it will perhaps not be out of place to lay down or touch upon a few of the fundamental axioms which more or less form the basis of systems of philosophy, ancient or modern, Eastern or Western, and especially in Kabbalah; such as "From out of nothing, nothing can proceed; therefore no substance that now exists has been produced from nothing, and whatever exists is in one sense untreated. All existing substances are emanations from one eternal substance." In the act of what is commonly termed creation the eternal Being drew from himself; consequently there is no such thing as matter in our sense of the word. Whatever we call matter is only another form or species under which the spirit comes into manifestation. Therefore the universe is a realization of the Infinite, an immanent effect of his ever-active power and presence. Though all existence flows front the divine, yet is the world different from the Godhead, as the effect is different from the cause. Nevertheless, as not separate, but abiding immanently in him, creation is evermore the manifestation of himself. The world is the mantle with which he clothes himself, or, rather, it is a revelation of the Godhead, not in his hidden essence, but in his visible glory. In giving existence to the universe the first act of the almighty was the production of a power and principle intimately and specially related to himself, to which are given the names of his holy spirit, his personal world, his first-begotten son and which the Kabbalists in general personify and term Adam Kadmon, or the archetypal Man, and who in turn caused to proceed from emanations from himself all the lower forms of actual existence in their several descending series and gradations.

According to Kabbalists, God is the author of the letters. Spirit is a revelation of thought and the form in which intellect or mind pronounces itself most distinctly. Letters are the organic elements of speech, and therefore he who taught man language or who made him, as one of the Targums expresses it, "ruach mamelella," a speaking spirit, must have been the author of the letters of the primeval language. The first ten numbers and the twenty-two letters of the alphabet, considered analogically as types of divine operation, are denominated the thirty-two paths of wisdom of which the almighty created the universe. "The works of God," says the author of "Cosri," another famous Kabbalistic work, "are the writing of Him whose writing is his Word, and whose word is his thought, so that the words, work and thought of God are one, though they seem to man to be three." As in the universe harmony reigns in manifoldness, so the letters and numbers constitute a system which has its centre and hierarchy. The unit predominates over the three. The three rules over the seven; the seven over the twelve. The centre of the universe is the celestial dragon. The circuit of the zodiac is the basis of the year. The heart is the centre in man. The first is elevated in the world like a king upon his throne. In the seven organs of the body there is a kind of opposition which sets the one against the other as in battle array. Three promote love, three engender hatred. Three bestow life, three lead to dissolution, and one cannot be apprehended by the mind without the other. Over the whole of this triple system, over man, the world and time, over numbers, letters and sephiroth, the only true king, the one God rules forever and ever. Such are the chief fundamental ideas which permeate the whole texture of the Zohar, which, as we have observed, forms the standard and code of Kabbalistic philosophy. The body of the books takes the form of a commentary extending over the five books of Moses, viz.: the Book of Genesis, Exodus, Leviticus, Numbers, and Deuteronomy, and is of a highly mystical and allegorical character, and which was the most general and favored method of teaching and imparting instruction in Eastern countries. In addition to these, there are eighteen supplementary portions, viz.:

1. Siphra Dzeniutha, The Book of Mysteries.

2. Idra Rabba, The Great Assembly, referring to the schoo or college of Rabbi Simeon's students in their conferences for Kabbalistic discussion.

3. Idra Seta, The Lesser Assembly, of the few disciples that that remained for the same purpose toward the end of their master's life or after his decease.

4. Sabba, The Aged Man.

5. Midrash Ruth, a mystical exposition of The Book of Ruth.

6. Seper Ha Bahia, The Book of Clear Light.

7. Tosephtha, An Addition.

8. Raia Mehima, The Faithful Shepherd (Moses).

9. Hechaloth, The Palaces.

10. Sithrey Torah, The Secrets of the Law.

11. Midrash Ha-Neelam, The Concealed Treatise.

12. Rose de Rasin, The Mystery of Mysteries.

13. Midrash Chasith, On the Canticles.

14 Maamar Ta chasi, a discourse, so-called from its first words, "Come and See."

15. Ianuka, "The Youth."

16. Pekuda, Illustrations of the Law.

17. Chibbura Kadma, The Early Work.

18. Mathuitin, Doctrines.

The commentary is sometimes called Zohar gadol, the Greater Light; the supplements, Zohar Katon, or the Lesser Light. Though the Zohar is said to be a commentary on the Pentateuch, it must be understood that the interpretation is Kabbalistic, and that the literal sense of the words is only a covering or garment of the true meaning. With the Kabbalists there are two ways of regarding and speaking of the Divine Being. When they speak simply and directly of his nature and attributes their style is severely metaphysical and abstruse, but at other times they indulge in the use of metaphor and allegory to a most extraordinary, if not extravagant, degree, at the same time declaiming against the possibility of any attempt to describe the incomprehensible (because infinite) Being. This is especially the case with the Siphra Dzeniutha, or Book of Mysteries, of which the following extract is a fair sample of its style:

"He is the ancient of ancients, the mystery of mysteries, the concealed of the concealed. He hath a form peculiar to himself, but he hath chosen to appear to us the ancient of ancients. Yet in the form whereby we know him he remaineth still unknown. His vesture is white and his aspect that of an unveiled face. He sitteth on a throne of splendors, and the white light streameth over a hundred thousand worlds. This white light will be the inheritance of the righteous in the world to come. Before all time En Soph, the boundless One, the unoriginated and infinite Being, existed without likeness, incomprehensible and unknowable. In the production of finite existence the first act was the evolution of the Memra, or the Word, which was the first point in the descending series of beings, and from whom in nine other degrees of manifestation emanated those forms which at once compose the universe and express the attributes and presence of its eternal ruler. To these nine forms is given the common name of Sephiroth, signifying Splendors. The whole or some of these Sephiroth constitute the universe, the manifestation of God, their names being:

1. Kether, Crown.

2. Chocma, Wisdom.

3. Binah, Understanding.

4. Chesed, Mercy.

5. Din, Justice.

6. Tiphereth, Beauty.

7. Netzach, Triumph.

8. Hod, Glory.

9. Yesod, Foundation.

10. Malkuth, Kingdom or Dominion.

The primordial essence is before all things. In his abstract and eternal nature and condition he is incomprehensible, and as an object of the understanding, according to the Zohar, he is nothing, the mystery of mysteries; but he took form as he called forth them all. The ancient of ancients is now seen in his own light; that light is his holy name, the totality of the Sephiroth. The order of their emanation is as follows: From Kether, the Crown, the primal emanation of En Soph, proceed two other Sephiroth--Chocma (wisdom), active and masculine; the other Binah (understanding), passive and feminine, the combination of which results in thought, of which the universe is the effect. The crowned Memro, or Kether, or primordial Logos, is the thinking power in creation, Chocma the act of thinking, and Binah the subject of the thinking. Says Cordovero, author of a famous Kabbalistic work, Pardis Rimmonim, or the Garden of Pomegranates: "The forms of all earthly beings are in these three Sephiroth, as they themselves are in him who is their fountain." The seven other Sephiroth develop themselves also into triads, in which two antithetical members are united by a third. Thus Chesed (mercy) is the antithesis of Din (justice), and both are united in Tiphereth (beauty). These terms, however, are not used as in our common theology and ethics in the moral or spiritual sense, but have rather a cosmological or dynamic meaning, Chesed signifying the expansion of the divine Will, and Din its concentrated energy. These two attributes are called in the Zohar the arms of God; and Tiphereth, whose symbol is the breast or heart, is the expression for the good they produce and uphold. The next three Sephiroth--Netzach, Hod, and Yesod--are also of a dynamical character, representing the producing power of all existence. Netzach, masculine, and Hod, feminine, are used in the sense of expansiveness and grandeur, and denote the power from which all the forces of the universe proceed and combine themselves in a common principle, Yesod, the foundation or basis of all things. Viewed under one aspect, these three Sephiroth or attributes reveal the Deity in the character in which the Bible speaks of him as Jehovah Zebaoth, or the Lord of Hosts. The tenth and last of the Sephiroth, Malkuth, sets forth the divine sovereignty and its never-ending reign within and by all the others. Thus we see that these Sephiroth are not mere instruments different from the divine substance. He is present in them; but is more than what these forms of being make visible. They cannot in themselves express the Infinite. While each of them has a well-defined name, he, as Infinite, can have no name. Whilst, therefore, God pervades all worlds which reveal to us his presence, he is at the same time exalted above them. His immutable nature can never be meted or scanned; therefore the Zohar compares these Sephiroth to classes of various colors through which as media the divine light shines unchanged as the sun-beam is unchanged, whatever medium transmits it. Again, these ten theogonic Sephiroth are resolved into three classes, and make what is termed olam atzoloth, the world of emanation. The first three are of a purely intellectual nature, and are exponents of the olam maskel, or "intelligent world," and set forth the absolute identity of being and thon ht. The second triad is of a cosmological and moral character, expressing the energy of rectitude and grace in the revelation of the beautiful. In them the almighty appears as the summum bonum. The remaining triad represents the divine architect as the foundation and producing cause of all visible being, and is termed olam hamotava, the physically developed world.

Furthermore, these worlds are divided in a fourfold manner, viz.: (1) Atzeloth, emanative world; (2) Bariah, creative world, referring to the higher order of spirits; (3) Yetsira, formative world, including all the heavenly bodies; (4) Asosah, or olam hamotava, terrestrial world, which latter, though containing the dregs of existence, is nevertheless considered as immaterial, for matter in the ordinary idea or conception of it, on account of its imperfection and inability, would be, as an emanation from God, an impossibility and a contradiction. The divine efflux of vivifying glory, so resplendent at its fontal source, becomes less potent as it descends in the scale of being, till, in the phenomenon termed "matter," it exists in its embers, or, as the Kabbalists describe it: "Like a coal in which there is no longer any light." The Zohar gives a beautiful illustration of the intimate and unique relation of three worlds from the flame of a lamp, the upper and white light of which symbolizes the intellectual; the lower and more shaded light, which insensibly blends itself with the upper one, represents the world of feeling; whilst the grosser material, which is beneath all, is the emblem of the physical world. That the above remarks may be better understood, we subjoin the following: Taking the three central Sephiroth as the highest manifestation of their respective trinities, the Zohar represents the crown as symbol of the one infinite substance; Tiphereth, or beauty, as the highest expression of moral perfection, and Malkuth, the kingdom, the permanent activity of all the Sephiroth together--the presence or shekinah of the divine in the universe. The ground principle of Zohar philosophy is that every form of life, from the lowest element of the organic world up to the purest and brightest beams of the Eternal Wisdom, is an emanative manifestation of God, and consequently that every substance separate from the first great cause is both a chimera and an impossibility. All substance must be ever with and in him, or it would vanish like a shadow. He is therefore ever-present, not with it only, but in it. In him it has its being, and its Icing is himself. All is one unbroken chain of Being, of which the Memra is the second and En Soph the first element. There can therefore be no such thing as annihilation. if evil exists, it can only be an aberration of the divine Law, and not as a principle. With the Kabbalists bereshith (creation) and beraka (blessing) are interchangeable terms. He believes that in the moral world wicked beings will eventually develop a better state of character and conduct; that Satan himself at some future time will regain his primitive angel name and nature. Cordovero asserts that "hell itself will vanish; suffering, sin, temptation and death will be outlived by humanity and he succeeded by an eternal feast, a Sabbath without end." Another teaching of the Zohar is that the lower world is an image of the one above it. Every phenomenon of nature is the expression of a divine idea. The starry firmament is a heavenly alphabet by which the wise and spiritually-minded can read the interpretation of the present and the history of the future. So with respect to man; he is the compendium and climax of the works of God, the terrestrial shekinah. He is something more than mere flesh and bone, which are the veil, the vestment, which, when he leaves earth, he throws off and is then unclothed. As the firmament is written over with planets and stars, which, rightly read, make the hidden known, so on the firmament of the human surface or skin there are lines and configurations which are symbols and marks of character and destiny. The inner man is, however, the true man. In him, as in the Divine self, there is a trinity in unity, viz.: 1, The Neshama (spirit); 2, Ruach (soul); 3, Nephesh (the sensuous or animal life), intimately related to the body and dissolving when it, the body, dies. The Nephesh never enters the portals of Eden or the celestial Paradise. Besides these elements in us, there is another representing an idea or type of the person which descends from heaven at the time of conception. It grows as we grow, remains ever with us, and accompanies us when we leave the earth. It is known as our ycchidah, or principle of our individuality. The temporal union of the two higher elements, spirit and soul, is not regarded, as with the ancient Gnostics, an evil, but a means of moral education, a wholesome state of trial, in which the soul or lower nature works out in the domain of sense, a probation for ultimate felicity. Human life, in its perfect character, is the complete agreement between the higher and lower selves, or, as the Zohar expresses it, between the king and queen. The soul at present is being schooled and disciplined to this harmony. It is like a king's son sent away for a time from the palace to fulfil a course of training and education, and then to be recalled home. Another prominent doctrine in the Zohar regarding man is the union of the masculine and feminine principles in him, and which in combination form one moral being. Before the earthly state the male and female soul, the two halves of our nature, existed then in union. When they came forth upon the earth to work out their probation they were at first separated, but eventually will come together and be indissolubly united. If probation of final bliss he not accomplished or successfully achieved in one life, another life is entered upon, and then, if necessary, a third. When the work of purification and enlightenment is completed and ended the soul attains to the consummate happiness in the fruition of the divine; that is, in the intuitive vision of his glory, in perfect love, and in that oneness with himself in which it will have the same ideas and the same will with him and like him will hold dominion in the universe as St. Paul himself affirms: "We shall judge the angels."

From this brief outline and sketch of the teachings of the Zohar we may sum them up as follows: Regarding the facts and words of the Scriptures as symbols, it teaches us to confide in our own powers in the task of interpreting them. It sets up reason in place of priestly authority. Instead of a material world distinguishable from God, brought out of nothing by his will and subjected to successive changes in fulfilling the purposes and plan of the creator, it recognizes countless forms under which one divine substance unfolds and manifests itself and all of them pre-existent in the divine intelligence; that man is the highest and most perfect of these forms, and the only one through whom God is individually represented; that man is the bond between God and the world, being the image of each according to his spiritual and elemental nature. Originally in the divine substance, man returns to it again when the necessary and preparatory process of the earthly life shall be finished and completed; for from the Divine have we come, and unto the Divine must we return at last.

The chief aim and object of all systems of philosophy has been to give a rational account of man's relation to the Divine; a right conception of which is the fundamental basis of all social, political, and spiritual growth and progress. Ignorant of this, the mind of man can never become imbued with clear ideas and conceptions as to the true object of his existence, of its whence or whither, and is therefore doomed to wander in a state of mental darkness and incertitude highly prejudicial to the exercise of those faculties by which he is able to investigate the real nature of things and understand the laws governing the universe in which, as a part, he lives and moves and has his being. In proportion that he has attained to the knowledge of nature, and extracted from her the secrets of his being, so has he succeeded in ridding himself from the errors of the past and marched with slow though steady steps towards a higher plane of life and thought, which, having gained, brighter and grander vistas of higher truths present themselves, inviting him to further research and investigation which, though attended with errors and mistakes, have been corrected by experience--the test of all true knowledge and the great and universal teacher of mankind. For this reason the history of philosophy may be described as the epitome of human errors and mistakes, of erroneous opinions and misconceptions; of cosmological systems based upon inadequate notions and imperfect inductions; all of whist had their day and then vanished into oblivion, the tomb of creeds, the grave of specious systems and dogmas that were unable to subsist and endure because they were not the true expositions of human life and destiny. To trace their origin and investigate their beginning is not without profit and advantage to those students who, comparing past and present systems of religion and philosophy, are thus able to divine and cull therefrom the truth that makes us free, that expands the mind and qualifies us to behold and view things not as they seem to be, but as they are in themselves; so that we catch glimpses of her majestic form not as in a glass darkly, but face to face.

In our preceding remarks on The Zohar, we gave in brief outline the substance of its teachings on the dogma of man's origin and existence, and his relationship to the Creator and the universe; teachings which in their nature and character are so different from the ordinary views both of Jews and Christians, that the question naturally rises, how was it that such a system of philosophy arose and became propagated amongst a nation whose conceptions of the Deity and Creation are so diametrically and radically dissimilar, as light to darkness? How came it about that a people so conservative in their religious notions, fostered within itself a feeling amounting almost to veneration for the teachings of The Zohar, or Kabbalah, as they were termed, as is evidenced by a long list of Jewish Rabbis, honored and still held in esteem for their great learning, piety and scholarly attainments'?

The answer to these questions compels us to take a comparative view of those systems of eastern philosophy amidst which Kabbalah sprang up and manifested such a vigorous growth as to outlast many of its competitors in the power and influence it has exercised over the minds of the thoughtful and studious. Ere, however, we do this, we shall have to dismiss, and put aside as erroneous, the common tradition that Kabbalah is of divine origin; first imparted to Moses on Mount Sinai, and then handed through him to the seventy elders, which could not be for the reason just advanced, that its teachings and philosophy are opposed to and bear scarcely any resemblance to Jewish theology. This being the case, we have to consider to what system of philosophy Kabbalah was related in the time that Rabbi Simeon Ben Iochai first taught it. We may reduce these to four, viz., the Platonic philosophy; that of the Alexandrian School in Egypt; of Zoroaster in Persia; and of the Brahmins in India.

Though there is in some respects a striking analogy between Platonism and Kabbalah, yet, after a comparison of their distinctive leading tenets, we are forced to the conclusion that Kabbalah did not originate from Platonism. In both systems the Logos, or Divine Wisdom, is the primordial archetype of the universe and acts a mediatorial part between the divine idea and the objects that are the manifestation of it. In both are to be found the dogmas of pre-existence, reminiscence, reincarnation and metempsychosis, so that some Kabbalists have supposed Plato to have been a disciple of Jeremiah the prophet, in order to account for this rather remarkable and coincident similarity of ideas. There are, however, great differences between the two that make it impossible to assert that the one is a copy of the other. The Kabbalists believed in one primal substance, Spirit. Plato acknowledged two, spirit and matter, the intelligent cause and the created material produced. Neither can the Kabbalistic Sephiroth be reconciled with the ideas and doctrine of Plato or his teaching respecting those forms or archetypes of things which existed in the divine Mind from eternity. Those ideas, according to him, abide in that Mind, are inseparable from it, are the divine Intelligence itself, and are the prototypes of all existing things; whereas the Sephiroth are divided into two classes and figuratively set forth as masculine and feminine, proceeding alike from the eternal fountain En Soph, then combining themselves in a common personified power called the Son, from whom they again become distinguished in a new and further form of development. It is impossible to compare this doctrine with Plato's triad of the Father, the Son, and the Soul of the World, without perceiving that Kabbalah and Platonism can never be identified and considered as one. We must therefore seek its origin from some other source than the Platonic philosophy.

Some writers have sought to prove that Kabbalah took its rise from what is known as the Alexandrian School of philosophy. the home of Neoplatonism. Here, again, though there are great resemblances and close coincidences between them, as, God is the immanent ground and substantial source of all being--all goes out from him and all returns to him again. They both recognize the necessity of a trinity and also agree in regarding the universe as a divine manifestation, also in their doctrines concerning the Soul and its final return to God; yet if there has been any copying we are warranted in supposing that the Neoplatonists copied and took from the Kabbalists. Kabbalah was developed in Palestine. Its very language, its composition and direct association with rabbinical institutions set this beyond doubt. The Jews of Alexandria held but little intercourse with their brethren in Palestine and never entered into intimate relations with the rabbis either of Palestine or Babylon, who were greatly averse to Greek wisdom and learning and forbade that children should be instructed therein. Whilst the Palestinian Jews detested and despised Greek philosophy, they took kindly and received Kabbalah, which was held in honor and esteem long years before Neoplatonism was ever thought of or appeared as a system of philosophy. It has also been said that Kabbalah was either directly or remotely the result of the teachings of Philo Judaeus, who resided at Alexandria at the beginning of the Christian era. This assumption, after a strict analysis of Philo's works cannot be drawn nor substantiated, inasmuch as they are totally and altogether opposite in their principles and systems of philosophy. Philo is more Platonic than Kabbalistic in his ideas. For instance, he posits the Platonic dualism; God, and a creation which once had a beginning, an active principle, divine Intelligence; and a passive one, matter pre-existent, shaped and conformed to an idea conceived in the divine Mind. "God," he says, "is not only the Demiurgos or Architect of the world, but also its Creator, calling all into creation by an act of his will, and as he pervades the universe by his presence in order to sustain it, he may therefore be said to be the place of the universe, for he contains within himself all things. He himself is the world, for God is All." To explain these assertions, he proceeds: "God is the unapproachable and incomprehensible Light. No creature can behold him-- but his image shines forth in his thought, the Logos, through which we can become acquainted with him." But to this first manifestation of the divine Being, Philo, like Plato, gives an hypostatic or personal character. He is God's first begotten. This first or elder Logos produces another Logos who exerts a creative power of which the world is a manifestation. In the exposition of his ideas of creation, we meet with many interspersed remarks on the nature of angels which are very different from the ideal principles as represented by the Kabbalistic Sephiroth. In his discourses on man, Philo distinguishes between the intellectual and the sensuous soul, which latter he affirms has its seat in the blood. In attempting to ascend to the intuition of divine and spiritual truth, it may be well, as he teaches, for the mind to occupy itself at first with merely human knowledge, just as the body requires milk before it can be capable of strong meat. But in the direct effort to obtain an insight into higher or heavenly truth, it is necessary to curb or place the senses in abeyance and let the intellect exercise itself independently of them altogether. When, however, such knowledge is attained, it is not by mere dint of mental labor or by the aid of philosophy, but by direct illumination from the Divine. He also believed in the possibility of the mind to attain intuitive perceptions of Deity himself, at the same time laying great stress on the exercise of faith, which he calls "the queen of all virtues." Faith lifts the veil of sense and conducts the spirit of man to an union with God, which has been exemplified more or less in the lives of all great mystics of ancient and modern times. From the study of early Christian and Gnostic writings, we arrive at the same conclusion, that though there may be found similarities and affinities between some of their teachings and those of Kabbalah, they are too slight to warrant the notion that the latter proceeded from Christianity. The dualism of the Christian faith, of a God and a created universe of matter and spirit as components of the universe, cannot be reconciled with the one substance of the pantheistic Kabbalah, In the Gnostic Bible, Liber Adami, the Book of Adam, or the Codex Nazareus as it is known to students (of which an account of its contents and teachings will be given for the first time in English, in the pages of THE WORD), we meet with scattered remarks on the degeneration of natures at each degree of remoteness from the Divine fountain of being, the production of actual things by the Logos; the four worlds--the male and female soul and their union--also the symbolism of numbers and letters of the alphabet, which, though showing some relationship, does not confirm the derivation of Kabbalah from it.

Whence then did Kabbalistic philosophy derive its origin, For the resolution of this question we must go eastwards to Babylon, whither the Jewish people were transplanted as captives at the fall of Jerusalem, and where the teachings of Zoroaster were exercising a wide influence over the popular mind. What those teachings were we are able to judge from the sacred book of the Persians, the Zend Avesta, a copy of which was first found and brought to Europe in the beginning of the 18th Century by Anquetil Perron, a learned Frenchman. In this sacred book may be found all the great primordial principles of the Kabbalistic system. Thus the En Soph of Kabbalah corresponds to Zeruane Akarene, the "Eternal Boundless One," of the Zend Avesta. Another epithet of the Deity amongst the ancient Persians was "Boundless Space" similar to the Kabbalists Makom or Place. The Logos, or Memra, or THE WORD, is the Honofer or Ormuzd of the Persian, by whom the world was produced and who is a Mediator between the boundless and incomprehensible Zeruane and finite beings. As the medium by which the attributes of the Deity become known, his throne is light, and like Adam Kadmon or "the heavenly man" in Kabbalah, he unites in himself true wisdom, the highest understanding, greatness, grace, beauty, power, and glory, and is the fashioner and sustainer of all things, of all beings, a most remarkable coincidence with the doctrine of the ten Sephiroth. Now Zoroaster flourished at the very time of the Jewish captivity, during which their rabbis first came into contact and under the influence of a religious philosophy which in many particulars was very similar to their own cherished teachings. In the Zend Avesta they found, as in the Book of Genesis, the tradition of the six days of creation, an earthly paradise, the demon tempting in the form of a serpent--the fall of the first pair who, before it, lived the life of angels, but after were obliged to clothe themselves with the skins of animals and delve in the earth to acquire the means of sustenance for their bodily wants. There also was found a prophecy of a future resurrection of the dead and a last judgment, which, in order to explain their presence in the Persian scriptures, some Biblical scholars assume that Zoroaster, their author or compiler, took them from the Jewish writings and incorporated them into his own theological doctrines. Be that as it may, it must always remain a supposition and a debatable question. There is, however, no gainsaying that the Jews appropriated some of his ideas which eventually were embodied in their Talmuds. In the rabbinical schools of Babylon there were esoteric teachings imparted, but only to a select few, some of whose names have been handed down as famous Kabbalists, such as Rabbi Chanina and Rabbi Oshaya. In this way Kabbalah was propagated, and at last found a home in Palestine.

Again, we must go more eastward still until we come to India, whence Zoroaster drew the fundamentals of the system of religious philosophy by which he is distinguished and regarded as one of the great teachers in ancient times. In that far off land beyond the river Indus, is found a people who at that remote period in the world's history had reached its zenith and attained to a high state of civilization never enjoyed by any other preceding nation. In its magnificent and stupendous monuments of architecture and sculpture which have escaped the ravages of time or of vandal conquerors-- in its profound systems of philosophy elaborated by Rishis, who were accounted as divine beings and renowned and venerated for their wisdom and learning--in their compositions of art and poetry, whose beauty, elegance and sublimity have never been surpassed by the productions of Western mind and thought, and beyond all these, in its solemn and mysterious religion with its esoteric doctrines and teachings, its imposing symbolic ritual and ceremonies, the Hindus, even in those ancient times, were far in advance (the Egyptians excepted) of all other nations. She was the ark in which were preserved the sacred remnants and fragments of a previous and now unknown civilization, which were systematized by her great Rishis and handed down for the benefit of humanity in succeeding ages. To her as to a great shrine of truth, great souls from out of all lands and countries, as Pythagoras and others, wandered and came for instruction and knowledge that would explain the great mysteries of life and being, ignorance of which is the great obstacle and barrier to human progress. Though through the all-prevailing law of change and the action of Karma which operates in the life of nations as of individuals, the glory of India has been eclipsed and her fair and fertile territories have been overrun and ravaged by ruthless and barbarous conquerors whose object was plunder anti rapine, yet lives she on, unconquered, unsubjugated in soul, in which still pulsate and throb those ideas and conceptions of beauty, and, working like leaven, silently, yet effectually, are both a prophecy and a guarantee of a future renovation of national life which will cause her to become again the paragon of nations and the teacher and instructor of the world. It is only since the beginning of the 19th Century that we have become acquainted with the religion and philosophy of India through the works of great scholars such as Sir William Jones, Schlegel, Bopp, Colebrooke, Max Muller, and others who by their excellent translations of Hindu Shastras, Puranas, etc., have made it possible for students to become acquainted with them and form a better and truer estimate of what India can teach us, The language in which her sacred scriptures are written is considered the most ancient of all, and distinguished beyond all others for its extensive vocabulary, its varied and perfect grammatical forms and inflections of speech by which it is adapted and able to express the most abstract ideas and metaphysical conceptions. Her sacred books, regarded as divine in their origin and revelation, are divided into Vedas and Puranas treating of a great variety of subjects, theological, legendary, ethical and devotional. In addition to these are the magnificent epic poems, the Ramayana and the Mahabharata, in the latter of which is found that gem of human thought, that flower of spiritual philosophy, which stands unique in the world's literature: the Bhagavad-Gita, the divine song, the song par excellence. We do not presume to assert that all the details of Kabbalistic philosophy are found in these most ancient documents. What we would assert after analyzing and comparing them is, that in these Hindu writings are to be found the radical principles of Kabbalah in unmistakable form. In both the systems, Indian and Kabbalistic, there is a recognition of a self-existent and eternal nature, indefinable, inconceivable, to which is given the appellation of Brahm, corresponding to Zeruane Akerene of the Persians, mid En Soph of the Kabbalists. There is also it filial emanation of this infinite nature who is as a firstborn son of Brahm and bears the name of Brahma. "From that which is," says Manu, "without beginning or end, was produced the Divine Man famed in all worlds," a personification strangely similar and coincident with the Memra, the Adam Kadmon, the heavenly man, prototype of mankind, of the Kabbalists. Again the universe is produced by Brahm. "From him proceeded the heavens and the earth beneath. In the midst he placed the subtle ether, the light regions, and the permanent receptacle of the waters." Yet the natural universe is considered to have been self-emanative, similar to the procession or development of the Sephirothic worlds from the first begotten son, who is at once the archetype and principle of all finite beings. In Hindu philosophy the soul, or rather spirit, is regarded as an efflux from the Deity, an emanation from the Light of Lights and destined ultimately to return to its great original. Subjected to the depraving effects of evil in time, the soul has to work out a purifying probation, and if it fails in this it reincarnates until the work be completed. With respect to creation we learn, "the entire world is an emanation from the Deity, and therefore of one substance. The one only has existed from eternity. Everything we behold and ourselves too are portions of him. The Soul, the mind, the intellect of man and all sentient creatures, are offshoots from the universal Soul, to which it is their fate to return. The human mind is impressed with a series of illusions which it considers as real, till reunited with the great fountain of truth." Of these illusions, the most potent is that of Ahamkara or the feeling of self. By its influence and action the soul, when detached from its source, becomes ignorant of its own nature, origin and destiny, and erroneously considers itself as a separate and independent existence, and no longer a spark of the eternal fire or part of the universal whole, a link in one unbroken and immeasurable chain. As in Kabbalah, the universe being of one substance and an emanation from the Divine, it follows there can be no such thing as matter in the gross and vulgar sense of the word. What we take to be attributes of matter are in effect so many manifestations of spirit. The substance we call matter is and yet is not eternal from the point of view whence we regard it,--eternal when considered in its relation to Deity, non-eternal with regard to its figured states or phenomenal development and manifestation. Such are the fundamental views and propositions of Hindu philosophy displayed with more or less clearness in the works above mentioned, the oneness and coincidence of which with those of Kabbalah is, as we have stated, too plain to be denied, and the only question remaining for explanation is, how came they to find a home in Palestine and become incorporated as elements in the Kabbalistic system of philosophy?

There are three ways by which we may account for their sameness: (1) from the intercourse of the Jewish rabbis during the Babylonian captivity with Zoroaster, who, as we have stated, drew his ideas primarily from India; (2) another probable mode of transmission was through the commercial intercourse between India and Egypt. It is not incredible that the scholars of Alexandria should have visited Persia in their quest after the scientific and esoteric learning of the East, nor is it improbable that Zoroaster himself, along with his monarch, King Gushtap, at whose court he resided and taught, should have made a pilgrimage to Alexandria as is stated in the Annals of Ammonius Marcellinus, an ancient Roman historian. This visit would afford opportunity to the sages and learned of that city of becoming acquainted and conversant with the peculiar tenets and principles of Eastern religious philosophy, which eventually found entrance into Palestine; (3) the most probable and likely is that it was conveyed thither by Buddhist propagandists, who inaugurated those secret lodges of esoteric schools or societies such as those of the Essenes and Therapeutae, as they were termed. Buddhism, as is well known, was an offshoot from Brahmanism and its adherents in accordance with the injunctions of their great founder, Gautama, to make known the Good Law, went forth into all the neighboring countries, Tibet, China, Japan eastward, to Syria, Egypt and Arabia westward, founding institutions and communities from which ultimately originated monkery and nunnery in all their different forms and customs. Everywhere, where they penetrated, they made proselytes and inaugurated rites and ceremonies and introduced modes of dress and ecclesiastical ornaments, which afterwards became the accessories in the rituals and worship of Christian churches. Through these Buddhist missionaries the basic ideas and principles of Kabbalah were first implanted in a soil favorable for growth and after development. It was a time when national decay had set in and old time systems of religion and philosophy were being shaken to their very foundations. The reign and regime of the old gods and goddesses and their worship were coming to an end and men's minds were craving after a purer faith, a nobler philosophy, a religion of light and truth, without which there is no real progress, no true progression in society. Kabbalah then sprung forth and manifested its existence, and whilst raising the mind above the phenomenal and temporal, introduced its followers, as did the Mystics afterwards in the dark ages, into a new world of thought, teaching them their true position in the universe and their real relationship to the divine Being in whom and through whom we live and move and have our being. Amidst this general darkness and mental uncertitude, this eclipse of faith and hope, Rabbi Simeon ben Jochai elaborated his philosophy of life, teaching the divinity of man as a derivation, or rather an emanation, from En Soph the "Boundless One," the one unknown yet omnipresent Being.

To whom, no high, no low, no great, no small,
He fills, He bounds, connects and equals all.
Sustains heaven's myriad orbs and all their suns
From seeming evil, still educing good

And better thence again, and better still
In infinite progression.

In doing this, and infusing into the mind and heart of man new and lofty ideas of human existence, Rabbi Simeon has done good service to humanity, and contributed both directly and indirectly to the overthrow of that system of polytheism which for long ages had enervated and depraved the moral life of nations. He lived not in vain, nor did his philosophy perish with him. Cherished and preserved by his followers, it was handed down and became the basis of all esoteric teachings imparted in the secret lodges of the Illuminati, Rosicrucians, and Mystics throughout the dark and mediaeval ages, so that his epitaph may well be "though dead, he speaketh still."

Having now sketched and outlined the theoretical part of Kabbalah as found in The Zohar, we will conclude by giving a short account of the practical, which is usually divided under two heads, viz., the Exegetical applied to the interpretation of the occult meaning of holy scripture, and the Thaumaturgic, comprising rules and methods for producing certain preternatural results in the cure of diseases and the exercise of Magical rites and practices. Exegetical Kabbalah is founded on the assumption as before stated that Moses received from the Lord on Mount Sinai not only the words of the law, but also the key to unlock and reveal the mysteries enwrapped and hidden in each section, verse, letter, point, and accent of the Pentateuch, and that this key has been handed down through wise men who had qualified themselves for its reception. This system of exegesis or explanation is threefold, and arranged under the heads of Gematria, Notarikon, and Temura, each of which we will now describe.

Gematria deals with the numerical value and power of letters, their forms, and sometimes their situation in a word, and is either arithmetical or figurative. In arithmetical gematria each letter has its numerical value. One word whose letters are equivalent to those of another may be accepted as an explanation of that other. For instance, Genesis, ch. I. V. 1, Brashith bara in the beginning created = 1116, also the words, berash hashanah nibra (in the beginning of the year was created) = 1116. Therefore the creation took place in September, in which month the Jewish New Year commences. So in Genesis xlix: 10, the words yabo schilo (shall come to Shiloh), = 358, and meshiach (Messiah) 358. Therefore Shiloh is the Messiah. Figurative gematria is employed in speculations on the letters which (from accident, but as the Kabbalists affirm, from divine design) are greater or smaller, reversed or inverted in the manuscripts of the Hebrew Scriptures. An instance of this occurs in Numbers x: 35. "And when the ark went forward," the letter nun in the word arun (ark) is written the wrong way of turned back to show the loving warning of God to the people, Again, in Genesis xi.: 1, "and the people became as murmurers." The nun in the word mthannanim (murmurers) is also written backwards to show the perverse turning of the people from God, and thus are these two places written in every true Hebrew Bible throughout the world. Another branch of figurative gematria is called architectonical, consisting of mystical calculations on the size, form, and dimensions of the holy temple, the tabernacle in the wilderness, and the future temple described in Ezekiel, of which some very curious and most interesting particulars are given in Sheckard's Bechinath Happerushim (select comments).

Notarikon is used when one letter is made to signify an entire thing or person. The term is taken from the practice of notaries in abbreviating words, though others derive it from notare, to note. Thus a single word is formed from the first or last letters of several words, as in Genesis i.: 3, the finals of the words bars elohim laasoth, which God created and made = amth. Another instance is the word agla, which, with the Tetragrammaton or holy name, was, as the Kabbalists say, inscribed on Magen David or the Shield of David, and is formed by taking the initials of the words atta gibbor leolom adonai (thou art, O Lord, eternally mighty).

Temura signifies permutation. That is, the interchange of letters by various methods, such as that known as Athbash, in which one word is composed that shall answer to another by inverting the order of the letters as they stand in the alphabet, making the last letter Th stand for the first and so answer to A, then Sh to correspond with B, and so on in the subjoined order:

Athbash

A,	B,	G,	D,	H,	V,	Z,	Bh,	T,	Y,	C,
Th,	Sh,	R,	K,	Ts,	P,	H,	S,	N,	M,	L.

By this method the meaning of Jeremiah li: 1, lb kmy (in midst of them that rise up against me) becomes Chasdim (Chaldeans). Another method is (there are 22 of them):

Albam

A,	B,	G,	D,	H,	V,	Z,	Ch,	T.	Y,	C,
L,	M,	N,	S,	H,	P,	Ts,	K,	R.	Sh,	Th.

By which the alphabet is divided into two equal parts, and the first letter interchanged with the eleventh, the second with the twelfth; thus Isaiah vii: 6, the word T B A L Tabeel becomes Ramla, the King of Israel. Sometimes letters of a word may be transposed as to compose another word as Mlachy (my angel) may be made Michael (the angel Michael).

Thaumaturgic Kabbalah is founded on the assumption that a certain virtue or energy is inherent in the words and letters of the Scriptures, which on the pronunciation of them with a specific and steadfast purpose will communicate itself to spiritual or heavenly powers, of which those names, words, and letters, are the symbols, producing effects which to those who have no knowledge of the occult power of vibrations would be altogether deemed incredible. Yet in our own experience have we met with instances of the occult power of words and symbols of a most extraordinary character, the results of which were most pronounced and beneficial. Kabbalists strongly affirm that by such means effects are produced in the higher or noumenal world which become expressed and manifested in the changes sought to be accomplished in this our phenomenal and lower life. It was and still is an article of Jewish belief that he who can rightly pronounce the Tetragrammaton, or holy name, is able to do wonders and produce miraculous effects. The parts of Scripture employed for this purpose are those which contain or are by the preceding modes made to be expressive of the divine names and those of angels and the Sephiroth, each of which corresponds with a part or member of the human body. The interrelation of these names is as follows:

Sephiroth	Divine Name	Angels	Parts of Body
Kether	Ehyeh	Chaioth	Brain
Hochma	Jah	Ophanim	Lungs
Binah	Jehovah	Arelim	Heart
Chesed	El	Chasmalim	Stomach
Geburah	Eloah	Seraphim	Liver
Tiphereth	Elohim	Malachim	Gall

Netzach	Jehovah Zabaoth	Tarsheesim	Spleen
Hod	Elohim Zabaoth	Beni Elohim	Reins
Yesod	El Chai	Cherubim	Genitalia, Mas.
Malkuth	Adonai	Ishim	Genitalia, Fem.

In the cure of diseases, the name of the heavenly power is invoked which corresponds to that part of the body affected, or the member to be healed. These names are sometimes, together with what are termed the signatures of the angels, inscribed on kemeoth or amulets of various kinds, and constructed according to certain rules, which Paracelsus in his magical works has outlined. They are also given in such Kabbalistic works as The Sixth Book of Moses, Shemosh Tehillim, and others. That part of practical Kabbalah relating to the conjuration and evocation of good spirits and angelic beings is denominated Theurgy or White Magic. That referring to the invocation of evil powers is called Goety or Black Magic, is found in the frightful grimoires of the Middle Ages. It must, however, be admitted that the most learned and enlightened Kabbalists ignore this latter entirely, holding it as an abomination, and denounce both the study and practice of it as having no connection whatever with the sublime Kabbalah elaborated by Rabbi Simeon.

Of the many learned Kabbalists who have written on this subject, the best and most esteemed are Rabbi Nachmanides, whose Shoshan Sodoth, "The Lily of Secrets," is a profound treatise on the powers of letters, names, and numbers. Gikatilla, author of Ganath Egos, "The Garden of Nuts," an introduction to the doctrines of Kabbalah, also of Sheaarey Zedek, "The Gates of Righteousness on the ten Sephiroth." On Kabbalistic philosophy the greatest and most famed are Moses Corduero, who composed Paredis Rimmonim, "The Garden of Pomegranates," and Isaac de Luria, who spent his whole life in the study, teaching and exposition of Kabbalah. His great work, entitled Etz Chaim, "The Tree of Life," edited and published by Vital, will ever remain a monument of his learning and knowledge of Kabbalistic Science. The Shefer Tal,, Shower of Dew," is a well-known and excellent work by Rabbi Shabbethai Horowitz, and is often referred to as a text-book by students, as also Chesed le Abraham, "Mercy to Abraham," by Abraham Asulai, a most remarkable work in seven gates or chapters, dealing with the mysteries of the law, the microcosm, hell, paradise, the transmigrations of the soul, demonology and guardian angels, hidden powers and forces, etc. Another important work, being the first printed book on Kabbalah, is Derech Emuna, "The Path of Faith," by Meir ben Gabbai, and treats in the form of dialogue on the Sephiroth, which will eventually appear in "The Word," for the first time in English. And last, though not least, is the Zohar itself, which, when first published in Europe by Leo de Modena in the twelfth century, produced a wide and profound impression in the learned world, including popes, ecclesiastics, professors in all the most noted universities. Scholars everywhere read and studied it, through whom its teachings and philosophy were adopted as appears in many theological works, published in that and the succeeding centuries, both Christian and Jewish. The chief non-Jewish authors of works on Kabbalah are Picus de Mirandola, "Conclusions Kabbalisticce"; Reuchlin, "de Arte Kabbalistica"; Brucker, "Historia Philosophiae"; Rosenroth, "Kabbalah Denudata," comprising Latin translations of large portions of the Zohar, with commentaries, glossaries, and a large mass of interesting information on the transcendental philosophy of the Jews; Basnage, "Historie des Hebreux," which has been translated into English. The works of Joel, and Jost, on Jewish sects, in German, are excellent for reference on Kabbalistic history. A French "Systeime dala Kabbalah," in French, is well worth reading. Count Mac Gregor Mathers--Kabbalah Unveiled--which, though embracing only a part of the Zohar, is a most excellent work, especially the introduction and very learned notes, which no one but a great Kabbalist could have compiled. To all these must be added the Edipus Egyptiacus, a really stupendous work by Athanasius Kircher, a most learned and profoundly erudite scholar, whose multifarious works comprise twenty-three folio volumes, chiefly on philosophical, scientific and literary subjects.

Having now emerged from out of the mazes of this labyrinthine subject of Kabbalah, the question may be asked, how is it that a work like The Zohar has been suffered to drop out of popular notice so as to become comparatively unknown, except to a few ardent and zealous students. During the last century a great amount of interest was exhibited by savants and scholars in the science of comparative Religion and the sacred books of all nations, especially those of ancient Persia, Egypt, and India, were subjects of profound researches and investigations by learned Orientalists such as Max Muller, Whitney, and a host of others, all noted for their philosophical and literary attainments. But The Zohar, the Book of Light, has been passed by, ignored and unappreciated, so that its existence is scarcely known. What is the reason for such neglect, so strange and anomalous? Among the many reasons that may be advanced in explanation of this universal neglect is the fact that the study and comprehension of this book demand, from students in general qualifications they do not possess, viz., a knowledge of occultism and an acquaintance with those correspondences and analogies which are an essential sine qua non in the acquisition of spiritual science and learning. The natural man, as St. Paul observed centuries ago, however learned and advanced in art and science, cannot understand the things of the spirit, nay, he will frequently have to quit or rid himself of many preconceived notions and prejudices, the result of his learning, and become as teachable as a little child ere he eau take a single step or advance in spiritual science and philosophy. The majority of students in public colleges and institutions, imbued with the commercial spirit of the age, are actuated in their labors and studies greatly by motives of gain, and the acquisition of wealth and position, are content and willing to follow in the world's train instead of becoming its leaders, its guides, and directors to a higher and truer knowledge of the philosophy of human life and existence. It has not always been so Great and learned and true men there have been, who in the study of The Zohar found a philosophy which expanded their minds and purified their natures from the defilement of those mercenary motives, which are at the present time so rampant and prevalent in all classes and grades of society. There are, however, looming up in the mental horizon of the world, indications of a deep and earnest desire and craving after a learning that shall ennoble human nature and not lead it into bypaths of error and illusion. Men are observing and detecting in the study of past systems of religion and philosophy something that was true, and therefore worth retaining and cherishing, and also recognizing that the end, the aim, and object of all of them, was the renovation and purification of human nature and its exaltation to a higher plane of thought and experience. This was their chief raison d'etre as formulated and expressed in The Zohar. In it, as in a deep mine, are to be found embedded veins and nuggets of valuable truths more precious than gold or rubies, but which must he delved for and excavated as miners toil and delve for gold and other minerals. All knowledge that is worth having, that which enriches and endows us with a wealth of power and strength to conquer nature and attain the goal of our destiny, implies labor and toil protracted and ofttimes wearying; involves self-sacrifice and self-denial, frequently painful and trying, but when acquired, gives us the right to take of "the tree of life" whose fruits and leaves in the symbolic words of the Apocalypse are for the healing of the nations. This knowledge it is that frees us from the trammels and bondage of sensual desire and indulgence and brings in its train self-conquest, the greatest of all victories, the noblest of all human achievements. Some years ago, a great general lay mortally wounded on his pallet bed within his tent, surrounded by brother officers and comrades on many a hard fought field of battle. The sands of life were fast running out. To cheer his last moments some one whispered, "Bring the record of his victories and read it to him ere he leaves us." It was brought and read. Scarcely was it finished when the departing warrior with a painful effort raised himself up on his elbow and said: "There is one victory unrecorded." And to their questions of astonishment, when and where it occurred, he replied: "On such a day I conquered myself," and with these words, the last he uttered, that great soul entered into the rest that remaineth for all of us who achieve the victory over Self. Let this be realized, then commences the true life within us, the great object of all our incarnations. May we learn the "open sesame" of the higher life, which is the ultimate heritage and acquisition to be enjoyed by all mankind. 'The struggle to attain to it is arduous and attended with conflicts of inward anguish and pain known only to the combatant. It is, however, a struggle that ennobles and strengthens us to hear and suffer, silently and uncomplaining, life's heavy burden of sorrows, and disappointments, to stand calm, steadfast and unmoved amidst the debris and wreckage of hopes blighted and withered, of fairy visions dispelled and faded away, of aspirations, desires, longings and anticipations unrealized, for the gold law, or, in other words, the divine is with us and in us, teaching us, educating us, preparing and qualifying us all for something better and grander, something more enduring and lasting than the fleeting hopes and dreams of the past, a something which in the words of the saintly Spinoza is the enjoyment and participation of the "One true, and immutable life," man's highest happiness and the source of that tranquility of mind and soul which springs from the intuitive knowledge and perception of the divine in nature as' also in ourselves. Then is it that old things pass away and all things become new, and to us again the words of that wonderful i and occult book, the Apocalypse, or the Book of Revelation, there is for us no more death, and sorrow and crying no more, for the tabernacle of the divine life is within us, transforming us into children of Zohar, or Light, that shall never become dimmed throughout all Lyons of time, then also, even in our present incarnation,

"Though too weak to tread the ways of truth
This age fall back to old idolatry,
Though men return to servitude a fact
As the tide ebbs, to ignominy and shame
By nations sink together, we shall still
Find solace--knowing what we have learned to know
Rich in true happiness, if allowed to be

Faithful alike in forwarding a day
Of greater Light, joint laborers in the work
Of their deliverance, surely yet to come,
Prophets of Nature, we to them will speak
A lasting inspiration, sanctified
By reason, blest by faith; what we know and love
Others will love, and we will teach them how;
Instruct them how the soul of man becomes
A thousand times more beautiful than the earth
On which we live and dwell above this frame of things
In light and beauty exalted, as it is itself
Of quality and fabric more divine."

       End of Introduction.

INTRODUCTION

THE LILY

THE students of Rabbi Simeon were assembled together and sitting in silence, waiting for the master to begin his discourse. At length Rabbi Simeon spake, and said: "As a lily amongst the thorns." This word lily, what doth it mean and symbolize? It symbolizes the congregation of Israel; and as lilies are either red or white in color, so the members of this congregation are divided into two classes, distinguished by their rigorous justice and uprightness, or by their gentleness, kindness and compassion. These are environed about with thirteen ways or degrees of mercy, as the lily has thirteen leaves surrounding it on all sides. Furthermore, intervening between the first and second Elohim or Alhim, mentioned in Genesis, are thirteen words corresponding to these thirteen leaves of the lily and the degrees of mercy surrounding the congregation of Israel. The divine name Alhim is mentioned again, and wherefore? In order to show the symbolic meaning of the five strong leaves which surround the lily, the occult meaning of which has reference to the five ways of salvation, corresponding to five gates of mercy. Respecting this mystery of five, it is written: "I will take the cup of salvation," which is the cup of blessing, and which must stand or repose upon five fingers only, similar to the lily supported and sustained by its five strong leaves. For this reason the lily symbolizes the cup of blessing, as there are five words between the second and the third Alhim mentioned in the Book of Genesis. One of these words is A U R, meaning light. This light was treated and became enclosed as an embyro in the Berith, or covenant, and, entering into the lily as a principle of life, made it fruitful, and this is what is called in Scripture "fruit tree, yielding fruit whose seed is in itself"; and as this life principle, entering into the Berith, caused itself to become manifested in forty-two kinds of second matter, so has it produced the Shemhamphorash, the great and ineffable divine name of God, composed of forty-two letters, which operated in the creation of the world.

THE REDEMPTION OF HUMANITY

Rabbi Simeon spake again: "The Flowers appear on the earth." By flowers is signified the appearance of created beings on the earth. When did they appear? On the third day, when it is written: "The earth first brought forth." Then the flowers appeared on that day. "The time of singing or of commingled voices and cries and noises is come," indicates the fourth day of creation, in which took place the excision of the Aretzim (the terrible one, or demons). For this reason the word Moroth (lights) is found without V and written M A R Th, meaning curse, or malediction. "The voice of the turtle" refers to the fifth day, when it is written: "The waters brought forth abundantly, and etc.," for the generation of created beings. On the sixth day it was said: "Let us make man," who in after-time would say: "Let us hear, before let us do or make." "In our land" is meant the Sabbath, symbol or type of the land of life, the world of spirits or souls, the world of resurrections or rising up to a higher life. "The flowers" were the fathers or pitris whose souls pre-existed in the Divine Thought, and, entering into the world to come, became concealed and hidden therein. From thence they came forth, becoming incarnated in prophets of truth. When Joseph was born they were concealed and unrecognized in him, and when he entered into the holy land he presided over them and ruled there; so then they became known. When did this occur? To this question Scripture gives answer: when the Iris, or rainbow, first appeared in the world. Then was the time of the excision or cutting of the brutal and savage and sinful from the face of the earth. Why, then, did they not perish? Why were they preserved? Because the flowers then appeared on the earth. If they had not appeared, they, the brutal and sinful ones, would have become extinct and the world would have ceased its existence. Who, then, established the world and caused the fathers to appear? It was the voice or cry of the little ones, or students of the law, and it was owing to them that the world now subsists.

EXPLANATORY NOTES AND REMARKS

In these two first sections of the introduction to the Zohar are abstruse intimations and references to the doctrine of Light, which enters so largely as an element in the systems of ancient Eastern philosophy, especially that of the Persians, with whom the Jews had at one time such intimate relations. Light is the primal emanation of the Divine, from which and by which all things visible and invisible have originated. From out of that Light have they all come forth, and into it will they return when the great drama of existence is completed and the tragedy of life comes to an end. Meanwhile the Light that enlighteneth every man that cometh into the world to play each his or her part, is accessible to all, irrespective of artificial conditions or the distinctions of human society. Upon our own measure of receptivity of it depends our inner development and evolution to higher planes of life; of loftier, clearer and more accurate views of truth that free us from the influence of external contaminations by purifying and spiritualizing the animal or lower nature within us. It is the one heritage common alike to king or peasant, noble or ignoble, learned or illiterate, rich or poor, and he who is endowed with and knows most of it ranks higher in the scale of existence and approximates nearer and closer to the Divine, in whom we all live and move and have life, whether we use it for the good and happiness of others or trifle and fritter it away as foolish spendthrifts who are ignorant of the value and worth of money. It was this Light that the great German, Goethe, in his last words, craved and desired: "Light! More Light!" And this is the Light that Rabbi Simeon refers to all through the pages of this remarkable book, in which we shall meet with many allusions to it of great interest, both to the general and the theosophic reader. Kabbalists affirm that there were thirty-two Alhim engaged in the work of creation as executors of the divine will. They correspond to the Dhyan Chohans in Hindu philosophy. By the lily, with thirteen leaves, is occultly meant the twelve avatars, or incarnations, of divine messengers, six of whom are Cabiri, ministers of karmic justice for the chastisement of nations; and six of them are Messiahs; their emblem is a lily, whose color is white, as seen in ancient paintings of The Annunciation, in which the Angel Gabriel holds a lily in his hand. The thirteenth is their great chief and lord, by whom they have been trained and commissioned and sent forth on the great work of spiritual enlightenment of the nations. In Eastern philosophy he is known as the "Great Sacrifice," the "Silent Watcher," who will not vacate his post until the last scion of humanity, agonizing and struggling with its weakness and infirmities to overcome self and accomplish its destiny, finds its way to him at last. We have also here hints of the state of mankind in its primary stages, when the cry of the Atzerim, the terrible or terrorizing ones, resounded on the earth, and which lasted until the fathers, or divine teachers, came and led humanity on to the upward track of light and civilization. Then the world became steadied or established, and students of the divine law of the universe and of the divine government of humanity became numerous, their voices and teachings going out unto the ends of the world; and then, as it is written: "Great was the company of the preachers" of truth and righteousness.

By the "little ones" are meant student initiates, of which class St. Paul was one. Before his initiation his name was called Saul, but after his initiateship be became known as Paulus--the little one. There are various other expositions of these two sections by Kabbalists, but so abstrusely worded and expressed in metaphysical terms and language that none but those who have a wide and extended knowledge of Hebrew and its cognate language would be able to understand and appreciate them.

For greater elucidation and a clearer understanding of the Briatic or creative Alhim, we give them in their order as set forth in Kabbalistic writings:

(1) In the beginning Alhim created. (2) And the spirit of Alhim hovered or brooded. (3) And Alhim said: "Let there be light." (4) And Alhim saw the light. (5) And Alhim divided between the light. (6) And Alhim called the light Day. (7) And Alhim said: "Let there be a firmament." (S) And Alhim made the firmament. (9) And Alhim called the firmament Heaven. (10) Alhim said: "Let the waters he gathered together." (11) Alhim called the dry land Earth. (12) And Alhim saw it was good. (13) Alhim said: "Let the earth bring forth." (14) And Alhim saw it was good. (15) And Alhim said: "Let there be lights." (16) Alhim made two lights. (17) And Alhim placed them in the firmament of the heavens. (18) And Alhim saw it was good. (19) Alhim said: "Let the waters bring forth." (20) Alhim created the whales. (21) And Alhim saw it was good. (22) And Alhim blessed them, saying: "Be fruitful and multiply." (23) Alhim said: "Let the earth bring forth." (24) Alhim made the beasts of the earth. (25) And Alhim saw it was good. (26) Alhim said: "Let us make man." (27) And Alhim created the man. (28) In the form or image of Alhim created he him. (29) Alhim blessed them. (30) Alhim said: "Be fruitful and multiply." (31) Alhim said: "Behold! I have given to you." (32) And Alhim saw all that he had made.

The English equivalents of the thirteen words intervening between the first and second Alhim are as follows: The heavens, the earth, earth was Tohu vabohu, darkness upon face, abyss (or great deep) Spirit. The five words between the second and third Alhim are: "Hovered, upon, face, waters, said."

The expression, "Congregation of Israel," in the first instance, refers to the first born sons of Light, or, as they are termed in the Book of Job, the morning stars, who, along with the Sons of Alhim, sang their song of praise at the creation of the world. In an extended sense, it includes the true children of light who have attained unto the Divine Life.

THE OCCULT ORIGIN OF ALHIM

RABBI Eliezar spoke, and said: "Lift up your eyes on high and behold who hath created these." Lift up your eyes on high. Where? To the place whither all eyes are turned. There is the pathakh azeen, or opening of eyes. There you will recognize the mysterious Ancient One who created these and is the object of research. And who is he? It is Mi (who) that is called the summit of the heavens above, for all things exist by his will. Because he is the object concealed and invisible after which all seek. Therefore is this mysterious being called Who (Mi), and beyond him search in vain. Rut at the other extremity is another being known as What! (Mah). What distinguishes the one from the other? Mi (who), the concealed and hidden One, is he whom all created beings are seeking to know, but after all their efforts and endeavors, by the gaining of knowledge, they only come at last to Mah (the what). Then, what do we know, What understanding of him have we? What have we found out or discovered, Truly, all is mysterious, as at first, and this is what the Scripture refers to where it is written: "Mah (what) I take thee to witness." "Mah (what) shall I liken thee to?" When the temple at Jerusalem was ravaged and destroyed there was heard a voice crying aloud: "What shall I testify concerning thee? For from the beginning of creation have I testified to thee." Also, is it written: "I call heaven and earth this day to record." "Mah (what) shall be likened unto thee." "I will crown thee with crowns of holiness and make thee to rule over the world." So that it shall be said: "Is this the city called Beautiful, etc?" "This is Jerusalem, the city most compacted in beauty." "Mah (what) shall equal thee?" That is, it shall ascend on high, where thou art sitting, and even as thou observest below, the holy people do not now enter the holy city; so I say unto thee I will not ascend there until the people have entered into thy walls below. Let this console and comfort thee. I will not ascend until, under the form of Mah, I become like thee in all things. If the overflow of thy afflictions be like that of the sea, and if thou say there is no healing or remedy for thee, thou thinkest wrongly. Mi (who) shall heal thee? This is the highest scale of the mystery--the mystery of the being, upon whom dependeth all things. He shall heal and strengthen thee. Mi of the heavens above is the highest pole, Mah of the heavens below is the lower pole, and the heritage of Jacob stands between these extremities of the heavens--Mi (who) and Mah (what). This is the meaning of the words "Who (Mi) created these?"

Then Rabbi Simeon, interrupting, spake, and said: "Eliezar, my son! cease thy interpretations of the words, for a profound mystery is about to be revealed, which the children of the world know nothing of, even onto this day." Rabbi Eliezar obeyed, and ceased speaking.

Rabbi Simeon for a moment was silent, and then said: "Eliezar, my son, what is the meaning of Aleh (these)? If thou sayest it includes the stars, constellations and other heavenly bodies which are visible and seen always to the eye of man and have been created by Mah, as it is written, "By the word of God the heavens were made." Aleh (these) cannot refer to things invisible, but to those that are seen. The mysterious meaning of the word was revealed to me one day that I was standing by the seashore, when Elijah, the prophet, suddenly appeared and said unto me: Rabbi! knowest thou what Aleh (these things) means? And I answered and said it means the heavens and their hosts, the work of the Holy One, blessed be He, which it behooves every man to study as it is written: "When I consider the heavens the work of that fingers, etc." "Oh, Lord, our God how excellent is thy name in all the earth!" Rabbi! said Elijah, this word is an occult word, and was revealed and explained in the heavenly college thus. When the Most Secret One wished to reveal himself, He first created a point, and it became a divine Thought, in which were the ideas of all created things and forms of all things, and also that holy, glorious Light wherein was the Holy of Holies--a structure of magnificent and lofty dimensions, the work of that divine Thought and the beginning, or cornerstone, to this structure, hidden and concealed in the name as yet ineffable find known only as Mi (who), who wished to manifest itself and to be called by a name and become arrayed and clothed with a precious and resplendent garment. He therefore created Aleh (these things), which then became a part of the divine name; for these words, joined and associated together, form Alhim, which is composed of Aleh (these things), and Mi reversed and which existed not previous to this conjunction.

To this mystery the worshippers of the golden calf alluded when they cried: "Aleh is thy God, Oh, Israel! As on the work of creation, Mi remains conjoined with Aleh (these), so in the name Alhim they are always inseparable. And by reason of this unity the world abides as it is having thus spoken, Elijah disappeared, and I saw him no more. It is from him I learned the meaning of this mystery of Mi, Aleh and Alhim."

Rabbi Eliezar and the rest of the students went, and prostrating themselves before their master, said: "If we had come into the world only to hear and understand the meaning of these words, we should be satisfied." Rabbi Simeon then commenced speaking again, and said: "Thus the heaven and all its hosts have been created by means of Mah, for it is written: "When I behold the heavens, the work of that fingers, etc. Oh, Lord, our God, Mah (what) that name is excellent in all the earth." Thou who hast set thy glory above the heavens, signifying and referring to the ascension of Aleh in Mi, after creating one for the other and forming one name. Thus mean the words berashith, bara. Alhim, God, in the beginning created Alhim. This junction of the two words being effected, the mother lent the daughter her garments of splendor and arrayed her in her jewels; and when was this? When all the males appeared before Alhim (God) as it is written: "All the males, three times a year shall they present themselves before the Lord, Alhim." Alhim is here called Adon, or Lord, as it is written: "Behold the ark of the covenant, Adon of all the earth." So the H from Mah, representing the female principle, went forth and was replaced by I (representing the male principle) from Mi, and thus Alhim is formed. This is the signification of the words "When I remember Aleh, I pour out my soul within me." "I have remembered this and have shed tears."

That the letters, emanating one from the other, might produce Aleh and then form Alhim, according as it is written: "I will bring them down from on high into the house of Alhim below," in order to form an Alhim like Alhim above. How? By songs and thanksgiving. Rabbi Simeon ceased speaking, and his son, Rabbi Eliezar, exclaimed: "My silence has resulted in the building of a temple above and a temple below, and the old proverb has been realized--'if speech is worth a shekel, silence is worth two.' If my speech was worth a shekel, my silence was worth two; for I have learned that two worlds have been created--the heavenly and the earthly--at the same tame."

Rabbi Simeon spake again: We will explain the words following those which have been quoted and explained: "That bringeth out their host by number." There are two personalities inferred, viz.: Mi and Mah---the one above, the other below. That above says "Bringeth out the host by number." It must be confessed there is none like unto hire, yet is he who bringeth forth bread from the earth, though below, one and the same. By number, amounting to six hundred thousand, "who stand together as one man." "He calls them by name." If you say by their own special name, He calls them. It is not so, because Aleh had not as yet entered into the divine name, and He was only known as Mi, and was then creating things in their own nature, and at the same time hidden and concealed in him. But as soon as Alhim was formed, as stated before, from Aleh, Mi, then, by virtue of this name, he created the universe. This is the meaning of the words: "He called by the name," his name. "By the greatness of his might"; that is, by the divine will, which in a hidden and mysterious manner and according to its good pleasure worketh and doeth all things both in the world above and the world below. "Not one faileth," meaning that of the host of six hundred thousand created and produced by the power of the name Alhim, not one is wanting or missing. Like the children of Israel, who, although punished and afflicted by plagues, yet always continued undiminished in number as they went out of Egypt, not one was missing of their six hundred thousand strong; and so shall it be with the host, both above and below, not one shall be wanting.

THE MYSTICISM OF THE ALPHABET

RABBI Chananya spake, and said: "Before creation began, the alphabetical letters were in reversed order; thus, the two first words in the Book of Genesis, berashith, bara, begin with B; the next two, Alhim, ath, with A. Why did it not commence with A, the first letter? The reason of this inversion is as follows: For two thousand years before the creation of the world the letters were concealed and hidden, being objects of divine pleasure and delight.

"When the Divine Being, however, willed to create the world, all the letters appeared before his presence in their reverse order. Th first ascended and said: 'Lord of the Universe! let it please thee to create the world by me, as I am the final letter of the word Emeth (truth), which is graven on thy signet ring. Thou thyself art called Emeth, and therefore it will become thee, the great King, to begin and create the world by me.' Said the Holy One (blessed be He): 'Thou, oh, Teth, are indeed worthy, but I cannot create the world by thee; for thou art destined to be not only the characteristic emblem borne by faithful students of the law, from beginning to end, but also the associate of Maveth (death), of which thou art the final letter. Therefore the creation of the world cannot, must not, be through thee.'

"After Th had disappeared, Sh ascended and said: 'I pray thee, Lord of the Universe, as bearing thy great name Shaddai (almighty), to create the world by me, by the holy name that becometh thee only.' Said the Holy One: 'Thou art truly, oh, Schin, worthy, pure and true; but letters that go to form lying and falsehood will associate themselves with thee, viz.: Koph (Q) and Resh (R), and with thee will make up SheQeR (a lie), Falsehood, in order that it may be received and credited, some first with the appearance of truth (Sh), which thou representest, and for this reason I will not create the world by thee.' So Schin departed and Q and R, having heard these words, dared not present themselves before the divine presence.

"TZ then went before him, saying: 'Because I mark the Zaddikim (the righteous), and thou thyself nearest me in thy name, Zaddik (righteous), and also it is written "The righteous Lord loveth righteousness," it will become thee to create the world by me.' Then said the Holy One: "Zaddi,

Zaddi, thou art truly righteous, but thou must keep thyself concealed, and thy occult meaning must not be made known or become revealed; and therefore thou must not be used in the creation of the world. Thy original form was a rod, symbol of the female principle, surmounted by Yod, a letter of the holy Name, and also of the Holy Covenant, and emblem of the male principle. (By this, reference is made to the first man, who was androgynous, with faces turning one to the right, the other to the left, as symbolized in the figure of Zaddi in the Hebrew alphabet). But the time will come that thou shall be divided, and thy faces shall then be turned to each other.'

"Zaddi then departed, and P ascended and said: 'I am the beginning of the salvation (Peragna) and deliverance (Peduth) thou will execute in the world. It will be fitting to create it by me.' 'Thou art worthy,' replied the Holy One, 'but thou also givest rise to Evil (Peshang), and in thy form resemblest those animals who walk with drooping heads, like wicked men who go about with bowed heads and extended hands. I will not, therefore, create the world by thee.'

"To the letter Ayin, the initial of the word Avon (iniquity), though it claimed the origination of Anava (Modesty), the holy One said: 'I shall not create the world by thee.' And forthwith Ayin departed.

"S then went and pleaded: 'I am near (Samich) to the fallen ones, as it is written: "The Lord upholdeth (soumekh) all them that fall."' 'Thou must return, Samich, to thy place,' was the reply of the Holy One, 'and must not leave it; for if thou dost, what will become of the fallen, who will need and look to thee for aid and support?' "Samich forthwith returned, and was followed by N, who said: 'Oh, thou Holy One! that thou mayest be venerated in praises (Nura tehillim), and also because the praise of the righteous will be a Nava (delight), let it please thee to create the world by me.' To whom he replied: 'Nun, return thou to thy place with the fallen (Nephelim), for whose sake Samich hath gone back to her place, and lean for support upon her.'

"M then followed after, saying: 'Thou wilt by me be called Melech (King).' 'Truly so,' said He, 'but I will not, for all that, create the world by thee. Go back at once to thy place with thy companion letters, L and CH; for there must be a King, and for the world to be without one would not be seemly.'"

THE MYSTERY OF THE ALPHABET

(Continued.)

AT that moment bh descended from off the throne of light and splendor, exclaiming: "I am thy glory, create the world by me." As it stood trembling with excitement before the Holy One, two hundred thousand worlds together with the throne itself were seized with a sudden tremor and seemed ready to fall. "Caph, Caph!" cried the Holy One, "what hast thou done? I will not create the world by thee, for thou beginnest bhala (ruin, loss). Return at once to thy place on the throne of glory and abide there!" Then Caph retired and went back to its place.

I next appeared and claimed that being the initial letter in the divine name IHVH, it was the best for the work of creation. But the Holy One replied: "Let it suffice thee to be what thou art, chief letter in my name and foremost in all my designs, thou must remain where and as thou art!"

Then came I and spake before the Eternal One: "Create the world by me, for in me alone is thy goodness (Tobh) and uprightness, both attributes of thee." "I will not, Oh Teth," replied the Holy One, "use thee in the creation of the world, because the goodness within thee is hidden and concealed from sight as it is written, "How great is thy goodness which thou hidest for them that fear thee." Seeing thou wilt remain invisible to the world, I am about to create, and furthermore because of the goodness hidden within thee, the gates of the temple will sink into the earth as it is written, 'Her gates are sunk into the ground,' and besides all this, thou with thy comrade the letter Heth (bh) composed sin. Therefore, these letters will never enter in the names of the twelve holy tribes." On hearing these words bh went not before the Holy One, but returned at once to its place. Z then went up and urged its claim, saying: "Thy children will through me keep the Sabbath, as it is written: 'Remember (Zecor) the Sabbath to keep it holy." "Thou, Oh Zain," replied the Holy One, "art of too warlike a form, resembling as thou dust a spear. I cannot use thee in the creation of the world."

When Z heard this decision, like N it retired and gave place to V, who said: "I am a letter in thy holy name." The eternal one answered and said: "Remain contented, Oh V that together with H you are in the great name. I shall not choose you by whom to create the world."

D, accompanied by G, went before the divine presence. To them it was said, "Let it suffice you, that so long as you are conjoined and associated, there will always be the poor on the earth who will need succor and help. Daleth (D)--poverty and Gimel (G)--help or the benefactor. Therefore both of you keep together, the one helping the other." (In the Hebrew alphabet G and D are successive letters).

Then came B and said: "Create the world by me, because I am the initial letter of beracha (blessing) and through me all will bless thee, both in the world above as in the world below." "Truly, Oh B," said the Holy One, "I will surely create the world by thee only."

Hearing these words, A remained in its place and went not into the divine presence, who therefore exclaimed "Aleph (A) Aleph! why comest thou not before me as all the other letters?" Then replied A: "Lord and sovereign of the universe, it is because I have observed that (B excepted) they have returned as they went, without success. Why, therefore, should I come before thee, since thou hast already given to B the great and precious gift we all of us craved and desired. Moreover, it becometh not the monarch of the universe to withdraw and take back his presents from one subject and give them to another." To these words the Holy One responded: "Aleph, Aleph! Thou shalt be the first of all letters and my unity shall be symbolized only by thee. In all conceptions and ideas human or divine, in every act and deed begun, carried on and completed, in all of them shalt thou be the first, the beginning."

Therefore did the holy one make the letters of the celestial alphabet, capitals, and those of the earthly, small, each corresponding to one another. Therefore also the Book of Genesis begins with two words whose initials are B, viz.: Braeshith, Bara (in the beginning created) followed by two others, whose initials are A, viz., Alhim, ath (God, the substance of) to show that the letters of these alphabets celestial and earthly are one and the same by which every creature and thing in the universe has been formed and produced.

THE INITIATION OF RABBI HIYA

BERESHITH, "In the beginning," said Rabbi Ionda, "what is the signification of this mystical word? It is hochma--wisdom, that wisdom by which the world was formed and still subsists. Like a globe it includes the six directions of space, viz., north, south, east and west, high and low, from which emanate six streams of existence, all of which flow at last into the great ocean of primal life. Another occult signification of Bereshith is this, Bara sith (he created six) and who was he? Though not mentioned, it was the mysterious though ineffable, the great unknown."

Rabbi Hiya and Rabbi Jose were walking together in the country and when they reached their destination, said Rabbi Hiya: "This occult meaning of bereshith is undoubtedly correct, since we find in the Book of Genesis that the creation of all things occurred and took place in six days and not more. In an ancient occult work on Genesis we have found many references to this account. Thus, the holy one at first formed a point in which was included and concealed, as in a palace, the forms or prototypes of all created things. Now though the palace contains them, the key of it is the most essential thing which closes and opens it. This palace, the world, is the receptacle or casket in which are enclosed many wonderful and secret mysteries, it has fifty gateways, ten on each of its four sides, nine opening heavenward and one, of which nothing definite is known about it, and it is therefore termed 'The Mysterious Gate.' There is also one kind of lock to all these gates and one key alone opens and closes them and gives entrance into the palace and the treasures therein. Bereshith, bara Alhim, these words are the palace, and Bereshith is the key that conceals or opens up their mysterious meanings. It opens and shuts, it reveals or obscures. Bereshith contains an opening word, shith, and a closing word, bara."

Said Rabbi Jose: "Truly this is so, and I have myself heard the master, Rabbi Simeon, say that this occult word bara closes but does not open, and thus explained it. "Ere the world became fixed and established, it was wrapped and enshrouded in darkness and chaos reigned supreme and as long as it endured, the world was Tohu (without form and solidity). When this key opened the gates, it became adapted for the generation and production of living beings. When was this? When Abraham came, as it is written: 'These (Aleh) are the generations of the heavens and the earth, behibaram' (when they were created) which word is au anagram of beabraham (by Abraham). The creation was brought about by the transposing of the letters of the concealing word, bara, into Abar, the sacred principle on which the world was founded and continues to subsist. Mi was the first aspect of the mysterious unknown who, when bara was transposed into Abr, created Alh (these). To Abr he took and joined the letter H, forming Abrh, to Alh. He took and joined I, forming Alhi, then of the two component letters of Mi, he took and added M to each of them and thus were formed Alhim and Abraham. Another explanation of the forming of these names is as follows:

"The holy one took Mi and joined it to Alh and this formed Alhim. He also took Mah, and joining it to Abr, formed Abraham. Now the name Mi (50) has reference to the fifty gates of Binah, the third sephira, and in it is also I, the first letter in the Shem Hamphorah or holy name IHVH, and Mah has also reference to the divine name, for the H thereof is the second letter in it. So the two worlds were formed, by I the world to come through H the present world through Mi, the world on high, through Mah the world below. But until the name of Abraham was formed, there was no generation of living creatures and things, and this explains what is written, Aleh produced the generations of the heaven and the earth bi-Abraham; that is, when the name of Abraham was formed, as it is written 'In that day the Lord God made the earth and the heavens.'"

Rabbi Hiya prostrated himself on the earth and kissing it, exclaimed: "Oh, earth, earth! how hard and unfeeling art thou! In thee lies buried everything delighting the eyes. All the lights of learning and wisdom thou causest to disappear and vanish from the world. How unfeeling thou art. The great master and teacher, the one shining light of the world, by which it was enlightened, has returned to the dust and now lies concealed in thee, even Rabbi Simeon thou hidest him and all things become subject to thee at last. Overwhelmed with emotion, for a moment he became speechless. Again he cried, earth! earth! exult thou not, for now I see the great masters of light are not delivered into thy hands, for Rabbi Simeon yet lives, and with eyes filled with tears of joy, Rabbi Hiya went on his way and Rabbi Jose was with him. For forty days he fasted that he might see Rabbi Simeon, but it was said to him: "It is not possible for thee to behold him." Then fasted he other forty days, at the end of which he saw as in a vision Rabbi Simeon, with Rabbi Eleazar his son, studying and meditating upon the words upon which Rabbi Jose had discoursed. They were surrounded by a multitude of listening and attentive students. Anon he observed mighty angelic beings, who descended from on high, taking Rabbi Simeon, and Eleazar, his son, with them, wended their way again upwards to the celestial school, where, when they arrived, they all became arrayed with garments of dazzling splendor, whiter and more glittering than the light of the sun.

Then spake Rabbi Simeon, and said: "Let Rabbi Hiya come up hither and behold how great joys the holy one hath prepared for the just and upright in the world to come. Blessed the lot of him who cometh hither with a pure heart and mind, blessed also are they who in the world abide steadfast and firm and unmoved as pillars of right and truth." Rabbi Hiya then ascended and after making obeisance to Rabbi Eleazar and the masters who were standing to receive and welcome him, went and sat down at the feet of Rabbi Simeon. A voice resounded and said: "Close thy eyes and bow thy head, so that thy mind may not be distracted or disturbed." He closed his eyes and there was, as it were, a great light shining afar off and another voice was heard saying: "Ye heavenly beings, high and exalted ones, who unseen and invisible to mortal vision, visit the world, attend ye! Teachers of the mysteries who in your lonely hermitages are sleeping, awaken ye! attend, as also those who before coming hither, have turned darkness into light and made bitter to become sweet, waiting and longing for the dawning of the day when the king should visit his loved ones, in and by whom he shall be glorified and hailed as the King of kings and Lord of lords. Such only have the right and privilege to be present here."

Then Rabbi Hiya saw his fellow students standing around the, masters and they wended their way to the celestial school. Some were ascending and others descending thither, and at their head was the great winged angel of the presence (Metatron), who was saying he had heard in the palace on high that the king, visits everyday and does not forget his lone and loved ones who are struggling towards the higher life unnoticed and unregarded by the world. At that moment three hundred and ninety worlds trembled and shook as with an earthquake. Stars as of fire descended from on high and fell into the great sea, whose ruler then stood up and swore by him that lives forever, that he would dry up all the waters of creation if ever the world and its powers should gather themselves against the children of light to destroy them.

As he ceased speaking, Rabbi Hiya heard a voice from heaven exclaiming: "Fall back! make room for the King Messiah coming to the school of Rabbi Simeon, whose students are all initiates and master teachers of the secret doctrine." Then came Messiah and visited all the celestial schools and confirmed the teachings and expositions of the mysteries given by their appointed instructors. As he entered the great assembly crowned with many crowns, all the great masters rose up and saluted. Turning to Rabbi Simeon, the emanation of whose light reached up to heaven, Messiah spake and said: "Blessed art thou, Rabbi Simeon, for thy mystic teachings are of the highest worth and valued and cherished by all. They only, along with those of Hesekiah, King of Judah, and Achiya, the Solonite, are marked and sealed with the approval of the holy one. I have come hither because I know that the angel of the presence visits no other school save yours."

As he ceased speaking, Rabbi Simeon raised his hand and repeated the vow of the angel of the great sea. Then spake Messiah words which made the heavens, the ocean and Great Leviathan tremble, fearing that the world was about to be destroyed and annihilated. Beholding Rabbi Hiya at the feet of Rabbi Simeon, "Who!" said he, "who has brought hither one clad in garments of the lower world?" "It is Rabbi Hiya," replied Rabbi Simeon, "a student skilled in the science of the mysteries." "Let him then, together with his son, be enrolled as members of thy school." "I pray thee," said Rabbi Simeon again, "that time may be granted for due preparation." The request was granted and Rabbi Hiya overwhelmed with feelings of joy, went forth exclaiming: "Blessed is the lot of the just in heaven, blessed also the lot of Rabbi Simeon ben Jochai, to whom the words of the scripture may be applied: 'I cause those that love me to be blest with substance, and I will fill their treasures.'" The following affecting and descriptive account of Rabbi Hiya's decease is not found in some of the early editions of the Zohar and is probably an interpolation from an ancient Kabbalistic work no longer extant.

Rabbi Hiya, perceiving the end of life approaching, exclaimed: "Return, my soul to thy home on high! Thou spark divine of heavenly flame, quit thou this mortal frame. Fearing, trembling, hoping the time has come for thee to mount up to the mansions of light and life. Sweet angelic voices are calling me. My strength is failing, my eyes grow dim; I cease to breathe; the earth is disappearing and heaven opens on my eyes. Me-thinks I hear the fluttering of angel wings. Ah! what do I see'? The tree of life radiating a perfume that fills the azure vault of heaven itself. I see descending the mystic heavenly dove. I recognize King Messiah, whom I saw in Rabbi Simeon's school. Oh! ye angelic beings, lend me your wings, that I may mount on high to meet him. Oh, my soul! can this be death'? How vain the fear and dread of the transports of ecstatic bliss and joys its presence brings! Oh, grave! where is thy victory? Oh, death! where is thy sting?"

A moment, and his soul had taken its flight--the life of Rabbi Hiya had ended.

THE MYSTERIOUS STRANGER

BERESHITH! Rabbi Simeon spake and said: "I have put my words in thy month, and I have covered thee in the shadow of my hand, that I may plant the heavens and lay the foundation of the earth." These words inculcate that man should study and acquaint himself with the mysteries of the secret doctrine by day and by night, and that the Holy One regards those whose delights are therein. Every new thought suggestive or explanatory of it is crowned by him, and by it he forms a new heaven. It is said that whenever a man gives expression to such a word it ascends at once into the divine presence, who taketh and embraceth it and adorneth it with seventy crowns, all engraveth with his holy name. This word of mystic wisdom then descends and visits the children of light, who are the life of the world. Then it flies through seventy thousand worlds and stands before the Ancient of Days, with whose words, enfolding the deepest mysteries, it then becomes united and together fly through eighteen worlds invisible to mortal eyes and known only to Alhim. Perfected and complete, it returns to the Ancient of Days and become to him a subject of delight as he takes and crowns it with three hundred and seventy thousand crowns, when at length it is transformed into and becomes a new world. So, with every such like word, it becomes a new world of hidden mysteries of heavenly wisdom, a new earth referred to in scripture. "As the new heaven and the new earth which I make abiding before me." Not which I have created, as in the past, but which I create in the present, by means of those holy words which preserve and renew the worlds, and this is the occult signification of these words. Observe, it is said, not the heavens, but new heavens."

Said Rabbi Eleazar: "What is the occult meaning of the words, 'In the shadow of mine hand have I hid thee?'"

Rabbi Simeon replied: "When the secret doctrine and its hidden mysteries was delivered to Moses on Mount Sinai myriads of angels endeavored, through jealousy, to consume him with their fiery breath. Then the Holy One covered him with his hand, so that they did him no hurt. Also, with the word of which we have just described proceeding from human lips, it also is covered and protected from the wrath and envy of angels, until it becomes a new heaven or a new earth; for then only become they uncovered and their meaning revealed. This is furthermore shown by the words, 'Say unto Sion Ammi Atha' (thou art my people). They should rather be rendered, 'Immi Atha' (thou art with me), with me as an associate, just as my word was with me when I created the world, as it is written: 'By the word of the Lord the heavens were made.' And so it is with words containing mysteries of the secret doctrine uttered by us. We become creators, and happy- am! blessed are I hey who consecrate themselves to the study and teaching of this holy science and knowledge. If, however, you say that such a word may proceed from or be spoken by one who has no knowledge or understanding of sacred mysteries, observe that, if this should happen, then the word spoken by one who is ignorant of the secret doctrine is seized hold of by a demon called aishtahphucoth (froward lips), who casts it into the great abyss when it becomes a false heaven, and know as Tohu (vanity). When this heaven of falsehood is formed, forthwith it becomes united with another demon named esithzenonim (or lady of seductions), who causeth the ruin and destruction of thousands and as long as this false heaven subsists and power and rule predominate. Therefore is it written: 'Woe unto you who draw iniquity (avon) with cords of vanity and sin (hatah), as with a cart rope.' What is Hatah? It is this seductress who, proceeding from this world of vanity, destroyeth the children of man. The cause of all this is the student who has not attained to the wisdom and science of an initiate or master. God preserve us from becoming such! See to it, therefore, that ye let not a single word escape your lips concerning divine mysteries without understanding or before consulting with a master that ye may not be originators of Hatah, and thus cause the destruction and ruin of many souls."

With one accord exclaimed the students of Rabbi Simeon: "God keep and preserve us from this!"

Continuing his discourse, Rabbi Simeon said: "Mark this also. It was by means of the secret doctrine that the Holy One created the world. Holy scripture affirms that it was with him and was his delight daily. He examined it attentively and minutely, and then uttered it, and thereby produced all his works in order to teach us to study occult science and sacred mysteries calmly and reverently, and thus avoid falling into error and causing many to stumble, to fall, to perish. It is written, "Then did he see it and declare it. He prepared it; yea, searched it out." in which verse are the words yaha (see), yesaphrah (declared), kenah (prepared), hakar (searched), showing what carefulness was exercised by the Holy One before creating the world. For ere doing so he formed the four words corresponding to those we have just particularized, viz.: Bereshith, bara, Alhim, ath, implying a fourfold examination of the secret doctrine ere he used it in Creation."

Rabbi Eleazar went one day to visit his uncle, Rabbi Jose, and Rabbi Abba was with him. A porter followed behind them.

Said Rabbi Abba: "As the time and opportunity are favorable, let us discourse and search a little into the secret doctrine."

Then spake Rabbi Eleazar, and said: "It is written, 'Ye shall keep my sabbaths.' Observe that in six days the Holy One created the world that each day was distinguished by a special production. But on what day appeared the production that was fruitful? On the fourth; for those of the three first days were unmanifested and hidden, viz.: fire, water, and earth. If you say that the earth was clothed with vegetation on the third. it was truly so. It was, however, really on the fourth day that the results became manifest and distinctive in themselves, and thus it became the fourth pedestal of the heavenly throne. All the works of creation were finished certainly on the Sabbath, as it is written: 'And Alhim created on the seventh day,' the Sabbath, which was the fourth day of the earth's fruitful production. But what meaneth 'Ye shall keep my Sabbaths,' as though there were two or more sabbaths? The scripture, by this plural word, designates the eve of the Sabbath and the day of the Sabbath, distinct yet not separate."

Then spake the porter who had followed them, and said: "But what is the signification of the following words: 'Ye shall reverence my sanctuary.'"

Rabbi Eleazar replied: "They refer to the holiness of the Sabbath."

"What do you mean by the holiness of the Sabbath?" asked the stranger.

"It is the heavenly holiness which cometh down upon the earth on that day," replied Rabbi Eleazar.

"If so, then you make not the Sabbath holy, but a something which is from above."

"That truly is so," said Rabbi Abba, "what Rabbi Eleazar has said, for it is written: 'Call the Sabbath a delight, and the Holy of the Lord honorable.' Therefore there is a distinction between the Sabbath day and the Holy of the Lord."

"What, then, meaneth the Holy of the Lord?" asked the stranger again.

"It is," replied Rabbi Abba, "as has been just said, a heavenly holiness coming from above on that day."

"Then," answered the stranger, "in that ease the heavenly holiness is glorious and hallowed, but not the day of the Sabbath; and yet the scripture says, "Glorify the Sabbath day."

"Men," said Rabbi Eleazar to Rabbi Abba, "let this man speak on, for he seems to be endowed with a wisdom and knowledge we do not possess."

"They turned toward the stranger and said: "Give us your opinion on the subject."

"It is written," he said to them, "'Keep my Sabbaths,' words which show plainly that there are two sabbaths--one heavenly and one earthly--yet are they but one, both alike in their esoteric meaning. There is another Sabbath--a third one, not mentioned in scripture, and which was unhonored. This Sabbath said to the Holy One: 'Thou art my maker, and I am called Sabbath. Now, there is no day without a night. Let there a Sabbath night or eve, as well as a Sabbath day, be kept.' To which the Holy One replied: 'My child, Sabbath art thou, and Sabbath thou shalt he called. I will yet adorn three with great honor and beauty.' Then made he proclamation, and said: 'Reverence my sanctuary.' That is to say, the Sabbath eve, which is also to be reverenced and kept; for the name of the Holy One is found in the word. I will now inform you how my father explained this to me. 'Imagine,' said he, 'a square within a circle, symbolizing two divine forms, which, though distinct, are not separate; for there is not division or separation in the divine essence. An earthly resemblance to this divine union is that between Jacob and Joseph. There is also a resemblance in the repetition of the word peace, in that verse of scripture, "Peace to those that are far off and peace to those that are near," those that are far off referring to Jacob and those that are near to Joseph, symbolical of the

Sabbath and the Sabbath eve, distinguished by 'Keep the Sabbath' and 'remember the Sabbath day.' But the words, 'Reverence my sanctuary,' designate a point in the middle of the square and circle which is the most sacred of all--he who violates and breaks this commandment is punishable with death, as it is written, 'Whoso violates it shall be put to death'; that is, who enters into the circle and square to the middle point and profanes it. Therefore is it said, 'Reverence ye,' for that middle point is called Ani (Me). which is but another term or name of the Great Unknown, the Divine Being."

After hearing these words from the unknown stranger, they embraced him, and said:

"Possessed of such knowledge of the secret doctrine, you must not follow behind, but go before us. What is thy name?"

"Ask me not," he replied. "But let us go forward discoursing on occult mysteries, each of us giving utterance to words of hidden wisdom which shall lighten the way."

Said they: "How came you to follow us'?

"Yod," he replied, "made war against two other letters, Caph and Samech (ch and S), in order that they might become attached to me. Koph was unwilling to be joined to one without whose help it could not subsist a single moment, and Samech was equally unwilling to become bound to Koph, and thus he unable to help those who stumble and fall. Then Yod, coming to me, embraced me, caressed me, wept with me, and said: 'My child, what can I do for you? I aim about to ascend on high, and shall acquire amongst many good things secret letters. all capitals, and valuable. I will then come back to thee and help thee and give thee other letters, better and stronger than those who have forsaken and left thee, even Ysh (blessing), who will he to thee treasures filled with good things. Go, therefore, my child, and mount thy ass.' And this is why I am here."

Rabbi Eleazar and Rabbi Abba were greatly pleased, and said: "Go on before and we will follow after thee."

Replied the stranger: "have I not told you it was through the King's orders that I have come hither?"

They said: "But you have not told us your name. Where de you dwell?"

"My habitation is a fine and strong one, a high tower, in which the Holy One and myself only reside. Just now I am here riding on my ass."

Then Rabbi Eleazar and Rabbi Abba pondered awhile and meditated on these sayings and the meaning of them, which to them were as honey and manna. Then said they unto him: "Who is thy father? If thou wilt tell us we will make obeisance unto thee."

"Wherefore should I?" he answered. "It is not usual with me to impart occult science to anyone. However, my father lives in the great sea, and was a great fish. He was great and strong and full of years, so that he swallowed up all the other fishes of the sea and then sent them forth living and filled with all the good things of the world. His power is such he can run through the sea in a moment, and he sent me forth as an arrow from the how of a skilled archer and concealed me in the place of which I have spoken; but he himself has returned, and remains hidden in the sea."

Rabbi Eleazar, after reflecting a moment, exclaimed: "Thou art the son of the great mystic teacher Rabbi Hammenuna, the Aged, the great initiate in the secret doctrine!"

Then they embraced him and went forward, saying: "Let it please thee, Oh, master, tell us thy name?"

"Then," said he, "it is written, 'Benaiah, Son of Jehoida.' We have already expounded the signification of these words. It will, however, be profitable to consider the deeply occult meaning of them, which has reference to human life. To continue, 'Son of a living man'; that is, of the just one--the life of the world. 'Who wrought many great works,' meaning Lord of all workers and of the heavenly hosts, all of whom are marked and distinguished by the letters of the divine name, Yehoval Sabaoth, the greatest of all names. 'The Lord of great works'; that is, the Lord of 'Mequabsel,' a mighty and most lordly tree. Where is its locality, and in what consists its magnificence? The scripture refers to it as being on high, where 'Eye hath not seen it, save thine alone, Oh, Lord.' In it is contained the life and essence of all existing things and living creatures, angels, archangels, heavenly hierarchies, principalities and powers, the universe with its unnumbered systems of stars and constellations; yea! all things are contained therein as in a glorious and magnificent palace, and from it come forth all things visible and reflective of its glory and magnificence. 'He killed two lions of Moab,' referring to the first and second temple of Jerusalem, which subsisted until the heavenly light which enlightened them was withdrawn from them; then were they destroyed and the holy throne demolished. Thus it is written: 'I was in the captivity'; that is to say, this divine glory or essence called Ani (I) was in captivity. Why does the scripture still proceed, saying: 'By the River Chebar?' Because Chebar is the mysterious river of the heavenly light which floweth forth, but became dried up and ceased to flow when I was in captivity, and this is the meaning of the words, 'The river decayeth and drieth up,' referring to the two temples of Jerusalem. With respect to the words, 'He killed two lions of Moab,' this latter word should be rendered Meab--of the father in heaven, having the same occult meaning. Again it is said of Benaiah, 'He went down and slew a lion in the midst of the pit in time of snow.' In former times, when the river of divine radiance and glory was flowing, the children of Israel flourished and lived in peace and offered up daily sacrifices for their sins, when a celestial being, with the emblematic form of a lion, was seen by them descending on the altar, consuming and devouring the offerings with the avidity of a hungry man, during which the demons of evil, like dogs, fled away and hid themselves. But, on account of the sins of the people, the Most High came down and killed the lion, if it may be so expressed. 'He killed it in a pit,' meaning in presence of the dog-like demons, living in dark subterranean places, that they might see they could seize and devour now the sacrifices, as they were of no worth in his sight. Now, the name of the lion was Ouriel, because lion-like in form, and the name of the demons was Baladan, or not human but dog-like. 'In the time of snow'; that is, when the children of Israel sinned and were consumed by divine justice. Such also is the significance of the words, 'She feareth not for her house of snow.' Why? Because arrayed with purple, and thus able to resist the fiercest flame. To proceed further, 'And he killed an Egyptian, a goodly man,' teaching that whenever Israel sins it loses the blessing and light of the divine presence which it once enjoyed. 'And he killed the Egyptian,' referring to the light which illuminated Israel, viz.: Moses, who was called an Egyptian by the daughters of Jethro, when they said to him: 'An Egyptian hath helped us.' In Egypt he was born and reared, and there he became initiated in the secret doctrine. 'A goodly man,' for he saw the Lord clearlyNum. 12:8 and not in dark speeches. He was a divine man, a man of God, a recipient of divine science as no other man had ever enjoyed before. 'And in hand of the Egyptian was a spear.' This was the sceptre or rod of God that was handed to Moses, as mentioned by scripture: 'And the rod of the Alhim was in my hand,' the rod which was made when the sun rose for the first time, and on it was engraved the Shem Hamphorash, or most holy divine name. By it he smote the rock, as it is written: 'And he struck the rock with his rod twice.' Then said the Holy One: 'Moses, my rod was not given to thee to be used thus. I swear, by thy life, from this moment thou shalt not retain it.' Therefore we read: 'He descended with the rod,' which proved a great affliction for Israel, for then the rod was taken away. 'And he wrested the spear from out of the hand of the Egyptian,' meaning the rod, and it was never seen again. Then, furthermore, he read: 'He killed him with his spear for the sin committed by a wrong use of the rod. Moses died and was not allowed to enter into the promised land, and that light was taken from Israel. The scripture further relates that he, Benaiah, 'Was more honorable than the thirty, but he was not one of the three.' 'More honorable than the thirty, referring to the thirty years he was separated from the heavenly powers on high, and who, at the end of life, took him to themselves again. 'But he became not one of the three, viz.: the Divine, under three hypostases or forms, and who gave him the desire of his heart. 'Nevertheless, David set him over his guard'; that is, David, being attached to him, retained his services, so that they might not be separated from one another, in the same way that the moon is attached to the sun, to which it addresses its song of praise as the center and source of its light."

Rabbi Eleazar and Rabbi Abba knelt and prostrated themselves before the stranger, and then--but where was he? He had suddenly disappeared. They looked around amazed, but he was not to be seen. They sat down and pondered, bewildered and speechless. At length Rabbi Abba spake, and said:

"True is it that whenever students of esoteric truths travel together, discoursing amongst themselves on the mysteries of the secret doctrine, then are they visited by spiritual masters and teachers from on high. This stranger was indeed none other than Rabbi Hammenuna, the Aged, who has taught us truths which have never been divulged and revealed to anyone before, and leaving us before we were able to recognize him."

Then rose they up to mount their asses, but were unable to do so. Again they tried, with no better success. Filled with a feeling of trepidation, they fled away and left their asses behind, and to this day that place is known and called Assfield.

ABUNDANT GOODNESS

RABBI ELEAZAR spake and said: "How great is thy goodness which thou hast laid up for them that fear Thee" (Ps. xxxi. 19). How exceedingly great the celestial happiness which the Holy One has prepared for those who are pure in heart and mind and delight in the study of the divine law, when they ascend into the higher and diviner life. The scripture does not only say thy goodness, but the great abundance of thy goodness. What do these words comprehend? It will be one of the great enjoyments of those who attain to the higher life, to live in the presence of the Eternal One who is known to them as "Abundant Goodness" and who in scripture is referred to as "the great good to the house of Israel, or children of light." Again, "How great is thy goodness," words wherein is contained the mystery of Hochma (Wisdom) which includes all mysteries and therefore is designated or called Mah (how.) "Thy goodness" is the light created on the first day. "Which thou hast laid up for them that fear thee" signifies the garden of Eden of which it is written: "The place, O Lord, which thou hast made for them to dwell in" (Ex. xv. 17). "Before the sons of Men," viz., the soul:; of the just who, on their ascension into Paradise, became clothed with bright ethereal raiment and in their forms resemble those they bore on the earth plane. After abiding there a short space of time, they mount up to the celestial college in the higher Eden, where, after bathing in perfumed rivers, they come forth at times, appearing to man, on whose behalf they perform miracles like the angels from on high and similar to what we have ourselves just experienced. We have seen the light of the sacred lamp, but alas! that we have not learned and acquired more of the secret doctrine of Wisdom.

Then spake Rabbi Abba. It is written: "And Manoah said to his wife, 'We shall surely die for we have seen God'" (Judges xiii. 22). Although Manoah knew not who had spoken to him, yet he imagined it was the divine Being of whom it is affirmed "No man can see my face and live." We ourselves have been blessed with the celestial light that has been with us on our way, and whom the Holy One has sent to us in order to make known and reveal to us secret wisdom. Happy are we!

Then went they on their way and arrived at a hillside as the sun was about to set. The leaves of the trees in a neighboring grove stirred by a gentle breeze began in sweet cadences to hymn their praises to the Creator and heard by the travellers wending their way, a voice cried: "Children of the great Divine who go down and mingle with mortals on the earth plane, and who reflect the light of your learning in the celestial college, assemble and gather yourselves together in your usual places for instruction in the secret doctrine." Then another voice exclaimed: "Ye great and honored teachers, behold, the Master sits on his throne!" Then another voice, in great and mighty tones, cried aloud: "The voice of the Lord breaketh the cedars" (Ps. xxix. 5). Rabbi Eleazar and Rabbi Abba at once prostrated themselves with their faces on the earth and trembled greatly. At last, rising, they fled hastily away and stayed not to listen longer, but proceeded on their way.

On arriving at the house of Rabbi Jose, son of Rabbi Simeon, son of Leconga, they beheld Rabbi Simeon ben Jochai there, and were exceeding glad. Said Rabbi Simeon: I know your journey has been a wonderful and marvellous one. We were sleeping when you went forth and we saw with you Benaiah the son of Jehoida and who had brought two crowns from the Aged One wherewith to bedeck you. Truly the Holy One was with you. Furthermore, if I had not seen this in a vision, I should have divined from your looks what has happened unto you. Said Rabbi Abba: What thou sagest is true, and the words of a sage are of more worth than those of a prophet. Rabbi Eleazar then recounted to his father all that had happened to them. Rabbi Simeon trembled and said: "Oh, Lord, I have heard thy speech and was afraid" (Habac. iii. 1). These words were uttered by the prophet Habacuc. After dying he was resuscitated and brought back to life by Elisha, the prophet and seer. Wherefore was he called Habacuc? Because of the words of Elisha to his mother: "About this season, according to the time of life, thou shalt embrace a son" (II. Kings iv. 16). In Hebrew the word embrace is expressed by the word habac. The prophet Habacuc was the son of the Shunamite woman and was so named because he was once embraced by his mother and again by Elisha as the scripture relates. "And he put his mouth upon his mouth" (II. Kings iv. 34). In an ancient book written by King Solomon, I have read that the seventy-two sacred divine names of the Holy One imprinted on the body of every mortal born into the world, had faded and become obliterated from the form of the Shunamite's son when he died. After Elisha the prophet had embraced him, these names containing two hundred and sixty letters reappeared, hence his name Habacuc, the numerical value of the letters composing it, being equal to 260. This is why Habacuc said: "I have heard thy speech and was afraid," that is, what I must experience or pass through in the world and was afraid. Oh, Lord! grant that thy work which time hast performed through me in my two lives may endure.

Pausing a moment, Rabbi Simeon exclaimed: After what I have heard from you I also am afraid before the Holy One. Then raising his hands on high he cried: How great is Hammenuna the aged, the renowned teacher of the secret doctrine! Blessed and happy are ye who have seen him face, to face, a favor I have never enjoyed. Prostrating himself upon the earth, Rabbi Simeon beheld in a vision Rabbi Hammenuna the aged, on his course and hastening to light up the temple of King Messiah. Observing Rabbi Simeon, he cried: "Thou shalt be associated and take thy place with the great teachers of the secret doctrine who ever stands in the presence of the Holy One." From that day Rabbi Simeon called Rabbi Eleazar his son and Rabbi Abba by the name of Peniel as we read of Jacob: "He called the name of the place Peniel, for I have seen Alhim face to face" (Gen. xxxii. 30).

EXPOSITION OF BIBLE MYSTERIES

"In the beginning," Rabbi Hiya spake and said: "The beginning of wisdom is the fear of Jehovah, a good understanding I have all they that do his commandments, his praise endureth forever" (Ps. cxi. 10). The beginning of wisdom has reference to the great object of wisdom, viz., to raise and elevate us into the higher and diviner life, as it is said: "Open to me the gates of righteousness" (Ps. cxviii. 19). This is the gate or way of the Lord through which everyone must pass in order to attain lento this life and live in the presence of the heavenly king. Ere this, however, there are several other gates on the upward course which must be passed through, each with their bolts and bars that have to be unloosed, and the last of which is that called "the fear of the Lord." It is the one only gate of access. There are in scripture two beginnings (bereshith) mentioned, and are united into one, viz., "the fear of the Lord" and "the beginning of Wisdom," both one and the same, and never found disjoined from each other. As it is written: "That men may know that thy name is Jehovah only." (Ps. lxxxiii. 18). Why is the first gate called the fear of the Lord? Because it is a tree of good or evil. When a man lives uprightly, it is a tree of good to him; if unjustly, a tree of evil. It is the gate or portal through which all blessing, spiritual or temporal, comes. The words: "A good understanding," refer to those gates which, as aforesaid, are one and the same.

Said Rabbi Jose: "A good understanding"; it is the tree of life without admixture or alloy of evil. "That do his commandments" are they who are true and faithful students of esoteric science. "His praise endureth forever" signifies that the throne of God or, in other words, the action of the good law, pervades the universe and endures throughout all ages.

Rabbi Simeon was sitting engaged in meditation and study of the secret doctrine during the night when the celestial bride becomes united to her bridegroom, for then, it is enjoined upon all the members of her retinue they should especially be present to accompany her to the nuptial dais and rejoice with her. On the eve of the heavenly union they must devote themselves to the study of the Pentateuch, the prophetical hooks, and the other parts of scripture, to the explanation of verses, and their occult meaning in which the heavenly spouse takes great delight. These students, with their acquired knowledge resulting from their studies, are "the marriage guests." When she ascendeth and seateth herself on the nuptial dais, the Holy One salutes her and blesses her attendants and presents them with crowns and garlands. Happy and blessed is their lot! Rabbi Simeon, together with his students, spent the night in study and acquiring deeper knowledge of esoteric science. Then said Rabbi Simeon: Blessed are ye! inasmuch as having spent this eve in meditation and study, your names will be enrolled and written in the celestial book, and the Holy One will endow you with faculties and powers more enlarged and receptive for the comprehension and understanding of divine mysteries.

Rabbi Simeon again spake and said: "The heavens declare the glory of God." (Ps. xix. 2). These words have already been explained, but they possess a deeper mystical meaning. At the time that the heavenly spouse is adorned in order to ascend the nuptial dais surrounded with the masters or teachers who have rejoiced with her throughout the night, beholding her husband, then is it "the heavens declare the glory of God," the heavens meaning the bridegroom who enters the nuptial chamber. The word "declare" (mesapherim) signifies sending forth glittering rays from one end of the wood to the other like a brilliant sapphire. "The glory of God" is the glory of the bridegroom who is called El (God) as it is written: "El judgeth the righteous, El is angry with the wicked every day." (Ps. vii. 12). During the whole of the year up to the eve of the celestial union, He is called El, but when the marriage day is consummated, he takes the name of Kobad (glory). These two names are a source of reciprocal light, power and joy to each other.

"And the firmament showeth his handiwork." His handiwork are the true and faithful followers of the holy law of whom it is said: "Let the beauty of the Lord, our God, lie upon us and establish thou the work of our hands upon us, yea, the work of [our hands establish thou it" (Ps. xc. 17), signifying or referring to the work of circumcision, which is a sign marked on the human body. Rabbi Hammenuna, the aged, has said: "Suffer not thy mouth to cause thy flesh to sin" (Eccles. v. 5). Never allow thy lips to give expression to evil words and thus sin against thy flesh which has been sanctified with the seal of the holy covenant, for by so doing thou incurrest the danger of being cast into the hell of evil and wrong-doing (Gehenna), the ruler of which is called Duma and is always attended with destroying angels, observing those who keep the covenant over whom they have then no power to injure or afflict. It is further written: "Neither say thou before the angel, that it was an error; that is, speak nothing that will cause the angel Duma to prevail against and overcome thee. "The firmament showeth his handiwork." These are the companions of the heavenly spouse, whose names are marked and inscribed in the firmament. What firmament? The visible heaven in which are the sun and moon, stars and constellations, and is the true Book of God. In it are found and written the names of all who have kept themselves pure and undefiled.

"Day unto day uttereth speech." This refers to the great holy day of the King who applauds his companions and commends the words of learning and wisdom uttered by each of them. "Night unto night showeth knowledge." That is, each night communicates to the following one the mystery of the esoteric knowledge which enlightens all intelligences. "There is no speech nor language where their voice is not heard," meaning they discourse not of worldly matters and vanities in presence of the King, who taketh no delight in such. "Their line is gone out through all the earth" refers to the dimensional archetypes according to which the heavens and the earth were measured and formed. If the question be asked who resides in them? Scripture declares: "In them hath he set a tabernacle for the sun," that is, the Holy One has fixed his mansion or tabernacle in the heavens wherein he is adorned and is then as a bridegroom coming out of his chamber rejoicing to run on his course, which when finished, he mounteth on high and runneth another course elsewhere. "His going forth is from the end of the heaven and his circuit unto the ends of it." that is, he descendeth from the higher to the lower world, which is expressed by the word outhqonphatha in which is included the idea of rotundity. For this reason the duration of a year is termed, thqouphatha-shana, for during that period the earth has travelled round the sun, and been the recipient of the whole of its rays of light and heat. "And there is nothing hid from the heat thereof." Every created thing, whether visible or not, is affected by the warming rays of the sun, which occultly represents the universality of the secret doctrine operating everywhere and is described as "the law of the Lord is perfect."

From the beginning of this Psalm (19th) the tetragrammaton or holy name I. H. V. H. is found six times, showing the mystery contained in the word Brashith (in the beginning), which has six letters. Bra-shith. (He created six) and these six letters correspond to the six first words of scripture which express the work of creation. Bra, Alhim, eth, hassamayim, veath, aaretzs

(Alhim created the substance of the heaven and the earth) or thus: Alhim created the substance of fire, water and earth.

At this moment Rabbi Eleazar and Rabbi Abba entered the assembly. On beholding them, Rabin Simeon exclaimed: Truly is the presence of the Schekinah with you and therefore I have called you Peniel, for ye have seen the Schekinah face to face, and now that I have explained the esoteric meaning of Benaiah, Son of Jehoida, I will explain to you the mystical meaning of yet another biblical verse: "And he slew an Egyptian, a man of great stature five cubits high" (I. Chron. xii. 23). The word Egyptian refers to Moses, of whom we said that he was very "great in the land of Egypt, in the eyes of Pharaoh's servants and the people of the land" (Ex. xi. 3), the mystical meaning of which is that he was distinguished more by his intellectual endowments and gifts than by his stature, similar to Adam, the first man, of whom it is metaphorically said that his stature was of the number of cubits separating the east from the west of the world. So when it is said of Moses that he was five cubits in height, it means that he was an adept practised in the five virtues leading to spiritual perfection, viz., love to God, chastity, charity, humility and perseverance in meditation and study of the secret doctrine. "And in the hand of the Egyptian was a spear like a weaver's beam," meaning the rod of God on which was engraved the holy name of forty-two letters, as was the shuttle of Bezaleel since we read: "He hath filled him with the spirit of God in wisdom, in understanding, in knowledge and in all manner of workmanship, and to devise curious works, in gold, silver and brass--all manner of work of the engraver, of the cunning workman, and of the embroiderer" (Ex. xxxv. 31-35). "Happy was the lot of Moses!" Come, therefore, dear friends; come and let us meditate and evolve new thoughts and ideas from out of the secret doctrine, for whoever on this night doeth thus shall be preserved from evil, and live in peace hereafter, "for the angel of the Lord campeth round about them that fear him and delivereth them. Oh, taste and see that the Lord is good. Blessed is the man that trusteth in him" (Ps. xxxiv. 8-9).

Again, on another occasion, Rabbi Simeon spake and said: "Bereshith bara Alhim" (In the beginning created God). These words require great thought and consideration, for everyone that says there is another God is cut off from the world, as it is written: "Thus shall he say unto them, the gods that have not made the heavens and the earth, even they shall perish from the earth and from under these heavens" (Jer. x. 11), for there is other God beside the Holy One.

This verse is in the Chaldee tongue excepting the last word, Aleh (these) which is in Hebrew. Why? It might be said, in order that the holy angels should not comprehend its signification of the divine unity. The true reason is that they might not become envious of man and thus cause him to suffer, for in the words, "the gods that have not made the heavens and the earth" have reference to certain angels who fell from heaven and set themselves up as gods.

Now the word earth which in Hebrew is arqa, in the Chaldee is arca; why so? Because it is one of the seven lower worlds where reside the descendants of Cain. After his expulsion from the earth, he went thither and begat children. This arqa was partly lighted and partly enshrouded in darkness and governed by two chiefs who were constantly warring against each other. On the arrival of Cain, however, they entered into an alliance of friendship for they perceived that it was to him they owed their existence. They became one body with two heads, the name of the one was Aphira, and Qastimon, the name of the other; this ruled over the dark, that over the light parts of Arqa. Before becoming joined together, they were like angels with six wings, Aphira having the form of an ox, Qastimon that of an eagle. On their union, they took on them the human form and begat offspring like unto themselves. When they found themselves in darkness, they became changed into the form of a serpent with two heads, and crawling as a serpent they plunged into the great sea, the abode of demons, where they found the decadent angels Azar and Azael and expelled them from their lurking places. These then fled and hid themselves in dark mountains thinking that the Holy One was about to execute vengeance open them for their evil doings and conduct. After this, the two chiefs Aphira and Qastimon swam through the great sea and went to visit Naamah, the mother of the demons, and the first deceiver and seducer of holy angels, who after their fall took different human forms and in their turn became corruptors of mankind. After roaming through the world they returned to Arqa, and now their great object is to corrupt the descendants of Cain and lead them into sin. Respecting this Arqa, the heaven with its various constellations and stars is altogether different from our visible heavens at night. The seasons for sowing and reaping are not the same as ours in their sequence and regularity, being separated by a considerable number of years; these two chiefs of Arqa are they to whom the Scripture refers, who posing as gods shall become exterminated from our Thebel or earth on which they shall not exercise any dominion, nor afflict the children of man during the night, but as saith the Scripture: "They shall be destroyed by Aleh, by whom the heavens and the earth have been created". This is why Aleh in this verse is written in Hebrew, designating the holy name untranslatable into the Chaldee language.

Then said Rabbi Eleazar to his father: What meaneth the words: "Who would not fear thee, Oh King of nations?" (Jer. x,, 7). Who is this King of Nations or Gentiles?

Said Rabbi Simeon: "This verse, my son, has been interpreted in various ways, but all alike erroneous, as is proved by the remaining portion of tine verse, "among all the wise men of the nations and in all their kingdoms, there is none like unto thee," which closes the mouth of the ungodly who imagine that the Holy One knoweth not and is not acquainted with the thoughts of their hearts. We will now refute their error.

A Gentile philosopher came to me one day, saying: You say that your God rules in the heavens on high and that all the angelic hosts cannot approach him or form a conception of his being. The words of this verse add no dignity to his glory. What glory and eminence can be ascribed to a deity who cannot be found and located amongst mankind. Furthermore, you declare: "And there arose not a prophet since in Israel like unto Moses" (Deuter. xxxiv. 10), from which it may be inferred that though no such prophet as he rose in Israel, yet it does not apply to the Gentiles, amongst whom I venture to maintain there have appeared many as great and equal to him. From these words of Jeremiah I conclude therefore that only amongst the wise men of the Gentiles there is none like unto God, but that in Israel there have been many like unto him; consequently, he could not be from this similarity their superior or master. Think well over my words and you will confess that I have reasoned logically and correctly.

My reply to him was thus: 'It is true what thou sayest, that in Israel there have been some sages like unto God. Who raiseth the dead to life again? Is it not God only? Yet both Elijah and Elisha brought the dead to life again. Who maketh the rain descend, but God only? Yet by his prayer Elijah caused it to cease and descend. Who is it but the Holy One that made the heavens and the earth? Yet Abraham came, and by him they were established. Who rules the course of the sun? Is it not the Holy One? Yet Joshua commanded it to stand still as it is written: "And the sun stood still" (Josh. x., 13). The Holy One gave decrees, so also did Moses, and they were established and conformed. Again the Holy One decreed punishments, but the just men of Israel caused them to cease or be turned aside, as it is said: "The righteous man ruleth in the fear of God" (II. Sam. xxiii., 3). Moreover, he commanded the just to walk in his way and to become like him. On hearing these words the philosopher turned away and went to the village of Shehalim, where he became known as the Little Joshua. There he applied himself to the study of the secret doctrine and eventually became one of the sages and chief men in that place.

Let us now return to the exposition of the words: "All the nations before him are as nothing." What do they mean? As also: "Who would not fear thee, Oh King of the Gentiles." What is their signification? Is God then the King of the Gentiles and not of Israel? Yea, the Holy One everywhere wishes to be glorified and worshipped by Israel and his name to be attached to Israel only, as it is written: "The God of Israel, the God of the Hebrews" (Ex. v., 3). "The King of Israel" (Is. xliv., 6). But the other nations of the world say: "We have other protectors in heaven. Your king ruleth over you and our king ruleth over us. The Scriptures say: "Who would not fear thee, Oh King of the Gentiles?" Now in heaven there are four great cosmokratores or rulers who derive their power and authority over the nations from the divine ruler and are unable to do anything except by his will and command. By the words: "Wise men of the nations," is meant the celestial rulers of the Gentiles, from whom these receive all their wisdom. Also the words: "Amongst all their kingdoms," have reference to the dominions of these rulers with their attendant hosts, who control the affairs of the world as executors of the divine will. "There is none like unto thee, Oh Lord, the holy and hidden one, who hath made the heavens and the earth." Of this Holy One we learn: "In the beginning God created the heavens and the earth," but to the nations and their dominions may be applied: "And the earth was without form and void."

Children! exclaimed Rabbi Simeon, let each of you prepar or procure a jewel for the heavenly bride; and thou, Eleazar, my son, be ready when the bridegroom cometh, to offer thy present to-morrow, when he ascendeth the dais with hymns and praises of his retinue.

Then Rabbi Eleazar read aloud: "Who is this that cometh out of the wilderness?" (Cant. III., 6). The two words "who" and "this" refer to two holy beings intimately associated and joined together by a tie which is termed olah (sacrifice). Though the literal meaning of this word is to ascend or come up, yet it occultly refers to the "Holy of Holies." Again "who" (Mi) is united to "this" (Zoth) in order that it, the Holy of Holies, may come from the wilderness. "Out of the wilderness" means mystically from or out of the word, and we are taught: "Thy word is comely" (Cant. IV., 3). Also by way of tradition has been imparted to us the signification of the words: "Who shall deliver us out of the hand of this mighty God?" This is the God that smote the Egyptians with all the plagues in the wilderness" (I. Sam., iv., 8). Why in the wilderness, when we read it was in their own land of Egypt? Now the term bemidhar (in the wilderness) in its real meaning is "by the Word," and everything that was done unto them was done by the Word of the Lord. And this is true generally.

When man rises in the morning he should utter or pronounce a blessing as soon as he opens his eyes, as did the holy men of olden time. They used to place near themselves a vessel of water. When waking they washed their hands and then commenced the study of the secret doctrine. At the time of cock crow, whether it be at midnight or break of day, the Holy One is found in the Garden of Eden, during which the defiled and impure are forbidden to pray or bless. When a man sleeps and his soul quits his body, an impure spirit comes and attaches itself to it and pollutes it. This is why it is forbidden to bless God before first washing the hands and engaging in the study of occult science. This applies also during the day when a man is awake; for then the impure spirit is unable to defile him except he is in some improper place. Even then it is unlawful when leaving it to bless God or recite a single verse of scripture without first washing his hands, though be may not have touched any impure thing. Woe to those who neglect and regard not this rite! They know nothing of the glory of their Lord; nothing of the law or principle upon which the world is founded. In every impure place there is an impure spirit whose delight is to dwell there and attach itself to man. Then spake Rabbi Simeon and said: Whoever gives not to God a part of his works or substance is guilty of avarice. Satan hates him, becomes his accuser and takes him out of the world. Great and terrible are the afflictions he has to endure! We give to God when we give to the poor as far as we are able, in the time of their need and necessity. If in times of our rejoicing and feasting the Holy One observes them ignored and forgotten and uncared for he grieves over and sympathizes with them and ascends on high, thinking to destroy the world. Then the souls of just men made righteous gather before him, saying: "Lord of the universe! thy name is called gracious and merciful. Have pity upon thy erring, forgetful children." And the Holy One replies: "Is it not upon mercy that I have founded the world as it is written: "The world is builded up on mercy" (Ps. lxxxix., 2). Then spake the angels: "Ruler of the universe! behold such a man eats and drinks and is able to succor the poor, yet refrains his hand." Then goeth forth the accuser, after obtaining permission, and hurries him out of existence. Who in the world was so great as Abraham, who did good and was kind to all creatures? Yet we learn from tradition that when Isaac, his son, was weaned, he made a great feast and invited thereto all the great men of the place to be present. At the festive gathering it is said that an accusing angel was there in the form of a poor unknown beggar, but no one recognized or took any notice of him. Abraham busied himself in attending to and waiting upon his royal and noble guests, whilst Sarah suckled the infants of all those who did not believe that she had given birth to a child and said that Isaac was some foundling who had been picked up on the roadside and brought to Sarah. When, therefore, they brought their own infants Sarah suckled all of them in their presence as the scripture states: "Who would have said unto Abraham that Sarah should have given children suck." The accusing angel happened to be entering the house when Sarah was uttering the words: "God has made me a subject of laughter." Forthwith he presented himself before the Holy One and said: "Lord of the universe, Thou callest Abraham thy friend. He has made a great feast, but has not remembered the poor and has not even offered a sacrifice of a single turtle dove. Sarah also says Thou hast caused her to become a subject of derisive laughter and jeers." Then replied the Holy One: "Who is there amongst men, kinder and more charitable than Abraham?" The accuser, however, was dissatisfied until he learned that the feast would be followed by sorrow and trouble to Abraham, which came to pass when God commanded Abraham to offer up Isaac as a sacrifice, and Sarah died through anguish of heart when she learned what God had commanded with respect to her son. All these misfortunes arose through neglect of the poor."

On another occasion Rabbi Simeon spake and said: it is written: "And Hezekiah turned his face toward the wall and prayed unto the Lord" (Is. xxxviii., 2). Observe how great the power and influence of a student of the secret doctrine. He is superior to all others, for he fears nothing, being in close touch with the tree of life, from which he receives counsel and instruction all his days. It teaches is in the way of truth and how to avoid evil that may assail us, and also how to direct our ways and walk before the Lord. Therefore, it is necessary we should study the secret doctrine day and night and observe its teachings and doctrines. By night, when reclining on our beds we ought to submit ourselves to the kingdom of heaven and make it our chief object to commend ourselves to the care and guardianship of the Almighty. Then become we freed from all evil influences and demoniacal powers have no sway over us. In the morning the student of esoteric science rises and gives thanks to his Lord and wends his way to the temple and there pours forth his soul in prayer and adoration. Afterwards he should take counsel from the holy patriarchs, as it is written: "I will come into thy house in the multitude of thy mercies, and in thy fear will I worship toward thy holy temple" (Ps. v. 7). We are taught from tradition never to enter the house of prayer before being instructed by the patriarchs, Abraham, Isaac and Jacob, who will inspire us with suitable prayers to be addressed to the Holy One, for the words: "In the multitude of thy mercy" designate Abraham; "I will worship in or toward thy holy temple," refer to Isaac; and "in thy fear," to Jacob. Then we render acceptable worship and of us it will he said: "Israel, thou art my servant in whom I will be glorified" (Is. xlix., 3).

Rabbi Pinchus used frequently to go and visit Rabbi Rechumi, whose dwelling was on the borders of the Sea of Genessareth. Rabbi Rechumi was very aged and had become blind. He spake and said to Rabbi Pinchus: I have heard that the son of Jochai, my fellow student in esoteric science, possesses a most precious stone, a pearl I have greatly desired to behold. It radiates rays of light like those of the sun and lightens up the world and will continue to do so until the Ancient of Days sits upon his throne. Thou art his grandson, therefore happy is thy lot. Go thou my son and search for this glittering and lustrous pearl, for now is the most propitious time for finding it.

Rabbi Pinchus with two others, went forth and embarked on a vessel. Observing two birds flying overhead, he cried aloud: Birds! birds! flying over the waters, have you seen the dwelling place of the son of Jochai? After a few moments again he cried: Birds! Birds! come and tell me. Then flew they away, but after a time returned and in the beak of one of them was a slip of paper on which was written: "The son of Jochai has quitted and left the cave in which he dwells with Rabbi Eleazar his son." Then he went and found Rabbi Simeon suffering from bodily sores. To his expressions of sorrow, finding him so ill and afflicted, Rabbi Simeon replied: I am glad, Rabbi Pinchus, thou hast found me thus. If it had been otherwise I should not be what I am. Suffering makes us wiser and better.

THE FOURTEEN PRECEPTS

THEN began Rabbi Simeon to discourse on the secret doctrine. "In the beginning created God" (Gen. i. 1). These words are included in the first commandment which is known as "the fear of the Lord," the first step in the acquiring of true wisdom and knowledge. It is also called the beginning because it is the true gate through which we enter into the higher mysteries of the divine life. and is the foundation upon which the world exists. There are three kinds of fear, two of which are of no avail in the search after truth, and have no reference except to bodily or physical enjoyment and delight, and the preservation of wealth, and therefore are altogether unmeritorious. True fear is that affection which arises from a feeling of reverence toward the Holy One as being all powerful, the rootless root of all life and existence and in whose eyes the illimitable universe with all its inhabitants are as nothing. This the fear which when exercised tends to bring nearer the time when the divine will shall universally prevail throughout the world.

In uttering these words Rabbi Simeon was affected to tears and said: Woe unto me whether I speak or keep silence! For if I speak, sinners will know how to worship and serve the Lord, and refraining therefrom will thus add to their guilt, and if I keep silent then I keep back knowledge that ought to be imparted to you. The man whose fear springs from a dread of affliction that may assail him, falls under the power and influence of evil that becomes his tormentor. The only right fear is that described by scripture, as "The beginning of wisdom and knowledge." Whoever begins the divine life with it, begins well and observes all the other precepts which are included in it. On the contrary, whoever exercises it not breaks and violates them, and to him may be applied the words of scripture: "And the earth was without form and void, and darkness was upon the face of the great deep, and the spirit of God moved upon the face of the waters" (Gen. i. 2). In this verse are designated the four kinds of punishments inflicted upon the ungodly: Tohu (without form), the punishment of strangulation referred to by the prophet Isaiah (Ch. xxxiv. 11) as the cord of Tohu. Bohu (void), which ejected great stones by which criminals are stoned, is the second kind of punishment. The third is darkness (choshek) or death by fire, as it is written: "When ye heard his voice out of the midst of the darkness, for the mountain did burn with fire" (Deuter. v. 23). The words: "And the spirit of God moved upon the face of the waters," refer to the fourth mode of punishment, viz., death by beheading with a sword. It is written: "And he placed at the east of the garden of Eden, cherubim and a flaming sword which turned every way to keep the way of the tree of life" (Gen. iii. 24). This flaming sword bears the name of "Spirit" and symbolizes the infliction of death meted out to transgressors of the commandments of the law.

Having described the first precept, viz., the fear of the Lord, come we now to the second which is intimately associated with it and never separated from it; that is, perfect love which everyone should cherish and entertain towards their Creator. If it he asked, what is perfect love, it is love of perfection, the one great love, as it is written: "Walk before me and be thou perfect" (Gen. xvii. 1). Furthermore, the scripture says: "And God said let there be Light" (Gen. i. 3). By the word Light is meant perfect love.

Then spake Rabbi Eleazar and said: My father, I have heard a definition of it which has just been given unto me. Rabbi Simeon said:

Then let Rabbi Pinchus hear it, now that he is here present. Said Rabbi Eleazar: Perfect love is that which manifests itself in two different ways or aspects and merits only to be called such. There are those who love God if he grants them wealth, length of days. offspring, worldly prosperity and success in their business enterprises, but hate and disregard him if the wheel of destiny or the good law brings them misfortune and suffering. Perfect love is that which changes not, but continues and abides the same in all circumstances, be they joyous or adverse. We should therefore love God even if he takes from us life, health, yea everything we hold dear.

When Rabbi Eleazar had ceased speaking, Rabbi Simeon, his father, embraced him, and Rabbi Pinchus thanked him and said: Truly the Holy One has brought me hither in order to behold the great Pearl whose radiant light will ere long illuminate the world.

Rabbi Eleazar began speaking again: The fear of the Lord is inseparable from his commandments, especially that of perfect love, and happy the man in whose life and conduct they are manifested and conjoined, as it is written: "Happy is the man that feareth alway" (Prov. xxviii. 14), for his fear and love are so associated that even if misfortunes assail and overwhelm, it matters not. He is unmoved and his heart becomes not hardened so that he falls into sin.

Again Rabbi Simeon spake and said: The third precept is that which teaches there is an all powerful Being who is Lord of the Universe, and also to proclaim his unity by the repetition of the six words of the Shema, which correspond to the six directions in space, with a fixed intention to do his will. The word One in the Shema should be equal in the duration of its pronunciation to the six words. This is the reason why the scripture saith: "Let the waters be gathered together in one place" (Gen. i. 9), that is, that the waters of the rivers running into the ocean may testify of the unity of the six directions. Stress should be laid also upon the letter "d" in the word echad (one), the numerical of it being equal to four and indicating the four directions of the rivers. For this reason this letter in the word echad occurring in this verse is always written larger than the others. The attestation of the six points or directions having been made, should be confirmed by six other words: "Blessed be his glorious name forever." In recognizing this unity symbolized by the letter d, man walks on dry land that brings forth trees and fruits. This also is why God called the dry land, earth, which is twice mentioned, land and earth being one and the same. "And God saw that it was good," symbolizing the unity above and the unity below. When this took place the earth was able to bring forth fruits and flowers.

The fourth precept teaches that Jehovah is Lord, as it is written: "Know therefore this day and consider it in thine heart, that the Lord he is God in heaven above and upon the earth beneath; there is none else" (Deuter. iv. 39). The word Alhim is in the divine name to show that they are one and the same, and without distinction in nature or essence as implied in the words: "Let there be Meoroth (lights) in the firmament of heaven" (Gen. i. 14). This word is written without a V, being singular in its form to show that they, Jehovah and Alhim, are a unity, and not a duality. This is also symbolized by the pillar of cloud by day and the pillar of fire by night going before Israel in the desert, representing the divine Being who giveth light and guidance to all the world. In this consisted the sin of the serpent; he acknowledged the divine unity below but promulgated a multiplication above, a doctrine which has wrought great mischief and strife in the world. Man ought to acknowledge distinction below but unity on high, that is, distinction of the divine Being from the world, but unity of essence and nature which when recognized and universally acknowledged, then will the demon of evil and strife disappear from amongst mankind and have no longer power and influence in the world. This is also the occult meaning of "Let them be for lights in the firmament of heaven" (Gen. i, 15). The word A U R (light) is also a symbol of the divine unity as its letters are in alphabetical sequence. A first, then U, followed by R. This, however, is not the case with the word Muth (death) in which the letters are found inverted. M being the thirteenth letter of the Alphabet, U the sixth and Th the twenty-second. Now Meoroth is compounded of the two words A U R and Muth. If or be taken from it, Muth remains the symbol of death and separation. It was by these letters that Eve became the cause of evil in the world as the scripture saith: "And then the woman saw the tree was good" (Gen. iii. 6), she took the letters M V from Meoroth and with Th thus formed Muth, death, which then first entered into the world.

Then said Rabbi Eleazar: My father, we have learned that when the letter M was left, V, the symbol of life, took its departure. Eve then took the letter Th and added it to M as it is said: "And she took and gave to her husband" (Gen. iii. 6), and thus formed Muth (death). In order however to counteract its effects it is necessary to add further to it the letter A, whose numerical value is unity and symbol of the divine Being. Muth then becomes Ameth (truth), by which the world is saved. Said Rabbi Simeon: Happy art thou my son for the same explanation of the word has also been imparted to me. The fifth precept. It is written: "Let the waters bring forth abundantly the moving creatures that have life" (Gen. i. 20). In these words are included three commands, having reference to the study of the secret doctrine, the multiplication of the human species and circumcision on the eighth day after the birth of a male child. He who addicts and gives himself up to the study and acquisition of esoteric science becomes eventually united to his higher self and equal to angels. Thus it is said: "Oh ye his angels, bless ye the Lord" (Ps. cxi. 20), signifying students of the secret doctrine who are called his angels upon earth as intimated in: the words, "and fowl that may fly above the earth" (Gen. i. 20), (also in Is. xl. 31): "But they that wait upon the Lord shall renew their strength, they shall mount up with wings as eagles" and so he able to go throughout the world as teachers and exponents of the truth that saves and purifies the souls and enlightens the minds of men. Thus the words, "fowl that may fly above the earth" refer to students of esoteric teaching called in scripture "waters." They are able to mount up to the great fountain of divine truth and partake of its living waters. That it might be so with him, David prayed: "Create in me a clean heart and renew a right spirit within me" (Ps. li. 10), that is, incline and open my heart for the study of the mysteries and occult meanings of thy word, and renew me with a right spirit, or, in other words, let my higher and lower nature become purified and unified.

With reference to the sixth precept contained in the words "Increase and multiply," he who conforms thereto increases the waters of the celestial river of life which never become dried up, but rather augmented by the birth of children. Every human soul, when it descends on to the earth plane, is accompanied by two attendant angels, one on the right side of it, the other on the left, as it is said: "He shall give his angels charge concerning thee, to keep thee in all thy ways." If, however, a man does wrong, they become his accusers.

Said Rabbi Pinchus: There really are three protecting angels to a good man as we read: "If there be a messenger or angel with him, or an interpreter, one among a thousand to plead his uprightness." "If there be an angel," refers to the first; "An interpreter," to the second; "One among a thousand," the third.

Rabbi Simeon replied and said: As a matter of fact there are five guardian angels to each person, for the scripture further proceeds: "He will be gracious unto him and will say." "He will be gracious," specifies the fourth; whilst "he will say," denotes the fifth.

Then said Rabbi Pinchus: Thy words are not altogether exact, for as much as "He will be gracious" refers to the Holy One, since compassion and graciousness belong only to Him. Thou speakest truly, replied Rabbi Simeon, for whoever ignores the precept "Increase and multiply" obstructs the flow or course of the celestial river of life and thus violates and profanes the holy covenant. Of such it is written: "They shall go forth and look upon the carcases of the men that have transgressed against me." "Against me," because this is a sin against God. The souls of such men will never enter unto the palace of the King, but be cast forth to live and dwell in the darkness and error of earth life.

The seventh precept has reference to the circumcision of male children on the eighth day of birth, by which, bodily impurity is taken away. Of the celestial regions whither souls come forth to be incarnated on earth, one of them, the eighth in order, is termed Haya (living). This is the reason why circumcision is performed on the eighth day of birth. In the ancient book of Enoch, the course of the celestial river of life is described as resembling the letter Yod (׳) which enters into the composition of the seventy-two divine names imprinted on the body of a child at time of birth, and denotes its purity. The words: "And fowl that shall fly above the earth" allude to Elijah, who is present whenever the rite of circumcision is performed, when a throne or seat is formed and set specially for him by pronouncing the words: "This is Elijah's throne." If this is neglected, he does not attend. Furthermore, we read: "And God created great whales or fishes," alluding to the two great fishes called Leviathan, symbolizing the male and female principle that manifests itself in every part of the creation. The words: "and every living creature" refer to the sacred name imprinted on the bodies of all incarnated souls coming from the celestial region called Haya. "Which the waters brought forth abundantly," denotes the letter Yod (׳) with which, as a sign, the angels above are distinguished from demons and also the children of Israel from other nations of the earth, viz., the impure and idolatrous. Blessed is the lot of Israel!

The eighth precept is that relating to the kindness to be shown to the proselyte who consents to be circumcised in order to enjoy the protection of the sheltering wings of the Schekina, or divine Presence, that guards and defends all those who, forsaking the worship of demons, give themselves up to the service of the true God. Thus it is written: "Let the earth bring forth, the living creature after its kind." The esoteric or mystical meaning of the words "after its kind," which are repeated twice in this verse of scripture, is as follows. The wings of the Schekina denote two celestial regions with many separate divisions or localities, whither the souls of proselytes return after separation from the body. The region included under the right wing contains two divisions through which pass the souls of the children of Israel, when after death they ascend to the celestial locality called Haya. The left wing with its two divisions is reserved for the nations of Ammon and Moab. All souls, however, whether they come forth from Haya, or Ammon and Moab, are living creatures differing in their kind, being those of Israel or those of proselytes who, as stated, ascend to the regions under the right wing of the Schekina. A further allusion to this mystery occurs in the words: "And ye shall be a delightful land." For this reason Israel is called ben yaqir (a dear son), because the Lord has given him a better portion than that of the proselytes. The children of Israel are also called "those whom I carry in my bosom," viz., the beautiful land to which, having ascended after death, they shall go out no more. The scriptures proceed further, "cattle and creeping thing and beast of the earth after his kind," teaching us that animals differ in their natures and forms, though animated with the same breath and life, so human souls, though differing the one from the other, nevertheless derive their origin from the same divine source.

The ninth precept has reference to the poor and indigent, ministering to their necessities as it is written: "Let us make man in our image, after our likeness." "Let us make man." Here the plural form of expression is used in order to point out that the creation of man was effected by the two divine essences symbolized as the male and female. "In our image," betokens the rich, corresponding to the male, "after our likeness," the poor, corresponding to the female. Now just as the two divine essences form a single whole, so amongst men ought these two classes, the rich and poor, symbols of the male and female principles in the divine nature, to form one mutually cooperative whole or community. "And let them have dominion over the fish of the sea, and over the fowl of the air, and over the cattle, and every creeping thing that creepeth upon the earth," the mystical meaning of which is given and explained in an occult work by King Solomon thus: "Whose has compassion on the poor, from his face and countenance will never fade away the reflection and glory of the divine likeness borne by the first man, by which he ruled and dominated the whole animal creation." As it is said: "And the fear of you and the dread of you shall be upon every beast of the earth, the fowl of the air, every creeping thing and the fish in the sea, etc." All these tremble and fear before the presence of man, because of the divine image imprinted thereon and is the only law of the creator enjoined upon the animal world that instills them with fear because of this image, first born by Adam. As long as man entertains and cherishes compassion and sympathy for the poor, he will continue to bear it. While he exercises charity he is truly human; when he ceases and refrains therefrom, he becomes and continues merely an animal. How can this be substantiated? From the life of Nebuchadnezzar, the Babylonian monarch, whose dream of his own downfall was never realized whilst succoring the poor. Immediately he ceased from deeds of charity and compassion and suffered himself to become filled with pride of heart and vainglory, then was heard the voice of the heavenly watcher: "The Kingdom is departed from thee," that is, the seal and stamp of the divine born by Adam, vanished from him and he ceased to be human. "His heart became changed and a beast's heart was given him and he was driven out from amongst men and dwelt with the beasts of the field." For this reason the scripture in order to express the creation of man, makes use of the words: "Let us make man," to indicate that to preserve the divine image, we should be charitable and compassionate, as was the rich and affluent Boaz to Ruth.

The tenth precept concerns the fixing and girding of the phylacteries. Said Rabbi Simeon; "Thy head upon thee is like Carmel (Garden)." These words have already been commented upon, but they have another and deeper meaning. "Thy head upon thee" refers to the phylactery of the head which represents the divine head, or, in other words, the divine name IHVH of which each of the letters stands for a verse of scripture which placed within the four sections of spaces of the phylactery of the head, correspond to the letters of the divine name. This is why we are taught by tradition that the words of scripture, "And all the people of the earth shall see that thou art called by the name of the Lord and they shall be afraid of thee," refers only to this phylactery. The first space or compartment contains the verse "Sanctify unto me all the first born whatsoever openeth the womb." Connoting the first letter of the Tetragrammaton, viz., I (') symbol of the first of all divine origins. This letter opens as it were the womb of the second, H, whereby it becomes fruitful. In the second space is enclosed the words: "and it shall be when the Lord shall bring forth into the land," referring to the second letter, H, whose womb as just stated is opened by Yod. In the Sepher Yetsirah we read, by fifty gates or openings of the celestial and concealed temple, the Yod enters and penetrates into H, that the sound of the schophar or trumpet may be heard. The schophar is securely closed until Yod comes and opens it and makes its sound heard, typifying freedom and the enfranchisement of the slaves and bondmen. It was by the sound of the schophar that the children of Israel marched out of Egypt, so will it always he, hereafter, the herald of freedom and deliverance. Such is the esoteric explanation of the letter H. The third space or section contains the Shema. "Hear Oh Israel, the Lord our God is one God," and is a commentary on the letter V (vau) which proceeds from the two letters before it and unities them. The fourth space contains words of blessings and menaces to the congregation of Israel, by the observance of which they should become the happiest and most powerful amongst the nations of the world. It connotes the final, H, fourth letter of the divine name and is formed from and includes in it the other three preceding letters. From these observations we may gather the occult meaning of the phylacteries. They are really explanations of the letters of the Tetragrammaton or divine name and therefore the scripture saith: "Thy head upon thee is as Carmel," and also: "The hair of thy head is like purple." Now the word used for hair in this verse is not the ordinary term Saar, but daleth, which comes from the root word dal, signifying poverty denoted by the phylactery of the arm, as that of the head denotes riches or wealth, and it is further added: "the King is held in its plaits or tresses," meaning that the divine name of God is in the four compartments of the phylactery. Whoever wears the phylacteries bears the divine likeness, for as the divine essence is expressed in the Tetragrammaton, so man becomes hearer of his image. Furthermore, it is said: "Male and female created he them," thus the phylacteries also symbolize the male and female, and taken together forth one unit or whole. Such is the symbolism of the phylacteries. The eleventh precept has reference to the levying and giving of tithes on corn, and the product of fruit trees. Regarding the first, scripture states: "And God said, behold, I have given you every herb bearing seed which is upon the face of all the earth," and of the fruit trees: "behold I have given the children of Levi all the tenth in Israel for an inheritance," and also: "All the tenth of the corn and of fruit trees are the Lord's and consecrated to him."

The twelfth precept concerns the tithes on fruit trees, as it is written: "every tree in which is the fruit of a tree, to you it shall be for food," or, in other words, though it is unlawful to keep what is consecrated to me I permit you to eat of the tenth of the products of the earth, whether of corn or trees, in order that they may serve as food to you and not to future generations.

The thirteenth precept relates to the redemption or purchase of the first born and thus making its life assured, for there are two angels, one of which is the lord of life, the other the lord of death, always hovering near and about at the time of birth. When a man redeems his child from the power of the latter then has it no power or influence over the life of his offspring. This is the esoteric meaning of the words: "And God saw every thing that he had made and behold it was very good." The word good designates the angel lord of life, the word very the angel lord of death. By redemption, the one is strengthened, the other enfeebled and has, as we have just said, no longer power over the child.

The fourteenth precept has respect to resting and ceasing from work on the sabbath day, as then God rested from the work of creation. This precept is subdivided into two others: one enjoining rest on this day, the other teaching us to keep it holy.

Concerning resting on the sabbath we have already said it was ordained, because the divine Being rested from his work which he then finished. When, however, the sabbath commenced, there were certain creatures who had not received bodies in which to incarnate. The question may here arise could not the Holy One have retarded the approach of the sabbath and thus have provided them with physical sheaths or bodies? The truth is, the tree of the knowledge of good and evil had excited them to revolt even before embodiment, through their great desire to descend into the world, or on to the earth, and make themselves lords and masters thereof. The Holy One then divided these into two classes of which he placed one, the good, by the tree of life, and the other, the had, by the tree, of knowledge of good and evil. Whilst intent upon providing for the former with bodily forms, the sabbath day dawned, and thus the work was interrupted and suspended.

If these rebellious and ambitious spirits had acquired bodies, the world would not have continued to exist even for a moment. The Holy One had, however, provided a remedy against this prospective catastrophe by hastening the coming of the sabbath and therefore the world exists and continues. What those wicked spirits thought of doing by the procreation of and filling the world with their offspring was accomplished by those good spirits by the tree of life who from the night of the first sabbath discharged this duty. This is why the wise and they who understand, restrict their connubial relationships to the day of the sabbath so that the wicked spirits may recognize how inferior they are to those who, whilst incarnated, are able to discharge marital duties. It is these wicked spirits who go forth in their hordes throughout the world with the hope of surprising anyone who violates and infringes the esoteric injunction respecting the conjugal act, the offspring of which becomes afflicted with epilepsy through becoming obsessed by Lilith, the great mother of the demons, who kills and destroys the child.

As soon as, however, the Sabbath day begins, and whilst it endures, these wicked spirits becoming filled with terror, fly quickly away and hide themselves, with the exception of one of them named Assimon who, with his attendants, is authorized to go through the world in order to seek and find out transgressors of the law relating to conjugal practice. When the night however has passed, he is obliged to go and hide himself in the great abyss of darkness. The sabbath ended, hosts of demons reappear in the world, and therefore to ward off and be proof against their evil influence and nullify their power, the reading of the ninety-first Psalm has been enjoined. As soon as the demons observe the children of Israel engaged in prayer, and the reading of it and holding in their hands a cup of wine, they hurriedly rush away and disappear in deserts and solitary places in which they make their dens and hiding places. May the Holy One ever keep and preserve us from their noxious power and influence!

Our masters and great teachers (their names and memories be ever blessed) admonish us that there are three different ways by which a man may incur guilt and attract evil: either by invoking curses upon himself, by wastefully casting bread or crumbs upon the ground, be they ever so small, and also at the conclusion of the sabbath by lighting a candle before first reading or reciting the psalm or liturgy of "separation" and by thus doing, causing the fires of Gehenna to be lighted before their time. There is in Gehenna a place reserved for those who break and profane the sabbath and who enjoy a respite from its fiery punishment whilst the sabbath endures and vent their maledictions and curses on them who light a candle before the prescribed time, saying: "May God hurl thee in his fury and bring thee hither and thus be tossed about as a ball so that thou becomest an object of shame and reprobation to thy kith and kindred."

The sanctity of the sabbath as long as it lasts imposes absolute rest both in the higher and lower worlds, during which, the punishments of the wicked cease and their overlookers remain inactive until the children of Israel have finished reciting the words: "Blessed art thou oh Lord who separateth the holy from the unholy." On him, however, who lights not his candle they invoke benedictions. Deut. 28: "God give thee of the dew of heaven and the fatness of the earth and plenty of corn and wine. Blessed be thou in the city and blessed be thou in the field, etc." "Blessed is the man that considereth the poor, the Lord will deliver him in time of trouble." Why does the scripture use the words "in time of trouble," in place of "the evil day?" Because the evil spirit then is able to obtain the mastery over the soul of a man, and then it is the Lord will deliver him. By the word dal (poor) is meant the humble sin-sick soul who repents of his sins against the Holy One. Another and further interpretation of the words: "The Lord shall deliver him in time of trouble" is that they allude to the last or judgment day.

GENESIS

CHAPTER I.

"BRASHITH." "In the beginning" was En Soph, the Divine, the self-existent infinite begin, without likeness or reflection, the incomprehensible, the unknowable One, the blessed and only Potentate, the King of Kings and Lord of Lords. who only hath immortality, dwelling in Light which no man can approach unto, whom no man hath seen or can see, before whom the great archangel with face beneath his wings bends in lowly reverence and adoration, crying, "Holy! Holy! Holy! who art and was and evermore shall be."

Tune had begun. Its great pendulum, whose beats are the ages, commenced to vibrate. The era of creation or manifestation had at last arrived. The nekuda reshima, primal point or nucleus, appeared. From it emanated and expanded the primary substance, the illimitable phosphorescent ether, of the nature of light, formless, colorless, being neither black nor green nor red. In it, latent yet potentially as in a mighty womb, lay the myriad prototypes and numberless forms of all created things as yet indiscernible, indistinguishable. By the secret and silent action of the divine will, from this primal luminous point radiated forth the vital life-giving spark which, pervading and operating in the great, enteric ocean of forms, became the soul of the universe, the fount and origin of all mundane life and motion and terrestrial existence, and in its nature and essence and secret operation remains ineffable, incomprehensible and indefinable. It has been conceived of as the divine Logos, the Word, and called Brashith, for the same was in the beginning with God. (All things were made by him, and without him was not anything made that was made. In him was life, and the life became the light of man.)

"They that understand (the secret doctrine) shall shine as the brightness of the firmament; and they who turn or lead many into the might path (of knowledge) as the stars forever and ever." (Dan. xii. 3.) The word zohar (brightness) designates that nekuda reshima, the central ray or point of light which was the primal manifestation of the Divine, En Soph. From it proceeded vibrations which made luminous the illimitable ether, from which was formed the universe that became the glorious temple or palace of the great Unknown. It was in a manner the holy seed or germ that gave origin and birth to the world, and is occultly referred to in the words: "The holy seed shall be the substance thereof." (Is. vi. 13.) Its analogue in nature is the silkworm which, unseen and in secret, elaborates and prepares a product that ultimately constitutes the material of the monarch's purple robe of splendor. Furthermore, for the manifestation of the glory of the divine Unknown to humanity, making use of verbal terms and letters, it has built for it the name alhim, or lord, as evidenced in the mystic sense of brashith bara alhim. "In the beginning, alhim created"; or, as it should be rendered by rushith, that is the primal zohar, the origin of all words, "God created alhim." The use of the word bara (created) need not excite surprise, for it occurs again in the words: "And he created alhim, the man, in his image." (Gen. i. 27.) This zohar, their, denotes the mysterious. One called brashith because the beginning of all things. In answer to the desire of Moses to know the name of the divine Being, it was given AHIH ASHR AHIH, "I am that or who I am." The sacred name AHIH is as a two-sided figure, whilst the name alhim is as a crown; and asher formed of the same letters as the word rash (head or crown) is a synonym of alhim and proceeds or comes forth from brashith. Whilst the primal zohar or divine ray of life was quiescent and unmanifested it was impossible for it to become known by any word or term whatsoever. But after operating in the boundless ether, the receptacle of all forms and prototypes of created things in the universe that was to be, then asher, representing the divine essence, took upon itself the form of a head or crown (rash) between the two AHIH's of the divine appellation, AHIH asher AHIH. Observe now, that the word brashith is composed of rash (crown), synonym of asher, and beth (house or palace). Hence the occult signification or rendering of the words "Brashith bara Alhim" is this: When rash the divine germ from which emanated and expanded the boundless ether appeared, and this ether became differentiated into form and color giving rise to the universe or palace of the great king, then was created alhim the great secret fructifying principle of nature, which was and is as a point that gives rise to lines which produce surfaces, or as the letter yod I, whence proceed all the other letters of the alphabet.

Again, from another aspect, when zohar the primal luminous point or ray gave rise to the emanating ether, it took. upon itself the form of the vowels holem (˙) shurek (·) and hirek (.) which are different dispositions of the one and same elementary point in their esoteric meaning.

When the primal vibration of the divine word took place it produced and impressed a wavelike motion throughout the boundless ether in which were contained all the sounds of the alphabet from A to Th. This operation and effect is symbolized by the union of these two letters forming the word ath as it is found written ath ha-shamayim (the heavens). Thus: Brashith bara Alhim ath hashamayim signify: He, the unknown mysterious One, created alhim the fructifying and generative principle of the heavens, one in origin but dual in operation. Hence it is seen that the divine word and essence designated by the word asher is found between the fecundative and generative principles, both of which are symbolized by the same name AHIH in the divine appellation AHIH asher AHIH.

The Zohar (brightness) also denotes the generative essence and includes all the letters taken as types and forms of creatures and things in its operation. Such also is the signification of the verse: "Jehovah, our God is one Jehovah" (Deut. vi. 4), containing three names expressive of the three gradations of the divine essence, as exhibited in the three first words of Genesis. "Brashith balm Alhim ath hashamayim." Brashith specifies the mysterious divine Being; bara, the mystery of creation: alhim, the mystery of preservation: ath hashamayim, the fructifying and generative principles considered as one. If to the word ath be added h from the following word hashamayim (heavens) we get the pronominal term athah (thou)--Alhim, the divine Being to which the scripture alludes. "Thou (Athah) givest life to all creatures." (Nehem. ix. 6). In this deeply mysterious ath, therefore, is comprehended the divine essence in its fructifying and generative form, and Alhim the point of union between them; and it may thus be regarded as a mystic analogue, though dimly and obscurely, of that majestic unknown Being that operated in the creation and production of the illimitable universe, whose goodness and beneficence are manifested in the preservation of the world with its myriads of creatures, who in their fructifying and generative powers and functions are finite replica of Himself, the "I am that I am." In concluding these remarks on this first verse in Genesis, observe that brashith (in the beginning) is equivalent to bra-shith (he created six) and refers to the scriptural words: "From one side of the heaven to the other," that is, to the six directions of space (north, south, east, west, above, and below), all converging to the three points representing the divine essence, which are one and the same, the mystery of which is included and hidden in the divine name composed of forty-two letters.

"They that are wise shall shine," i.e., those who are initiated into the secret doctrine. They are like the notes and accents in music by which musicians and singers are guided and led in their playing and chanting, as troops that follow their leader and chief. The consonants and vowels are the chief elements in the formation of words, but the wise alone by their understanding give life and meaning to them. "Those who turn many into the right way (of knowledge) shall shine as the stars forever and ever." By the word stars is meant the signs of punctuation used to separate the parts of a sentence and render the words intelligible, and thus are teachers and students of the secret doctrine. Who, by their intellectual and spiritual enlightenment and knowledge of esoteric science, cause earth's ofttimes weary wandering and belated pilgrims to find the true path of light that leads them to the higher and diviner life. Happy are they engaged in the work of guiding others into the right way! Around them is a halo which the prophet Ezekiel beheld in vision encircling the heads of cherubim, the brightness and refulgence of which shall never become faded or dimmed but endure forever.

"And the earth was tohu and bohu" (Gen. i. 2), that is, without form and void. The word "was" relating to the past, is here used to indicate the primeval state of the earth at the time of its creation. The water covering the earth was cold as snow and impregnated and contaminated with mud and debris which by the action of a strong fire congested and hardened and the space or place it occupied in becoming separated from the water was called Tohu, or the place of waste and dregs, and corresponded to the evil demons that made it their abode. Bohu, on the contrary, was that part or portion of the earth that became purified. If it be asked: by the action of what power was this purification accomplished, the scripture answers: "Darkness was upon the face of the deep." The term darkness refers to the fire or light which, though of divine origin, existed like a nebulous dark cloud at the beginning of creation. "And the spirit of God proceeded from the lord of life and hovered or moved upon the face of the waters." (Gen. i. 2). After impregnating them with the breath of life, and causing them to become purified and fructified, then from out of the state of Tohu came forth a great and mighty wind that overthrew mountains and broke into pieces the rocks, similar in its effects to the sight beheld by the prophet Elijah, as it is written; "after the wind, an earthquake" (I. Kings xix. 12), that dispelled the darkness in which was the hidden and concealed fire that transformed the world from tohu into Bohu, and from a state of chaos made it receptive of seeds and germs of life. This is expressed in the words; "and after the fire a still small voice" (I. Kings xix., 12).

Tohu was thus a state of chaos in which the world existed for ages after its first creation, enshrouded in darkness and immersed in water. By the action of fire, in its qualities of heat and flame, and the concomitant operation of the divine spirit, the constituent elements became differentiated and each imbued with energies and powers of attraction and cohesion, as also of repulsion, and thus prepared to be taken up and used in the elaboration of material forms and bodies in which pre-existing spiritual entities or beings might incarnate and manifest themselves in accordance with laws regulating and governing their birth, growth and development. This preparatory and progressive stage in the world's physical history was what is termed bohu, a state of darkness which was at the same time an allotrophic form of the divine light that in its infinite modes of energy and operation pervaded the vast expanse, making it pregnant with the germs of life that eventually came forth out of the earth's mighty womb and began their ascent on the spiral curve of evolutionary existence; until, after aeons of upward struggle and ceaseless endeavor, they attained their destiny, becoming children of Light, assimilated in the grandeur of their expanded faculties of mind and heart with the great Father of Light, the Holy One (blessed be He), whose love and beneficence to all his creatures are as great as his power, and who knows neither measure nor end.

"And the spirit of God moved upon the face of the waters"; and then went forth the fiat of the divine word: "Let there be light and light was" (Gen. i. 3), light radiant and glittering with a thousand different colors and rays, fringing and embellishing all objects with a halo and sheen of beauty and splendor, entering into and informing each atom and evoking its latent life and energy and exciting it to the display and exercise of its inherent properties and functions in the great economy of nature.

In all the various phases of development from tohu to bohu, through countless ages of silent, secret and ceaseless progression from lower to higher stages and states of being, the Divine has manifested itself under many and different aspects or characters corresponding to and symbolical of them. Thus, whilst the earth was in a state of chaos, it manifested itself as Shaddai, the Almighty; and when it passed from the state of tohu to bohu, as Sabaoth, or Hosts. When darkness disappeared, then became it known as Alhim. But not until the life-giving word was spoken, did it become known as Jehovah, the "I am that I am." This is wherefore the scripture states in the vision of Elijah: "Jehovah was not in the earthquake" (I. Kings xix. 2), but Shaddai. Jehovah was not in the fire (I. Kings, xix. 12), but was "Sabaoth." "After the fire a darkness made visible," it manifested as Alhim; then was heard the still small voice and the name Jehovah was complete, the four letters of which serve as symbols of the divine essence as the hands and feet represent the human frame.

Taking now the tetragrammaton or holy name, AHIH, manifested in these three aspects or forms of cosmic development, we find the divine appellation of twelve letters, AHIH asher AHIH, the name revealed to the prophet Elijah. "And God said: Let there be light and light was."

Proceed we now to investigate and acquaint ourselves with the hidden mysteries and teachings of the secret doctrine regarding creation which have just been outlined in a general manner. Hitherto we have dwelt upon the secret operation of En Soph or the unknown infinite and eternal Being in preparing the earth and impregnating its substance with a mysterious divine virtue or power which rendered it capable of becoming the medium for the enfoldment and manifestation of pre-existing spiritual entities and beings. These effects achieved, there was needed the omnific, life-giving Logos or Word to originate and utter the symphonal vibration that should impart life and breath and motion to the universe. Then and not till then was it spoken; then and not till then the celestial and terrestrial worlds becoming bound and associated together by a reciprocal influence, a new and a living way was opened for the incarnation and exhibition of life upon the earth. This is why in the antecedent primal stages of development in the world's history the expression "God said," is not found in scripture. At first he willed, as the Arabic version gives it, and his will operated silently, slowly, yet surely and effectively. The primary substance of the earth being thus prepared, it was through the mysterious action of the Word that it became endowed with vital properties and attributes through the divine vibration imparted to it. This is what scripture affirms: "And God said," that is, Alhim manifested himself by and through the divine Logos; and thus by and through the Word, produced motion or vibration under the laws of which created matter, or substance, resolved itself into an infinitude of different forms.

"Let light be." Now the word yehe (he) is composed of three letters, IHI, yod being the first and third letter and H coming between them. The yod, or I, represents the male and the female principle. The full word is therefore a symbol of the divine Father and Mother, the final yod being the same as the first in order to show that all the three aspects or forms as stated, under which En Soph operated in the creation and production of the universe, were only the manifestations of one and the same divine Being. The first yod also designates the Father, the engenderer of light; the second letter H denotes the Logos; the third letter yod, the primal light. The divine aspects are further symbolized by the three vowel points, holem (˙) shurek (·) and hirek (.) the Father, the Word and the Light. Before the manifestation of the Logos seven other letters were formed, but the primal light proceeding from the Father was too ethereal and empyreal to receive and become impressed with their forms and signatures. When, however, the state, of tohu gave place to that of bohu, other seven letters were formed; but, again, as matter was not sufficiently condensed, it could not retain them. At the manifestation of the creative Logos, eight others completing the letters of the alphabet were formed, which endured because by the action of the Logos, the barrier between the spiritual and earthly was done away and they began to exercise a reciprocal influence on each other. This is the occult meaning of the words: "Let there be a firmament" and thus form a medium, a point of union between the higher and lower worlds. This taking place was the prelude to the appearance of life upon the earth.

"God saw the light that it was good" (Gen. i. 4), for then the universe became lighted up and pervaded throughout with the divine life which preserves it for the common weal and happiness of created and animated beings.

"And God called the light Day" (Gen. i. 5). Why is it written: "He called"? Because Alhim wished or willed an emanation distinct from the Logos, which should constitute the world-soul, the foundation root of universal life. This light emanation, the life of the world, is termed Day, representing and corresponding to the first AHIH in the divine appellation "I am that I am." "And the darkness he called Night." That is, He produced from out of the primal darkness a passive or reflected light like that of the moon and called it Night.

It was by the union of Day and Night, symbolizing light and darkness, the male and female principles, that the Logos or creative Word proceeded. This mystery is also symbolized by the vowel points (˙) (·) (.). When the creative and passive light blend and unite, that is, when the active male principle unites with the passive female principle, an equilibrium is established and procreation takes place. The union of these two lights or principles gives rise to a sense of pleasure and delight which has been personified as the goddess Venus, and is known and termed in the secret doctrine as "Musaph" (something additional, augmentation) without which life would not be worth living. This it was that caused all as yet unembodied spirits and holy souls to be filled with a joyous longing and desire for incarnation on the earth plane and thereby attain to higher states and stages of existence and thus approximate nearer to the great Being who in scripture is termed Jehovah, Zebaoth, the Lord of Hosts, God of all the countless myriads of created souls and Lord of all the earth. From what has just been said it will be perceived that the words Day and Night in scripture are symbols of the heavenly or divine lights from the synthesis of which creation, as it exists, has resulted.

"And God said let there be a firmament in the midst of the waters" (Gen. i. 6). In these words the scripture begins to unfold and display in detail the various processes in mundane creation which began by dividing the waters above from the waters below. Amongst the many antinomies of existence by which we are able to distinguish their nature and thus attain unto truth, the conception of right and left will hest assist us in understanding and grasping the secret doctrine contained in these words, the right corresponding to light, goodness, harmony; the left, to darkness, evil, discord, from which has proceeded that state called Gehenna or Hell, a subject upon which Moses himself pondered and thought deeply and long in his studies on this part of Genesis. In the work of creation there was a differentiation of the divine essence resulting in two states of the primal substance, called light and darkness, connoted also by the terms right and left. When Alhim, the creative mean, or word, appeared and became a point of union between them, they began to blend harmoniously together and thus gave occasion for the appearance of vegetable and animated existences. Discord vanished and peace universally prevailed. This primal discord between the light and darkness, the right and left, may be illustrated by the quarrel and contention that arose between Korah, and his associates, and Aaron, the high priest. After his studies on the great problem of the origin of Gehenna, Moses thus reasoned to himself: I must adjust and harmonize this difference and discord between Korah and Aaron on the principle of reconciliation that prevailed and operated between light and darkness at the time of creation, that is, I must become a mediator between them. Finding, however, that the contention on the part of Korah was of a stubborn and inflexible character, he said truly: This opposition and difference between the two parties, Korah and Aaron, is altogether different from what prevailed between primeval light and darkness, and though willing to mediate and make peace and harmony between them, Korah and his company have rejected and refused my counsels and thus have instituted and made a Gehenna or Hell into which they must eventually fall. In refusing to accept and comply with the proposition of Moses, Korah demonstrated that his fend and dispute had not for its object the advancement of the divine glory. He thus became an apostate and renegade to the divine rule or principle of reconciliation, by which opposites blend and work harmoniously together. In this consisted the sin of Korah and his company, which caused Moses, though of great meekness of character, to be filled with wrath and anger, not because of their rejection of him as a mediator, but on account of their adverse opposition and antagonism to the principles of reconciliation, the existence of which they failed to perceive or ignored as operating in the preservation of the world.

The following remarks are from an ancient occult work entitled Liber Adami, or, The Book of Adam. "When the passive light, termed in scripture 'darkness,' became blended and unified with the active light, there were myriads of spiritual beings or existences, part of whom were fully developed and ready for incarnation, the rest but imperfectly so. Believing that the light and darkness were antagonistic in nature and principle, there arose a division of opinion amongst them, some declaring themselves partisans of light, others its opponents and advocates of darkness. When the mediating Logos had blended light and darkness and thus symbolized the perfect unity of the divine essence, the advanced and enlightened amongst them embraced and received the fact, whilst those only partially developed remained obdurate in their ideas and opinions and thus by their contrariety and differences of thought and the contentions and quarrels that arose therefrom, Gehenna or Hell came into existence." This discord and dissension has found an entrance and reflection in the world and is distinguished by the object in view, whether it be actuated by desire for truth or motived by selfishness and a hankering and craving to rule and dominate over others. Examples and instances of these two classes of individuals are found in the history of mankind. Of the first class, were the famed teacher Hillel (nasior president of the school of Jerusalem at the beginning of the Christian era) with his colleague Schammai. Their only object was the research of truth and the advancement of the divine glory, and though their disputes were very keen and sharp, yet friendship and good will always existed between them. Of the second class, an example has just been given in the case of Korah and his party in their contention with Aaron for supremacy, which resulted in their destruction and descent into Hell, the limbo and native place of dissension and discord.

We can now discern the reason why God made the firmament and separated the waters that were above from the waters that were beneath, that is, he caused a clear distinction to be made between those who, entertaining different views and opinions, were actuated by the desire for truth, and those whose object, through crass, self-willed ignorance, was the rejection of and antagonism towards it. In connection with Korah and his company, cut off or separated from the congregation of Israel, the same word, yabdel (separated), is used by Alhim in dividing the waters above and the waters beneath the firmament, as also by Moses when he spake: "Seemeth it to you a small thing that the God of Israel hath separated yon from the congregation," etc., and further, "the Lord separated the tribe of Levi to bear the ark of the covenant of the Lord."

Here the question may arise: If on the second day of creation the separation between light and darkness occurred, how was it that the quarrel arose with Levi the third tribe of the children of Israel? Should it not have been in connection with Simeon, the second tribe? The fact of the case is this: the tribe of Levi though reckoned the third, in the eye of Jacob, was accounted as second. The form of service called separation recited by the children of Israel at the close of the sabbath has for its object the separation of the spirit ruling during weeks days from the spirit that rules and presides over the sabbath day. When the sabbath closes, the wicked spirit is filled with the desire to acquire ascendency over Israel, but as soon as it hears the recitation of the verse: "Let the beauty of the Lord our God he upon us; and establish thou the work of our hands upon us; yea the work of our hands establish thou it" (Ps. xc. 17), it betakes itself to flight, and when with the sprig of myrtle and cup of wine in hand the word of "separation" is spoken, it hurries away and returns to Gehenna whence it came, its own place, where dwell Korah and his company as it is written: "They and the accomplices went down alive into the pit" (Num. xvi. 33). They were not, however, swallowed up until the congregation of Israel had separated itself from them, even as the descent into hell of the wicked and contentious angels occurs only after the repetition of the formula of separation at the close of the sabbath. There are two Gehennas; one above, where are the wicked and rebellions spirits; and the other, whither Korah descended and is the pattern of the former.

"Let there be a firmament in the midst of the waters" (Gen. i. 6). The word Alhim, God, is composed of two words AL-HIM, which signify God, water, or sea. This last word has the same letters as yamah, by which the scripture teaches that all division of opinion, symbolized by the term sea, is right and just when its object is the glory of the divine, as then AL becomes united to HIM. When, however, this is not so, AL remains separated and detached and yamah, or HIM, then symbolizes the great ocean or abyss of darkness in which Hell is enshrouded and concealed. When the waters became separated, then Alhim interposed and became the point of union between them, and harmony prevailed and dissension ceased. The waters above the firmament, the male part; those below, the female. Those above were designated Alhim, and distinguished by the first H in the divine name IHVH; those below were called Adonai, and characterized by the second H. Although the mediation of Alhim took place on the second day, unity and harmony did not begin to prevail only on the third day when, as the scripture states: "God saw that it was good," which is not affirmed of either the first or second day of the work of creation. It was then the letter V entered in the divine name and took up its position between the two H's. This interposition and mediation of Alhim, between the waters above and those below the firmament, is further symbolized by the waters of the river Jordan when they became separated to allow of the passage of the children of Israel into the promised land. The waters flowing down to the place of passage formed into a heap, whilst those below flowed into the sea and the children of Israel passed over between them. In order to distinguish and emphasize the separation of the waters which, had not Alhim become mediator between them. would never have proved fruitful and brought forth abundantly the living creature, the scripture repeats five times the word raqiang (firmament).

Now the time essential for this correlative union was a period of five hundred years, during which the waters above and those below flowed unitedly by the tree of life, serving as a point of contact and junction, so that by their reciprocal action they might give rise to vegetable and animal life upon the earth plane. This union or blending together was thus necessary ere their proper distribution could take place, as it is recorded of David after gathering together food and provisions, he afterwards distributed them to all the congregation of Israel. It is also written: "That thou givest them, they gather" (Ps. civ. 28), and again, "She riseth also whilst it is night, and giveth meat to her household" (Prov. xxxi. 15).

CHAPTER II.

WHEN discord prevailed between the elements, a preternatural and extraordinary degree of coldness predominated throughout the world and the waters below became congealed and arid, giving birth to two demons, one male, the other female, who engendered myriads of beings similar to themselves in order to add to and increase the forces of disorder and disruption. Herein consists the secret symbolism of circumcision. One of these demons is called Apheth (viper) and the other Nachash (serpent.) They are one and the same in their natures. After union with Nachash, and seven years of gestation, Apheth deposited offspring on the earth. Herein also is the mystery of the seven names of Gehenna, as also of the seven names of the tempter spirit. Thus everything emanating and proceeding from the sphere of darkness is a medley of good and evil. That the good, the pure and undefiled might subsist and continue as the base and foundation of the world, it was essential that from it should emanate the divine name of eighteen letters, the source and origin of all the benefactions and blessings by which the world is sustained and upheld.

"And God said, let the waters under the heaven be gathered together into one place" (Gen. i. 9). By the term waters is also meant the ten sephiroth, kether, hochma, bina, etc., whose origin is derived from the great Being who in himself is both male and female. And who is He? The eternal One, En Soph, the boundless One, from whom hath proceeded all life and breath and all things. The waters above the firmament designate these sephiroth, who came forth from H the fourth letter in the tetragrammaton, IHVH. In order, however, to arrive at and obtain some conception, though it be inadequate, of En Soph, through them, it was necessary that the sephiroth should be arranged and posited in a certain order, or sequential series and relationship to each other, and thus become a reflected image of the Eternal. This then is the meaning of the words "into one place," i. e, that by the union of the sephiroth we might be able to ascend to the supreme point of origin, the Eternal One, as saith the scripture, "Jehovah is One and his name One." One above and One below; above, the unity of the boundless One in whose essence is contained and concentrated all celestial and terrestrial existence; One below, yet the same unity needing the intermediary of the sephiroth in order to be apprehended and conceived of. When this takes place, it is perceived that there are not two gods, but one God; one in unity of essence, above all and in all. The visible reflection of the divine unity is referred to in scripture as follows: "I saw also the Lord sitting upon a throne" (Is. vi. 1), and, "they saw the God of Israel" (Ex. xxiv. 10), "The glory of the Lord appeared" (Num. xiv. 10), "As the appearance of the bow that is in the cloud in the day of rain so was the appearance of the brightness around about" (Ex. i. 28). This was the appearance of the likeness of the glory of the Lord. That is, as the light of the rainbow, though refracted into different colors, is one and the same, so the divine light and splendor, though refracted and reflected by the sephiroth, is only one and the same. This mystery is also contained in the words: "Let the dry land appear" (Gen. i. 9), for by the word yabash (earth or dry land) is signified the eternal One, the life of the world, from whom come forth all creatures and existences, as from the earth spring forth all flowers, fruits and seeds. Furthermore, by the words "I do set my bow in the cloud" (Gen. ix. 14), is denoted and symbolized the sephiroth called Malcuth (kingdom), since "I have established it from the creation of the world." Reverting to the conflict between the primal elements of light and darkness, it is written, "Rachel travailed and she had hard labor" (Gen. xxxv., 16), the esoteric meaning of which is this: When conflict commenced, the angel Michael took up a position on the right of Kether, the supreme sephiroth, Raphael on the left and Gabriel in the front, thus giving rise to the three different colors. So is the divine glory surrounded with circles of colors which are but reflections of it and connoted by the three words, Jehovah, Alohenu, Jehovah, Deut. 6:4 appellations of the divine One who, concealed and invisible to human vision, is but One, as are the colors of the rainbow; and whose unity is expressed in the verse: "Blessed be the name of his glorious and everlasting kingdom." The beauty of the three colors in the verse: "Hear! oh, Israel, the Lord our God is one God" (Deut. vi. 4). The lower is copy or pattern of the higher. The unity above is expressed by a verse containing six words. Shema Israel, Jehovah, Alohenu, Jehovah, Achad. (Hear, Israel, Jehovah our God, Jehovah is one); the unity below, by the verse Mi, mdd, beshahuloi mim. "Who hath measured the waters in the hollow of his hand" (Is. xl. 12), both referring to one Being, the transcendently glorious equilibrator or adjustor, creator of the world, IHVH. Kadosh! Kadosh! Kadosh! (Holy! Holy! Holy!) "Let the waters be gathered together," or as it may be rendered: "let the waters become equilibrated and blended harmoniously together, then will the earth become filled with the glory of God and then will the dry land appear," i.e., the mystery of the divine unity expressed in the occult formula imparted to and made known only to initiated students and adepts of the secret doctrine, CHUZU BMUCHSO CHUZU.

And God said: "Let the earth bring forth grass, the herb yielding seed" (Gen. i. 11). When the waters had been thus brought into one place, or when the strife of the contending elements had subsided and ceased, then began the work of generation and procreation resulting in the appearance of created beings innumerable, delighting in the service of their Lord. This is expressed in the words: "He caused the grass to grow for the cattle" (Ps. civ. 14) on a thousand hills, for whose sustenance it shoots forth daily. By the word chatzir (grass) is denoted those angelic beings appointed and ordained to administer to the necessities of cattle and supply them with food. "And herb for the service of man" designates and refers to the ministering angels called Ophanim, Hayoth and Cherubim, whose special and peculiar mission and service is to aid and assist in the celebration of sacrifices and worship of the Creator, which constitutes the true service of man. Included under the sane terms are those spiritual beings whose study it is to supply the needs of those whose works are good and their worship acceptable to the divine Being, and also to look after their means and sustenance, as it is written: "To bring forth food out of the earth," which connotes the herb seeding seed (not seed of the grass) for the good and welfare of the world. All these various orders of spiritual beings by the divine prevision have been delegated for the service of humanity, that it may enjoy the greatest benefactions and blessings from on high. "And the fruit tree yielding fruit" (Gen. i. 11). The word fruit here repeated twice indicates the male and female sexes, for as one tree is fructified by another tree, so is the female made prolific by the male. Who amongst these angels then were male and female! They are those called cherubim and thimroth. Who and what are the thimroth? They are angelic beings who are present in the incense of burnt offerings and are therefore called thimroth aschan (columns of smoke) and are thus helpers to man in his worship. "Yielding fruit," that is to say, angels in male and female forms resembling human beings with this special difference, they are of majestic form and noble countenance, whilst the cherubim are smaller in stature and of frailer build. Scripture saith of them, "they have the figure of a man," which is the synthesis of all figures and forms, because bearing the impress of the Holy Name whose four letters correspond to and symbolize the four quarters of the world, North, South, East and West. Michael is stationed at the north and the faces of all the angelic hosts are directed towards him as being their chief. Scripture further states, they have the forms of a man, a lion, an ox and an eagle. By the face of a man is meant the face of the male and female blended into one. This form of the human figure is that which is graven on the heavenly chariot [1] surrounded with myriads of angelic beings, as it is written: "The chariot of God is encompassed about with thousands upon thousands of shinan (angelic beings)" (Ps. lxviii. 18), by which word is meant the four differing figures and features of the angels. The first letter of it, Sh, is the initial of the word shor or ox; the second letter, N, is the initial of nesher, an eagle; whilst the third letter, A, is the initial of aryeh, a lion; and the fourth letter is N, final; thus symbolizing the form of a man that stands erect and is always understood to include both the male and female figure. All the myriads upon myriads of angelic beings spoken of by the Psalmist derive their particular forms from the mystery expressed by the Psalmist, each according to their group. Yet notwithstanding their diversity of form they have all one common character, so that whether they bear the form of the ox, eagle or lion, they all exhibit the trait of the human which is synthesized by the four sacred names graven and imprinted on the divine chariot. Those with the figure of an ox are endowed with special power which is called el (power). Those with the form of au eagle, with that degree of grandeur called gaddol (greatness); those with a lion's form, that degree of strength called ghibor (strength). As the supreme He, in the likeness of a man, regards them all, they look to Him and receive an impress, peculiar and belonging to man only, and called nora (fear) and which inspires the animals with a feeling of terror and fright. All these

---

[1] By this expression Is meant the divine humanity whose transcendent glory, majesty and splendor are beyond the powers of human comprehension and language to express. He is the Augoeides of the Platonists. By theologians and in Christian creeds, he is called the Unigenitus, Light of light, very find of very god, begotten, not made, the brightness and reflection of the great divine Father of Light and love and the express image of his person. In Kabbalistic philosophy, he is termed the heavenly man, Adam Kadmon, Merkava (the chariot). Few are they who have enjoyed the high privilege of beholding him. It is only the pure is heart that see him, and that only occasionally. The glory surrounding him is too overwhelming for human eyes to behold An ancient seer and prophet. Ezechiel, says: "And when I saw it, I fell upon my face." Another equally Illustrious seer relates: "And when I saw him, I fell at his feet, as dead. And he laid his right hand upon me, saying unto me, 'Fear not; I am the first and the last.'" Another says of him: "To Him every knee shall bow and every tongue shall confess that He most reign until all things become subject to Him, and then will He deliver up His Kingdom to the Father, and God shall be All and in all."

angelic forms thus synthesized in the human form reflect its traits and features, as it is written, "they had the face of a man" (Ez. i. 10). For this reason the Holy One (blessed be He) is called powerful, great, mighty and terrible, which four names are symbolized by the four letters of the tetragrammaton, IHVH, which includes all names.

These four forms are graven on the divine chariot, thus: on the right side, the face of a man; on the left, that of an eagle; on the front, of a lion; and behind, of an ox. These forms are likewise graven on the four quarters of the world. Like a great branched tree laden with fruit, the divine chariot marked with these forms sends forth all souls which are the seeds or germs of life to the world, as is implied in the words: "The herb yielding seed" (Gen. i. 11), that is, angels called "herb" who cast their seed into the world from which come human creatures. "Fruit tree bearing fruit after his kind whose seed is in itself." These words designate the man who conserves his seed to advantage. "Upon the earth" refer to him who lives a dissipated life, the which is therefore unlawful and forbidden. The angelic beings symbolized by the word grass are not fruitful, having no seed, and therefore vanish and fade away as they have not the signature of any of the letters of the divine name and become consumed by the primal fire out of which they came forth.

Human beings possess not the same stability and endurance of form as the higher angels in their classes, who have no need of a material covering which a man wears as long as his soul is bound and attached thereto. At night when man sleeps, his soul, quitting the body, ascends into the region of "the consuming fire" [1] and returns thence at the moment of waking refreshed and strengthened, and enters again into the body. The reason of this is, that his soul has not the same powers of endurance and stability as

---

[1] This expression is not to be taken in the vulgar and material sense as is common in Christendom. It Is rather to be considered as the great alchemical fire that transmutes the baser metals into silver and gold, or, in other words, that by its action upon our lower self, changes our evil and defiled human nature so that it becomes like unto the divine nature. It is described in the words of the great and saintly mediaeval Kabbalist, Count Pious do Mirandola: "There is the element of fire in the material world, the sun is the fire of heaven, and in the supersensual world is the fire of the divine Intelligence." The elementary fire burns, the heavenly fire vivifies, the Divine loves, that is, makes us lovable and loving so that we become, as one expresseth it, partakers of the divine nature. Happy and blessed is our destiny, the destiny of every created human soul.

higher and more exalted spiritual beings. To these refreshed souls the scripture alludes. "They are new (or rather renewed) every morning" and further adds, "great is thy faithfulness" (Lam. iii. 23), the import of which is that the divine faithfulness is as illimitable as his goodness and like a mighty ocean into which all rivers and streams flow, yet it is not full, and which also sendeth them forth again to the place from whence they came. Oh! truly great is the beneficence and faithfulness of the divine Being who draweth up the souls of men into the great purifying fire and flame of his love and returneth them again and again until they have accomplished their destiny--final union with Himself.

"And God saw everything that it was good" (Gen. i. 13), because on the third day of creation harmony and peace between all contending elements and forces generally prevailed, which beholding, the sons of the morning or the first born children of light, the angels on high, sang their joyous song of "peace and concord throughout the universe." Only on this great day, is the word "vayomer" (and God said) repeated twice, an occult word containing the mystery of the twelve transformations of the letters of the sacred name IHVH, symbolizing the four cherubic forms graven on the divine chariot.

CHAPTER III.

AND God said "Let there be light" (Gen. i.14); the word meoroth (lights) is defective in the Hebrew, being written without vau and therefore is it that offspring suffer from epilepsy and similar complaints. When the primal light was as yet invisible or unmanifest, a qalepha [1] (sheath or covering) formed itself around it, which, becoming enlarged, produced a second that extended itself to "little form" [2] with which it wished to be united and bear its form permanently. The Holy One dismissed and sent it below. When he created Adam in order that the "little form" might appear in the world, the qalepha, seeing Eve was conjoined with Adam, flew towards the paradise above desiring, as at first, to be joined with and form part of "little form," but the angel watchers on high would not allow her to enter and the holy One, having rebuked her, cast her into the depths of the vast abyss of space. When Adam sinned, however, she was permitted to ascend thereout and allowed to have power and influence over the offspring of "little form," who are punishable for the actions of their progenitors. Thus she goes throughout the world. When she dune to the gate of the earthly paradise and saw it guarded by cherubim, she seated herself next to the one that wielded the flaming sword, but, on observing its threatening attitude towards her, fled back to the world and finding these little ones as just described, killed them when the moon was on the wane. This is wherefore the word meoroth (lights) is, as has been stated, defective. Until the birth of Cain took place, she was unable to get near Adam, but eventually succeeding in doing so, she brought forth evil offspring and flying or winged demons.

This association with Adam continued a hundred and thirty years until the coming of Naamah, by whose great beauty Aza and Azael, sons of God, were seduced and fell from their high state of light and purity. From them came forth a brood of evil spirits into the world. Naamah it is who

---

[1] A term applied to the world of elementals void and destitute of mind who desired to become united and associated with humanity.

[2] Little Form, denoting the world of forms and beings before incarnating as human beings on the earth plane. The psalmist, speaking of man, says "thou hast made him 'littler' than the angels, that is, in form and mind."

wandereth through the world at night time, causing men to lose their virility, and wherever they are found sleeping alone in a house she acquires power over them, especially in times of physical weakness and ill health, whilst the moon is waning. When, however, the moon is increasing, the letters of the word meoroth are changed into the term imrath (the word), as it is written: "Imrath Jehovah, the word of the Lord, is refined" (Ps. xviii. 30) as gold tried in the fire. "He is a shield and buckler to all them that put their trust on him," a buckler and shield against evil and malignant spirits who roam and fly about in the world during the decadence of the moon, to such as those whose trust is in the Holy One.

When King Solomon went down into the garden of nuts, as saith the scripture: "I went down into the garden of nuts" (Cant. vi. 11) he took up a nutshell, that gave rise to reflections and ideas that enabled him to understand the reason and cause why anything that is pure and holy becomes environed by what is evil, as the nut enclosed within a shell. He perceived that evil spirits attach themselves to the pure and good, environing them similar to shells by exciting and producing certain kinds of pleasing emotions and feelings, the tending of which is to defile and corrupt, as it is written: "The pleasures of man produce and bring forth evil spirits" (sadah and sadoth) (Eccle. ii. 8) which occurs during the hours of sleep. It was necessary that the Holy One should create them in the world in order that it might be complete.

The universe as a whole is a system of worlds, enveloping the other from the lowest to the highest, from the most material to the highly spiritual, from the darkest and most dense to the most luminous and ethereal, all is a scale of graduated worlds of being and existence, and therefore the saying: "as above so below, and as below so above." Each world is a garment or envelope to the next in sequence. From the primal point of light issue forth luminous rays which extend through and pervade all the separate encircling worlds of existence, converting them into palaces of the great king, the splendor, beauty and magnificence of which are beyond description, and, as with these worlds rising in their order one above the other, so is it with regard to the human form, which in its grace and beauty of contour is the highest expression and approximate image of the divine, more than all other physical forms below it in the scale of being. All this is in accordance with the divine plan of creation, man himself being a microcosm or miniature of the universe, and composed of a series of coverings or envelopes, one within the other, as spirit, astral form and physical body. As long as the substance of the moon was conjoined with that of the sun, it shone with its own light, but becoming separated and disjoined from it and independent, it reflected a diminished luminosity and became itself enveloped with zones of decreasing light, so that we may now understand why the scripture saith: "Let there be lights," using the defective word meoroth, by which is designated occultly the zones or planes of existence of varying degrees of light which encircle each star and planet in the universe, as also this, our earth, through whose circumambient envelopes of more ethereal substance the primal life-giving light is reflected, and thus differentiated and adapted to become a blessing to man and every animate and inanimate creature.

"And God made two great lights" (Gen. i. 16). The Hebrew word vayas, "and he made," refers to the creation as a whole, everything in its kind being subject to its law and order. These two great lights were at first joined together and formed one whole and were of equal light, being both of them impressed with the two same sacred names, Jehovah and Alhim, though this latter name was as yet manifested only in an occult manner; yet scripture calls them both by the word great, in the plural, with the article of distinction, hagedolim (the great), because of their absolute identity, each bearing the same mysterious name Matspats, understood only by students of the secret doctrine, and which form the two highest of the thirteen degrees of divine mercy and goodness upon which the world is founded. The moon, unable to rule along with the sun, and feeling its loss of dignity in becoming disjoined from the sun, said: "Where feedest thou" (Cant. 1, 7), or "whence derivest thou thy light and glory?" The sun answered and said: "Where thou restest thyself at midday." The light of the moon was therefore diminished in order that the light of the sun might be greater and more manifest at noon, and accordingly the scripture further adds, "that I may not be as one that turneth aside from following in the path of the flocks." Constrained to be similar to the sun, the moon humbled herself, diminished her light at midday, as it is written. "Go thy way in the footsteps of the flocks" (Cant. 1, 8). The Holy One said to the moon: "Go and humble thyself," after which she lost her own light and now reflects only that of the sun though at first she was the same in rank and dignity with it, thus intimating occultly that the female can never fulfil her destiny and discharge her function except in joint union with her husband. The greater light designates Jehovah; the lesser light, Alhim; the one being a reflection and manifestation of the other as a word is of thought.

At first Alhim was expressed by the four letters of the sacred name, or tetragrammaton, but afterwards through manifesting on lower planes of existence, was known and distinguished by this name; yet nevertheless it radiates its power and glory in all directions in boundless space, as the mediator between the known and the Great Unknown, between the spiritual and material, the celestial and terrestrial scales and grades of life and existence as indicated esoterically by the letter H, which in Alhim conjoins Al with im, Al denoting God and im (or yam) the sea as symbol of matter. Thus Alhim becomes the word or Logos mediating between the world of pure emanations and the worlds of creation. The former being higher or prior in existence, is termed the light that rules by day, the latter, the light that rules by night.

The scripture further states: "He made the stars also," referring to the countless and innumerable hosts of angelic and ministering spirits existing in and by him who is the light and life of the universe, as it is written: "And God set them in the firmament of the heaven to give light upon the earth" (Gen. i., 17); that is, upon this lower world which is a replica or reflection of the world above it, and on the fourth day became illuminated with divine light and termed the Kingdom of David, the Asiatic world of effects, the fourth pillar of the divine throne of glory. This being completed, the four letters of the sacred name became adjusted one to another in their place and position in creation. Notwithstanding this, the throne was not completed till the sixth day, when the form of man was created and all the worlds throughout the realms of space were fixed in their relative orders and position and classed under the four letters of the divine name, viz., the Atzilatic, Briatic, Ietziratic and Asiatic worlds. The fourth day is called in scripture the day rejected by the builders, as it is written: "The stone which the builders rejected" (Ps. cxviii., 22), and also "My mother's children were angry with me" (Cant. i., 6), the esoteric meaning of which is: the light of the moon became diminished on that day and the enveloping worlds were established in their relative positions around the glittering and resplendent orbs of light in the firmament, in order to support the throne of David.

All these worlds send forth reflections of their light upon the earth which they receive from other worlds higher and more glorious than themselves, which in their totality form the Grand Archetypal Man, whose image, all who bear it, are called Man. This is the signification of the words: "Ye are men" (Ez. xxxiv., 21); that is, ye are called by the name of Adam (man). This, however, does not apply to the idolatrous nations. Every living spirit is therefore called Adam, for it is a divine emanation of which the body is a raiment or covering, as it is further written: "Thou hast clothed me with skin of flesh" (Job. x., 11), showing that the flesh of man is only a garment, and does not constitute the man. The souls that became incarnated on the earth plane in animals are in form similar to the garment that covers them, some of them being pure animals as mentioned in scripture, the ox, the sheep, stag, wild goat, giraffe and others.

Those souls who have been created and appear as men take upon them the human form and are called human souls, whilst the tens, "flesh of beast" signifies that the soul that has incarnated in this form has the name, the qualities and nature of a beast. For instance, the ox is a soul residing in an ox form, the flesh being its garment. This same applies to the rest of animals, and as idolatrous nations are not in scripture called men, so those impure souls have nothing in common with the truly human.

The bodies of idolatrous people are called impure flesh, as it is defiled by the soul of which it is the covering. The body is impure so long as the impure stall resides within it. As soon, however, as the soul quits it, it becomes pure again, being only a shell or covering. The souls of idolaters who incarnate on the earth plane take upon them the forms of unclean animals, such as the camel, swine, coney, and others. It is for this reason that animals have been distinguished into two classes, the pure and impure. Each have their peculiar tendencies and natural inclinations, and gravitate to the source whence they first originated. The heavenly lights suspended in the firmament are types and figures of things in the world, as it is written: "And God placed them in the firmament" (Gen. i, 17), the greater light to rule by day, the lesser light to rule by night. By the greater light scripture denotes the males who rule by day in that they provide for and look after the household and its necessary requirements and needs. On the arrival of night the sway of the female begins, as the proper manageress of the household, for, as saith the scripture: "She riseth also while it is yet night and giveth meat to her household and a portion to her maidens" (Prov. xxxi. 15). She and not he. Thus the light ruling by day signifies the male, or husband; the light ruling by night, the female, or wife. We further read: "He made the stars also." When the wife relinquishes domestic cares and duties in order to attend to her husband, she leaveth the direction of them to her maidens who abide at home to carry on the management, which again reverts to the husband when day begins.

"And God made two lights"; that of the sun is termed "flames of light" and go upward; that of the moon is termed "flames of fire" and descend upon the earth, and exercise their power and influence during week days. This is why at the close of the Sabbath, the blessing of the fire is pronounced. "Blessed art thou, Oh Lord, who has created the flames of fire," for then its rule and influence begins again. The fingers of the hand are occult symbols of a deep spiritual mystery the back of them being furnished with nails. It is therefore lawful to regard and fix attention on them at the close of the Sabbath, for the light of the fire whose rule begins at that moment is represented by the exterior part of the fingers, whilst the flame of light that comes from above must only be meditated upon by regarding the interior part of the fingers to which it corresponds. This mystery is expressed in Scripture thus: "Thou shalt see my back part, but my face shalt thou not see" (Ex. xxxiii. 23). Therefore a man should not regard and meditate upon the interior part of the hand at the close of the Sabbath when he repeats the prayer ending with the words: "Who hast created the flame of fire." The words "Thou shalt see my back part" refer to the back of the fingers symbolizing the light that rules and prevails during week days. "My face shalt thou not see," to the front part, the "flames of light," which rule during the Sabbath, on which day the Holy One himself presides over the invisible hosts of spirits surrounding his throne of glory, who are under his special charge. Therefore, on the Sabbath, rest from toil and labor is granted to all the worlds. The holy nation is the only one upon the earth that inherits and enjoys this heritage of the "flames of light" proceeding from the primal light and manifested only on the Sabbath day, and from which also emanate all the lesser lights that prevail below. At the departure of the Sabbath these "flames of light" become invisible, but the flames of fire, each of them in their appointed place and manner, rule and prevail during the week days. For this reason the nails of the fingers should be only regarded and meditated on by the glare of a fire.

It is written: "And the living creatures (hayoth) ran and returned as flashing flames of light" (Ez. i. 14). No human eye is able to view these angels going to and fro. They are the angels of "The Wheel," the occult meaning of which is this: Metatron is the chief and highest among the angels. Above him at a distance of five hundred leagues are those hayoth, or living moving creatures, whose flight through the realms of space is so rapid as to be indistinguishable to mortal eye; they are concealed beneath the two supreme letters of the divine name, Y and H, which rule and dominate the two remaining letters, V and H, that form their chariot. The great mysterious, the Unknowable, ruleth over all these hayoth, of whom those that are invisible rule over those that are visible and reflect their light end glory down upon them. All these living creatures are placed n the firmament of heaven, and respecting them it is written: "Let there be lights in the firmament of heaven" (Gen. i. 14), that is, let the living creatures called hayoth be in the region called the firmament of heaven. Above and beyond them, however, is another heaven as it is written: "And the likeness of the firmament above the heads of the living creatures was as the color of the terrible crystal" (Ez. i. 22).

It was the higher firmament of heaven whose glory and magnificent splendor (like that of the starry mist of the Milky Way, which includes within its dim and remote recesses innumerable and countless worlds of ineffable brilliancy and beauty) dawned upon the prophet's vision, and there it exists a universe of light and love hidden and concealed from mortal gaze like the thought of the Divine Mind, ineffable, transcending all human comprehension and powers of conception. As man has never been able to divine and understand the nature of thought, much less can he gauge the thoughts of Ain Soph (who is as a mighty ocean in which all thought is drowned) the Infinite and Boundless One, the concealed of all concealments, without beginning and without end, the great invisible center and fount of all life and motion existent in worlds known and unknown, careering in their mighty orbits in the fathomless abysses of space, the Great Being the smallest portion of whose glory and might and majesty is reflected and seen in sun and moon and the splendid galaxies of stars and constellations, all glittering and flashing in a midnight sky, and in the mystic music of the spheres are forever singing as they shine: "The hand that made us is divine."

In the present world of shadows and uncertainties, man must have wandered and lived ignorant, uninstructed and unenlightened, unable to acquire the faintest glimmer or notion of the mind and nature of the Divine Being but for the intermediation of the Logos or Word that, operating through the sephiroth kether (crown) produced the letters of the alphabet which, in their forms, simple and multiplex, are symbols of spiritual ideas by means of which we obtain conceptions, though inadequate, defective and incomplete, of Him in whom we live and move and have our being.

The letter aleph symbolizes the beginning and the end. Throughout the universe, all classes of beings are impressed with its signature, both those in heaven and those on earth. Though it includes many forms, yet they are but one full letter. By the higher part of it is symbolized the divine mind and thought, as also the upper firmament of the spiritual world. Beneath it and in the middle of aleph is the letter vau, the numerical value of which is six, denoting the six degrees between the Supreme Mind and the firmament above the hayoth, or "the hidden living creatures." The light emanating from the Divine is expressed in the word "brashith," of which the first part, bra, contains the initial letters of the name Abraham, to which scripture refers: "And the Lord appeared to Abraham as he sat at the door of his tent in the heat of the day" (Gen. xviii. 1), the esoteric meaning of which is as follows: When Abraham sat at the door of his tent; that is, at the gate separating the higher and lower world, symbolized by the letter aleph, he felt the great heat of the day; that is, he became mentally and spiritually enlightened by the divine light of the First Logos.

The light of the Second Logos was beheld by Isaac when, in the cool of the evening and the sun was going down, he prayed for the coming of this light, as it is written: "And Isaac went out to meditate in the field at eventide" (Gen. xxiv. 63). It was then he foresaw the contention that would arise between Jacob and Esau.

The light of the Third Logos, that proceeds from the other two, was that seen by Jacob, as it is written: "And as he passed, peniel the sun rose upon him and he halted upon his thigh" (Gen. xxxiii. 31). At eventide he beheld the light called and known as the Netzach of Israel (victory of Israel), and he halted on his thigh, because this light of sephirothic origin constitutes the thigh in the sephirothic figure. His thigh, not thighs, for as just said, he beheld the light of netzach, which is only' of the fourth degree.

For this reason, after Jacob no one was endowed with the gift of prophecy until the coming of Samuel, as scripture states: "The netzach, the strength or victory of Israel" (1 Sam. xv. 29). "And he touched the sinew of his thigh." When the angel of Esau who struggled with Jacob saw he could not prevail against him because he derived his power and strength from the two first sephirothic degrees or emanations; that is, from the supreme light and that called Adam Kadmon, the archetypal man, he touched the sinew of his thigh in which was contained the force symbolized by netzach (denoting firmness, inflexibility), and from that time as we have observed, prophecy was not found in Israel until the coming of Samuel, when it is said: "The netzach or strength of Israel is not a man"; that is to say, comes not from that sephirothic degree called man, but from that named netzach. Joshua indeed prophesied but only in an inferior manner because of his intimate and close association with Moses, as it is written: "And thou shalt put some of thine honor upon him" (Num. xxvii. 20). This was the case with David, as he says: "At thy right hand are the pleasures of Netzach" (Ps. xvi. 11). Not in but at thy right hand, that is netzach.

CHAPTER IV.

WHY was the thigh of Jacob weakened? Because impurity attacks a man on his left side and deprives him of his power and strength, and this state of weakness prevailed till the coming of Samuel, who reminded the people that netzach was the light of Jacob, the netzach that triumphs in Israel. This also is why the Prophecies of Samuel during his lifetime were denunciations of wrath and judgment. Furthermore, the Holy One endowed Samuel afterwards with the sephirothic power called hod. When? After he had anointed Saul and David as kings, which made him the equal of Moses and Aaron who rejoiced, the one in Netzach, the other in Hod.

All the sephiroth are bound together in orderly sequence as it is written: "Moses and Aaron were his priests and Samuel amongst those that call upon his name" (Ps. xl. 6). All are united and joined the one to the other, as were Jacob, Moses and Joseph. At first Jacob was lord of the house, then after his death Moses took possession. Joseph only ruled it during his life and that through Jacob his father. When he died Moses then ruled, for when the Divine Presence went out of Egypt, Moses became joined to Joseph, as it is said: "And Moses took the bones of Joseph with him" (Ex. xiii. 19).

Why is it said, "with him?" Because as a man cannot enjoy the female except through means of a body, so with the body of Joseph as a link, Moses became united with the Schekina, which thus in a manner of speaking had three husbands, being united at first with Jacob, then Joseph and Moses. Jacob died, and his body was buried in the holy land. Joseph died, but his body was not buried there, only his bones. Moses died, but neither his bones nor his body were interred in the holy land. After his death, the Schekina entered into Palestine and returned to her first husband, Jacob. From this we infer that a woman twice married after her decease becomes joined to and cohabits with her first husband. Moses entered not into Palestine, yet was he more favored than Jacob, who became joined to the Schekina on high after death, whilst Moses was honored by her presence with h in earth life. If it is said the pre-eminence is with Jacob, it is not so, because when the children of Israel went forth out of Egypt, they were subjects of Jubilee, the lowest stage of knowledge leading to divine wisdom and knowledge, and therefore wandered they in the wilderness, being unable to enter into Palestine. Their children, however, entered in, because they were children of the Schekina. During life Moses lived with her and followed her commands, but when he departed out of the world he ascended to the mount of the Holy Spirit, and through it to Jubilee on high where were gathered the six hundred thousand souls that along with him had come out of Egypt. With Jacob this was not the case. He, through the spirit, attained to that degree in the divine life termed Shemita, corresponding to the period of demission in connection with the year of Jubilee. He did not enjoy communion with the Schekina in his lifetime because he had to concern himself too much with the cares of his household. The holy land could only be gained and entered by divine aid and assistance. This is why those who are spiritually minded only become united with the Divine, whilst those engrossed with the cares, duties and anxieties of married life are only partially so. The life of the former is spiritual, that of the latter is carnal and worldly. There can be no point of union, no association with one another.

Between those who died in the wilderness and those who entered into the promised land is only a physical resemblance. Those who died in the wilderness attained to that degree of spirituality which enable them to behold the Divine in all his wondrous works and marvellous doing with their own eyes, whilst those who entered into the Promised Land and had lived in the wilderness were worldly minded and thus unqualified for the attainment of spiritual light and life. Jacob, whilst he lived, was attached to his wives, but after death his spirit became united with the Divine. Moses separated himself from his wife and attached himself to the Divine whilst in the body, and after death became united with the great mysterious Being who is above all and in all.

All the separate grades and degrees of spiritual life for one great and vast whole. The soul of Moses belongs to that called Jubilee, his body to Shemita. The soul of Jacob belonged to Shemita, his body to his wives. All these celestial degrees of light have their types on the earth plane and are suspended and posited or placed in the firmament. Though the scripture uses two different words to denote heaven, yet are they synonyms one of the other and mean the same thing, being included in one name, the mysterious name containing all names, of Him who can only be the object of all our thought and subject of all our faith.

And God said: "Let us make man" (Gen. i. 26). "The secret of the Lord, that is, the secret of the divine life, is with them that fear him."

Rabbi Simeon was sitting surrounded by his students and meditating on these words when suddenly a voice audible only to himself cried "Simeon! Simeon!" what signify these words "Let us make man?" Who was he that spake thus to Alhim? It was the voice of the great celestial Being known as the Aged of the Aged who, making himself visible for a moment and speaking these words to Rabbi Simeon, disappeared then from view and was seen no more.

Divining from the exclamation Simeon! Simeon! and not Rabbi! who it was that had addressed him, Rabbi Simeon turned to the students and made known to them who and what he had just seen and heard.

"It is evident," said he, "that the Holy One whom the scriptures describe as The Ancient of Days (Dan. vii. 9) has just spoken and now is the time to unfold and make known a profound mystery which up to the present has never been divulged and revealed to mortal man."

Pausing a moment as one enraptured and overwhelmed, and filled by the sudden influx of a great invisible spiritual force and power, the students gazing in breathless silence and speechless wonderment, in low and solemn tones Rabbi Simeon spake again.

"In ages long gone by lived a great and powerful king whose design it was to build palaces wherein to dwell and live in a manner becoming his royal grandeur. In his retinue of servants and attendants was found an architect, of great abilities and lofty genius in the art and science of construction, who made it the chief aim of his life to acquaint himself with the plans and ideas of his monarch and carry thorn into execution and doing nothing except by his authority and command.

The king was the Divine Being personified in scripture a heavenly Wisdom. Alhim was the celestial architect personified as "the heavenly Mother." Alhim was also the architect of the world below and was designated and known as the Schekina, and as a woman is not allowed to do anything without the consent and against the wish and will of her husband, all the palaces have been built by emanation. The father, through the Logos or

Word, said to the mother: "Let this be done!" and it was done at once, as it is written: "And God said let there be light and light was," that is, the Logos said to Alhim, the creative Logos, "let there be light." The master or lord of the palace speaks and the architect forthwith executes and thus were all the palaces or worlds made and produced by emanations, as, "let there be a firmament," "let, there be lights in the firmament," all were done on the moment. Regarding the present world, the world of separation, that is to say where all things appear to be independent of each other, the architect said to the master of the palaces: "Let us make man in our image and after our likeness." Certainly replied the master, it will be good to make him, but he will surely transgress and commit wrong against thee, in that he will be ignorant and foolish, as it is written: "A wise son is the joy of his father, but a foolish son is the heaviness of his mother" (Prov. x. 1). A wise son denotes man who came forth by emanation, a foolish son, created man."

Rabbi Simeon ceased speaking as all the students before him rose up and cried: Rabbi! Rabbi! Master! Master! Was there then a division between the Father and the Mother whether man should come forth from the father by emanation or from the mother by creation?

No, replied Rabbi Simeon, because man by emanation is male and female as he proceeds from the father and mother conjoined, as it is written: "And God said let there be light and light was." "Let there be light" connotes the part of man that emanated from the father; that is, the male principle; "and light was," refers to that part that emanated from the mother, the female principle. Man therefore was created androgynous with two faces. The emanative man possessed no special form or likeness, but the heavenly mother it was who wished to produce and provide the created man with a special image. Now the two lights emanating from the father and mother, called in scripture, light and darkness, the form of created man must of necessity be compounded from the active light proceeding from the father, and the passive light (termed darkness) that proceeded from the mother. As, however, the father had said to the mother that the emanated man if placed in the world would through frailty transgress and sin, he refused to take part in the formation of a human form for him. For this reason the light created on the first day was concealed and hidden and treasured up by the Holy One for the righteous, as also the darkness was created and reserved at the same time for the evil and wicked, as it is written: "The wicked shall be silent in darkness" (I Sam. ii. 9). And it was also on account of this darkness that man would, as foreseen, sin against the light, the father was unwilling to take part in the creation of man below on the earth plane. This also is why the mother said: "Let us make man in our image," that is of light, "and in our likeness," of passive light or darkness (which as has been stated is a materialized allotrophic form of light itself), which serves as a garment of the light as the body serves as a covering for the soul, as it is written: "Thou hast clothed me with skin and flesh" (Job x. ii).

As Rabbi Simeon ceased speaking for a moment, the students, one and all, pleased and delighted with their master's teaching, exclaimed: "Happy oh Master is our lot, in that we have had the privilege of hearing and listening to teachings that have never been delivered and imparted to anyone until now."

Resuming his discourse, Rabbi Simeon spake and said: "See now! that I even I am He and there is no Alhim with me" (Deuter. xxxii. 39). Give attention, oh students, to the expositions I am about to give of teachings handed down from ancient masters which I am permitted to impart and make known to you. Who was he that gave expression to the words: "Behold I even I am He"' It was the Supreme Being, the Highest of the high, the Cause of all causes, the one and only originator of the universe, without whom nothing was made that was made, in heaven above or on earth below, as we have already expounded in our remarks on the words: "Let us make man." From the plural form of this expression, we perceive that in the divine essence there are two hypostatic beings or Logoi who speak the one to the other at this moment. The second said to the first: "Let us make man" because it did nothing from itself, but by the permission of the first. He it is who said: "Behold I even I am He and there was no Alhim with Me"; that is, there was no Alhim with whom I consulted and took counsel, therefore, the logical conclusion is that Alhim who said "Let us make man" was a hypostatical Logos made for the creation of man. Master! cried the students as they stood up, pardon our interrupting thee, but hast thou not said that the Cause of all causes said to the first hypostatic being or Logos, called Kether (Crown), "Let us make man."

Then answered Rabbi Simeon and said, note well the explanation I am about to give unto you. I have not said that He who is Cause of all causes is the same as the Alhim, or that He is not the same. In the divine essence there is no conjunction of persons or natures whatever as commonly understood. What conjunction there is in the divine essence is similar to that which exists in the male and female principles which are as one, as it is written: "For I called them one" (Is. li. 2). Because in the divine essence there is no multiplicity nor conjunction, therefore is it that God said: "Behold I even I am He and no Alhim is with me"; that is, I am Alhim and Alhim is I.

Then rose up all the students and bowed themselves before their master, Rabbi Simeon, and said: Happy and blessed is the man whom his Lord hath chosen and permitted to reveal and make known mysteries that have never been divulged even to the angels themselves.

Rabbi Simeon continuing his discourse spake and said: We must bring to a close the interpretation of the esoteric meaning of this most mysterious part of scripture. It is further added: "I kill and make alive, I wound and I heal, neither is there any that can deliver out of my hand" (Deuter. xxxii. 39). The words "I kill and make alive" have reference to the sephiroth found on the right hand of the sephirothic tree of life, viz., hochma (wisdom), chesed (grace), and netzach (victory); those on the left hand being binah, (understanding), geburah (justice), hod (glory). From the former proceed principles conducive to life, from the latter those that tend and converge to death. If these pairs of opposites had not been united by the mediating sephiroth, viz., tiphereth (beauty), yesod (foundation), and malkuth (kingdom), there could not have been any equilibrium of principles in the world, no balance of justice, inasmuch as every perfect tribunal consists of three judges who in their official capacity and jurisdiction are considered as one. When the three Logoi constitute themselves as a tribunal for the dispensation of right and justice, the right hand is extended to receive penitents and on the sephirothic tree this hand, termed the Schekina, the right hand of God, is associated with chesed (grace or mercy). The left hand is associated with the sephiroth geburah (justice). The hand called on the above mentioned three, Jehovah or Schekina, corresponds to the mediating sephiroth, tiphereth (beauty, etc.), so that when a man repents of his sins and wrongdoings, this hand is outstretched to save him from the exacting justice and severity of the tribunal; but when the Cause of all causes judges, then as scripture states, "there is none that can deliver out of my hands." Still further, in this verse, the word I (ani) is repeated three times and thus there are three alephs, a, a, a, and three yods, i, i, i which letters form part of the tetragrammaton, or Sacred Name, written in full. The verse also contains three vaus (v-ahayeh, v-ani, v-en) that are also found in the divine name. The masters have explained the occurrence of the word Alhim in this verse as meaning Alhim acherim, other, that is, false Gods. According to this view the interpretation of it is this. "Behold I, even I, the Holy One am He, or I am the Schekina and Alhim is not with me; that is, the demons Samuel (prince of darkness) and Nachash (serpent) are not with me. I kill and make alive by the Schekina; I destroy the guilty and unrepentant and I make to live him that is just and upright; and there is none who can deliver out of my hands; that is, from the hands of Jehovah, from the three Logoi whose essence is denoted by and concealed in the fourteen letters of the mysterious word Chuza Bmuchso Chuza. Such is the truth."

The interpretation we have given and the remarks we have made concerning the Supreme Being, the Cause of all causes, and his relation to the Logoi have never been hitherto vouchsafed and imparted either to prophet or sage. Ponder over and observe the mysterious gradations of the Divine essence or life obscurely and dimly connoted by the sephiroth who are its raiments and coverings and as there is an ascending series of worlds beyond worlds in infinite succession profusely scattered throughout the boundless realms of space each with their motions, periods of duration and their laws, in one grand scheme involved and in a perfect whole united, so with the sephiroth in the highest world of emanations. Though differing in their relationship to the great center and source of Life and Light, yet are they each of them mirrors of the glory and beauty, the splendor and power, the might and majesty of the divine attributes and reflections of the Cause of all causes, the great Being dwelling in light ineffable, in presence of which all other lights become dimmed and disappear as fades and vanishes the darkness before the rising sun. "Let us make man." Another and altogether different interpretation and meaning has been given of these words by the learned of former times, and is as follows: They apply them as spoken by ministering angels who, endowed with a knowledge both of the past, the present and future, foresaw that man would fall and therefore they opposed his creation. Furthermore, at the moment that the Schekina or creative Logos said to the Holy One: "Let us make man" the angels Aza and Azael objected and said: Why create man since thou foreseest that he will sin and break thy law, along with the woman who will be formed from the passive light called darkness, as the man from the active light? Then spoke the Schekina and said in reply to them: Through woman, against whom ye object, shall ye yourselves fall and lose your glory and state, as it is written: "And the sons of Alhim saw the daughters of man were fair and they took them wives of all which they chose" (Gen. vi. 2).

Said the students to Rabbi Simeon: Master! were not Aza and Azael correct in saying that man through the woman would sin and transgress?

To this remark Rabbi Simeon replied: It was on this account that the Schekina said unto them: "Before accusing them ye should see to it that ye are better and stronger and purer than they. Man will fall and sin by one woman alone; ye will fall and be seduced by many. He will repent, but ye will become obdurate and hardened in your sin."

Said the students again to Rabbi Simeon, since sexual desires and impulses were the cause of sin and transgression, wherefore do they exist?

Said Rabbi Simeon: If the Holy One had not created a spirit of good that emanates from the active light, and spirit of evil that emanates from the passive light or darkness, man would have been a neutral ignorant kind of being unable to distinguish and contrast things essential to mental growth and spiritual development and progress; therefore was he created dual in nature, endowed with sexual feelings and rational functions, from the right and orderly discharge of which, or otherwise, he enjoys or suffers, as it is written: "See I have set before thee this day, life and good, death and evil" (limiter. xxx. 15).

Why then, said the students, was man thus created with a power of choosing and determining his future? Would it not have been better to have formed him with no desires and inclinations except for the just, the true and good, and thus have avoided becoming the cause of such disturbance in heavenly regions?

Said Rabbi Simeon in reply: It was necessary that man should be created thus in order that the good law might operate and be an incentive to spiritual progress and development. Now the law in its jurisdiction operates in two ways in the dispensation of justice, promising rewards to the righteous and decreeing punishment to the guilty and sinful; therefore is it written; "Verily there is a reward for the righteous and punishment for the wicked," and man must therefore be created and adapted for the reception of these different effects, viz., rewards and penalties. The Divine Being desires that good should prevail throughout the world, as the scripture saith: "He hath not created the earth in vain, he formed it to be inhabited" (Is. xlv. 18). Furthermore, the good law is as it were a judicial robe to the

Schekina, and if man had been created without moral tendencies and with an inclination liable to be diverted to evil as well as good, then would the Schekina have been like a poor man without garb or raiment. He who commits sin despoils in a manner the Schekina of its robe and incurs punishment and condemnation; as on the other hand, he who observes and practices the commandments of the law, is accounted as meritorious as one who arrays the Schekina with a robe or garment. This truth is symbolized by the garment with fringes or borders (zizith) as it is written: "For that is his covering only, it is his raiment for his skin when he shall sleep" (Ex. xxii. 27) referring to the Schekina. When anyone offers up an insincere prayer, destroying angels pursue after it, as saith the scripture: "All her persecutors have overtaken her" (Lam. i. 3), therefore we pray that "He being full of compassion, forgiveth our sins and destroys us not utterly" (Ps. lxxviii. 38).

THE KING'S PALACES

THE word sin refers to Samuel, who is the serpent; destroys means the destroying angel, his anger, the Holy One who wishes not that these angels should seize hold of our prayers. The destroying angels are under the control of seven chiefs, each having seventy others subject to his orders and authority. These are always ready to seize a man's prayer as it proceeds from his lips, and there are myriads of them. When a man with fringed garment and phylacteries girded upon his head and arm, uttereth a sincere prayer, scripture saith: "And all the people of the earth shall see, thou bearest the name of Jehovah and shall be afraid of thee" (Deuter xxviii. 10). As we have before stated, the name of Jehovah is contained in the phylactery on the head of every suppliant, and when thus seen these destroying angels fly quickly away as it is written: "A thousand shall fall at thy side and ten thousand at thy right hand" (Ps. xci. 7). When Jacob by divine clairvoyance saw the afflictions and the captivity his descendants would endure and suffer in the later days, it is said that he was greatly afraid and distressed (Gen. xxxii. 7). This was why he divided the people into three companies, as it is written: "And he divided the children unto Leah and unto Rachel and unto the two handmaids, and he put the handmaids and their children foremost, Leah and her children in the middle and Rachel and Joseph hindmost" (Gen. xxxiii. 1, 2). By these three companies or divisions were prefigured the three captivities: the handmaids and their children referring to the captivity of Edom or Egypt, Leah and her children, and Rachel with Joseph, to the other two captivities.

Foreseeing the anguish and misery that would be endured by his descendants in the future, this is why he prayed and vowed, saying, "If God will be with me, and will keep me in the way that I go, and will give me bread to eat and raiment to put on so that I come again to my father's house in peace, then shall the Lord be my Adonai (Gen. xxviii. 20-21). David also alluded to the captivity of the Schekina, foreseeing the children of Israel returning with joy to their fatherland and in the exuberance of his joy, composed ten different songs, the last of which is entitled "A Prayer of the afflicted one, when overwhelmed, he poureth out his complaint before the Lord" (Ps. cii.). The prayer of the poor and suffering has precedence with the Holy One and is regarded before the prayer of all others. And what is the Poor man's prayer? It is the evening prayer which he is privileged to utter when by himself and alone. The upright poor man is the descendant of Jacob under the power of other nations, and resembles the evening prayer in that he is in the night of captivity. The prayer of the Sabbath day is a charity or good deed done to the poor, and is as the rising sun that beams upon everything and is a benefit to all. For this reason a man should regard himself as a mendicant at the King's gate or door, as humility of heart and mind should be the chief feature in praying during the week days especially when, girded with the phylacteries, a man stands as a suppliant and mendicant before the palace gates of Adonai, the Great King, and prays: "Open my lips, Oh Adonai, and my mouth shall show forth thy praise" (Ps. li. 17). During week days, an angel like an eagle descends as soon as the evening prayer begins and taking it between his wings ascends and presents it then to the Holy One.

This ministering angel is called Ouriel (light of God) when the prayer is an act of piety and love, and Nouriel (fire of God) when it proceeds from earnestness of heart and feeling which is as a fiery glow coming forth from the soul within, as it is written: "A fiery stream issued and came forth" (Dan. vii. 9). During morning prayer, the ministering angel who descends is in form like a lion, and after taking it, ascends again heavenward. During vespers, or evening prayer, the ministering angel is in form of an ox and under the rulership of Gabriel. On the Sabbath day the Holy One descends Himself from heaven accompanied by the patriarchs, in order to welcome his only daughter. This is the mystery and occult meaning of the word Sabbath, She-Bath, the signification of which is, for she is his only child.

When the Sabbath dawns, the Holy One descends from his throne of glory to greet its coming, and myriads of angelic beings assemble and sing their hymn of praise and adoration: "Lift up your heads, oh ye gates, and be ye lift up ye everlasting doors, and the King of Glory shall come in."

Who is the King of Glory! The Lord, strong and mighty; the Lord mighty in battle. Lift up your heads and be ye lifted up, ye everlasting door, and the King of glory shall come in. Who is the King of Glory? The Lord of Hosts! He is the King of Glory. (Ps. xxiv. 9.) Then are opened the gates of the seven palaces, the first of which is the palace of love, the second of reverence, the third of mercy, the fourth of the luminous mirror, the fifth of the non-luminous mirror, the sixth of justice, the seventh of judgment. These palaces are alluded to in the words Brashith bra Alhim. (Gen. 1. i.) Brashith divided into Bra-shith signifies He created six, viz., the six palaces, and Alhim along with them forms the seventh. Corresponding to them are also seven palaces here below on the earth plane, an allusion to which is made in the psalm beginning with the words, "Give unto the Lord, oh ye mighty, give unto the Lord glory and strength." (Ps. xxix. 1.) In this psalm the words, "the voice of the Lord," are found repeated seven times, as also the divine name Jehovah eighteen times, corresponding to the number of worlds that the Holy One visits, as described in Psalm lxviii. 18. The chariot of God, viz., the divine form in which He manifests his glory, is surrounded by tens of thousands and myriads of angels, and in this form of manifestation He visits the eighteen systems of worlds in the universe. The gates of the palace whither prayers ascend are strongly guarded, but they find no entrance unless sincere and the result of meditation, whilst the palace of the Shekina or Divine Presence is always open, and it is of prayers sent up to it that the Psalmist refers. "They shall not be ashamed, but they shall speak with the enemies at the gate" (Ps. cxxvii. 5), that is, the King's gate, or gate of the Divine Shekina, to whom all prayers from our Higher Self, or the divine within us, should be addressed direct and without any intermediary; because what cometh from the divine, unto the divine returneth, like the Scripture with all its positive and negative commandments and precepts which came direct from the name of Jehovah, as it is written: "This is my name for ever, and this is my memorial unto all generations." (Ex. iii. 15.) The word shemi (my name), augmented with the two first letters yod and he (I and H) of the divine name has the numerical value of 365, equal to the number of negative precepts or prohibitions of the law. Also the word zicri (my memorial). augmented with i the two last letters of the same name, vau and he (V and I1), in its numerical value represents the 245 positive precepts or commandments of scripture. It is for this reason that the liturgy of the Shema, containing 248 words, is repeated before the benediction, "Blessed be thou, Oh Lord, who hast chosen thy people Israel in love."

ON ISRAEL OR THE CHILDREN OF LIGHT

NOW the children of Israel are all included and summed up in the name Abraham, of whom God spoke as "his friend," and which also applies to Israel, for Israel is contained in the divine name written in full, IV D, HA, VAV, HA, the numerical value of which is 45, equaling that of Adam (man). The scripture states that "He created man (Adam) in his image," signifying Israel who existed in the divine thought or mind before the creation of the world, and afterwards was created in the likeness and image of God. Offspring, life and the means of subsistence proceed from the middle column of the sephirotic tree of life, called in scripture, "My first born, even Israel" (Ex. lv. 22), and that nourisheth all the world. The support of Israel since the destruction of the temple is prayer, which is accepted in lieu of sacrifices. Its cry since the time of the first captivity has been: "Give me children or else I die" (Gen. xxx. 1). When the Shekina vanished from the temple, the ten sephirotic splendors also departed with it, and, becoming blended and united together they ascended on high and surrounded the throne of glory that they might still continue to receive prayers that go up on high. When man therefore desires that his prayers may ascend to heaven as a sweet and pleasing melody, or when he yearns to break the yoke and bondage of the old serpent who seeks always to disturb and thwart his prayers, he ought first of all to unify himself with the Divine Presence or heavenly Shekina, and use it as a sling wherewith to combat against and overcome his spiritual adversary. This living consciousness of the Divine within us and about us it is that endows us with strength and fortitude to tread the path of duty calm and unperturbed, and thus become better able to accomplish life's great mission and achieve its greatest victory, self conquest, the prelude to the realization of our destiny, i.e. union with the Divine. The teachings of Theosophy on this subject of the secret doctrine are contained in the names of the accents used in sacred chanting, such as Zarka (a sling), Shophar (a trumpet), Segolta (a bunch of grapes), etc.

THE PRAYER OF RABBI SIMEON

THE students had assembled and waited for the master to begin his daily discourse and exposition of the secret doctrine. Rabbi Simeon, after a few moments of meditation, prayed and said:

"Oh ye angels on high and ye great teachers of the secret doctrine taught and expounded in the sacred schools above, assemble yourselves and be present to note the words and their esoteric meaning that I am about to make known, and thou, oh Elijah, I conjure by the bond of our brotherhood, and pray thou mayst be allowed to descend and be present whilst I explain the mystery of the great struggle between good and evil in the world, as also of the conflict between light and darkness that has been, and still is, waged from the beginning; and thou Enoch, great angel of the Divine Presence! come thou and be present also, along with the masters of the school over which thou presidest. This I entreat and supplicate not for my own self, but for the honor and glory of the Shekina." Then began Rabbi Simeon his discourse.

"Oh Zarka," he said, "it is indeed through thee that our prayers ascend and reach their destined place on high. As a slinger slings and directs his stones to a certain mark or object, so should we, whilst praying, direct and address our prayers to the Divine in a manner of which thou art the symbol. Therefore the teachings of our forefathers instruct us that all our desires should be expressed before the pronunciation and utterance of the divine name, and by standing up cause them to ascend on high. Prayer should be direct and uninterrupted by anything whatever, even though it be a serpent entwining itself about our lower limbs, and always addressed to the Infinite One as we have been taught. At the repeating of 'Blessed be thou, oh Lord,' every knee should be bowed, and never by word or act of inattention should the union between himself and the Divine Being be disrupted. The union of the Shekina with its heavenly spouse is sometimes effected by passing through six degrees of the lower limbs of the sephirotic tree. It is for this reason that during prayer, the knees should be bowed and the six joints of each of the legs may be emblematic of this union, which is sometimes effected by passing through six degrees of the arms of the sephirotic tree. Occasionally, the Shekina ascends on high between the father and the mother symbolized by the letters yod and he. When it ascends it attains to the highest position, so that, losing sight of it, the angels themselves ask, "Where is the place of its glory?" When it rises above aleph, it forms and becomes a crown, which is called kether (crown). When, however, the Shekina descends below, it takes the form of a vowel beneath aleph, and then is called nekudah (point), as the crown above is called taga in the esoteric science of the accents. When this taga becomes joined to the Shekina, the letter zain is formed, a symbol of the union denoted by the seventh shephira, and in its form an emblem of the foundation stone of the universe. This is why it is written; "Thou shalt have a perfect and just stone" (Deuter. xxv. 15). There is no musical accent which has not its corresponding vowel point,--thus segoltha coincides with segol, the accent zakeph with seheva. Those who are acquainted with the esoteric meaning of the accents will easily find the correspondents of all the others, such as athnach, munach, etc.

PREVIOUS WORLDS AND RACES

"These (aleh) are the generations (children or races) of the heavens and the earth" (Gen. xi., 4). It has been stated that in every passage of Scripture that the word aleh occurs, there is no connection with what precedes it. This is the ease with the passage just quoted. Its logical reference and connection is with the words "tohu," and "bohu" (without form and void) in the second verse of Gen. i. There are those who say that the Holy One created worlds and then destroyed them. Why were they destroyed? Because, as the Scripture says, "the earth was tohu and bohu," indicating the state of former worlds before their destruction. But would it not have been better if he had not created them? Most certainly it would, and the explanation involves a great mystery. if you ask an explanation of what and wherefore He destroyed them, our reply is this: In the first place the Holy One never has destroyed the work of his hands. The scripture referring to the heavens, states: "The heavens shall vanish away like smoke, and the earth shall wax old as a garment, and they that dwell therein shall die in like manner" (Is. li. 6), from which it has been inferred that the Holy One creates and destroys worlds with their inhabitants according to a certain law. The fact is, that the Holy One created the, world and its population through the law expressed esoterically in the word "brashith," and referred to in the following passage:

"The Lord possessed me in the beginning of his way, and before he had created anything I was with him" (Prov. viii. 22); and by this brashith (beginning) he created the heavens and the earth, the foundations of which were based on "berith" (law or covenant), the letters of which are contained in br(ash)ith. It is of this berith that scripture speaks: "If the law (or covenant) I have made had not existed, there would have been no day nor night, heaven nor earth" (Jer. xxxiii. 25), and it is of this law the Scripture further states: "The heavens are the Lord's," and he has given the earth to the children of men. (Ps. cxv. 16.) By the earth the Psalmist means our earth or world, which is one of seven worlds or earths referred to by David: "I will walk before the Lord in the lands or earths of the living" (Ps. cxvi. 9). If, therefore, the Lord created worlds and destroyed them by reducing them to a state of tohu and bohu before the creation of the heavens and the earth, it was because the berith or law of such creation was not yet elaborated or existent. This is why the earth has escaped the fate of previous worlds.

At first God made known this law by the symbolism of circumcision to the heathen nations of antiquity; but, as they were unwilling to accept it, the earth remained barren and unfruitful. This is the esoteric meaning of the words, "Let the waters be gathered into one place" (Gen. i. 8), signifying the secret doctrine or knowledge of the divine law; "into one place" designates Israel, whose spiritual derivation is from the place of which it is said, "Blessed be the glory of the Lord in his place" (Ez. iii. 12), meaning by "the Glory of the Lord" the lower Shekina, and "in his place" the Shekina on high. As the souls of Israel are unified with it, therefore Jehovah is with them and over them, for it is written, "The portion of the Lord is his people" (Deuter. xxxii. 9). For this reason, the Scripture also saith, "Let the waters be gathered together in one place"; that is, Israel who accepted the law, and "let the dry land or element appear"; that is, the idolatrous nations who, unwilling to receive it, have remained barren and sterile.

This, then, is the explanation of what has been erroneously said: "God created worlds and destroyed them" through caprice. It was because of their rejection of and non-conformity to the law of nature. According to traditions that have been handed down, they, that is, the early races and their offspring, were created and called into existence by the second Divine Form, or hypostasis, symbolized by the letter H, as it is written "behibaram" (whom he created), a word which the most ancient teachers maintain ought to be divided and written "behi baram," meaning, God created them by the he. This is why the letter H in this word (an anagram of the name Abraham) is found written in the Pentateuch smaller than the other letters, and implying the barrenness and infertility of the heathen during the fifth or He millenium after creation, which led up to the destruction of the first and second temples.

Moses, because he wished to bring these nations to a knowledge of the Divine, believing they had been created by the Divine Form called He, was greatly disappointed and grieved when God said to him: "Go, get thee down, for thy people have sinned" (Ex. xxxii. 7), in that they have failed in love to H and reverence to V that were due unto them, and have fallen from that high state of spiritual elevation represented by V, the letter which proceeds and is derived from the L and H, and descended from on high along with H in order that not a single soul should be lost of those who had inhabited previous worlds that had entered into pralaya, symbolized by the captivity of Israel. The souls of the Antediluvians (ereb rah) emanated from those to whom Scripture refers. "For the heavens shall disappear like smoke and the earth wax old as a garment, and they that dwell therein shall die in like manner" (Is. li. 6). They are also those for whom Noah was unwilling to intercede, and therefore it is written of them, "And they were destroyed from the earth" (Gen. vii. 23). They were the same souls of whom it is also written, "Thou shalt blot out the remembrance of Amalek from under heaven" (Deuter. xxv. 19).

Unthinkingly, Moses caused to descent the being called H among these men, and was therefore denied the privilege of entering into the Holy Land until He returned to its former place on high. When He descended from above Vau came down also. Who shall raise He again on high? It is Vau whose presence was not with Moses (the word Moses is written without a Vau). This is why the letter He in "behibaram," an anagram as stated of Abraham, is written smaller than the other letters in the book of the law, and to which scripture alludes. "He brought them forth out of Egypt" by means of the Vau who, at the same time, brought out the He. When the Vau and He became conjoined, the vow was made. "The hand of God upon his throne shall be raised against Amalek, the Lord will have war with Amalek from generation to generation" (Ex. xvii. 16), "yod al cas Jah milehamah la Jehovah beamalek."

What is the signification of the words, "from generation to generation"? They allude to the time of Moses. We have been informed by ancient masters that a generation is in number equivalent to 600,000 souls, and there exists a tradition that in the time of Moses each woman bore in her womb potentially the same number of embryos.

After the deluge the souls of the antediluvians incarnated in five different races or nations, viz., the Nephilim (fallen or degraded), Giborim (mighty ones), Anakim (tall ones), Rephaim (the giants), and Amalekim (Amalekites). It was through the last of these that He fell from on high. Balaam and Balak were descendants of Amalek. Take Ain and Mim (a and m) from the former, L and K from the latter, and the remaining letters form the word Babel, and the subtracted letters the name Amalek. It is of them that Scripture refers, "therefore is the name of it called Babel because the Lord did there confound (babel) the language of the earth" (Gen. xl. 9). And they were they who survived the catastrophe of the deluge of whom it is said: "He destroyed every living thing on the face of the earth" (Gen. vii. 23).

These five races survived till the time of the fourth captivity of Israel, whose chief enemies they were, and therefore called instruments of iniquity. They are denoted in Scripture by the words, "And the earth also was corrupt before God, and the earth was filled with violence" (Gen. vi. 11). Of these, the first race was the Amalekites. Of the Nephilim it is recorded, "And the sons of God beheld the daughters of men that they were fair" (Gen. vi. 2). They were also the second in rank of the angel hosts that were cast out of heaven and became incarnated.

CHAPTER IX.

WHEN the Holy One wished to form man and said: "Let us make man in our image. " He intended to set him over the angelic hosts who should be subject to his commands. The revolting angels, however, protested and said: "What is man that he merits Thy regards? (Ps. viii. 5); he will most certainly sin against Thee and disobey Thy commandments." Said the Holy One unto them: "If ye were on earth below you would become more wicked and culpable than he. And so it happened, for as it is written, as soon as "they beheld the daughters of men that they were fair, they took them wives of all which they chose" (Gen. vi. 2). Therefore, the Holy One hurled them into the abysmal darkness, where they abide unto this day.

Such was the doom of Asa and Azael, from whom originated and were engendered those angelic beings who, through sexual intercourse with their fair and beautiful human wives, became the fallen ones and thus forfeited the joys of the heavenly world, exchanging its eternal happiness for the fleeting pleasures and delights of earthly existence, as it is written, "He repayeth them that hate him, to their faces to destroy them" (Deuter. vii. 10). The Giborim (mighty ones) formed the third race, and were they whom Scripture describes as "mighty men which were of old, men of great renown" (Gen. vi. 4). They it was who, at the building of the tower of Babel, said: "Go to and let us build us a city and tower whose top may reach unto heaven, and let us make us a name" (Gen. xi. 4). Becoming incarnated, they were those who built mansions, colleges, and founded oracles and temples, not for the worship and glory of the Divine Being, but for their own self-exaltation, and then tyrannized over Israel as though they were dust of the earth, by plundering and robbing them of every thing they possessed. Concerning them the Scripture states, "And the waters prevailed and were increased greatly upon the earth" (Gen. vii. 19).

The fourth race was that of the Rephaim or Giants, who, whenever they beheld the children of Israel in sore straits or distress and afflictions, scoffed and derided them and treated with contempt the good law and its students and followers, but regarded with favor and indulgence the idolatrous and ungodly. Of them it is written, "The Rephaim (giants) shall not rise again" (Is. xxvi. 14), and when the redemption and deliverance of Israel shall appear, then will be accomplished the words of scripture respecting them, "Their memory shall perish."

The fifth race was the Anakim (tall ones), a despicable people, of whom it is said: "The Rephaim were like unto them" (Deuter. xi. 11). It was through them that the earth reverted back to its previous state of tohu and bohu, occult words in which is contained the epitome of their history and final disappearance from off the face of the earth, which occurred when the light divine appeared in the world.

Another explanation of the words, "These are the generations or offspring of the heavens and the earth," is gathered from the words, "And Aaron took them and cast them into the furnace and formed of them a calf." Then said the Israelites: "These (aleh) be thy gods, oh Israel" (Ex. xxxii. 4). On the day that all these different races were exterminated, the Holy One along with the Shekina created the heavens and the earth anew, as it is written, "For as the new heavens and the new earth which I make shall remain before me" (Is. lxvi. 22), which words are the complement to "on the day that God created. . . ."

Then it was that God also made to grow out of the groun every tree that is pleasant to the sight and good for food" (Gen. ii. 4). But not until the extermination of the above mentioned races did the secret doctrine appear in the world, and the children of Israel flourished and sprung forth as the trees and green herb out of the ground alluded to in scripture; for till then "the Lord God had not caused it to rain upon the earth and there was no man to till the ground" (Gen. ii. 5). The esoteric meaning of which is, the children of Israel were not there to do sacrifice and render worship to the Holy One. A further exposition is that the words, "And every plant of the field," denote the first Messiah; and the words "every herb of the field" a second Messiah.

What was the reason for the appearance of these Messiahs? Because there was no Moses to make intercession with the divine Shekina, and therefore is it written, "There was no man to till the ground." This esoteric meaning and interpretation is also that of the words, "And the Sceptre shall not depart front Judah" (Gen. xlix. 10), referring to the Messiah son of David; whilst the words, "nor a prince of his posterity," denote Messiah the son of

Joseph,--"Until the coming of Schiloh, "--signifies Moses; the numerical value of these two names being the same. The Hebrew words "velo iqhath" (to him shall the nations look) are composed of the same letters as "velevi, qehath" (hevi and Qohath) the ancestors of Moses. Also, "every plant of the field," signifies the righteous whose souls emanated from him who is termed "The Just One," who is the life of the world and abideth forever. The word "shiah" (plant) is composed of the letter Sh, the branches of which symbolize the three Patriarchs and "hai" (life) denoting the Eternal One who alone hath life and immortality. The following word "eaheb" (every herb) denotes the union of the seventy-two branches of the celestial tree, and which only became united with the Shekina on the appearance of Adam (the man) whose name in its numerical value is equal to that of Jehovah. The words, "and every herb of the field before it grew out of the ground" denote also The Just One, of whom it is written, "Truth shall spring out of the ground" (Ps. lxxxv. 11), and "The Truth shall be sent down upon the earth" (Dan viii. 12.) These passages signify that students of the secret doctrine, like the green herb, will spring up during the period of captivity; that the truth will become recognized and prevail when Moses cometh again, of whom it is written, "The jaw of truth was in his mouth" (Mal. ii. 1); so that no one was better able to unfold and expound Divine mysteries than he. When he returns, "a mist shall go forth from the earth and water the whole face of the ground" (Gen. ii. 1); that, is. Ad (a mist). shall be taken from Adonai (Lord) and V and N becoming added to it shall form Adon, master or lord of the earth, by whom it shall be watered. Then will Israel understand the full meaning of the secret doctrine. The word Ad, translated in the targum or Chaldean paraphrase a cloud, designates also him who is referred to in scripture as "The cloud of the Lord was upon the tabernacle by day" (Ex. xl. 38). It is by him that the masters of the secret doctrine and all students of the good law shall be enlightened and flourish when He cometh again.

SYMBOLISMS OF MAN

"And the Lord God formed man" (Gen. ii. 7), that is, Israel. Here the word vayitzer (formed) is written with two yods or I's, indicating that the Holy One formed him with two natures, the higher and lower self; the one divine, the other earthly, and impressed upon his form the divine name, I V I, expressed by the two eyes and the nose between them, thus: I. The numerical value of these letters is 26, which is also that of the divine name, Jehovah.

It is on this account that scripture saith, "From the top of the rocks I shall see Him" (Num. xxiii. 9). The word zurim (rocks) denotes also forms, so that Balaam who uttered these words, meant that in viewing the form of Israel, he beheld and recognized the divine name.

Another comparison of Israel with this Divine name is in the two tables of stone containing the law and representing two I's, the letter V symbolizing what is written on them. Man also in himself represents the union and blending together of the higher and lower Shekinas, symbolized by the repeating of the Shema, morning and evening.

The union of the two natures in man is also referred to in the words, "Bone of my bone and flesh of my flesh" (Gen. ii. 23). We also read that God planted man, that is, Israel, in the sacred garden of Eden, as it is written, "And the Lord God took the man and put him in the garden" (Gen. ii. 15). Jehovah Alhim, the Lord God; that is, the heavenly father and mother; "garden," the lower Shekina; "in Eden," the heavenly mother; "the man," the middle column of the sephirotic tree; from which was formed his wife, and who being his delight should never be separated from him.

It was then that the Holy One planted Israel, who are the holy branches of the world, or, in other words, a race purer and better than those that had formerly existed; as it is written, "The branch of my planting, the work of my hands, that I may be glorified" (Is. lx. 21). "And out of the ground made the Lord God to grow every tree that is pleasant to the sight and good for food" (Gen. ii. 9). "The Lord God denoting the celestial father and mother; "every tree that is pleasant to the sight," the Just; and "good for food," the middle column consisting of the sephiroth kether, tiphereth, yesod, etc., and from which proceed those stores of food by which the righteous are sustained and which, when mankind becomes purified and enlightened, will contribute to the life of the world. Then will every one take of the tree of life in the midst of the garden, and eat and live for ever more.

The tree of the knowledge of good and evil symbolizes those whose intellectual faculties are directed only to phenomenal objects that can be seen and handled, and by whom the presence and operation of the Shekina in nature, in the life of nations and in the soul of man himself, are unrecognized and ignored; and thus it will be until the times of error and darkness pass away; then will they also become proselytes of the divine life of whom it will be said: "The Lord alone is their leader and there is no strange god in their midst" (Deuter. xxxii. 12); and, human nature transformed and enlightened and purified, mankind will become as a tree that, in its stately form and beauty, is pleasant to the sight. The tree of the knowledge of Good and Evil occasioned Israel to fall into error which they should have avoided and remembered the divine command admonishing them to "Eat not of the tree" of Good and Evil, on pain and penalty of spiritual death involving loss of union with the Divine, without which there can be no interior enlightenment, no spiritual development. This command with its twice repeated warning, "thou shalt die, thou shalt die," refers also to the children of Israel who endured two great calamities, the destruction of the first and second temples, and the loss of the higher and lower Shekina or manifestation of the Divine presence in their midst, as expressed and typified in the words, "And the river shall be dried up" (Ia. xix. 5), and which then became resolved in Ain Soph, the Boundless One, whence it emanated at first.

This aridity or state of dryness will not however continue always, for when Israel comes out of captivity then will the river that was dried up and wasted go forth again out of Eden to water the garden, and divine knowledge cover the earth as the waters cover the seas.

This recurrence and reappearance of the Divine Presence amongst mankind is mystically referred to in the words, "Then shalt thou delight thyself in the Lord" (Is. lviii. 14). The word anag (delight or joy) in this passage of scripture is composed of the initial letters of "Eden," Nahar (a river), and Gan (a garden.) Then also shall be accomplished and fulfilled the words of scripture: "Then Moses and the children of Israel shall sing" (not sang, as generally translated--Ex. xv. 1) for error and idolatry symbolized by Pharaoh and his hosts will he destroyed and pass away forever. Furthermore, we read, "the river that went forth out of Eden to water the ground was parted and became into four heads" (Gen. ii. 10). These four heads or channels are symbolized on the sephirotic tree by chesed (mercy) which forms the right arm, teaching that he who desires to become wise should always turn himself to the south, the quarter presided over by Michael and his hosts, along with Judah and two other tribes of Israel, whilst he who prays for wealth should turn towards the north where is stationed Gabriel with his hosts, along with Dan and two other tribes. The third channel is symbolized by Netzach (triumph or victory), the right limb of the sephirotic tree presided over by Nuriel with his hosts, along with Reuben and two other tribes. The left limb is Hod (splendor). It is to this sephira that, what is said of Jacob, is applied, "And he halted upon his thigh (Gen. xxxii. 31). The fourth head is presided over by Raphael and his hosts, along with Ephraim and two other tribes. The mission and work of this ruler is the healing and assuagement of the afflictions of the captivity.

The words, "and became parted into four heads" refer also to four individuals who gained entrance into the mysterious garden of Eden, or Paradise. The first entered it by the channel Pishon, that is, "Pishoneh halakhoth" (the mouth that teaches the good law). The second, by Gihon (the place where is buried he who creepeth on his belly--Levit. xl. 42). It is under the presidency of Gabriel whose name is composed of the words Gebra, al (divine man), and who is alluded to in the words, "the man who walks on a hidden path and whom God has covered as with a veil" (Job. iii. 23), and also in the following passage: "No man knoweth unto this day the place of his sepulchre" (Deuter. xxxiv. 6); the esoteric signification of which is understood only by those initiated in the secret doctrine. The third individual entered by the channel called Hiddekel or Had qal (the adapting word), the third part of the secret doctrine imparted to initiates and known as Darash (exposition). The fourth entered by Phrath, the channels through which flows the principle of fecundity. Ben Zoma and Ben Azai, who penetrated into and attained to the knowledge of the secret doctrine concealed within its esoteric covering, by their wrong use of it found it a curse instead of a blessing, whilst to Rabbi Akiba it became a blessing and a source of joy, tranquillity and power.

THE STRANGE VISITOR

AS Rabbi Simeon concluded his remarks, Rabbi Eleazar, his son, spake and said: My father! I along with other students were one day discussing in the college a remarkable saying of Rabbi Akiba to his novitiates, viz., "When you come to places paved with pure white marble glittering in the sunlight, you should not say here is water, for then ye will expose yourselves to the danger expressed in the words, 'He that speaketh lies shall not tarry in my sight'" (Ps. ci. 7).

Suddenly there appeared in our midst an aged and venerable looking man who said unto us: "What may be the subject of your discussion." Having informed him thereof, he said: "Truly it was a most dark and abstruse saying and had been a subject of discussion in the celestial college. In order that you may grasp and comprehend its latent meaning, I have come hither in order to give you an explanation which has not heretofore been granted or given to any man of this generation. Stones of white and glittering marble symbolize the pure waters that spring forth and take their origin from the fountain. Aleph (A) denotes the beginning and end or sum total of created life. The letter vav, separating the higher from the lower yod, symbolizes the tree of life, the fruit of which gives immortality. The two yods have the same meaning as in the word vayitzer (and he created) denoting the two appearances of the Divine Presence under the form of the higher and lower sephiroth called hochma (wisdom) and symbolized by the two yods or I's. This hochma is found just below the sephiroth kether (crown) and denotes the beginning and end of all things. The two yods also symbolize the two eyes of these sephiroth from which fell two tears unto the great abyss of primal matter. Why did they fall? Because of the two tables of the law which Moses brought down from on high, which the children of Israel were unable to appreciate to their advantage. They were therefore broken and destroyed. The same cause occasioned the destruction of the first and second temples, for the vav had taken flight and disappeared. Other tables of the law were then given with affirmative and negative precepts, rewards and penalties corresponding to the sephiroth on the right and left sides of the Tree of Knowledge of good and evil, from which the law as now promulgated, came forth. The sephiroth on the right side symbolize life; those on the left, death.

This then was why Rabbi Akiba said to his students: "When ye behold pavements of pure white marble, ye shall not say they are water, or to be more explicit, do not confound together the law of the lower nature (the flesh) with that of the higher (spirit), for the one inflicts death, the other gives life. Do not fall into the error of imagining that they are one and the same, lest convicted of inexactitude, ye come under the category of those mentioned in Scripture. "He that speaketh lies shall not tarry in my sight" (Ps. ci. 7). The difference between the two sets of tables of the law was this; the first that was broken and destroyed proceeded from the tree of life, the other from the tree of the knowledge of good and evil, and corresponded, as we have stated, to the right and left sides of the sephirotic tree, and this is why it is said, "A wise man's heart is on the right hand, but a fool's on the left hand" (Eccles. x. 2).

At the conclusion of these words we all crowded round the venerable stranger to embrace him, but he suddenly vanished out of sight and we saw him no more. Resuming his discourse Rabbi Simeon spake and said:

"There is yet another exposition of the words 'And a river went out of Eden.' This Edenic river symbolized the tree of life in the spiritual world; that stands fair and beautiful amidst all that is pure and holy, as it is written, 'Evil shall not dwell with thee' (Ps. v. 4); 'went out of Eden,' denotes Enoch or Metatron the great angel of the Divine Presence and who came from the higher Eden of the Holy One (which is never infested with inferior orders of angelic beings) to take charge of the lower or earthly Eden and protect it from the assaults and ingress of demons. It was the garden into which Ben Azar, Ben Zoma and Elisha, found an entrance; and from the tree of good and evil planted in it came forth the law inscribed on the two tables of stone containing on one side positive precepts and on the other negative commandments, respecting what ought to be done and what left undone, what is pure and lawful and what is impure and unlawful."

As Rabbi Simeon ceased speaking, there rose up in the midst of his audience an aged stranger grave and venerable in appearance and aspect and exclaimed:

"Rabbi! Rabbi! what thou hast just spoken is true. The tree of good and evil is not the tree of life. The esoteric doctrine of the two yods in the word vayitzer is this: They denote and symbolize two separate creations, one good, the other evil; one of life, the other of death; of things commanded and things forbidden, and are alluded to in the words, "And the Lord God formed the man out of dust from the earth and breathed into his nostrils or soul the breath of life," the divine Shekina. Man is a threefold product of life (nephesh), spirit (rauch), and soul (neschamah), by the blending and union of which he became a living spirit, a manifestation of the Divine."

Having uttered these words, the unknown stranger suddenly vanished out of sight, leaving the students lost in wonder and amazed. Then spake Rabbi Simeon and said:

"We have been honored with the presence in our midst of a great adept, and what he has spoken is in strict conformity with the words and teaching of Scripture."

SYMBOLISM OF THE DIVINE LIFE AND HUMAN DESTINY

"AND the Lord God took the man and put him into the garden of Eden to dress it and to keep it" (Gen. 11:15). The question may be asked: "Whence did He take him?" The answer is: "From the four elements, fire, air, earth and water, which form the basis of man's physical body and are symbolized by the words 'And a river went out of Eden to water the garden, and from thence it was parted and became into four heads'" (Gen. 11:10). That is, the Holy One formed man from these four elements and placed him in the garden of Eden, into which a man enters again whenever he repents of his wrongdoing and conforms his life to the good law, until at length, divested of mortality, he is placed again in the heavenly garden; that is, he enters into and becomes a conscious participant of the divine life and clothed with immortality. "To dress it and to keep it," meaning to keep and observe all the precepts of the good law, obedience to which imparts to and endows him with power to control these elements and drink of the river of the water of life--as disobedience causes him to drink of the bitter waters flowing from and by the tree of evil, symbolizing the tempter, so that instead of ruling and controlling the elements he becomes their slave.

Then occurs what is written concerning the children of Israel when they came to the waters of Marah: "They could not drink of the waters for they were bitter" (Ex. xv. 23). Disobedience to the good law of rightdoing always, sooner or later, results in bitterness of life, thought and feeling, and only by rightdoing can the words of scripture be accomplished.

"And the Lord showed him a tree, which, when he cast into the waters, the waters, though bitter, were made sweet." The tree here spoken of is the "Tree of Life," the Divine or Higher Life. "And if thou wilt diligently hearken to the voice of the Lord thy God and wilt do that which is right in his sight and will give ear to his commandments, I will put none of these diseases upon thee which I have brought upon the Egyptians, for I am the Lord that healeth thee" (Ex. xv. 26). What does all this mean, What is the secret doctrine or teaching inculcated in these words? It is that when this our human life becomes dark and embittered with sorrow and sadness through weakness and failing to live in accordance with the good law; there is only one agent or power that can clarify it and cause it to become again pure and sweet and clear; it is the Divine within us, "healing all our diseases, redeeming from all evil, and satisfying with good things, so that our youth is renewed like the eagles" (Ps. ciii. 4, 5). It was through the instrumentality of Moses that the waters at Marah were made sweet, and he therefore represents the Messiah.

Of Moses it is said: "And the rod (mateh) was in his hand." The word rod designates Metatron, the angel before the throne or Divine Presence and from whom cometh life or death. When it is changed or transformed into a rod, it is a source of help and assistance to man, as it then comes from the side of good. When, however, it is transformed into a serpent, it is then not a blessing, but otherwise to him, and this is why Moses in his fear fled from it. The Holy gave it into the hand of Moses and so was formed and came forth the oral and written law relative to things lawful and forbidden. But immediately Moses struck the rock with it; then was it taken from him as it is written: "And the Egyptian had a rod in his hand and Benaiah plucked it out of his hand" (2 Sam. 23:21). The rod of Moses symbolizes also the serpent or tempter, who was the cause of the captivity of Israel. The words "And from thence it was parted into four heads" have yet another symbolical and occult meaning. Blessed is he whose study is in the secret doctrine, for, when the Holy One takes his soul unto himself, it leaves the body formed out of the four elements, and rising on high is placed at the head of the four Hayoth, or living creatures, to whom the words refer: "In their hands shall they bear thee up" (Ps. xci. 12).

"And the Lord God commanded the man, saying: 'Of every tree of the garden thou mayst freely eat, but of the tree of the knowledge of good and evil, thou shalt not eat of it'" (Gen. ii. 16, 17). Now, wherever the word zav (commandment) is found in Scripture it is to forbid idolatry, the tendency toward which comes from the liver (chabad), which word signifies hard, bitter, or grievous, and therefore idolatry is called or termed a hard service. The liver moreover is the seat of rage and wrath, and this is why it is said that whoso giveth way to anger and rage is as culpable as he who commits an act of idolatry. And this is the meaning of the words "And God commanded the man," that is, in forbidding idolatry he also forbade the indulgence in anger, for they proceed from one common source and lead to the shedding of blood and "whoso sheddeth man's blood, by man shall his blood be shed" (Gen. ix. 6). The penchant for murder comes from the liver and is as a sword in the hand of the angel of death, and "The end or results of it is bitter as wormwood and sharper than a two-edged sword" (Prov. v. 4). The word "saying" signifies the spleen, of which it is said "she eateth and wipeth her mouth and saith, 'I have done no wickedness,'" (Prov. xxx. 20). This organ has no orifice nor canal, but is a solid substance with veins and arteries and absorbs dark blood from the liver. Adultery is therefore in scripture symbolized by the spleen, as its perpetration leaves no traces behind it, whilst murder becomes quickly detected by bloodmarks and therefore men fear to commit murder more than adultery.

When these sins of idolatry, murder and adultery, cease to prevail among mankind, in that day there shall be one Lord, and his name One. On this account a man who is a true Israelite will find his unity in the secret doctrine, which is as a tree of life to them that lay hold of it, and "happy is everyone that obtaineth her" (Prov. lv. 18). This tree of life is the Matrona, symbolized by the tenth Sephira Malcuth (Kingdom). This is why Israelites or children of light are called Beni Melchim (sons of kings). It is also why the Holy One said: "It is not good that man should be alone. I will make him a helpmate for or against him" (Gen. ii. 18), by which is meant the Mischna, which is as a helpmate to the Schekina and proved of great benefit during the captivity by teaching what was lawful and what forbidden, what was pure and what impure. If Israel, however, should cease to respect the Mischna as a spouse, then instead of a helpmate to him, it would become a helpmate against him and there could never he harmony between them until the cause of dissonance were done away by purity of life and worship.

This is the reason that Moses was not interred within the precincts of the Holy land and no one knoweth to this day the place of his sepulchre. The sepulchre signifies the Mischna which was prevalent over the Matrona in the early days of Israel, during which the King and Matrona became separated from the celestial spouse. Therefore saith the scripture: "For three things the earth is disquieted and for four which it cannot bear. For a servant when he reigns; and a fool when he is filled with meat, for an odious woman when she is married, and a handmaid when she takes the place of her mistress" (Prov, xxx. 21, 23). The servant that reigns refers to Samail or Satan. The handmaid that takes the place of her mistress, designates the Mischna, whilst the fool filled with meat denotes the strangers living in the camp of Israel who were ignorant and foolish.

Again Rabbi Simeon spake and said: "And out of the ground the Lord God formed every beast of the field and every fowl of the air" (Gen. ii. 19). Woe unto those whose hearts are hardened and eyes blinded so that they are unable to understand and appreciate the teachings of the secret doctrine and know not that the "beast of the field" and the "fowl of the air" symbolize those who are ignorant and, though possessing life (nephesh) and soul (haya), are of no advantage or benefit either to the Schekina whilst in captivity, or to Moses who never quitted or forsook her for a moment, or, in other words, who recognize not the reality of the Divine Life nor the existence of the Higher Self.

Here Rabbi Eleazar asked a question: "What was the great object of life with an Israelite during the time of Moses?"

"Eleazar, my son," replied Rabbi Simeon, "why dost thou ask such a question as this? Hast thou not read and studied the words of Scripture? 'I am he who declares the end from the beginning and from ancient times the things that are not yet done'" (Is. xlvi. 10).

"Yes," replied Rabbi Eleazar, "and I recognize them as true."

This is why we are taught by tradition that Moses is not dead and is therefore called "man," of whom it is said: "There was not found a helpmeet for him" (Gen. ii. 20). But everything was against him and he found no help in bringing the Schekina out of captivity as it is written: "And he looked this way and that way and he saw there was no man" (Ex. ii. 12). At that moment, scripture saith: "And the Lord God caused a deep sleep to fall upon the man and He took one of the ribs and closed up the flesh thereof" (Gen. ii. 21). "The Lord God" denotes the Divine Being as father and Mother; "a deep sleep" the captivity, which is also the meaning of the words "a deep sleep fell upon Abraham" (Gen. xv. 12). "And He took one of the ribs"--from whom? From the virgins of the Matrona. The divine Father and Mother took a virgin from the white or right side of her, designated in scripture as "fair as the moon" (Cant. vi. 10). "And closed up the flesh in its place," signifying the union of the celestial with the animal nature of man. The words "for that he also is flesh" (Gen. vi. 3), refer to Moses, whose physical form radiated light golden hued like that of the sun, as it is written: "The face of Moses was as the face of the Sun," whilst that of the virgin of the right side was like the moon. Therefore scripture saith: "Thou art fair as the moon and clear as the sun" (Cant. vi. 10). Another signification of the words, "And closed up the flesh in its place" is that the Father and Mother wished to protect (vaisgor) her, as it is written: "And the Lord shut (vaisgor) him in (Gen. vii. 16).

"And of the rib which the Lord God had taken from man, made he a woman, and brought her unto the man" (Gen. ii. 23). In this verse is an allusion to the mystery of the marital affinity. We are taught that when this affinity is ignored and disregarded the consequences are most injurious. The Holy One in his operations has worked on the law of affinity, as it is written: "The Lord (IHVH) hath built Jerusalem" (Ps. cxlvii. 2). The V in the divine name IHVH is the son or child of I and H, the Father and the Mother, to whom scripture refers: "And the Lord God made of the rib which he had taken from man." This rib denotes the middle column in the sephirotic Tree of Life symbol of the virgin, of whom it is written: "For I, saith Jehovah, will be unto her a wall of fire round about, and will be the glory in the midst of her" (Zech. ii. 5).

It is for this reason that the future temple, glorified and perfected humanity, built and formed by the Holy One, will endure forever. It is of this temple that scripture speaks. The glory of this latter house shall be greater than that of the former (Hag. ii. 9), which was built by man's hands, but this shall be built by the Holy One, and is alluded to by the Psalmist: "Except the Lord build the house, they labor in vain that build it" (Ps. cxxvii. 1). The words "And the Lord God formed the rib he had taken" equally apply to Moses, who, when building the tabernacle in the wilderness, foresaw the future tabernacle God would form, as it is written: "And for the second side (rib) of the tabernacle on the north side there shall be twenty boards" (Ex. xxvi. 20). The north side here refers to the side of the sephirotic tree called Chesed (mercy), and known as the white side. "And closed up the flesh thereof." The word flesh signifies the red side of the tree which is called Geburah (power), and at this time were fulfilled the words: "His left hand is under my head and his right hand doth embrace me" (Cant. ii. 6), as also the words: "This is now bone of my bone and flesh of my flesh." She shall be called ashah because she was taken from aish (man), that is to say, that the virgin humanity is a union of the man or father representing the male principle, with the mother, representing the female principle.

When the temple just referred to is completed, each individual will find his companion or mate-soul predestined from the beginning to become united with him, and then will be realized the words of the prophet: "And I will also give you a new heart and a new spirit will I put within you" (Ezech. xxxv. 26), as also the words of another prophet: "And your sons and your daughters shall prophesy, your old men shall dream dreams, your young men shall see visions" (Joel ii. 28), alluding to the renewed state of humanity in the future, as tradition expresses it. The son of David or the Messiah will not appear until all souls now incarnating shall have reached perfection and accomplished their destiny, and those who have lost their Higher Self and have failed to become united with it shall be exterminated from the world. "And they were both naked, the man and his wife, and were not ashamed" (Gen. ii. 25), referring to the time when licentiousness and sensuality shall disappear and vanish out of the world and nothing exist causing a sense of shame and immodesty.

CHAPTER XIII.

NOW the serpent was more subtle than any beast of the field which the Lord God had made" (Gen. iii. 1). "Beast of the field" signifies the idolatrous nations who are the offspring and progeny of the old serpent who tempted and seduced Eve to do evil by exciting selfishness and other animal propensities within her. Under their influence she conceived and brought forth Cain, who killed Abel his brother, the shepherd of whom the scripture terms "beschagam," "because he is flesh." This word also is used of Moses, who killed the Egyptian. Moses may also be regarded as the eldest son of Adam. When the children went up out of Egypt, a great multitude of strangers went with them and became intermingled with them. Also, during their sojourn in the wilderness and on their journey to the promised land, strangers belonging to another nation, such as the Kenites of whom Jethro, the father-in-law of Moses, was the head, flung in their lot with and dwelt amongst the Israelites. These strangers or aliens Moses wished to convert and make one with the children of Israel. The Holy One who counts a good intention as a good action, said unto him: "Thou desirest what is impossible. Through them thy descendants will suffer. It was such as they who caused Adam to sin and disobey after it had been said unto him: 'From the tree of knowledge of good and evil shalt thou not eat,' and it will be they who will cause the children of Israel to go into captivity, and also through them thou wilt not be able to enter into the promised land."

The failure of Moses to enter along with the Israelites into the Holy land was owing to the murmurings and cries of these strangers causing him, in a moment of anger, to strike the rock with the rod God had given him, instead of speaking to the rock as he had been commanded (Nunn. xx. 8). Like Adam, in his disobedience, so Moses too had to suffer the penalty for his act of disobedience. But as the Holy One rewards the good intention equally as the good deed, therefore He said to Moses: "I will make of thee a greater nation and mightier than they" (Num. xiv. 12). The Holy One said: "Whoso hath sinned against me, him will I blot out of my book" (Ex. xxxii. 33), which words apply to the descendants of Amalek, of whom it is written: "Thou shalt blot out the remembrance of Amalek, for they it was that caused the tables of the law to be broken."

"And their eyes were opened and they saw they were naked" (Gen. iii. 7) refers to Israel when they were living amidst the mud and clay of Egypt and had no knowledge of the secret doctrine. Therefore spake the prophet concerning them: "Thou art naked and bare" (Ezek. xvi. 7). This is also why Job repeated the word "naked." "Naked came I out of my mother's womb and naked shall I return thither" (Job i. 21.). He used the word shameh (thither), which has the same letters as Moseh (Moses), to show that he, Moses, wished to convert the strangers and that hereafter he will reincarnate and appear again to Israel in order to proclaim and make known the Schekina. These words of Job also refer to the time when Israel in captivity would perceive they were naked or devoid of the secret doctrine, and therefore said: "Jehovah hath given, Jehovah hath taken away, may the name of Jehovah be blessed."

And they sewed figleaves together and made themselves aprons" (Gen. iii. 7). The meaning of these words is, that man will cloak himself with the frail coverings of his own sinful propensities when he perceives himself naked and has nothing to hide and cover what should be hidden. The garment with which Israel covers himself is the legal robe with its fringes and borders and also the phylacteries and sandals, and therefore scripture saith: "And the Lord God made unto Adam and his wife coats of skins and clothed them" (Gen. iii. 21). The hagoroth (coats or coverings) is here used in order to distinguish the legal robe, and therefore it is written "hagor." "Gird thy sword upon thy thigh and make thy glory and majesty appear" (Ps. xlv. 3), referring to the Shema repeated when each one is arrayed in the legal robe when "the high praises of God are in their mouth and a two-edged sword in their hand" (Ps. cxlix. 6).

"And they heard the voice of the Lord God walking in the garden" (Gen. iii. 8). These words allude to the voice of God heard by Israel when at Mount Sinai, and as scripture saith: "Did ever a people hear the voice of God speaking out of the midst of the fire?" (Deuter. iv. 33). On hearing this voice the strangers or aliens (Ereb. Rah) in Israel perished, for they it was who said: "Let not God speak with us lest we die" (Ex. xx. 19). After their death the law was given. The ignorant of the present time who know not and recognize no other law than that of selfishness, are incarnations of these strangers and are indicated by the words: "Cursed is he that lieth with any manner of beast" (Deuter. xxvii. 21), because they derive their origin from the serpent to whom it was said: "Cursed art thou above all cattle and above every beast of the field" (Gen. iii. 14).

Many impurities exist in Israel and are as dangerous and noxious as snakes and serpents. There are those that originated at first from the tempter, also those of idolators who resemble the wild animals and savage beasts of the field. There is also the impurity arising from wrongdoing in daily life and still more, the impurity of the evil-minded. All these are found afflicting Israel, yet is there no greater impurity than that of Amalek or that personified evil called and known as "The God of this world." It is that "which poisons all within and hardens all the feeling." It causes the death of the soul and transforms it into an idolater, a worshipper of the world and its golden image of wealth. Its occult name is Samael, "The poison God." Though Samael was the name of the serpent that tempted and seduced Adam and Eve, yet are they one and the same and are both cursed alike.

"And the Lord God called the man and said 'Where art thou?'" (aicha). In this verse God showed to Adam the destruction of the temple or holy place, causing great sorrow and anguish of heart, as alluded to in the verse of scripture beginning with this word "aicha." "How doth the city sit solitary that was full of people" (Lam. i. 1). In both these passages of scripture this word "aicha" is as a mournful note in a bar of music. It will not, however, always be so. The time will arrive when the Holy One shall banish and destroy all evil in the world as it is written: "Death is swallowed up forever and the Lord God will wipe away tears from all faces and the rebuke of his people (humanity) shall be taken away from off all the earth" (Is. xxv. 8), and in that day Jehovah shall be One and His name One.

We are taught by tradition that all which Solomon wrote in the "Song of Songs" has reference to the King of Peace who, though he rules below, yet has his kingdom on high and thus is king of both worlds. This is occultly signified by the letter B, whose numerical value is two, placed at the beginning of the word hochma in the Scripture, "be-hochma, by wisdom is the house built" (Prov. xxiv. 3), and also in the verse "King Solomon made himself a sedan of the wood of Lebanon" (Cant. iii. 9). By the word sedan (thequna) is meant the renovation of the lower world by the action, and influence of the higher world, the action of the Higher Self on the lower nature. Before the creation the existence of the Divine Being was unknown and his attributes nameless and unrecognized, and, as there was no speech or tongue to express his glory and being, His name was hidden and concealed in Himself. When the Holy One created the universe He impressed upon it marks of design and formed worlds which did not endure, but perished and passed away. Then the Divine, Ain Soph (the boundless One) surrounded or enveloped Himself with a garment of light of transcendent brilliance, from which emanated and came forth the great and lofty trees of Lebanon, and the twenty-two letters became the sedan or chariot of God. The law by which the world was created (the ten words) was established and confirmed so that it changeth not. This is the meaning of the above verse, as also of the words "The trees of the field together with the cedars of Lebanon which the Lord hath planted, are full of sap" (Ps. civ. 16), for they have been planted by the King of Peace for his glory in order that every one may know and recognize that He is One and His name is One--that His name is Jehovah the most High above all the earth.

By this manifestation of the Divine a way of access has been opened and the light thereof has become visible throughout the universe and is the light that enlighteneth every man that cometh into the world. It is circumambient as the air and, like the ocean, rolls all round the world. From it hath proceeded all things and unto it all things shall return as it is written: "All the rivers run into the sea, yet the sea is not full--unto the place whence the rivers come, thither shall they return again" (Eccles. i. 7). The light divine attracts and draws all other lights, so that they become at last blended and unified with it. This final consummation is alluded to in the words "I am the rose of Sharon and the lily of the valley" (Cant. ii. 1), the word Sharon signifying field or rather the ocean that absorbs all the rivers) of the world which proceed from and return into it again.

Be-hochma, "by wisdom the house has been built." The letter Beth or B, whose numerical value, as we have stated, is two, signifies the two kingdoms, celestial and terrestrial, of heaven and earth (the lower and Higher Self). It is by the establishment of the celestial on the terrestrial, or of heaven upon earth, that the house of the King (humanity) will become united and the King will rejoice thereat, for then the two kingdoms will become one and then the new and living way will become opened to those who make themselves susceptible and receptive of the Higher and Diviner life. Therefore is it written "Brashith, bra Alhim" (Gen. i. 1). The two kingdoms created by Alhim (B--two, rashit--kingdoms) for the kingdom is called reshith (beginning) according to the words "Reshith Hochma." Before the manifestation of Alhim, the celestial or primal light resembled a great frozen ocean and rivers could not flow into it, as they like it were frozen also. It was this great congealed ocean to which Job referred: "Out of whose womb came the ice?" (Job xxxviii. 29). As long as the ocean remained frozen, so long was it of no benefit to man, and the rivers ceased running their courses into it. When the north sea is frozen it continues so until the advent of the south wind with its heat and warmth. The rivers and streams then begin to flow again towards the south and from their waters, the beasts of the field, as scripture saith, do quench their thirst.

Thus will it be when the Higher Self of humanity rules over its lower nature. The ice will dissolve and melt away, the waters of divine life will flow continuously, and every voice shall sing and give thanks to heaven for its deliverance from Self. This glorious consummation is symbolized by the sounding of the shophar or trumpet, the prelude of the great deliverance. There is a further allusion to this union of the higher and lower kingdoms (the human with the divine life) in the words "As long as the son of Jesse liveth upon the earth" (I. Sam. xx. 31), for divine life upon the earth is only possible through the Messiah, the son of Jesse. He it is who is master and lord over all, and from him the earth (humanity and individual life) receiveth its nourishment and sustenance.

This is why the scripture says, ve-ath haaretz (and the earth). The letter V joined to ath designates the nourishment of the world which comes from Alhim. The ath, composed of the first and last letters of the Hebrew alphabet, denotes also the Alhim who dwelleth in the heavens as it is written "Go forth ye daughters of Sion and behold King Solomon with the crown wherewith his mother crowned him on the day of his marriage" (Cant. iii. 11). As Alhim, by the operation of the two supreme sephiroth, the one male and the other female, descended below, therefore is he lord of the heaven and earth by conjoining and making them one, He it was who, attracted heaven to earth whilst the King on high attracts the earth to heaven, each of which has its own special way or path, that of the earth being broad and wide and referred to in scripture as "The path of the just is as the shining light" (Prov. iv. 18), whilst that leading to the Kingdom of heaven (the higher life) is referred to in the words "There is a path which no fowl knoweth and which the vulture's eye haft not seen, the lion's whelps have not trodden it, nor the fierce lion passed by it" (Job xxviii. 7, 8).

The mystery of these two different ways is expressed thus: "Who maketh a way in the sea and a path in the mighty waters (Is. xliii. 16), and also by the

Psalmist: "Thy way is in the sea and thy path in the great waters" (Ps. lxxvii. 19). When these two worlds become united and blended together they are symbolized by the union of the male and female, the one being then the complement of the other. It is also written: "Lift up your eyes on high and behold! Mi (who) hath created aleh (these)" (Is. xl. 26). In these words is expressed the whole work of creation, for by Mi above and Aleh below everything has been formed and made. And this is why at the very beginning of the book of Genesis, the letter B is repeated twice, as also the letter A in the consecutive words "Brashith Bra, Alhim, Ath;" B representing the female and A the male principle. It is from these two letters that all the other letters have proceeded, the total of which is denoted by the Hashamayim (the heavens). The letter V prefixed to the word ve-ath haaretz (and the earth) shows that the H gives birth to heaven, and a way to it, whilst V gives birth to earth, and provides it with nourishment and everything that it needs to sustain it. The word ve-ath also indicates that the V takes the A and Th, symbolical of the beginning and end, and by their conjunction the earth is fed and supported. The occult mystery of this is expressed in the words "All the rivers run into the sea" (Eccles. i. 7).

There is no effect without a cause, is a truth that cannot be denied. Yet our judgments concerning effects are often erroneous. For instance, the sound we hear when an anvil is struck by a hammer does not proceed from the anvil, as imagined, but is the result of their concussion which causes vibration in the air. Also volcanic flames are not due to the earth from which they come forth, but to the fire in the interior of it. When scripture saith: "And Mount Sinai was enveloped in smoke, because the Lord descended thereon in the midst of the fire" (Ex. xix., 18), it signifies the conjunction of heaven and earth, the bringing together and union of the spiritual and material. Everything that takes place on earth has its cause in the invisible and noumenal world, which in scripture is described as, and said to be, the right hand of God, while the earth or world of effects is described as the left hand. "Mine hand also hath laid the foundations of the earth, and my right hand hath spanned the heavens. I will call them and they shall stand up before me" (Is. xlviii. 13), the heavens representing the male principle on the right hand, earth the female principle, on the left hand, both of them found together before Him.

Such is also the meaning of the words "Lift up your eyes and behold Mi (who) hath made Aleh (these)," Mi and Aleh being the complement of each other. Before creation it was impossible to form any conception of the creator, as hochma (wisdom) was hidden and unrevealed as the Primal Being. Only after the apparition of the Divine light in the universe and its rays beamed forth and became visible, could its existence be cognized and perceptible, its nature and quality being transcendently bright and pellucid. When, however, its apperception began, then the question arose Mi (who or what is it?) Without this Mi or Who? Aleh (these or that) could not have come into existence. The mystery of the origin of all things is adverted to in the words, already quoted, "Out of whose womb came the ice?" or rather "Out of the womb of Mi came the ice?" that is the world. Mi therefore is the progenitor of the earth and impregnated it with life and vitality. It was therefore only after the creation that Mi became the subject of thought. Again, the word Brashith, what does it signify? Does it mean that "by two words," that is, by K equal to "two" and rashith equal to "words," Alhim created, or by the word Alhim created, taking Brashith as a single word? The real meaning is that before the creation of the world there was no distinction between the Supreme Principle and the Creative Logos or Word, they being one and the same, and only after creation became they distinguished the one from the other. It is written "While the King sitteth at his table, my spikenard sendeth forth the smell thereof" (Cant. i. 12). The King signifies the Supreme or First Principle, the spikenard sending forth its odor, denotes the creative Word or Logos who is King below having formed the world on the model or pattern of the world on high and "the smell thereof" is the divine light. There were two creations, viz., the heavens and the earth, and they were concomitant in time with each other; the creation of the former was effected by the right, that of the latter by the left hand, and extended over six celestial days as it is written: "For in six days the Lord made the heavens and the earth" (Ex. xxxi. 17). These six days correspond to the six outlets through which the waters of life flowed into the world and also the six channels by which they return again on high. Through the six outlets it is that peace cometh into the world.

"And the earth was Tohu and Bohu, without form and void." The constituents of the primal matter of the earth at first were impure and shapeless and without form and continued in this state until, becoming impressed with the Divine name of forty-two letters, they took upon them different forms, qualities; and separated into the four elements of fire, air, earth and water. After their purification and combination in different proportions, these contributed to the formation of the physical and natural world, the four cardinal points, and to the infinite variety of forms and colors, existent therein and all on the pattern of the higher world. Ere this was accomplished and before the Divine name of forty-two letters had been impressed upon the primal matter of the earth when in a state of chaos, the great serpent alone and his demon hosts of elemental beings, leaving the chaotic world of Tohu and Bohu penetrated into the higher world to the height of 1,500 cubits, but were eventually expelled and hurled headlong into the abysmal darkness where they abode until the primal heavenly light shone upon the earth and dispelled the obscurity in which it was enshrouded, therefore is it written: "He discovereth deep things out of darkness and bringeth out to light the shadow of death" (Job xii. 22).

Before the advent of the light, universal darkness prevailed and the waters were congealed so that the earth was without rivers or streams. On the appearance of light, however, they were liquefied by its rays and became fluidic and the arid earth refreshed by them was rendered fertile and adapted for vegetable and animal life. The celestial light of which scripture speaks existed from all eternity. As soon as it dawned its splendor was visible from one extremity of the world to the other, but foreseeing that it would he unappreciated and unregarded by mankind in general, the Divine Being concealed it, so that it should be accessible only to those who walk in the straight and narrow path leading to its discovery and enjoyment. Happy they who find it, for then they become sons of God and children of the Light.

"And God saw the light, that it was good." It has been handed down from our forefathers that dreams in connection with a good object are presages of peace and blessings, especially when letters composing words are seen by the dreamer in their right order and sequence. For instance, the letters T, O, bh of the word Tobh seen in their order denote good, so that he who sees the initial letter T may take it as a favorable sigma or token, and as a synonym of Tab, signifying peace. The numerical value of T, initial letter of the word T-v-b, is nine and symbolizes the ninth Sephira Malcuth, which receives its light from the first Sephira Kether (crown). The letter V is a symbol of the light proceeding from the first two sephiroth and B is the symbol of the first sephira and therefore it is the first letter with which scripture commences, Brashith. Thus each of the letters in this word T-v-b are symbols of the three highest sephiroth and designate the just and upright in the world who unite in themselves the heaven and the earth, therefore it is written: "Say unto the righteous it is good" (Is. iii. 10), as the divine light and life dwelleth within them, manifesting as goodness from above and mercy and compassion or unselfishness from below as saith scripture: "The lord is good to all, and His tender mercies are over all his works" (Ps. cxlv. 9). In the words "to all" is expressed the prophecy that the day will dawn upon the world when every man's eyes shall be opened and the light he seen by all. Such is the mystic meaning of these words. "Brashith bra Alhim," in the beginning.

The occult meaning of these first words of scripture is adverted to in the verse: "When ye come into the land whither bring you, it shall be when ye eat of the fruit of the land, ye shall offer up as a sheave-offering to the Lord your first fruits" (Num. xv. 19, 20). The first fruits are a symbol of Hochma, the divine wisdom, the first sephira or manifestation of the Divine Being on the earth plane, and thus may be considered the first fruits. Brashith signifies then, "by the first fruits," and B, its initial letter, denotes the world watered and refreshed by the mystic river mentioned in the verse: "And a river went out of Eden to water the garden" (Gen. ii. 10). This river, proceeding out of the secret place of the Most High, never ceases to flow down upon the world or the garden, as it is termed. This secret place of its origin or fount is symbolized by B, the first letter in the book of Genesis. It includes in itself all the other letters and symbolizes also the river which gives life to all things. The secret place resembles a narrow path most difficult to discover and walk therein, yet bestudded with many priceless gems. From it proceed two great life forces, indicated by the word ha-shamayim (the two heavens) and used in scripture to denote the source of this mystic river. The words that follow after, viz., "veath haaretzs" (and the earth) possess a mystical meaning, implying that the mystic river flowing down from the heavens on to the earth will bring with its waters peace and salvation to mankind, which will in their realization be the first fruits when heaven and earth become united and blended together.

At the time of creation there was no distinction, no dark deep gulf or rent between heaven and the earth. When, however, they became separated, the earth fell into the state of chaos and confusion (Tohu and Bohu) and only by the action and silent operation of the heavenly light can they again become united. When the light from the right hand of God fell upon the earth, darkness from the left hand also went forth and encompassed it. Thus they became blended together, the light being hidden within the darkness. In order, however, that the earth might be blessed and become fertile and fruitbearing, God divided and separated them, only to unite them again eventually as they are the complement of each other and from the evening and the morning shall be an eternal day. There is no day without night and no night without day in this world, and this sequence of the great law of the universe (growth and decay, life and death) will endure until the accomplishment and realization of the Psalmist's prophecy: "The darkness and the light shall be both alike" (Ps. cxxxix. 12).

A KABBALISTIC SYMPOSIUM BY RABBI SIMEON'S STUDENTS

RABBI ELEAZAR spake and said: "It is written 'the voice of the Lord is upon the waters. The God of glory thundereth, the Lord is upon mighty waters' (Ps. xxlx. 3). These words allude to the celestial river whose life-giving waters circulate and flow throughout the world and give life and strength to every creature that breathes and moves upon the face of the earth. 'The God of glory thundereth' signifies the sephiroth Geburah (power) as expressed in the words, 'but the thunder of his power (Geburah), who can understand?' (Job xxvi. 14). This awful power it is that proceeds from the left side of the sephirotic tree, by and through the God of glory that is on the right side. 'The Lord is upon mighty waters' alludes to the sephiroth Hochma (heavenly wisdom) described as God upon mighty waters, that is upon the secret place from which they flow forth, as it is written, 'Thy paths are on the mighty waters'" (Ps. lxxvii '19).

After this brief interlocution, Rabbi Simeon resumed his discourse find said: "It is written, Over against the border, shall the rings be for the places of the staves to bear the table' (Ex. xxv. 27). What is the esoteric meaning of the word 'border' (misghereth)? It refers to the secret place in the tabernacle kept continually closed to everyone except to him whose duty it was to enter therein and light the lamps. It was therefore called the 'closed place' and symbolized the world to come or the hidden and unseen world. The rings here mentioned, of which there were three linked one with the other, signify the sacred chain of the three elements, water, air and fire. The water proceeds from the air, the air from the fire and fire from the water. Thus these elements, though apparently different, are radically the same. 'Places of the staves' denote the modal combinations which these elements assume in the various types of things and creatures existent in the universe, the modus operandi, of which, Nature's great secret, is not imparted to a worldly minded man to fathom or understand. He remains ever in the outer court and is never permitted to enter her adytum and view the mysteries of the inner temple or Holy of Holies, inasmuch as the sight only of them would prove fatal to him. And this is why it is written 'the stranger that cometh nigh, shall be put to death'" (Num. i. 51).

"The letter B in the word Brashith is written larger than any other letter in the Pentateuch. What is the reason of this?" asked Rabbi Jose, "and what is the esoteric explanation of the six days of creation which has been handed down by preceding adepts and teachers?"

Replying to these questions, Rabbi Simeon said: "As in Scripture is found the expression 'The cedars of Lebanon,' distinguishing them from all other cedars, so the six days of creation are separated and characterized especially as the days of Brashith (creation). With reference to these important days the Scripture thus refers to them: Thine Oh Lord is the greatness (gedulah), the power (geburah), and the victory (netzach), for all things in heaven and earth are thine. Thine is the kingdom (malcuth) and thou art exalted as head above all" (1 Ch. xxlx. 11). The word "All" in this verse signifies the just or the good law which prevails throughout the universe. The targum paraphrases these words thus: "The All (or the good law) binds together heaven and earth. It is the basis on which the universe is built. In heaven it is symbolized by the sephira Tiphereth (harmony or beauty) and in the world by the children or sons of light. This is the reason why the Scripture begins with the letter B (the numerical value of which is two) in the word Brashith, B---'two,' rashith--'beginning,' that is to say, by the second 'beginning,' or, in other words, by hochma (wisdom), the second in the first sephirotic triad, and which is the signification given by the targum of Jonathan Ben Uzziel to this word. Brashith, for though hochma is placed second in the manifestation of Ain Soph (the boundless One), it is in essence one and the same with Kether (the crown), the supernal or higher sephira. The signification then of the initial words of Scripture, Brashith bra, Alhim (translated in the English version, 'In the beginning God created'), is this: By hochma (wisdom), the second manifestation of the Divine, or, in other words, the Creative Logos or Alhim created the heavens and the earth. From it proceeded the light which enters as a principle of life into every living existent thing and creature, as it is written, 'A river went forth out of Eden to water the garden,' that is, to prepare and qualify the earth for the production, growth and development of animated existences. By the word Alhim is signified the ever-living eternal Alhim.

"Now the words 'bra Alhim' created Alhim seem to indicate that Brashith, the supreme Alhim or Logos, created the lower Alhim. And this is true, for, owing to the celestial river from which all life has flowed into the universe, the first and the third sephiroth, viz.: Kether (crown) and Binah (understanding) in an ineffable manner, becoming united, gave rise or origin to the lower Alhim, who created the world and was thus the proximate source of all life necessary for its subsistence and endurance. To this Alhim was entrusted all power, both in heaven and earth, after they had been called into existence. The words 'athhashamayim' (the heavens) indicate that it was only after the ever-living and eternal Alhim had manifested as hochma the creative Logos that the third manifestation or Logos descended from on high upon the earth. Then it was that the three supreme Logoi became blended and unified in the work of creation, and then was it also that the sacred chain of three rings became complete and the resplendent light was manifested on creation as intimated in the words 'Brashith bra Alhim, ath hashamayim vatha aretz.' In the beginning God designed the world. By the second 'beginning' (hochma), wisdom, He formed it, and by the third 'beginning' (Binah), understanding, He manifested it and caused the light to descend from on high upon the world below. I now understand and grasp the esoteric meaning of the strange enigmatical words, 'Shall the axe magnify itself against him that heweth therewith' (Is. x. 15). It is to the hewer and not to the axe that honor must be ascribed, so to the first and supreme Logos who created the world by the other Alhim, or Logoi, should and ought to be attributed honor and glory."

Said Rabbi Jose: "This is the interpretation of the mystical words, 'What nation is there so great that hath God so nigh unto them as our Jehovah Alhim' (Lord of the Alhim) (Deuter. iv. 7), alluding to the supreme and other Alhim, or Logoi, who were the Pachad whom Isaac the patriarch worshipped and which, though differing in their manifestations, were one and the same in essence. The allocution of the words Brashith to the ten sephiroth is as follows: Brashith bra refer to Kether (crown), and Hochma (wisdom), Alhim to Binah, ath to gedulah and geburah, hashamayim to Tiphereth, vath to Netzach, Hod and Yesod and ha-aretz to malcuth.

CHAPTER XV.

"AND God said let there be light and light was.' To whom spake Alhim these words, 'let there be light?' It was to the dwellers on the earth; but 'light was' refers to the light made for the world to come. The higher light, the light of the eye was created first by the Holy One who caused Adam, the protagonist, to behold it so that he was able to view the world at a glance. This was the divine light enjoyed by David, who in a moment of spiritual ecstasy exclaimed, 'How great is thy goodness which thou hast laid up for them that fear thee' (Ps. xxxvi. 20), and it was the self-same light by which God showed Moses the promised land from Gilead unto Dan. From the beginning, this divine light was hidden and concealed, as the Holy One perceived that the generations of men who lived in the time of Enoch and Noah, and also during the building of the tower of Babel, would use it for selfish purposes. He imparted it to Moses, who made use of it three months after his birth, as it is written, 'She hid him three months' (Ex. ii. 7), after which he was brought into the Presence of Pharaoh. Then the Holy One took it away from him until his ascent of Mount Sinai in order to receive the law. On that occasion it was again imparted to Moses and enjoyed by him during his lifetime. To such an extent was its manifestation, that it is said, 'the skin of his face shone, so that the children of Israel were afraid to come nigh unto him' (Ex. xxxiv. 30). Moses was so invested with this divine light that it seemed like a talith or garment about him. This same divine light is referred to by the psalmist. 'Who coverest thyself with light as with a garment' (Ps. civ. 2). 'Let there be light and light was.' Wherever in the Scripture this word yehe (let there be) is used, it refers to or signifies this divine light, both in this world and the world to come."

Said Rabbi Isaac: "The light created by God in the work of creation, filled the world with its splendor, but was eventually withdrawn and concealed, why? In order that transgressors of the good law might not participate in it, and therefore the Holy One conceals and preserves it for the right-doers as it is written, 'Light is sown for the righteous and gladness for the upright in heart' (Ps. xcvii. 11). When it shall prevail again throughout the world humanity will become renewed and live the Higher life and make it one with angelic life. Till then, however, this divine light is concealed in darkness which is as a covering to it. And this is why God called the light 'Day,' and the darkness He called 'Night,' the one being only a diminution of the other as it is written, 'Light and darkness are both alike to thee. He discovereth deep things out of darkness'" (Job xii. 22).

Said Rabbi Jose: "The meaning of those words is this, that the great mysteries of life, at present veiled and hidden in darkness, become revealed to the 'Illuminate' or enlightened by the adaptation of their modes of thinking, and thus comprehensible to the human understanding with its limited powers of expression, so that the words of Scripture are realized, 'And the light of the moon shall be as the light of the sun' (Is. xxi. 26). That this might become actual, there was needed language or audible speech. This speech is that known by the term Sabbath: and because of its purity, it is forbidden to give utterance to any idle or profane word on that day. This is why Rabbi Simeon used to say to his mother, whenever he heard her speaking on secular and profane subjects during the sabbath day, 'Mother, remember it is the holy day and do not indulge in idle discourse, for that is forbidden!' This form or kind of language it is, that should prevail everywhere because, as it symbolizes the union of the active principle of light with the passive principle of darkness, it is the only means for giving expression and form to the hidden mysteries of life." Said Rabbi Isaac: "If this is to be, wherefore is it then written, 'And God divided the light from the darkness?'"

Rabbi Jose replied: "In order that light might give rise to day and darkness to night. Afterwards He associated them together and made them as one, wherefore it is written, 'And the evening and the morning were day one (one day) (Gen. i.) the evening, morning and day forming one whole.'"

Said Rabbi Isaac: "Until the manifestation of Alhim, the creative Logos, the male principle was in the light, and the female principle, in the darkness. In the work of creation they became unified, and formed the necessary complements of each other. If it be asked, why were they separated and disjoined) it was that there might be a distinction between them; and they became united in order that the true light might be found in its complement, the darkness, and the true darkness in its complement, the light. Though at present there are many different shades and degrees between them, yet, notwithstanding, they form but one whole, as it is written, 'Day, one.'"

Said Rabbi Simeon: "It is on this union of light and darkness that the whole universe is based and formed. In Scripture it is referred to and spoken of as a covenant. Thus it is written, 'If my covenant be not with day and night and if I had not appointed the ordinances of heaven and earth' (Jer. xxxiii. 25). What is this covenant? It is the good law of justness, right and harmony, that form the basis of all existence throughout the universe. The import and mystery of it is expressed in the word zacor (remember). Day and night in their adjustment to each other symbolizing the great law of harmony and unity, it follows that it lies as the root of all created existence and therefore saith the Scripture, 'but for this covenant or union between day and night, I should not have established the laws and ordinances of heaven and earth,' and which in all worlds throughout the universe form one and the same rule of life."

Rabbi Simeon again spake and said: "It is written, 'By the voice of the Mediator or Harmonizer, amongst those who draw forth water, shall be proclaimed the divine law of Justness' (Jud. v. 11). The voice of the Mediator (Kol mkhtztzim) here signifies the voice of Jacob, the word mkhtztzim being equivalent to ash ha-benaim. 'Those who draw forth water' are they who draw the water of life flowing from an inexhaustible fountain on high, that gives strength and vitality to every animated being. It is further added, 'and the clemency or goodness of God shall be poured in abundance upon Israel, and the people of God (those who live conformably to the good law) shall appear at the gates.' Israel here signifies the children of light to whom as a heritage the Holy One has laid up and reserved this divine life forever when they become circumcised in heart, the sine qua non of its enjoyment. When this is not the case, then are realized the words of Scripture, 'They forsook the Lord God of their fathers' (Jud. ii. 12). This apostasy lasted until Deborah, the prophetess, appeared and led them back into the true path; so that it is said, 'The people willingly offered themselves' (Jud. v. 2). Furthermore, it is written, 'The inhabitants of the villages, ceased, they ceased in Israel until that Deborah arose, that I arose a mother in Israel' (Jud. v. 7).

"What is the esoteric meaning of 'a mother in Israel?' The phrase refers to the celestial mother by whom the heavenly waters of life were made to flow into the world, so that the children of light might be strengthened and established and the true source of it be made known and manifested. This great unknown truth is referred to in the words, 'The righteous One hath founded the world' (Prov. x. 24). The three come forth from the one. One is in three and stands between two, forming a triad from which has proceeded everything; so that One is all and all is One; as it is written, 'It was evening and it was morning, day one, for the day, with its evening and morning, is one.' This mystery is further expressed. It is written, 'And God said let there be a firmament in the midst of the waters and let it divide the waters from the waters'" (Gen. i. 6).

Said Rabbi Jehuda: "Seven firmaments are there on high founded on and governed by the great law of universal harmony, of which the Tetragrammaton or sacred name is a symbol. The firmament here mentioned is established in the midst of the waters. It is above the Hayoth or living creatures and divideth the waters above from the waters below and serves as an intermediary between them. When the waters below call to the waters above, it is through it that the latter descend and give life and strength to all creatures as hath been stated. It is written, 'a garden enclosed is my sister, my spouse; a spring shut up, a fountain sealed' (Cant. iv. 12). By 'a garden enclosed' is meant, the spouse congealed therein, the universal mother of existing things, from whom floweth forth the great river of the water of life, which if it should cease to flow the waters below would become congealed and infertile. As rivers and streams become frozen when the north wind blows, and remain so until the south wind comes and dissipates by its warmth and heat the frost, in like manner, the waters of the river of life do not flow into the world of humanity except under the influence of the life divine. Such is the esoteric meaning of the firmament existing between the higher and lower regions of life. Scripture saith not, "let there be made a firmament and let it be placed in the midst of the waters, i.e., between the waters above and those below; for the firmament here mentioned existed before the beginning of the creation of the world and was only placed between them, that is, above the Hayoth or living creatures."

Said Rabbi Isaac: "In the human body, there exists an organ called the diaphragm, separating the heart from the abdomen, so that what the former receives or takes in is transmitted to the latter. So is it with the firmament in the midst of the waters, or the higher and lower spheres of existence. What it receives from the higher it transmits to the lower spheres for the maintenance and continuity of human and annual life. There is an allusion to this in the words, 'And the veil shall divide between the holy place and the holy of Holies'" (Ex. xxvi. 33).

Said Rabbi Abba: "'Who hideth himself in the waters and maketh the clouds his chariot and walketh upon the wings of the wind' (Ps. civ. 3). By the waters is signified the waters on high by which the house was built, as it is written, 'Through wisdom (hochma), the house is built, and by understanding (binah) it is established' (Prow. xxiv. 3). 'Who maketh the clouds his chariot.' Rabbi Yessa the aged separated the word 'abim' (clouds) into ab (cloud), and im (ocean), denoting that the darkness proceeded from the left side of the sephirotic tree of creation. 'And walketh upon the wings of the wind' refer to the holy Spirit from on high, symbolized by the two golden cherubim placed at each end of the mercy-seat, as it is written, 'Thou shalt make two cherubim of gold, of beaten work shalt thou make them' (Ex. xxv. 18). Of these cherubim we also read, 'He rode upon a cherub and did fly, yea, He did fly upon the wings of the wind' (Ps. xviii. 10). Whilst the manifestation of the Divine is confined and limited to the higher or heavenly spheres He is said to ride upon a cherub, but after its appearance in the world, then He rides upon the wings of the wind."

Said Rabbi Jose: "It is written, 'He weigheth the waters by measure' (Job xxviii...25). These words refer to that just proportion or measure of the life principle necessary for the development and perfection of all animated creatures, and which proceeds from the sephiroth Geburah (Justice or Justness)."

Said Rabbi Abba: "The ancients relate that when the great teachers descended and came upon earth, they began their meditations on the mysteries of creation by observing the strictest silence, impelled thereto by the fear lest by a single word they should divulge what was revealed to them and thus subject themselves to condemnation."

Said Rabbi Eleazar: "At first the initial letter of the alphabet, alternately ascending and descending, impressed on the surface of the lower waters the forms of all the other letters, and they became the complement of each other. After the formation of these letters they became the foundation of the world. Then the waters above mingled with those below, giving rise to the words called Beth (house). This is why Scripture commences with the letter B in order to teach that the origin of the world is due to the mingling and blending of these waters which continued until the firmament which now separates them was established and fixed. This separation took place on the second day of creation and on that day was also created Gehenna, which continues to exist as the place of the devouring fire reserved for the wicked and wrongdoers.

A SYMPOSIUM OF RABBI SIMEON'S STUDENTS

IT IS written, "Let the waters bring forth abundantly the moving creature that hath life, and let the earth bring forth the living creature after his kind" (Gen. i. 20, 24). Said Rabbi Eleazar: "The waters below, like the waters above, brought forth creatures after their kind and similar to themselves."

Said Rabbi Hiya: "The waters above sent forth the living creatures. What is the meaning of these 'living creatures?' It was the soul of the first human being as it is written, 'And man became a living soul.' It is also added, 'and fowl shall fly above the earth,' denoting the angelic messengers who appear to man in dreams, as also those who manifest themselves in various forms and different aspects. Of these latter it is that Scripture refers to, 'And a river went out of Eden, and from thence it was parted and became into four heads' (Gen. ii, 10). 'And God created great whales (fishes), meaning Leviathan and its female.' 'And every living creature that moveth' in all parts of the earth. What is this nephesh hayah (living creature)? It was Lilith, the mother of the elementaries, which the waters brought forth abundantly and ministered to their growth and increase. As when the south wind begins to blow, the frosts disappear, streams become swollen and rivers flow in all directions into the seas, so was it with these creatures, as it is said: 'There go the ships, there is also that Leviathan whom thou hast made to play therein' (Ps. civ. 26). The words, 'And every winged fowl after his kind,' signify those creatures of whom it is written; 'For a bird of the air shall carry thy voice and those that have wings shall tell the matter'" (Eccles. x. 26).

Said Rabbi Jose: "All these beings have six wings, never more nor less, and therefore the words 'After his kind' are applied to winged angelic creatures. In their rapid flight through the world they observe and note the actions of men and report them on high, and thence it is written: 'Even in thought, curse not the King and curse not the rich in thy bed chamber'" (Eccles. x. 20).

Said Rabbi Hezekiah: "Scripture here useth the word haromeseth (moving creature) and not hashoretzeth (creeping creature). Wherefore? Because it refers to Lilith, as has been stated, who is also denoted in the words; 'Thou makest darkness and it is night, wherein all the beasts of the forest do move' (thirmos). These words also include and denote those angelic beings called hayoth (living creatures) who predominate and exert an influence equalling that of Lilith, and during the three watches of the night chant their hymns of praise until the morning dawns. It is of them that the prophet Isaiah speaks; 'They who remember the Lord and keep not silence'" (Is. lxii. 6).

Here Rabbi Simeon rose up and spake: "After long and protracted meditation on the origin of mankind, I have gathered that when the Holy One wished to create man, all the worlds throughout the universe were greatly affected and disturbed until the sixth day, when the divine will and intention became realized. Then the supernal light of all lights shone forth in its glory and splendor issuing from the gate of the east, spreading and enveloping the whole world with a garment of ineffable brightness, truly magnificent and indescribable.

"Then spake the great Kosmocrator of the east to his fellow rulers over the other quarters of the world: 'Let us make man in our image' that he may he receptive and enjoy the effulgent glory of the light that is streaming forth and enlightening the whole world. Then became conjoined the east with the west, engendering and bringing forth man on that part of the earth whereon the Holy Temple was afterwards founded and built. According to another ancient tradition the meaning of the words, 'Let us make man,' is given thus. The Holy One spake and made known to the angels the mystery and occult signification of the word Adam (man), the letters of which indicate his relation to both worlds, the seen and unseen, the known and unknown. By the letter M, which is written as a final or closed mem, is found thus contrary to rule in the word lemarbeh, occuring in the verse, 'Of the increase of his government' (Is. ix. 7). Man is connected with the higher world, whilst daleth or the letter D, closed on the west side, indicates his relation to the lower and sensible world. The principles of which these letters are the symbols ultimated in their manifestation on the phenomenal plane of existence and the production of a blended and harmonious whole, viz., of man in the form of male and female until the Lord God caused a deep sleep to fall upon him (Gen. ii. 21). The Holy One then separated them and having clothed the latter in a form most fair and beautiful brought her to man, as a bride is adorned and led to the bridegroom. Scripture states that He took one of the sides or parts (of the androgynous form) and filled up the place with flesh in its stead. In a very ancient occult book we have found it stated that what God took from the side of Adam was not a rib but Lilith, who had cohabited with him and given birth to offspring. She was however an unsuitable helpmeet for Adam and therefore Scripture states, 'But for Adam there was not found a helpmeet for him' (Gen. ii. 20). After the disappearance of Lilith and Adam's descent into the world plane of existence, then it was, as stated, 'The Lord God said, It is not good that man should be alone, I will make him a helpmeet for him.'"

On another occasion Rabbi Simeon spake and said: "It is written, 'And every plant of the field before it was in the earth, and every herb in the field before it grew, for the Lord God had not caused it to rain upon the earth' (Gen. ii. 5). By the phrase, 'Every plant of the field' is meant the preexisting ideal forms of great forest trees before their actual appearance in the world. Note that Adam and Eve were at first created androgynous. Wherefore were they not created face to face, or separated individuals? Because, as Scripture states, 'The Lord God had not caused it to rain upon the earth.' The union of man and wife is a type of a great spiritual fact, viz., the union of heaven and earth which could not be accomplished until the rain which united them descended. Then Adam and Eve ceased to be androgynous and gazed into each other's faces, as is the case with heaven and earth, the one reflecting the image of the other. If it be asked: whence or how do we know that things above are formed and modelled after things below; we say, from the mystical signification of the words; 'And the Tabernacle was reared up' (Ex. xl. 17), meaning the heavenly tabernacle which existed not until the earthly tabernacle had been erected. This is why the scripture states, 'And there was no man,' that is, until the creation of Eve, man was an imperfect being; which fact is indicated occultly by the absence of the letter Samech (denoting aid, help) in every passage relating to the creation of woman. Although members of the celestial college--those that have been initiated and enlightened in the secret doctrine--affirm that the word 'Ezer' (help) denotes that woman was created to be a help to man, she became so only when from androgynes they because separated and thus able to behold each other face to face. This is occultly referred to in the words; 'They are brought together forever and are made in truth and uprightness' (Ps. cxi. 8). By the term 'brought together' is meant that the union of male and female whose coming together is for mutual help, will continue even in the supernal worlds forever. 'For the

Lord God had not yet caused it to rain upon the earth' signifies that complete and perfect union between man and woman did not then exist because it had not as yet become a fact in the natural world, for it is added; 'And a mist went up from the earth and watered the whole face of the ground' (Gen. ii. 6), which refers to the sexual desires experienced by the female towards the male. Mists rise at first from the earth, heavenwards and, after forming clouds, heaven causes them to descend and water the earth. This applies also to the offering up of sacrifices, the smoke and fume of which ascending on high are caused to descend in blessings on mankind. If the congregation of Israel had not first offered up sacrifices, blessings would never have been showered upon tine world."

Said Rabbi Abba: "Wherefore is it written, 'And the tree of life in the midst of the garden and the tree of knowledge of good and evil?' We learn from tradition that the height of the tree of life attained to 1,825,000 miles and from its root flowed forth all the waters of creation in their various directions and courses. The celestial river, after refreshing the garden of Eden with its perfumed and crystalline waters, descends on to the earth below for the sustentation and refreshment of every living creature on the earth, as it is written, 'He sendeth the springs into the valleys, which run among the hills. They give drink to every beast of the field, the wild asses quench their thirst' (Ps. civ. 10, 11), 'And the tree of the knowledge of good and evil.' Wherefore was it not planted in the midst of the garden and what is the mystical meaning of this tree? Its nature or essence was two-fold, being bitter or sweet, according to the character of those who take and appropriate its fruits. Those who are selfish find that what they thought good, becomes evil to them. Thus many are seduced and go astray from the path of rectitude, and therefore is it called 'the tree of knowledge of good and evil.' When man ceased to be androgynous and became separated as at present male and female, it is said, 'And He closed up the flesh in its stead' (Gen. ii. 21), in which words occurs the letter S or Samech (help). The Holy One, like the judicious gardener transplanting trees and flowers, after sundering the two forms, placed them where they could behold each other face to face and thus begin on their course of physical and spiritual development and perfection. Furthermore, how know we that such was the origin of man and woman as at present constituted? Because it is written, 'The branches of my planting, the work of my hands, that I may be glorified' (Is. lx. 21). 'The work of my hands' refers to a special formation that should characterize man from other creatures. It is also written, 'In the day thou plantest, thy seed shall only produce wild fruits' (Is. xvii. 11). We are taught that plants, like the fragile wings of locusts or grasshoppers, are void of color. It is only after attaining to full growth that they become distinguished and conspicuous by variety of form, shape and color, such as the cedars of Lebanon. It was the same with the protagonists Adam and Eve, for, as plants before transplantation, so was it with them. They did not become perfect until they were transplanted onto the earth plane. It is also written, 'And the Lord God commanded the man, saying, of every tree of the garden thou mayest eat, but of the tree of knowledge of good and evil thou shalt not eat, for in the day thou eatest thereof, thou shalt surely die' (Gen. ii. 16, 17). From tradition we learn that the word tzav (commanded) denotes idolatry in general, the name Lord or Jehovah refers to blaspheming the holy name, whilst Alhim or God indicates the denial of justice in the world. 'The man' refers to the crime of murder, 'saying' to fornication, 'from every tree in the garden' to theft, 'mayst eat' to the prohibition from cutting flesh from a live animal. In saying, 'From every tree of the garden thou mayst eat' God indicated that even if man should commit all these sins, he was not to despair. Thus we see that the patriarchs, Abraham, Isaac and Jacob, and also prophets, have eaten of it and died not at once. He wished to warn man against tasting of the tree of death, as it is written, 'but of the tree of knowledge of good and evil eat thou not of it, for whoever does so dies as if he had taken poison.' 'But of the fruit of the tree which is in the midst of the garden,' God has commanded, 'We should not eat.' 'The fruit of the tree' denotes the woman. Thou shalt not eat thereof, because as scripture states, 'Her feet go down to death and her steps lead into Hades' (Prov. v. 5). There is fruit that is salutary when gathered from one tree and lethal when plucked from another tree. This latter was the fruit Eve referred to, viz., that of the tree of death and is described by the words of scripture just quoted.

"It is written, 'Now the serpent was more subtle than any beast of the field which the Lord God had made'" (Gen. iii. 1). Said Rabbi Jose: "The tree of which we have been discoursing was nourished by supernal light, by which it became great, fair and beautiful to the light. It is also written, 'And a river went forth out of Eden to water the garden.' The garden here mentioned denotes the female, whom the river made fruitful. Then man and woman became again one, in the sense as it is said, 'Jehovah is one and his name is one.' After disobeying the divine commandment, a deterioration in their heavenly state took place and they became separated from the higher and diviner life as intimated by the words, 'And from thence, it (the river), was parted'" (Gen. ii. 10).

Said Rabbi Isaac: "The serpent of which scripture speaks is The Tempter."

Said Rabbi Jehuda: "It was a real serpent." Going to Rabbi Simeon and making known to him their different views, he replied:

"Your interpretations are really one and the same and are both correct. Samael, when he descended on the earth plane, rode on a serpent. When he appeared under the serpentine form, he is called Satan. Whatever his name, he is the being known as the spirit of evil. It is said that when Samael descended from on high as just described, all the other animals fled away frightened and terrified. By his persuasive and guileful words, he deceived the woman and thus caused death to enter into the world (that is, the lower nature then ceased to be amenable to and obey the dictates and supremacy of the higher Self). He succeeded in doing this by means of the Sephira Hochma (wisdom), prostituting and using it for his evil purposes and thus caused the world to become accurst, and the tree which the Holy One had planted to become destroyed. What man lost Samael gained and enjoyed until the apparition of another sacred tree in the person of Jacob, who, by means of wisdom, acquired paternal blessings which neither Samael on high nor Esau below should be able to enjoy. He was therefore an after type of the first man; and here we see that as Samael deprived man of blessings proceeding from the first tree, so Jacob deprived Samael of blessings above and below proceeding from a tree having a human form. This is the mystic meaning of the words, 'And there wrestled a man with him' (Gen. xxxii. 24). 'The serpent was more subtle than any beast of the field.' These words refer to the Tempter, the angel that brought death into the world, and knowing this, we can understand the meaning of scripture, 'And God said unto Noah, the end of all flesh is come before me' (Gen. vi. 13). The angel of death having destroyed the divine life in man, who now had become wholly physical, governed and controlled by his animal or lower nature, and therefore dead and impervious to the heavenly influence of the Higher Self.

"And he said unto the woman, Yea, (aph) hath God said, ye shall not eat of every tree in the garden?" (Gen. iii. 1). Said Rabbi Jose: "The serpent began his discourse with aph (poison) and thus cast it into the world. What he said was this, 'By this tree the Holy One created the world, eat ye therefore of it and become equal to Alhim and able to distinguish between good and evil.'"

Said Rabbi Jehuda: "Not so spake the serpent, for then he would have spoken truly and the tree would have been recognized as the means by which, like a tool in the hands of an artisan, the Holy One had formed the world. What he really meant and did say was this, 'The Holy One himself has eaten of this tree and was thus able to create the world. Do ye therefore eat of it and ye will also have power to do the same as He. Alhim knows this and hence his prohibition.'"

Said Rabbi Isaac: "The words of the serpent were a tissue of falsehoods. At first he said, 'Yea hath Alhim said, ye shall not eat of the tree?' He knew well that God had said, 'From every tree of the garden thou mayest eat.'"

Said Rabbi Jose: "Tradition states that this command of God related to the sin of idolatry, denoted by the word 'commanded,' to blasphemy, by the name Jehovah, the denial of divine justice, by that of 'Alhim,' by the word 'Adam,' the crime of murder, and fornication, by the words 'said unto him.' In answer to the question that may arise, were there so many men in the world that the Divine Being saw fit to ordain these commands on man, it can be said that in this tree were involved all the negative behests, so that whoever violated them became numbered with transgressors guilty either of idolatry, murder, or fornication; of idolatry through denial of the lord above this tree; of murder, for he cuts short life that proceeds from the Sephira Geburah on the life side of the tree; and under the domination of Samael of fornication, as this tree is the female principle. Now it is known that the law forbids a man to be with any woman except in presence of her husband, so that there may arise no feeling of suspicion whatever. Whoever eats of this tree is culpable of a like offence. God in all these commandments to Adam, forbade him to eat of the tree of good and evil, wishing to preserve him from all the sins and their penalties which it contained."

Said Rabbi Jehuda: "Truly whoever eats of this tree transgresses, as he who is found alone with a woman when her husband is absent. This therefore is what the serpent said to Eve: 'Behold! I myself have touched this tree, and still I live, do ye the same and ye will find you will not die, for Alhim has only forbidden you eating therefrom.' We read that the woman at once saw that the tree was good for food (Gen. ii. 6). How did she see and discover this?"

Said Rabbi Isaac: "The tree was exceedingly fair and beautiful and odoriferous as it is written, 'The smell of my Son is as the smell of a field which the Lord hath blessed' (Gen. xxviii. 27), and she was therefore induced to take and eat of its fruit."

Said Rabbi Jose: "Eve saw the tree that it was good for food, because it had the power of opening the eyes of all that approached it."

Said Rabbi Jehuda: "Not so, as we learn that only after eating of the fruit thereof their eyes were opened."

THE DEVACHANIC OR HEAVENLY SPHERES

SAID Rabbi Simeon: It is a tradition from the most ancient times that when the Holy One created the world he engraved and impressed on it in letters of brilliant light, the law by which it is sustained and governed. Above, below and on every side of it, it is engraved on every atom that man, by research and discovery, might become wise and conform himself to it as the rule of his life. The world below is, in shape and form, the reflection and copy of the world on high, so that there may be no discontinuity between them, but reciprocally act and react upon each other. This being so, we purpose to show that the same principle or law that operated in the creation of the physical world, operated also in the origin of man, and that both alike are manifestations of one and the same law. That this great fact may be more fully perceived, let us first consider the esoteric meaning of the words, "But they, like Adam, have transgressed the covenant, there have they dealt treacherously against me" (Hos. vi. 7).

When the Holy One created man he invested him with a form so transcendently glorious and perfect in its proportions, and with mental endowments so great, that all other creatures trembled and stood in awe at his presence amongst them; for on his visage he bore the imprint or reflection of the Divine, their creator. Furthermore, the Holy One placed him in the garden of Eden, that there he might enjoy the pleasures and delights of angelic existence. In this beautiful abode, angels came round about him and made obeisance to him and revealed unto him their occult knowledge respecting the Divine Being, whom they regarded and worshiped as The Lord God of the universe, in order that he might unite and join them in His worship and service. Instructed in and taught the most profound celestial secrets, man became initiated in the mystery of wisdom (hochma), the first of the Sephiroth, in order that he might become imbued with an adequate idea and conception of the honor and glory due unto his maker.

In the invisible world, (or heaven, Devachan), there are seven spheres or states of existence, in which operate all those principles of life and existence which can only be matters of faith to the generality of mankind as at present constituted. Corresponding to them there are seven spheres or states, appertaining to and surrounding the lower world of humanity. Of these seven spheres, six can be apprehended by the human mind and only by those initiated into the highest mysteries. As the lower spheres belonging to the terrestrial world are formed after the pattern of those of the celestial world, the highest of the terrestrial spheres which comes between them is that which was at first designed by The Holy One as the abode and dwelling place of man in his primeval state of purity and sinlessness. After his expulsion from this Edenic sphere of existence, it became reserved by His Creator for the souls of the righteous in which they might enjoy the happiness of the beatific vision, or divine presence, and take on them the form and appearance of Adam before his fall.

THE FIRST, of these seven lower terrestrial spheres, is that from which proceeds an influence that prepares and qualifies dwellers on the earth plane to acquire a state of perfection, approximate and similar to that which distinguishes angelic beings. In it are found gathered together students of the Good Law, engaged in the study of that secret wisdom and doctrine that is never imparted except to just, upright and unselfish souls, who are admitted therein that they may enjoy a knowledge both of heaven and earth, and thus be better able to meditate on Divine mysteries and become receptive of heavenly delights and enjoyments. It is altogether invisible to ordinary human perception and the way of access to it unknown and undiscoverable save to those who, amidst the afflictions and distress attendant on earth life, render a faithful obedience to the Divine law.

It is written, "A virtuous woman is a crown to her husband" (Prow. xii. 4), in which words there is an occult reference to this sphere which as stated is a subject of faith and not of sight. A man ought therefore always to cleave unto and be faithful unto the Divine within him or his Higher Self and never deviate either to the right or left from its dictates and injunctions through menace or fear which in scripture is termed "the adulterous woman or a woman of fornications." Therefore is it written: "Say unto Wisdom, thou art my sister, and call understanding (binah) thy kinswoman, that they may keep thee from the strange woman, from the stranger which flattereth with her words" (Prow. vii. 4, 5). In this sphere also are gathered the souls of those who have commenced on the upward track or path to the Higher Life, for when they quit and go out of earth life, they rest and abide in it for a period more or lese prolonged, and necessary to prepare them for ascension into the higher or celestial Eden.

In each of the lower spheres are found souls in various and different states of progression each arrayed in garments and vestments corresponding thereto in brightness and color which they continue to wear until they attain unto the angelic state of existence, when they are discarded and thrown away. Ere this however takes place they enjoy the privilege of beholding the denizens of the higher celestial spheres and contemplating the glory of their Lord. Here are found those who, though heathen by birth, embraced and conformed their lives to the good law and from them emanates an aura, so bright that when they ascend, they become invisible to beholders. This sphere is more splendid and glittering than gold or precious stones. Through an opening on one side of it glimpses are obtained of the miserable state and unhappy condition of the inmates of Gehenna or Avitchi, into which they have been hurled by destroying angels, because in earth life they were rebels and disobedient to the good law. Through this same opening, a beam of celestial light penetrates into their dark abode three times daily, when for a short period they enjoy an assuagement of their misery and pain. Again, in this first sphere are upright proselytes such as Obadiah and Onkelos, who are held in honor above others. When any inmate is judged worthy to ascend into a higher sphere he retains the rank that distinguished him from his fellows. THE SECOND SPHERE is more interior than the first and is the abode and resting place of the fathers of humanity. It is illuminated by a light of many variegated colored rays descending from on high and its effulgence is far beyond that emitted by the most glittering diamonds. In it dwell those who were tormented and afflicted in the world yet renounced they not their worship of and trust in The Divine, nor ceased in their service to humanity. There too are those who, at all times and with all their power and strength, hallowed the divine Name, their daily prayer being, "Let His great name be blessed forever and ever." These, dwelling more in the centre of his sphere, are more recipient of the light by which it is illuminated and are better able to catch glimpses of higher and more supernal rays of light which, singly or in combination, flash down from the next higher sphere where abides the Messiah, who occasionally descends in their midst in order to direct and guide them in the path of ascension.

THE THIRD SPHERE; in it are assembled those who in earth life were subjects of great suffering and grievous trials, also those who died in early childhood. Here also are those who mourned and sorrowed over the destruction of the Holy Temple and are consoled and strengthened by the Messiah, so that eventually they ascend into the glory and Light of

THE FOURTH SPHERE, which includes those who mourned over the destruction of Jerusalem and were slain by idolatrous nations. When beholding them, and thinking over the miseries they endured, the Messiah weeps sympathetic tears so that the chiefs of the house of David gather round him in order to share in and thus mitigate his sorrow. In it the Messiah abides and dwells and in the time of the new moon his cry ceases not until it is responded to by the voice divine from on high. When he descends and visits the lower spheres, he is girded with garments of dazzling light, the sheen of which radiates in all directions, imparting renewed vigor and energy to those who died and suffered grievously for his sake. Ere he ascends again he arrays himself in a purple robe into which are woven the names of those who were slaughtered by idolaters for and which, after he ascends, are transcribed and impressed on the purple robe of the great king; and there cometh a time, when the Holy One will envelop Himself with it and judge the nations as it is written: "He shall judge amongst the heathen" (Ps. ex. 6). Ere, however, this comes to pass, the Messiah with an aureole of light, and accompanied with hosts of angels in their chariots, visits his martyrs to console and comfort there. Within this same sphere live and dwell the ten famed Rabbis of Israel, Rabbi Akiba and his associates together with others who all acquire here the faculty of beholding the reflection of that transcendently Divine light that no mortal can approach unto, of which it is written: "No eye but thine, oh God, has seen it" (Is. lxiv. 3).

THE FIFTH SPHERE includes all those souls who in earth life repented of their evil ways and attained a state of purity, and with them are those who sacrificed their lives for the glory and honor of God. At its entrance sits Manasseh. the king of Judah, whose repentance The Holy One graciously accepted and restored unto him His divine favor. Here also are they who deeply regretted their deeds of selfishness and evil ere they died, and now enjoy along with the rest, its joys and delights. There comes a time when the celestial light descends from the sphere above, filling every one with that degree of happiness of which he is receptive. It is a sphere of joy so exalted and great, that even the souls of just men made perfect are unable, through its intensity, to enter and abide therein, those servants of the Divine who had attained to the unitive stage in the Higher Life being only admitted into it and occupy the highest rank.

THE SIXTH SPHERE is the peculiar abode of these latter and of the most exalted of divine and holy men and women whose love for their Lord proved itself true and lasting. At its entrance are all those who proclaimed the word of the Lord and when the time of ascending higher comes they are the first. At another entry, Abraham, the right hand of the Holy One, is found, and there too is Isaac who was hound upon the altar as a perfect offering unto the Most High. At the third entry is Jacob, surrounded by the chiefs of the twelve tribes each with the halo of the divine Shekina encircling their heads. When the children of Israel suffer affliction, all these patriarchs are likewise afflicted and implore the Shekina to protect them, which then descends and places a crown over Israel that defends them from all trials and troubles. All these six spheres are variously connected with each other.

THE SEVENTH SPHERE is the complement of all the others and, being the most central, its existence is a subject of faith and not of knowledge to human beings. In this most secret and most interior of the spheres is a most magnificent column of light of many colors, green, white, red and black predominating. Each soul, at the end of each incarnation on earth ascends for a moment into this sphere, and, according to the color that he first beholds, so is he located in the sphere corresponding to it. The mystery of these six spheres is expressed in the word Sheth (six) and occultly alluded to in the first word of holy scripture, Brashith, bra, shith, He created six lower spheres and their corresponding higher antetypes, both being included in this word Brashith.

Said Rabbi Jehuda: There were two temples, the first and the second; one above and one below and one the type of the other, so in the Divine name I H V H there are two H's. The letter Beth (B) hath this peculiarity. It represents a house, which is its meaning, with a door or way of entrance that in whatever way it is turned, remains open, therefore, is this letter the gate to the scriptures and in a mystical sense symbolizes Him who is janua vitae, the gate of life.

Said Rabbi Isaac: It has been said by Rabbi Eliezar that Brashith synthesises the universe and everything contained in it, and as such is referred to in scripture. "This was the appearance of the likeness of the glory of the Lord" (Ez. I. 28). It was the likeness in which was contained that of six others. The word Brashith may thus be interpreted and rendered, bra, shith, that is to say, after the form of brashith, God created six other worlds or spheres of existence.

Rabbi Jose spake and said: It is written: "The flowers appear on the earth, the time of the singing of birds is come, and the turtle dove is heard in our land" (Cant. ii. 12). The occult meaning of the word flowers, refers to the six higher and lower spheres; "appear on the earth," refer to their representatives, Abraham, Isaac, Jacob, Jachin, Boaz, and Joseph; "the time of the singing of birds," denotes the worship and glory rendered by man to the Divine Being after attaining to a knowledge of these spheres, as scripture saith, "that my glory may sing praise to thee, and not be silent" (Ps. xxx. 12); therefore is it that the Psalm containing these words, is termed mizmor (a song), which term is applied only to those psalms that David composed under the direct inspiration of the Divine Shekina.

HIGHER DEVACHANIC OR HEAVENLY SPHERES

SAID Rabbi Abbi: "The higher or celestial world with its accompanying spheres, though invisible to mortal sight, has its reflection and analogue, namely, the lower world with its circumambient spheres, according to the saying, 'As above, so below.' The works of the Holy One in the celestial world are the type of those in the terrestrial world. The meaning of the words, Brashith, bara Alhim is this: brasahith, i.e., the celestial world, gave rise or origin to Alhim, the visible divine name that then first became known. Thus Alhim was associated with the creation of the world, as Brashith was connected with the creation of the celestial or invisible world, that being the type, thus the antetype, or in other words, one was the reflection and analogue of the other, and therefore it is written, 'Ath hashamayim, veath ha-aretzs' (the heavens and the earth). The heaven on high produced and gave rise to the earth below."

It is written, "And the earth was without form and void" (Tohu va Bohu). The signification of these words has already been given. The word aretzs here refers to the earth in its primal state when void of light. By the word "was," scripture teaches that it existed at its creation in a state of chaos and confusion. It is also said "and darkness," which was the deprivation of the light emanating from the antetypal world, owing to the matter of the earth becoming condensed and thus less receptive of its reflection. These words, Tohu, Bohu and darkness, together with a fourth, "wind," represent the four elements composing the substance of the earth. Another version gives "ve-ath ha-aretzs," referring to this world and its several divisions that are altogether different from those of the celestial world and which are as follows: Aretzs, Gia, Nesia, Zia, Arga and Thebel, which latter is greater than all the others as it is written: "And He shall judge the world (Thebel) in righteousness" (Ps. x. 9).

Rabbi Jose having asked the question: "What kind of world is that which is called Zia?" Rabbi Simeon replied:

"It is the place of Gehenna or Hell, 'a land of draught and of the shadow of death' (Jer. ii, 1). It is mystically referred to in the words, 'and darkness was upon the face of the deep' (Gen. i, 2), alluding to Zia, the abode of Hell and of the Angel of death, and is so called because the faces of those who are banished there become blackened on account of their wicked lives when on earth. The earth of Nesia is that the inhabitants of which become oblivious of the past; whereas, in that of Bohu, the faculty of memory is vivid and active."

Said Rabbi Hiya: "The word Bohu denotes the earth, Gia, whilst the words, 'and the spirit of Alhim moved upon the face of the waters,' designate that of Thebel, which is nourished and sustained by the spirit of Alhim, as is also Aretzs, our own abode of earthly existence, which is circumscribed and surrounded by seven spheres analogous to those of the celestial world, all of them being under the domination and control of their particular lords and guardians. The seven spheres of the celestial world are prototypes of those that surround our world and are inhabited by angelic beings who sing the praises of the Holy One, and use their own individual forms of worship. Their rank and order are indicated by the sphere they occupy.

"The first of these higher or celestial spheres and nearest to the earth, is altogether void of light and is the abode of angels who are like tempestuous winds, never seen, but felt, and are always invisible as they are void of light and darkness and undistinguished by any color. They are wholly without self-consciousness and without form or shape. Its chief and ruler is an angel named Tahariel, who has under him seventy subordinates. Their motion is manifested by the glittering of fiery sparks, the appearance and disappearance of which constitute day and night. "The second celestial sphere is distinguished from the first by the possession of a modicum of light, and is inhabited by angels appointed to watch over humanity and guide it into the path of uprightness whenever there is danger of its falling into error and wrong doing. When righteousness prevails in the world, they are filled with joy and delight. Their chief and ruler is called Qadmiel. When Israel commences its worship of the Holy One, they then manifest and make themselves visible in forms of intense brightness, and three times daily they bless and hallow the divine name. When they observe Israel studying and meditating on the law or secret doctrine, they ascend on high before the Holy One, who takes account of what they have seen and heard.

"The third celestial sphere is pervaded and filled with fire and flames. In it the fiery river Nahar dinur takes its rise and flows into Gehenna, overwhelming and engulphing in its course those mortals whose lives on earth were given up and addicted to evil and wrongdoing. Over these are placed destroying and tormenting angels, also accusing angels who, however, have no power or influence over Israel when it repents and does what is just and right. The abode of their chief is on the left side of this sphere in which darkness prevails, as it is written, 'and darkness was upon the face of the waters.' It is also the abode of Samael, the angel of darkness, the great transgressor.

"The Fourth celestial region is splendidly luminous, being the abode of angelic beings of great honor and dignity who, unlike those of the first sphere, begin and finish their worship of the Holy One without interruption. They are not subject to any change or declension, being angels of mercy and compassion of whom scripture speaks 'Who maketh his angels as the wind, and his messengers as flames of fire' (Ps. civ. 4). Their great mission work is on the plane of human existence and are invisible save in visions of the night, or on extraordinary occasions according to the degree of intelligence of those to whom they manifest themselves. Their great chief is named Padiel by whose orders they hold the key and open the gates of mercy through which pass the prayers and supplications of those who sincerely repent and live the Higher and Diviner life.

"The Fifth celestial sphere is one of still greater and more intense light. Therein are angels, some of them ruling over fire, others over water, and are messengers either of mercy or judgment, and as such become manifested as heralds of light or darkness. Their worship of the Holy One takes place at midnight. They are under the control of a chief named Qadashiel. When at midnight the north wind begins to blow, the Holy One, blessed be He! enters the garden of Eden and holds converse with the righteous. Then begin they their service of praise which resounds throughout the whole of this sphere and lasts during the night until daybreak and the sun appears. At that moment these angels join in a grand and glorious song of thanksgiving that peals also from all the hosts of heaven, from angels and archangels, seraphim, cherubim, above and below all uniting in the ascription of blessing and honor, glory and power to Jehovah, the Lord of Hosts that liveth forever and ever; as it is written, 'When the morning stars sang together and all the sons of God shouted for joy' (Job. xxxviii. 7). This their great anthem ceases not until Israel begins its song of praise.

"The Sixth celestial Sphere is nearer to the Kingdom of heaven. In it are seas covered with ships, also rivers and lakes abounding in fish. Its denizens are under the rule of presidents, the chief of whom is named Uriel, who enter on their official duties at certain fixed times. When the time arrives for the ships to go south, Michael is their ruler; and when they go north, Gabriel assumes authority and direction; as these two archangels occupy the right and left sides of the Mercaba, or celestial chariot. When, however, the ships go eastward, Raphael rules, and Uriel when they sail westward.

"The Seventh Celestial Sphere is the highest and accessible only to souls of the greatest purity and thus qualified to enter into its joys and delights. None other are found there. In it are laid up treasures of peace, blessings and benefits.

"All these seven spheres are inhabited and filled with beings like in their form to man, who cease not to worship and give thanks to the holy One. None of them, however, are so conversant with the glory of the Holy One as the inhabitants of the sphere of Thebel, who are perfectly pure in body, mind and soul. In the seventh celestial sphere there are those who have attained to the highest degree of holiness as in the seventh sphere belonging to earth below, are found the just with purified bodies. Moreover, above and beyond all these spheres there are seven others the existence of which is a subject of faith and not of experience, and in each of them are spiritual beings of the highest order.

"The first of these mysterious spheres is inhabited by lofty angel named Rachmiel, who has the charge over those who have forsaken idolatry to become worshippers of the Holy One. By him they are prepared to look in the Luminous Mirror, or Beatific Vision.

"In the second higher sphere dwells Ahinael, who receives under his care all who died ere being initiated in the secret doctrine, and instructs them in its teachings.

"The third is that where abides Adrahinael, a spirit under whose care and guardianship are those who in earth life had resolved to change their evil habits, but being suddenly overtaken by death, were unable to do as they had willed. Such souls find themselves cast first into Gehenna, out of which, however, they are taken by this spirit and prepared for the enjoyment of the divine light emanating from their Lord and Creator, the Holy One. The joys of such souls are inferior to those of others. They are known as 'children of the flesh,' and of them it is written, 'From one new moon to another, and from one sabbath to another, shall all flesh come to worship before me, saith the Lord' (Is. lxvi. 23).

"The fourth of the spheres is inhabited by a spirit named Gadrihael, presiding over all those who were slain by idolaters. His office is to guide them unto the palace of the king clothed in robes of purple, in which their names are inwoven and where they abide until the day when the Holy One shall avenge their sufferings, as it is written: 'Hs shall judge amongst the heathen. He shall fill the places with dead bodies and shall wound the heads of many' (Ps. cx. G.).

"Adiriel is the presiding spirit in the fifth higher sphere and is in charge of those souls who through their lifelong penitence, attained to a high degree of holiness and purity in which they surpass all others, even as their abode excels all others in grandeur and glory.

"All the aforenamed presidents are under the rule and authority of the archangel Michael, captain of the myriad hosts of heaven, whose office it, is to fill with joy and delight the souls of the faithful and true servants of the Lord, by causing them to view and behold the light, clear as crystal, that marks the course of the river of the water of life flowing into the world to come." [1]

---

[1] The conclusion of this discourse is wanting."

RABBI SIMEON'S DISCOURSE ON PRAYER

RABBI SIMEON said: "Who is he that knoweth how to address his prayers to the Almighty as did Moses in all the circumstances of his life, whether long or brief in their duration. We have found in an ancient book, that prayer, in order that it may become effective and enter through heaven's gates without hindrance or obstacle, should be expressed in terms suitable and corresponding to existent circumstance, otherwise it is ineffective and of no avail. Blessed are they who learn and acquire the true secret of prayer, by which they succeed in obtaining through the Schekina their requests, and those blessings by which evils are assuaged or averted and judgment becomes tempered with mercy." For a few moments, Rabbi Simeon ceased speaking and then, as one inspired, he slowly rose and standing up, exclaimed: "Who can utter the mighty acts of the Lord, who can show forth all his praise and teach us the mystery and secret of prayer, but Abraham the patriarch sitting now on the right hand of God? He can tell us, he to whom were revealed in raptured vision the glorious mansions of the Great King. Seven are they in number and each with their entrances, through which the prayers of mankind may ascend up to the throne of the Eternal from the lips of those whose souls are in harmony and union with the Lord of the universe, who embraces worlds above and below with his love and regards them as a glorious whole. Such souls are they of whom scripture speaks, 'when trouble came they visited thee, and poured out their prayer when thy chastening was upon them' (Is. xxvi. 16).

"The first of these sacred mansions is referred to in the words, 'And they saw the God of Israel and there was under his feet, as it were, a paved work of a sapphire stone, like unto heaven in its clearness' (Ex. xxiv. 10). Its existence is the greatest of mysteries. It is the abode of a great spirit named Saphira whose radiant form is white and in its brilliancy like unto the precious sapphire stone. The light of this mansion sendeth forth rays in two directions, glittering and flashing like sparks from a candle, and though apparently separate and distinct, yet are they but emanations and scintillations of the one divine light; as it is written, 'like the color of burnished brass' (Hz. i. 7). This spirit Saphira is stationed on the right side of the mansion whilst on the left is stationed another spirit whose color is red and named Lebanah. The rays of these two spirits become blended and mingled together, the red absorbing the white as the cows of Pharash, of whom we read that when the lean had eaten up the fat kine it could not be discerned that they had eaten them (Gen. lxi. 20). There are two gateways to this mansion leading to the sphere termed 'the heaven of heavens.'

"From the emanations of these two spirits, Saphira and Lebanah, are created and formed those angelic beings called Ophanim, who in their holiness are accounted equal to the Hayoth, or living creatures, described by the prophet (Ezechiel i. 20). The appearance of the Ophanim was like unto the color of Beryl, but that of the Hayoth was like that of coals of burning fire and amidst them were fiery flames, glittering and scintillating like sparks, referring to the Holy Spirit from whom they all emanate and by whom they shine as it is further written, 'and the living creatures went and returned as the appearance of flashing lightning.' When a spirit becomes united and blended with another, there flashes forth above the four Ophanim a great white and dazzling light, each of whom takes the form of a lion with the wings of an eagle and rules over a thousand and three hundred myriads of subordinate spirits like unto themselves.

"These Ophanim form the wheels of the heavenly Mercaba, or chariot, by whom it is moved in four directions. In each wheel of his chariot appear the three different colors of the supreme light, thus twelve altogether. These Ophanim also constitute the four mystic beings of the Divine Chariot having the forms of a man, a lion, an ox and an eagle, facing the four quarters, but when the wheels of the chariot begin moving, they become faced to each other, as it is written. The loops held together each to each' (Ex. xxxvi. 12). At the time that the wheels begin moving, a voice sweet and harmonious is heard resounding by the dwellers in the lower world. The light emanating from this mansion is perceived by angels extending to the star Sabathai (Saturn), and is a source of nourishment and sustentation to all who behold it as it is written, 'Everywhere is the spirit, and wherever it went the wheels also went, for the spirit of the living creatures, or life, was in the wheels.' (Ez. i. 20). Some behold this light bright and ebullient as the rays of the sun reflected in clear water, by others it is perceived blended with the light of Lebanah.

"Blessed is he who by the intensity of his prayer is able to ascend into this mansion for, then by the exercise and performance of rites and ceremonies that symbolize union with the Divine and the oneness of the living spirit, his soul becomes filled with a heavenly joy, and he is encircled by a bright aura by which he is led to the silent contemplation of the mysteries of the second mansion. By the prayers of such souls, the four Ophanim become as one, and blended together as fire with water, and water with fire, as the North with the South and the South with the North, and also as the East with the West and the West with the East. Such is the power of a just man's prayer to accomplish the union of opposites; so that the human becomes Divine, and the Divine is blended with the human, which union is symbolized by a tall lofty column of light that extends and reaches from the lowest to the highest spheres, attracting the attention and regards of all spirits inhabiting there and by their meditation becoming united with the Divine Spirit as it is written, 'They have all one breath' (Eccles. iii. 16) that is one and the same indwelling spirit.

The Second Mansion is that alluded to in scripture, "like to heaven itself in brightness" (Ez. xxiv. 18) and is the abode of an angelic being termed Zohar (splendor) who in the luminous brightness of his form, is ever the same and changeth not. The light in this mansion is transcendently white and illumines it in all directions. Happy the lot of those to whom it becomes visible. With the spirit Zohar is associated another, the color of whose aura resembles that of the hyacinth more than the pearl or diamond and causes the light of this mansion to be more pronounced and noticeable by its contrast. From this light emanate the Seraphim, heavenly things having six wings according to the number of the mansion which is the sixth from the highest. It is they who consume up all those who have no respect nor regard for the worship and glory of their Lord and they are therefore termed "Consumers." The mystery attending their office and service is referred to in an ancient tradition that states, dasthmsh btga chlph, i.e., whoever makes a selfish use of the Crown, thus profaning it shall be consumed. He, however, who studies Scripture and the six orders of the Mishnah is as he who by reverential worship becomes unified with his Lord. To all such, the Seraphim become adjustants by consuming in their flames all the descendants of the great Serpent by whom death entered into the world. These seraphim are under the government and authority of the presiding spirit of the mansion, When the wheels of the Mercaba or heavenly chariot begin moving, they fall back and many of them are consumed in their own flames, but eventually they are resuscitated and, gaining their pristine state, take refuge beneath the wing of the eagle, one of the four living creatures surrounding the Divine chariot. When the divine light is seen beaming within the four living creatures, each of the wheels begin moving. The wheel belonging to the East, in moving in that direction becomes hampered by the other three, turning each in their own direction. This occurs alike with the other wheels of the North, South and West. Only when their individual motions are equilibrated, can the Divine chariot be raised and turned in any direction by the mystical Column of light that unites the higher and lower spheres. This same Column, according as the chariot is at rest or in motion, closes or opens the gate of prayers.

DEVACHANIC SPHERES AND MANSIONS

IN the third mansion or higher sphere is the spirit Nogah (splendor), whose aura is of the most absolute whiteness and purity and without a shade of color, by reason of which it takes its name. It is altogether invisible to the lower spheres except when tempered and blended with the rays that proceed from them. The light of this mansion is most wonderfully manifested in the appearance of a great and mighty sheaf of fire, emitting sparks of twenty-two different shades of color, corresponding to the twenty-two letters of the Hebrew alphabet. This luminous sheaf, however, remains invisible and undistinguished until the time that prayers ascend from the lower spheres, when all these star-like sparks become united and form a column of light and give rise and origin to holy and powerful Hayoth or living creatures that separate themselves into two groups, one having the form of a lion, the other, that of au ox. Above these are seen the four Ophanim or wheel-like spiritual beings, under whose rule and control are myriads upon myriads of subordinate spirits. Each of these Ophanim has eight wings and derives its power and sustenance from the Hayoth above them and are stationed at the four cardinal points of the world. Each have four figures or forms, two of which are turned towards the Hayoth and two are covered by their wings, that they may not behold the Mercaba or celestial chariot in its circular motions, and thus avoid being consumed and annihilated. Their reverence and veneration of the Divine Being give rise to unnumbered hosts and legions of angelic beings who chant praises and sing hymns continually to his honor and glory. To this mansion there are four entrances and gateways, corresponding to the four quarters of the world, and each of them guarded by ten chiefs. When prayers ascend from the lower mansions and spheres these gates are opened, when a general blending and fusion takes place, of chiefs with chiefs. Ophanim with Hayoth and Hayoth with Ophanim, of angelic hosts and legions with other hosts and legions, of lights with lights, and spirits with spirits, all blended together become at length unified with Nogah, the ruling spirit of the mansion, into one mighty, harmonious whole. In this mansion is a place glittering and shining like burnished brass, wherein are vast hosts of angels who are unable to go out therefrom and ascend on high until this mansion becomes united by prayer with the next higher or fourth mansion.

These particular hosts of angels are the executive messengers of Karmic law and sent forth by the chief justice of the tribunal in the fourth mansion. They are termed Generals because they lead their hosts against nations and inhabitants of the world who violate the good law of right and justice. On the sixty walls of their abode they suspend their shields of gold, in number six hundred thousand, are entering into the fourth mansion from which when they return they descend into the lower worlds and spheres as far as the planet Mars, in order to execute the decrees and sentences entrusted unto them. Here they remain until the time of prayer, which ascends on high from the lower spheres, when they blend and mingle with the angelic messengers of mercy and goodness, and, together with them, enter into the great effulgent column of light beaming down from on high, and ascend into the fourth mansion. Happy he who understands and comprehends the mystery of this column by which he comes into union with the Divine, thus escaping all affliction and becoming participant of the blessings conveyed and imparted to him by these Karmic angels. He is verily the just man, and a world upholder, for his prayers are always effective and prevail with heaven, whence he receives his recompense and becomes enrolled amongst the children of light.

Take note that all these spheres and mansions with their living creatures, their legions of angels and all their spirits of light, are coordinate and bound together and linked by indispensable and indissoluble ties, and as the coats and parts of the eye are necessary and essential for sight, each of them being unable to operate without the aid of the other, working together in perfect harmony, so is it with all these angels and spirits. But for the many gradations in their orders, prayer would be unable to ascend on high and become effectual. By this series of gradations it is that prayers proceeding from the throne find an entry into the fourth mansion and attain to that degree of holiness which distinguishes true worship and adoration of the Divine Being.

The fifth mansion varies from all others in that it is a combination of four mansions, one within the other. Its president spirit is called Zacouth (righteousness) and rules over those who by their lives and deeds have become justified. Out of this mansion go forth seventy light rays corresponding to the number of the chiefs that guard its gates, who, along with two others, constitute a sanhedrim to which Karmic angels and spirits bring and submit their reports of human action on the earth plane. These two superior rays are known as "the witness." The mystery respecting them, their existence and office, is indicated in the words, "Thy belly is as a heap of wheat, set round about with lilies" (Cant. vii. 2). By these seventy light beings, all actions are weighed and each man adjudged. On their decisions becoming ratified by the two witnesses, they are carried out, executed by Karmic ministers whether for good or otherwise, and this is why this mansion is termed Zacouth, whose president bears the impress of the letters of the divine name, I. H. V. joined together similar to the juncture of the male and female and give forth a light that illuminates all sides of the mansion, and also three other rays corresponding to the three judges necessary to constitute a legal tribunal. Their jurisdiction extends to all questions and matters relating to wealth and poverty, sickness and health. Myriads of angels attend to receive their decisions and forthwith proceed to execute them throughout the world.

Above this tribunal are seated four flaming Seraphim from whom stream forth seventy-two bright and shining rays corresponding and similar to those before mentioned. Beneath them flows a fiery river that consumes everyone that approaches it. In it are thrown and consumed those angels who in any way incur condign punishment. It never flows into the fourth mansion because of the letters I. H. V. borne by the president, for wherever they are visible no punishment can he inflicted. All decrees, whether for good or otherwise, affecting mundane affairs, go forth from the mansion, saving those relative to fecundity, which are adjudicated on in the higher mansion. In the middle of it exists a place where assemble all spirits ascending from lower spheres.

This mansion has also twelve gateways at which are stationed chiefs, who make known to their subordinates the decrees and mandates they have to discharge and execute in the world, as it is written, "He cried aloud and said thus; Hew down the tree and cut off his branches, shake off his leaves and scatter his fruits" (Dan. iv. 14). Having received their orders, these Karmic angels speed their flight to the firmament of the Sun, and when it rises despatch them to all quarters of the world to be executed by demons and elementals of fire, air, earth and water, as also by birds and other creatures. Until they are carried out they return not to their abode on high.

In this same mansion, when anyone in the world becomes ill, it is determined whether and when he shall recover or die. It may be asked: How so? We have just said that decrees relating to life and death are not in the jurisdiction of the mansion. This is truly so. Though the sentence be decreed in it, the final fiat is given from above and is invariably conformable to it. Happy he who attains unto union with the Divine, for then his prayers rise on high and return with the blessings from the mansion symbolized by prostration of the face upon the ground at the time of prayer, an attitude by which we supplicate that judgment may be tempered with mercy as it is written, "He is a God of truth and without iniquity, just and right is He" (Deuter. xxxii. 4). The fifth mansion is the abode of a spirit named Beraqa (lightning) because the light reflected by it upon the lower spheres is similar to lightning, purple hued in color. It is a combination of different colored rays, such as white, black, red and green, yet to sight they appear as one. Beneath it, stand four Ophanim with faces turned to the four cardinal points and each with its own peculiar color. In proportion as these Ophanim approach and come into contact with one another, so do their colors become fused and blended the one with the other. When this occurs their forms become visible within each other, as it is written, "An Ophanim in the midst of an Ophanim" (Ez. i. 16). The various colors prevailing in this mansion are due to the flaming sword mentioned in scripture, "He placed at the east of the garden of Eden Cherubim and a flaming sword" (Gen. iii. 24).

CHAPTER XXI.

THIS sword is suspended over the judges presiding in the fourth mansion and is alluded to in an old saying, "Let every judge when delivering judgment remember, that the sword is suspended above his own head." It is continually turning and when the Ophanim become fused together, two fiery rays proceed from it and going outside the mansion, station themselves before the gate thereof, taking the form of a man and a woman. At other times they appear as spirits or as superior angels. The male ray characterizes angels engaged on missions of mercy and goodness in the world, therefore need they the intense light of the male form; whereas, those angels who as to their form have been consumed, need the light of the female form, on their reappearance. The spirits presiding in these two lights become united at the time of prayer. The force that produces this union is the affection of Love and when it is effected the name of this mansion becomes changed from Beraqa into Ahabah (love), for in it is accomplished the union of all beings by their common love to the Supreme Being, of which scripture speaks, "There will I give thee my love" (Cant. vii. 12). Furthermore, when these two rays become blended, there spring forth and become manifested unnumbered myriads of angelic beings metaphorically named, Manchakes, Raisins and Pomegranates, whose plane of existence lies between the fifth mansion and the planet Venus. Thus it is written, "A man would give all his substance for Ahabah" (love) (Cant. viii. 7); that is, to draw to himself angels from this palace so named, but they would not be induced to leave it. This mansion is symbolized in the act of prayer, by prostration of the body, with extended hands indicative of the desire to become united by love with the Divine. The sixth mansion is presided over by a spirit named Khute Hashne (threads of scarlet) and is occultly alluded to in the words, "Thy lips are like a thread of scarlet" (Cant. iv. 3). It is also termed, the mansion of aspiration and is that which angels of the lower spheres ardently desire to attain unto and become united with in spirit by the nesheqath rakhunutha (the kiss of love), who is in intimate relationship with all the lower spheres. Another reason why this mansion is so called, is, that everyone who succeeds in coming into relation with it attracts to himself divine energy from on high through the unitive power of love. In this mansion is Moses who died by a kiss of this love and it is therefore called by his name. Its presiding spirit is a spark of love and unifies the lights of the higher and lower spheres and makes them one, when sparks flashing out of it give rise and form to living creatures holy through goodness and love and are therefore called the GREAT HAYOTH and enter into union with those of the lower spheres similar to the husk and shell of a nut, as it is written, "Hayoth great and small" (Ps. civ. 25). It is for this reason it is termed Zanath Egoz (the garden of nuts) and is so referred to in scripture, "I went down into the garden of nuts" (Cant. vi. 11), i.e., into this mansion of love in order to unite the male and female principles. These Hayoth are divided into twelve, and trios of them are stationed at the four gateways, and on them are dependent all inferior spirits so that throughout the whole of the spheres concatenation of all the various grades and orders of beings, all dependent one upon the other and forming a grand family of spirits throughout the universe from which is formed a mighty angelic spirit who ascends on high to adore and worship the Supreme Spirit and become united with it. This union of spirits with the Divine is occultly alluded to in the words, "Let him kiss me with the kisses of his mouth" (Cant. i. 2); that is, with the kiss of love expression of the universal ecstasy and the eternal delight experienced by every animated being in its union with the Divine, by which partially developed spirits become eventually perfect and spirits in darkness become illumined with the light proceeding from the eternal Spirit, supreme over all. And this is effected by prayer coming from a sincere and loving heart. Happy he who prays, so that these spheres and mansions and their indwelling spirits become united together in love and thus able to climb the ladder whose top rests on the throne of the Eternal. The mystery of this mansion of love is alluded to in scripture, "And Jacob kissed Rachel" (Gen. xxiv. 11). Abraham, who is on the right hand of the Most High, is the president of this mansion. Ahabah, his great aim having been to confirm himself with the divine will, hence his words: "Behold, I know now that thou art beautiful" (Gen. xii. 11).

Now the beauty of a woman is her breast, the seat of love. Isaac, who is on the left hand, presides over the Beth Din or tribunal of Justice, whence are issued decrees and judgments. He attained to union with the Divine through the spirit of Zacouth (righteousness). The other prophets preside in the mansions of Nogah and Zohar and are mystically indicated in the words, "The joints of thy thighs are like jewels" (Cant. vii. I).

Joseph, the just and pillar of the world, presides in the beautiful mansion of Saphira which is of great beauty and splendor, notwithstanding the words of scripture that allude to it, "Under his feet" (Ex. xxiv. 10), that are written to enhance the divine glory. It is through this mansion that spirits, by means of the shining column of light, ascend into the seventh, the most mysterious of all, and here as radii in a circle converging to the centre; so in it spirits from all spheres ascend and form a vast united family in perfect and eternal union with the Divine, which is referred to and indicated in the words, "Jehovah is Alhim, Jehovah is Alhim" (I Kings, xviii. 39). Blessed in this life and in the world to come are they who are able to attain unto this union, symbolized by the bending of the knees in the act of prayer and adoration, together with prostration of the body, extension of the arms and hands and abasement of the face on the ground, these gestures indicating their desire to become conjoined and unified with the Supreme Spirit, the Soul of all souls, the infinite and eternal Being, primal fount of all light and blessing.

When this glorious union is accomplished and consummated, of worlds below with worlds on high, earth and heaven will become conjoined in the Divine life and then will judgment be changed into mercy and goodness and the Divine will be done on earth as it is in heaven, as it is written "And He said unto me, 'Oh Israel thou art my servant in whom I will be glorified'" (Is. xlix. 3). Happy the people whose "God is the Lord" (Ps. cxlix. 15).

CHAPTER XXII.

THE seventh mansion is without visible form, being the highest and most mysterious of all, enshrouded with a veil which separates it from all other spheres and mansions, so that no one can perceive the two Cherubim standing behind it and therefore it is termed The Holy of Holies, for therein is the, Supreme Spirit that imparts life and light to all creatures. When the union of all spirits with the Divine takes place, then the light of this mansion descends out of the Holy Place and illuminates all worlds. All light coming down from on high is like the seed of man that unites the male and female, and so is it with this mansion which unites the higher with the lower spheres. Happy the man who accomplishes this union, for then is he wholly blessed and beloved both on high and below. When the Holy One decrees judgments such a man is able to appease and allay them and yet does not act contrary and in opposition by so doing, but through his intimate union with the Divine Being all penal judgments and decrees become self annulled and innocuous. Oh blessed is he both in this world and the world to come; as it is written, "The righteous man is the foundation of the world" (Prov. x. 25). Whilst he lives a voice from on high is ever speaking unto him, saying: "Thou shalt rejoice in the Lord, thou shalt glory in the Holy One of Israel" (Is. xli. 16). As the chief priest officiates at the altar of sacrifice and the Levites chant, the cloud of incense ascends on high; so is the ascent of spirits to the higher spheres and mansions, until at length they become unified with the light of light, and abide forever, perfected and wholly divine through the power of prayer. It is then that all spirits like lesser lights are blended with the great divine light, and entering within the veil of the Holy of Holies are overwhelmed with blessings proceeding therefrom as water out of an inexhaustible and ever-flowing fountain. In this mansion is the great Mystery of Mysteries, the deepest, most profound and beyond all human comprehension and understanding, the eternal and infinite Will, that governs, sways and rules all worlds throughout the universe, the mighty causal Will, known only by its effects and silent operations, and that through all ages to come will ever act until the human and divine wills are blended together in one eternally harmonious whole, and humanity attains to the Higher and Diviner Life. Blessed are they who have entered into the enjoyment accruing from this union of wills as it is written, "Thy father and thy mother shall be glad and she who hath born thee shall rejoice" (Prov. xxiii. 25). When perfect union prevails, everything is centered in and proceeds from the Divine Thought or Mind. All forms and ideas give place to and disappear in the Divine Mind, that alone animates, vivifies, sustains and enlightens every human soul. The supreme Will, residing and acting through pure thought, it follows that by prayer man effects this union with the Divine Will and attracts it to himself, and therefore it is written, "Happy is that people who enjoy this greatest of blessings, whose God is the Lord," for then the world rejoices in mercy and goodness that come from above, through the prayer of union, which never proves in vain or resultless. It avails with the Lords as that of a child with its father and is answered. The suppliant becomes girded about and endowed with a power felt and feared by all inferior creatures. It ordains and the Holy One fulfills its behests, as it is written, "Thou shalt desire a thing and it shall be established, and the Light shall shine upon thy way" (Job xxii. 28). [1]

---

[1] Note by translator. These mansions in their totality correspond to the third heaven mentioned by St. Paul in the Epistle to the Corinthians. The reader will find some very interesting information on these spheres and mansions in the works of St. Dionysius the Areopagite. He will also find a very interesting reference to the "two witnesses" in Revelation, XI, 1, pointing to the Kabbalistic origin of this book.

CHAPTER XXIII.

SAID Rabbi Isaac: "It is written, 'And God said, let there be light.' (Gen. 1-3). This was the primeval light that illuminated the world on all sides and which the Holy One withdrew and hid, that it might not beenjoyed save by the righteous--"

Said Rabbi Simeon: "By the words, 'And God saw the light that it was good' is signified that the divine light in itself is a source of joy and delight; the word 'good' being the same used in connection with Balaam, thus, 'When Balaam saw that it pleased,' in that it was both (good) in the eyes of the Lord to bless Israel' (Num. 24-1); and therefore at the end of the verse, 'And God divided the light from the darkness' in order that the upright might live in the light and the wicked in darkness. Note that it is from this primal celestial light emanates the light which shineth and illumes the world and becomes a source of joy to every living creature. It was with this higher light that the Holy One with his right hand formed and engraved crowns as we have formerly described. It is written, 'How great is Thy goodness which Thou hast laid up for them that fear Thee, which Thou hast wrought for them that trust in Thee, before the sons of men.' (Ps. 31-19.) 'How great is thy goodness' refers to the primal light the Holy One hid and reserved for them that fear him, even the righteous in life. It is written, 'and the evening and the morning were day, one.' The evening arises out of darkness and the morning from light and from the conjunction the day is formed."

Said Rabbi Jehuda: "Wherefore is it written of each day, 'It was evening and it was morning?' It was to show that there is no day without night, and no night without day and therefore are not to be separated."

Said Rabbi Jose: "'The primal celestial light of the first day is that which lightened the other days of creation,' and therefore the word YOUR day is repeated." Said Rabbi Eleazar: "For the same reason, the scripture uses the word boqer (morning) in connection with all the days of creation, as it designates the primal light."

Said Rabbi Simeon: "The first day of the creation is the synthesis of all the other days, for as there is really no separate fractional moment in time, they only formed part of the whole. It is written, 'God said let there be light' meaning angelic beings who are emanations from the light on high that shineth forth on the world below and were created on the first day and took up their position on the right hand of the Holy One. 'And God saw the light that it was good.' The word ath before good, refers to the luminous and non-luminous mirror, the one 'being the light by which the Beatific Vision is acquired by prophets, the other that which enlightens the mind of man for the perception of truth."

Said Rabbi Eleazar: "The word ath indicates that in the light that God called good, are comprehended and included all the angelic hosts that emanated from it and also when perfect harmony prevails amongst all orders of beings, will regain their pristine splendor."

Said Rabbi Jehuda: "It is written, 'Let there be a firmament in the midst of the waters,' by which is meant the interior man who is receptive of the knowledge of spiritual truths (the waters above), and of earthly things or scientifics (the waters below)."

Said Rabbi Isaac: "On the second day, Gehenna was formed whilst the work of creation was yet incomplete; the term 'good' is not applied and used until the third day, when it is repeated twice, as then all discord and clashing of elements ceased and the lot of the wicked in Gehenna became alleviated through the decreased intensity of its fiery heat. Wherefore the second day is considered an incomplete period until junction with its complement, the third day, took place."

Rabbi Hiya was sitting before Rabbi Simeon and said: "Light coming from the right appeared on the first day, but darkness from the left attended with division of the waters and discord amongst the primary elements, why did not the first day contain and make up what was wanting in the second?"

Said Rabbi Simeon: "Because as there existed no harmony between the first and the second day, the third was necessary to equilibrate them and cause union between them. It is written, 'Let the earth bring forth.' It was by the green herb that the waters above and below had become blended and made fruitful, representing thus the union of male and female principles, therefore is it true that what is above is as what is below.'"

Said Rabbi Jose: "That being so, there must be a God above and a corresponding God below: If you affirm this, I should say that the God on high is called the living God, whilst the God below is Ahhim, designated in scripture by the term toldoth (productions), as it is written, these are the products of the heavens and the earth which are created (Behibaram). Now we learn from the secret doctrine that this peculiar word should be divided and read thus, behi-baram; meaning that God created the heavens and the earth by He. Now He who is above is the universal Father, who created all beings. He made fruitful the earth so that it brought forth toldoth (products), in the same way that the female is made fruitful by the male."

Said Rabbi Eleazar: "All the fructifying powers were present in the earth, potentially, at the time of its creation, but only became manifested in the various productions of the six days; as it is written, 'And God said let the earth bring forth the living creature.' If, however, it be said, the words of the scripture are 'Let the earth bring forth grass,' our reply is that the earth from the third day was then imbued with generative forces that remained dormant and hidden until the appointed time for manifestation. The earth was void and empty, as it is affirmed, of all life, as the targum renders the meaning of the words 'tohu vabohu,' but it became adapted for the reception of those generative forces necessary in the production of grass, herbs and trees, that manifested their existence on the sixth day. This was the same with the light created on the first day of creation, but did not become visible only at the appointed time, viz., on the third day. It is written, 'Let there be lights in the firmament of Heaven.' The word Meoroth (light) is here written defectively, indicating by this that the evil serpent is the author and originator of discord and separation of what should always be united and blended harmoniously together viz., the sun and the moon. This word also denotes the malediction by which, through the serpent, the earth became cursed, as it is written, 'Cursed is the ground because of thee' (Gen. 3-17), and being found in the singular, signifies that the moon, designated by the words, 'Let there be light,' and the sun by the words, 'In the firmament,' were originally created together and formed one, in order to give their united light upon the earth, but through the serpent they became separated; hence it is written, 'Let them be for lights in the firmament of the Heaven,' to give light upon the earth, instead of 'Let them enlighten the earth,' and therefore we conclude that both in heaven above and on earth below, time is measured by the courses of the moon."

Said Rabbi Simeon: "By the moon's courses, the solstices and days are reckoned and determined."

Rabbi Eleazar objected to this statement and said: "Is not frequent mention made of fractions of time in the world on high?"

Said Rabbi Simeon in reply: "Only in the angelic world is there no need of the lunar courses as elements for calculating time, and when any mention is made of them it is by way of accommodation to the understanding of the dwellers on earth."

Again Rabbi Eleazar made objection and said: "It is however written, 'Let them be for signs and seasons,' that is, for the measurement of time, and these words being in the plural, we may infer that they apply to both worlds having the same unit of measure."

Said Rabbi Simeon in reply: "The word othoth (signs) is written defectively to show that divisions of time exist not in the world above as in the world below."

Said Rabbi Eleazar: "Why then is it written, 'Let them be for signs and for seasons,' and from which we may gather that the sun and moon together were to be used for this purpose that the moon is only needed."

Said Rabbi Simeon: "The moon is designated by a plural term, as it resembles a casket filled with various jewels that is ofttime spoken of in the plural. Observe that every numerical calculation begins with unity, whatever its value and worth may be or whatever it represents. Now the Divine Unit is that in which everything is included and therefore beyond and above all mathematical calculation. It is the basic unit from which all things in the world take their origin and beginning, and its analogy in the phenomenal material world is the moon, which is the base of all calculations in connection with the solstices, feasts, sabbaths; and therefore it is that Israel, who belongs to the Holy One, begins the division of time from the various phases and aspects of the moon, symbol of the divine point or unit; and therefore it is written, 'Ye are attached or joined unto the Lord your God' (Deuter 4-4). It is written, 'And God said let the waters bring forth abundantly the moving creature that has life' (Gen. 1-20)."

Said Rabbi Eleazar: "The occult meaning of these words has already been unfolded. They refer to the waters below that signify the lights above, which are both alike fruitful and generative, 'and fowl that may fly above the earth.' Why is it not written, 'who fly?'"

Said Rabbi Simeon: "The esoteric meaning of the word bird refers to the archangel, Michael, as it is written, 'And one of the seraphim flew towards me' (Is. 6-6). The word 'fly' refers occultly to Gabriel, as scripture saith, 'And the man Gabriel which I saw at first in vision, being caused to fly swiftly' (Dan. 9-21). The words 'above the earth' refer to the prophet Elijah who descends from on high, reaches the earth in four flights or steps; of him it is written, 'The spirit of the Lord shall carry thee whither I know not' (Kings 18-12). The first step is indicated by the words 'The spirit of the Lord,' the second by 'shall carry,' the third by 'whither,' and the fourth by 'I know not.' Moreover, the scripture adds, 'in the open firmament of heaven,' referring to the angel of death who, as we learn from tradition, is sometimes on earth and sometimes present in heaven, to seduce and tempt men or accuse them of their misdeeds."

Said Rabbi Abba in reply: "The angel of death was created on the second day, whilst the words just expounded are written of the fifth day. The fact is that the angel Raphael, who is appointed to heal the earth of its evil and affliction and the maladies of mankind, was created on the second day; the words, 'In the open firmament' denote the angel Uriel, as indicated by the words that follow, 'And God created great whales or fishes.'"

Said Rabbi Eleazar, "The words 'great fishes' refer to the seventy rulers appointed to rule over the seventy nations of the world, but the words 'Every living creature that moveth' signify Israel whose souls (nephesh) proceed from 'hahaya' (the living), and therefore is it that in scripture they are termed, 'The only nation or people.' The words, 'Which the waters brought forth abundantly after their kind,' signify those who devote themselves to the study of the secret doctrine. 'And every winged fowl after his kind,' are the righteous in Israel, because they are really 'The living creatures' (living the higher life). Another exposition of these words explains them as referring to the messenger angels sent on earth."

FURTHER KABBALISTIC EXPOSITIONS OF THE SIX DAYS OF CREATION

SAID Rabbi Abba: "'Nephesh hahaya' (living soul) truly denote the souls of Israel. They are the children of the Holy One and holy in his sight, but the souls of the heathen and idolatrous nations whence come they?" Said Rabbi Eleazar: "They emanate from the left side of the sephirotic tree of life, which is the side of impurity, and therefore they defile all that come into contact with them. It is written, 'Let the earth bring forth the living creature after his kind, and creeping thing and beast of the earth after his kind' (Gen. 1-24). Wherefore does the word 'lemina' (after his kind) occur twice? It is to confirm what has just been stated, that the souls of Israel are pure and holy, but the souls of the heathen being impure and unholy are symbolized by the creeping thing and beast of the earth, and therefore, like the foreskin in circumcision, are cut off. It is written also, 'Let us make man in our image and after our likeness,' indicating that in man exist forces and powers coming in all directions from on high, which by 'hochma' (wisdom) will finally attain their culmination within him. The words 'Let us make man' include and contain the mystery of the male and female principles, of which every act and function is effected by supreme wisdom. 'In our image and after our likeness,' denote the dignity of man, as he alone amongst the animal creation is a complete unit in himself and is thus able to rule over all creatures below him. 'And God saw everything that he had made and it was very good.' Here scripture supplies, what was not said of the second day, the term 'good' not being affirmed of it, because on the second day death was created. If it be asked, was it necessary that God should see everything he made before pronouncing it to be good? The answer is that God being omniscient knows all things and to him the past and the future are as the present; the past with its countless generations of men and the future enfolding everything that shall be in the course of ages to come, and this is the meaning involved in the above words, for everything created and made by God cannot but be good. The scripture adds, 'And it was evening and it was morning the sixth day.' Why is it that the definite article is joined to this day and not to the others? Because when the creation of the world was completed and finished, the union of male and female principles was established, through the letter H and therefore it is said, 'The heaven and the earth were finished' (Gen. 2-1), having become harmonious to each other."

Said Rabbi Eleazar: "It is written, 'How great is thy goodness which thou hast laid up for them that fear Thee' (Ps. 31-19). Remark, that the Holy One created and placed man in the world, so that by an upright life and service he might attain to and enjoy the heavenly light that has been laid up for righteous souls, of which it is said from the beginning of the world, 'men have not heard, nor heard by the ear, neither hath the eye seen Oh God! what thou hast prepared for them that trust in Thee' (Is. 64-3). How can we attain unto this heavenly light of the higher life? Only by the study and the knowledge of the secret doctrine, for he only who meditates therein, conforming and fashioning his life to its teachings, attains unto it and becomes regarded as though he had created a world or a new life, as it was by the secret doctrine creation originated and by it still subsists, as it is written, 'The Lord by wisdom (hochma) hath founded the earth and established the heavens by understanding (hinah) (Prov. III-19); and further it is said, 'I was with him as one brought up with him and I was daily his delight, rejoicing always before him' (Prow. 8-30). These words signify that whoever makes the study of the secret doctrine his delight contributes to the welfare and subsistence of the world, for the spirit by which the Holy One created and still sustains the universe is the same that operates in the hearts and minds of all true students of the higher life, as also of young learners. 'How great is Thy goodness' refers to the special good or blessing the Holy One has reserved for them that fear Him, and scripture adds, 'Which Thou hast wrought for them that trust in Thee before children of men.' What is the meaning of the words 'Which Thou hast wrought?' They refer to the work of creation."

Said Rabbi Abba: "They refer also to the Garden of Eden, the Holy One planted on earth after the pattern of the celestial paradise, for the just to dwell therein, and therefore it is written, 'Which Thou hast wrought for them.' There are, therefore, two paradises, one heavenly, the other earthly."

Said Rabbi Simeon: "The scripture certainly speaks of a celestial paradise, and with reference to the words 'before the children or sons of men,' they mean that those who delighted in the worship and service of their Lord will dwell therein. The words, 'The heavens and the earth' denote the written and unwritten or traditional law. 'And all their host' refer to the expositions and commentaries on them, amounting in number to seventy. The words, 'were finished' designate the union of these, the one being complementary to the other. Whilst, 'with all their hosts or constellations' refer to the divers interpretations of these laws, as also to things lawful and non-permissible. 'And on the seventh day God ended his work which he had made,' these words signify the traditional law, which is the foundation of the world. 'The work which he has made'; it is not said, 'all his work,' because the written law which emanated through hochma (wisdom) was not included in it. Therefore is the term 'seventh day' repeated three times, (1) 'And on the seventh day God finished,' (2) 'and God rested on the seventh day,' (3) 'and God blessed the seventh day.' The first has reference to the traditional law, containing the mysteries of creation, the second, the foundation of the world. In the book of Rah Yeba, the aged and venerable, this also refers to the Jubilee and is therefore followed by the words 'from all his works,' for from the second day everything was produced and brought forth. The third expression relates to the high priest who blesses all the world and has the preeminence in all things, as we learn from tradition that in all offerings the high priest receives the principal part."

Said Rabbi Jose, the aged: "The two words, 'seventh day,' denotes the basis of the world and the middle column of the sephirotic tree of life, whilst the words, 'and sanctified' show the place of the temple; as it is written, 'and shew me it and his habitation' (2 Sam. 15-25). Therein reside and abide all the saints above, and thence comes the sweet delicious bread which is the delight of the congregation of Israel, as it is written, 'Out of Asher, his bread shall be fat and be the delight of kings' (Gen, 49-20), signifying that from Asher shall come forth the covenant of peace and the bread of the poor shall become 'lechem panneg' what kings (viz., the congregation of Israel) delight in as a dainty. It is from this abode on high come all joys and delights and everything regarded as Holy and sacred in the world, there 'He hallowed it' (vayikadesh otho), oth here meaning the covenant; 'because in it He rested, 'therefore, on the seventh day, every creature above and below rests also, 'from all his work Asher bra Alhim lausoth, which Alhim created and made.' We know that the injunction 'remember ye' leads to obedience, that the creative work may become perfected, and the meaning of these words is that God created the good law that through study of and obedience to it, man might attain to perfection."

Said Rabbi Simeon: "It is written, 'Who keepeth covenant and mercy with them that love Him and keep His commandments, to a thousand generations' (Deuter 7-9). The words, 'who keepeth' refer to the congregation of Israel, while 'covenant' designated the foundation of the world, but 'mercy' here means Abraham. Thus all the works of God were wrought to be a benefit and blessing to every one of his creatures, above and below, to all souls, together with elementals and demons. If it be said these latter are no blessing to the world, our answer is that every created thing or creature hath its proper use, and this is so with elementals and demons, for they act as the executors of karmic law on criminals and wrong doers and transgressors.

CHAPTER XXV.

REMARK what is said of Solomon, 'And if he act unjustly I will chastise him with the rod of men and with the stripes of the children of men.' (II Sam. vii. 3). What mean the stripes of the children of men? They are the elementals or demons. Furthermore, at the time of the creation of the world and when the sabbath appeared, there were spiritual beings who had not as yet become incarnated in a body. They emanated from the left side and had nothing in common with those that came forth from the right side of the sephirotic tree of life, as they were the residuum of created beings and so are incomplete and undeveloped creatures with out the impress of the divine name before which they quake and tremble and flee away. It should be remembered that every man is incomplete who does not beget and leave a son behind him in the world, and is not impressed with the divine signature of the Holy Name and does not ascend into the vestibule of paradise. Like a tree uprooted and that must be replanted in order to grow and bear fruit, so must he become reincarnated in order to bear the complete Holy Name which is never impressed on anything that is imperfect. Observe also, of these unembodied beings some are in the world above and some in the nether world, and because they are unincarnated they can never accord either with angels or human beings.

"If it be asked, how is it that those above are imperfect seeing they are all pure spirits? the reply is, whether above or below, they are only partially developed owing to their derivation from the left side of the tree of life. Though invisible to man, yet are they continually around and about him for his hurt. They have three things in common with angels and three in common with human beings, as stated before. After the creation and apparition of these imperfect elementals, they remained hidden and concealed in abysmal darkness during the evening and morning of the sabbath, and when it ended they came forth and entered into the world and are now to be found everywhere. In order that mankind might be protected from the assaults of these spirits of the left side, Gehenna with its fire and flame was created. These elemental beings ardently desire to become incarnated, but are unable to do so. We ought therefore to take care and guard and protect ourselves from their influence by use of the prayer in the liturgy for the warding off their afflictions.

"Observe that the canopy of peace was extended over the world as soon as the holy sabbath commenced. What is the canopy of peace? It is the sabbath during which all spirits, demons and elementals, together with foul infernals, go and hide themselves in the great darkness, for when the holiness of the sabbath prevails in the world no unclean spirit is able to endure it and flees from it. Wherefore on the sabbath day there is no necessity for reciting the prayer for protection, 'Blessed be thou, oh Lord, ruler of the universe, who protected thy people Israel . . .' a formula of prayer ordained to be recited during week days because then the world needs protection, but on the sabbath day the canopy of peace is raised and outstretched over the world and thus protected on all sides. Even the wicked in Gehenna are also protected on that day, together with all beings and creatures above and below, and enjoy peace and rest whilst the sabbath lasts. For this reason its holiness is acknowledged in the prayer, 'Blessed be the Lord who covers us, together with all his people Israel and Jerusalem, with the canopy of peace.' But why Jerusalem? Because there it is raised and first pinned up. We ought, therefore, always to pray that it may ever be over us to guard us, as a mother guards and protects her children so that they may live in fear of nothing. Again, at the time when Israel pronounces this benediction and prays for this canopy of peace to rest upon them, the Holy Spirit descends from on high and covers them as a bird its young, with its wings. Then flee and depart all evil spirits out of the world and Israel abides safe under the protection of its Lord. Also it is then that this 'canopy of peace' or the Holy Spirit imparts to each of its children new souls or a new life. Why? Because it is the lord and giver of life which emanates from it."

CHAPTER XXVI.

SAID Rabbi Simeon: "Furthermore, we learn that the Sabbath is an image of the world to come; and so it is, for the sabbatical year is a type of the year of Jubilee. The new life which is imparted during the sabbath is hinted in the word zacor (remember), and when it enters into the soul of man, joy and gladness prevail throughout the world, everything ungodly and profane becomes banished and sorrow and sighing are done away; as it is written, 'In that day the Lord shall give rest from thy sorrow and from thy fear and from the hard bondage wherein thou wast made to serve' (Is. xiv. 3). On the Sabbath evening, therefore, ought everyone to eat of the different articles of food that have been prepared, symbolizing thereby the universal canopy of peace which includes under its cover everyone, if there be no encroachment on the food prepared for the morrow. The lighting of the Sabbath candle is devolved on the wives of the holy people, the reason of which is that as by a woman the heavenly light became extinguished, so by woman must it be made to reappear. Another and more important reason is, the canopy of peace signifies the Matronutha of the world, or the Holy Spirit whose emblem is a woman, whose expressed desire it is that a woman should be charged with lighting the Sabbath candle, as being not only an honor, but a great benefit for the procreating of good and holy children who shall become as lights in the world and distinguished for their knowledge of the secret doctrine. By it, wives will obtain long life for their husbands and will also become sources of light and instruction in their household and marital duties. Remark also that the Sabbath consists of a day and a night. The words 'remember' and 'keep' have one and the same meaning as it is written, 'remember the Sabbath day to hallow it' and also 'keep the Sabbath day and hallow it' (Deuter v. 12). The words zacor (remember), shemor (keep), referring to the male and female considered as a whole. Blessed the lot of Israel whose hospitality the Holy One deigns to accept and enter into the place they provide for Him! As it is written, 'Happy the people who enjoy these blessings! happy the people whose God is the Lord'" (Ps. cxliv. 15).

Said Rabbi Simeon: "It is written, 'God understandeth the way thereof and He knoweth the place thereof' (Job xxviii. 23), What signify the words, 'God understandeth? . . .' They have the same esoteric meaning as the words

'And the rib which the Lord God had taken from man, mode be a woman' (Gen. ii, 22), which have reference to the oral law designated by the term 'way,' as it is written, 'Thus saith the Lord who maketh a way in the sea' (Is. xliii. 16), but the words 'He knoweth the place where it is' refer to the written law, which is designated by the word daath (knowledge). The name Jehovah Alhim is here written in full to show that the oral or traditional is the complement of the written law. These when combined are sometimes termed hochma (wisdom), and sometimes binah (understanding). They are also symbolized by the combined divine name, Jehovah Alhim (Lord God). The rib taken from the side of man refers to the non-luminous mirror or light of human intellect, as it is written, 'But on mine adversity (or rib) they rejoiced and gathered themselves against me' (Ps. xxxv. 15).

"The words 'had taken from man' signify that the tradition proceeded, from the written law; 'made he a woman and brought her unto the man,' mean that these two kinds of law must of necessity be united together, as they cannot exist apart, the one supplying what the other lacks. These words also refer to the attachment of man and his wife that should always subsist between them. Another interpretation of the words 'God understandeth the way thereof' is, that as long as a daughter abides with her mother she is the object of maternal care, but when married it becomes her duty to look after the needs and wants of her husband, and therefore it is added 'and he knoweth the place where she dwells.'

"It is written, 'And He formed man.' In these words is expressed the mystery of the formation of man from the right and left sides of the sephirotic tree of life. Man was composed of two natures, the animal or lower self and the spiritual or higher self, and this because the former is necessary to the development of the latter. It is the lower nature of man that excites the female principle. It is a tradition that the north that symbolizes the evil principles seeks attachment with the female and therefore is she called ishah, a term compounded of two words, ash (fire, man) and H, signifying the yoni or female principle. The higher and lower self cannot become united and harmonized so long as sexuality and carnal desire are dominant. The term man has already been explained, that at first it designated androgynous man, but afterwards became sundered and separated.

"We will now explain further the esoteric meaning of the phrase, 'the dust of the earth.' When a woman marries she takes the name of her husband, therefore is he called ish and she ishah. He is designated zedek and she zedek, also he is described as ophar and zeb, she as ophar and zabiah; as it is written, 'The glory (Zebi) of all lands' (Ezek. xx. 15). It is written, 'Thou shalt not plant thee a grove of any trees near unto the altar of the Lord thy God' (Deut. xvi. 21).

"Is it not permissible to plant groves in any places not contiguous to the altar of God? In reply we say that the word ascher (groves) designates the husband and ascherah, the wife; as it is written, 'Bring forth out of the temple of the Lord an the vessels that were made for Baal (husband) and for ascherah (wife). The esoteric explanation of these words is this: the altar designates her, the Schekina, or divine spouse, and therefore it is forbidden to raise or build any other altar and present a spouse to God beside it. Note that the worshippers of the sun are termed worshippers of Baal, but the adorers of the moon, the adorers of Ascherah.

"The wife is called ascherah, derived from the word ascher, designating her husband. Why then are not they used any longer to distinguish a man and his wife, and also the celestial husband and spouse? Because the word ascherah comes from asher in the same sense as found in the words, 'And Leah said, Happy am I, for the daughters will call me blessed, and she called his name Asher' (Gen. xxx. 13). Now the altar of God on the earth is not honored and blessed by heathen nations, but despised, therefore the terms Ascher and Ascherah are not longer applied to the altar symbolizing the celestial husband and spouse, nor to a man and his wife; and this is the signification of the words, 'Thou shalt not plant the ascherah near the altar,' that is thou shalt not present to God any other spouse than the legitimate one, the altar of Adamah (earth), as it is written, 'An altar of earth shalt thou make unto me' (Ex. xx, 24).

"It is also written, 'And breathed into his nostrils the breath of life,' meaning that the earth was then made fruitful as is the female by the male, for it is animated with life-giving principles and force. Furthermore, man is endowed with a two-fold nature and thus able to develop the lower self, by which his earthly frame is animated. 'And the rib which the Lord God had taken from man, made he a woman.' The full divine name Jehovah Alhim is here used, and are the father and the mother who prepared her and brought her unto the man. The word 'rib' denotes the mystery expressed in the words, 'I am dark, but comely as the tents of Kedar and as the curtains of Solomon' (Cant. i. 5); for before marriage a woman resembles the non-luminous mirror, that becomes radiated after the marital union for which her father and mother have prepared her, and so the scripture adds, 'and brought her unto the man' from which we infer that the duty of the parents of a bride is to give her into the keeping and care of her husband according as it is written, 'I gave my daughter unto this man for wife' (Deuter xxii. 16). From that time she goes with her husband into his house that is now hers, and it is his duty to consult with her on all matters appertaining to domestic affairs. Therefore it is written, 'And he lighted upon a certain place and tarried there all night, because the sun was set' (Gen. xxviii. 11), meaning that Jacob took the permission he enjoyed: and therefore from these words we infer that the conjugal union should be the result of consent and permission on the part of the wife after listening to her husband's voice of loving affection. If, however, there be no feeling of reciprocation, no conjunction ought to take place, for conjugality should always be voluntary and unaccompanied with unwillingness. 'And he tarried there all night for the sun was set,' teaching that conjugal duties should always be nocturnal. 'And he took up the stones of that place and put them for his pillow,' meaning that though a king possesses golden couches and fine robes, he prefers the bed prepared by his beloved spouse, though composed of stones; as it is written, 'And he laid down in that place to sleep.'

"Note what is further written. 'And Adam said, this is now bone of my bone and flesh of my flesh' (Gen. ii. 23). These were the words of Adam to draw Eve unto him and incline her to enter into nuptial union and thus show that they are one and now undivided and unseparate in a higher sense than before. Then he begins to praise her that there is none like unto her, that she surpasses all other beings, the one deserving the name of woman; as it is written, 'She shall be called woman, words that pleased her,' as it is written, 'Many daughters have done virtuously, but thou excellest them all' (Prov. xxxi. 29). 'Therefore shall a man leave his father and his mother and cleave unto his wife and they shall be one flesh' (Gen. ii. 24). That is to say that Eve was induced by these loving words of Adam to consent to enter into marital relationship with him and as soon as this was effected we read, 'Now the serpent was subtle' (Gen. iii. 7). In the moment that Adam and Eve became thus associated, the lower nature became excited and aroused by sexual desire in which it delights, as scripture saith, 'And when the woman saw that the tree was good for food she took of the fruit of it and did eat' (Gen. iii. 6), denoting that hitherto their love had been angelic and pure, but was now changed into carnal desire first arising in the woman and leading them to conjugal relationship, for a woman is the inspirer of love whilst man is the receptacle of it and in this resembles angelic beings whose actions are determined by pure love unblended and unmingled with carnal desire."

Said Rabbi Eleazar: "How can this be, will the lower nature with its passions and emotion remain attached to the female on high?"

CHAPTER XXVII.

RABBI SIMEON answered and said: "The lower or passionate nature is always striving to imitate the actions of the higher, with this difference, that what is spiritual and pure it changes into the carnal and impure. The higher nature takes its origin from the right side of the sephirotic tree of life, but the lower from the left side, and is embodied in the female and becomes unified in it, as it is written, 'His left hand is under my head and his right hand doth embrace me' (Cant. ii. 6). Hitherto we have discoursed on a subject, exceedingly esoteric and unknown to ordinary minds, but now we will speak more clearly so that every one may comprehend and understand them." On hearing this the student novitiates expressed their great desire to learn more of this mystery of sex.

Rabbi Simeon was journeying to Tiberias and there were with him, Rabbi Jose, Rabbi Jehuda, and Rabbi Hiya. Whilst on the way, they beheld Rabbi Pinchus coming to meet them. After exchanging greetings, they all sat down under a great shady tree by a hillside.

Then said Rabbi Pinchus: "Since now I have met with thee, oh Rabbi Simeon, and am seated by thy side, let it please thee to instruct me further in the Secret Doctrine."

Then spake Rabbi Simeon and said: "It is written, 'and he went on his journeys from the south even to Bethel unto the place where his tent had been at the beginning between Bethel and Hai' (Gen. xiii. 3). The scripture saith, 'He went on his journeys' instead of 'his journey.' Wherefore? Because there is here an occult reference not only to his own journeying, but also that of the Schekina, who always went with Jacob, and therefore we learn that whenever a man leaves his home and wife, he ought not to think or imagine that the Schekina forsakes him in any way, for though it has been said a man ought always to cleave to his wife that the Schekina may always be with him, yet it is possible he may go alone on a journey and the Schekina still abide with him, and when so doing he ought to direct his prayer to the Holy One that this may be, and in this way the male and female will always be associated in union with each other, whether going from home or otherwise. Therefore it is written, 'The Just One shall walk before him and set him in the way of his steps' (Ps. lxxxv. 14). Whenever anyone goes on a journey, he should always be mindful and circumspect and careful of his words and actions, in order that his lower and higher selves may not become separated and disunited from each other, so that when he returns home their union may be intact and complete. This ought also to be the case when a man returns home, for then he should attend to the discharge of his conjugal duties which is lawful and right and a source of delight both to the Schekina and his spouse; as it is written, 'and thou shalt know that thy tabernacle shall be in peace and thou shalt visit thy habitation and thou shalt not sin' (Job v. 24). When, however, he neglects these duties, he transgresses against the divine ordinance. On the other hand, by attending to them, his enjoyment is enhanced by the knowledge that he is carrying out his charging, the dictates of the marital law, which is known as the covenant of the Holy One.

The occult meaning of these remarks is this: that followers and students of the good law should always, in the discharge of their conjugal duties, fix their minds and thoughts upon the Schekina that never quits or leaves the house on account of the spouse; as it is written, 'and Isaac brought Rebecca into the tent of Sarah, his mother' (Gen. xxiv. 67). Now we learn from tradition that when this occurred, a candle was lighted in a very marvellous manner, because at the same moment the Schekina entered into the tent along with Rebecca,--the mystical meaning of which, is, that showers of blessings from on high descend on the right discharge of conjugal duties, for then the male and female become truly one and not till then, and the male becomes associated both with the Schekina or heavenly mother and his spouse; to which the words refer, 'They shall endure until the desire of the everlasting hills be accomplished' (Gen. xlix. 26). The word ad (desire) designates the pleasure all men experience in becoming united with the Schekina above in order to attain unto perfection and the blessing resulting therefrom, and also with his spouse who receives from him her nourishment and affection.

Again Rabbi Simeon spake and said: "The secret doctrine and its teaching have relation to two baith (houses), or more explicitly the human and divine, the lower and higher self, as it is written, 'for the two houses of Israel' (Is. viii. 14). Of these one is a mystery beyond human comprehension, the other, though exceedingly occult, is within the range of the understanding. The first is symbolized by the Great Voice mentioned in

(Deuter v. 20). 'The Great Voice that ceaseth not,' that is always resounding and speaking within us though unheard and unrecognized by the external ear. By it hath been delivered and spoken the esoteric teachings known as 'the voice of Jacob' that they may become known. Now this great interior voice and the word which expresses it are as it were two houses, the one visible, the other invisible. One is the eternal Wisdom (hochma ilaah) hidden and concealed in the divine mind and sendeth forth the great interior voice; the other the Voice of Jacob or esoteric teachings expressed by words, especially by the term Brashith, or as it may be differently written and explained by the words baith reshith, meaning the house or doctrine called reshith or beginning."

Pausing for a few minutes, Rabbi Simeon began again discoursing: "The scriptures beginning with the words, bra Alhim, the mystical meaning of which is the same as is contained in the words vyeben Jehovah Alhim ath azla (the Lord God formed the rib). The mystic signification also of the words, ath hashamayin (the heavens), is the same as vayebah al ha-Adam (and brought her unto the man). The words ve-eth ha-aretz (and the earth) also have the same occult meaning, atzm matzmi, (bone of my bone)."

Said Rabbi Simeon: "It is written, 'The Lord said unto my Lord, sit thou on my right hand until I make thine enemies thy footstool' (Ps. ex. 1). These words refer to the Supreme, saying to Adonai next in being to Him, 'sit thou on my right hand, that the West may become joined to the East, the right to the left, so that the power and might of the idolatrous nations (or evil) may not prevail, but become broken and dissipated. 'The Lord said unto my Lord,' have also the same signification as 'Jacob said unto the Lord' as is seen in the words, 'the ark of the covenant, the Lord of all the earth' (Josh. iii. 11). Another exposition of the words 'the Lord said unto my Lord' is, that they are significant of the holy state called 'the year of Jubilee' addressing the state called 'the Sabbatical year,' saying, 'sit thou on my right!' Observe that this latter holy state or condition of the world, namely, Sabbatical year, has not from the beginning yet become united to the highest sephira on the right and left, who at the creation of the world took it then and joined it to its left side. For this reason, the world will not last or endure beyond seven thousand years. At the end of that period, however, this state of holiness in the world will become joined to the supreme sephira on the right hand and the earth then will become perfected forever. Then will be realized the words, 'The new heavens and the new earth which I will make shall remain before me or exist always' (Is. lxvi. 22). If this exposition be correct, what then is the sense of the words 'sit thou on my right hand?' They were spoken provisionally to Adonai 'until his enemies were made his footstool'; that is, until all opposition and disobedience to the divine law shall cease and peace and harmony prevail throughout the universe, when all antinomies and antithesis of right and left, good and evil, angel and demon, shall be done away and the knowledge of the Lord shall cover the earth as the waters cover the seas, and heaven and earth so long separated and disjoined shall become one and united forevermore, which glorious consummation is implied in the conjunction of the words, 'the heavens and the earth.'"

RABBI SIMEON'S ANALOGIES OF THE DIVINE LIFE IN MAN

AS Rabbi Simeon ceased speaking the students rose up to depart, but ere they left he himself stood up and said: "I have still a few further remarks to make before going, on two passages of scripture, which seemingly are somewhat contradictory in expression to each other. The first is, 'The Lord thy God is a consuming fire' (Deuter iv. 24); the other is, 'but ye that cleaved unto the Lord your God are alive every one of you this day'" (Deuter. iv. 4).

"If the Lord be a consuming fire as here stated, how could the children of Israel on becoming joined unto the Lord escape from being consumed, and continue to lived? It has been explained how the Divine Being is a fire that consumes every other kind of fire, for there are flames of fire more intense in their nature than others. To this statement I wish to add a few supplementary remarks. Whoever wishes to understand the mystery of union with the Divine will do well to reflect and meditate upon the flame proceeding from a lighted candle or a burning coal, in which may be recognized two kinds of flame or light, one white and the other dark or bluish in color. The white flame ascends upwards in a straight line, the dark or blue part of the flame, being below it and forming its basis. Though these be conjoined together, the white flame is always seen clearly and distinctly, and of the two is the most valuable and precious. From these observations we may gather somewhat of the occult meaning of the thekheloth (blue fringes) mentioned in scripture. The dark or blue flame is connected and conjoined with that above it, namely, the white, and also below it with the candle or coal in a state of combustion. It becomes sometimes red, whilst the superior white flame never varies in color and remains invariably the same. Furthermore, it is noticeable that the dark or blue flame consumes and wastes the substance of the coal or candle whence it emanates, but the white pure light consumes nothing and never varies. Therefore, when Moses proclaimed the Lord to be a consuming fire, he alludes to the astral fluid or flame that consumes everything similar to the dark flame that wastes and destroys the substance of the candle or coal. In using the term thy God, not our God, Moses refers to the white or

Divine light which destroys nothing, in which he himself had been and came down from Mount Sinai out of it uninjured and intact. This is the case with everyone who lives in the Divine light of the higher life. He lives, then, the true or real life, and the astral light of the lower earthly life cannot harm or injure him. Therefore, to the children of Israel who had sanctified themselves and attained to this life, Moses could truly say: 'ye cleaved unto the Lord, your God, and are alive as at this time.' Above the white flame there is yet another arising out of it, yet unseen and unrecognizable by human sight and has reference to the greatest of mysteries, dim gleamings and notions of which are revealed to us by the different flames of a lighted candle or a burning coal."

As Rabbi Simeon ceased speaking, Rabbi Pinchus embraced him, exclaiming: "The Lord be praised! the Merciful One, who has led me hither." Rabbi Simeon, along with his students, went and accompanied Rabbi Pinchus on his journey for three leagues, and then bidding him adieu returned homewards.

CHAPTER XXIX.

SAID Rabbi Simeon: What I have discoursed on has reference to the secret doctrine and its teachings of the mystery of the divine wisdom united with the divine essence. Thus the final H in the tetragramma-ton corresponds to the dark or blue flame united with the three letters preceding it, I H V, making the white flame a light. Sometimes the dark is designated by the letter D, and other times by H. When Israel below is not living the divine life, it is characterized by D; but when it becomes con-joined with the white light, then it takes on itself the letter H; as it is written, 'If a damsel, a virgin, be betrothed' (Deuter. xxii-23). The word Naarah (damsel) is here written without the feminine termination H contrary to grammatical rule, naar being the male and naarah the female. Wherefore is it so written? Because she has not as yet come into union with the union with the male, and whenever this is the case the final H is found wanting. For a similar reason the dark or blue flame is designated by the letter Daleth, or D. When, however, it becomes conjoined with the white flame above it, it is represented by the letter He or H, for then a perfect union is effected in this sense, that the two become blended together (symbolizing thus the union of the lower and higher nature).

"Similar is the occult meaning of the smoke ascending from altars whereon sacrifices are offered up. It provokes into flame the blue light beneath it which, when it flashes forth and burns, becomes conjoined with the white flame above it and then as in the flame of a candle becomes or forms one whole and perfect light, and as it is the nature of the blue flame to consume that from which it emanates so does it consume the sacrifices placed on the altar; as it is written, 'When the fire of the Lord fell and consumed the burnt sacrifice' (I Kings, xviii-38). From the appearance of a perfect light or flame we may gather that the blue and white portions of it have become united into a whole when the grease of the sacrifices and burnt offerings has been consumed and then priests, levites, and all the rest of Israel becoming united with it join in the singing and chanting of hymns and psalms, and the world above and the world below are again united and blended as the flame of a candle and become blessed in the one great Divine Light of the universe. Such is the mystical meaning of the words: 'But ye that cleaved unto the Lord your God are alive,--every one of you--this day.' But wherefore doth scripture say 'but you' (veathem) and not 'you' (athem)? It is to show that whilst the sacrifices are consumed as soon as the blue flames touch them, yet Israel (living the divine life) though attached to it is not consumed, but are preserved in life unto this day.

"All colors seen in dreams are of good omen, except blue; because, as in the flame, we have observed it consumes and destroys the body beneath it. It is the upas or deadly tree that overshadows the world, and is lethal to everything beneath it. If it be objected that there are angelic beings on high who, along with mankind are equally under the blue flame and yet are not consumed, our reply is that they, as existent beings, are celestial in their essence and, therefore, different from human existences who are to the blue flame what the candle is to the light.

"In space there are forty-five divisions or directions, each of which is distinguished by different colors. The seven colors of the white light penetrate the seven abysses, and by the effect of their vibrations upon the rocks therein, cause water to flow forth, which is an allotrophic form of the air contained in the white light; light and darkness are really the producers of air and water according as the essential part or element of matter unites with one or the other. Light in passing from its primal state descends into this material world through sixty-five channels or avenues through which, when it courses, a voice is heard that makes the abysses tremble and shake, exclaiming, "Oh, matter! let light pass through thee!" as it is written, 'deep calleth unto deep at the noise of thy waterspouts (or channels)' (Ps. xlii-8). Below these there are three hundred and sixty-five smaller channels or rivulets, some of which in their color are white, some dark and others red. Each of these rivulets, of which there are seventeen, as it meanders in its course, resembles a rose in its outlines with its layers of petals. Of these rivulets rose-like in form, two are like streams of iron and two, like copper. On the right and left of them, in the eastern and western quarters of the world, are two thrones connected and communicating with each other by means of these intermediate rivulets and channels. These thrones form each of them a heaven, that on the right being dark colored and that on the left being variegated in hue. As the light passes from one to the other throne through the various channels between them, it becomes more powerful and stronger in its circulatory course, similar to the blood in the veins of the body. Such is the region on high that gives rise to the seven different colors which, in their totality and blending, constitute the great mystery of that unknown something termed light. There are also seven other different colored lights, which, on flowing together and thus becoming blended, form one great ocean of light which then streams forth from its seven different outlets; as it is written, 'and he shall smite it in its seven streams' (Is. xi-15.). Each of the seven outlets or streams becomes divided and forms into seven reservoirs, and each of these into the source or fount of seven rivers and which subdivide again and form seven brooklets; thus forming a vast circulatory system by which the waters of each separate and then meet again and become blended together."

THE TWO SERPENTS, ASTRAL FLUID AND THE ANIMAL NATURE

"A great fish coming from the left swims through all these waterways to poison and corrupt them. Its scales are as steel. From its mouth comes forth a lurid flame and its tongue is like a sharp sword. Its object is to force its way into the sanctuary of the great ocean to pollute and defile it and thus extinguish light, and causing the waters to become frozen, and the great circulatory water system may cease to operate.

"The occult meaning of this mystery is expressed in the words of scripture, 'Now the serpent was more subtle than any beast of the field which the Lord God had made,' (Gen. iii-6). This evil serpent wished to accomplish his aim by first corrupting the brooklets below (mankind) and making them impure and bitter, so that flowing back to the great ocean their fountain head, it might become polluted. This is why he first seduced man and brought death into the world and entered into the heart of man from the left side. "There is, however, another serpent that comes from the right. These two serpents are they that are closely attached to man during his lifetime (the astral fluid and animal nature), as scripture saith, 'of all the beasts of the field that the Lord God had made,' these two are the most cunning, crafty and subtle in tempting and destroying man. Woe unto him who allows himself to be led on and seduced by the serpent, for death irretrievable is his doom, physically, morally and spiritually, both to himself and to those associated with him, as in the case of Adam who wished to know and become expert in nature's secrets and occult science. In revealing them and exciting within him a fictitious joy and happiness, the serpent acquired that influence and control over Adam that contributed to and brought his ruin and downfall and thus caused him to suffer, as also his successors. From the day that Israel came to the foot of Mount Sinai, the impurity and corruption wrought by the serpent has not disappeared from the world.

"Hear what saith scripture when Adam and Eve ate of the fruit of the tree by which death entered into their souls or lower nature, 'And when they heard the voice of the Lord of the Alhim walking in the garden' (Gen. iii-8), or, as it ought to be rendered, had walked (mithhalech). Note further that whilst Adam had not fallen, he was a recipient of divine wisdom (hochma) and heavenly light and derived his continuous existence from the Tree of Life to which he had free access, but as soon as he allowed himself to be seduced and deluded with the desire of occult knowledge, he lost everything, heavenly light and life through the disjunction of his higher and lower self, and, the loss of that harmony that should always exist between them, in short, he then first knew what evil was and what it entailed, and, therefore, it is written, 'Thou art not a God that approveth wickedness, neither shall evil dwell with thee' (Is. v-5); or, in other words, he who implicitly and blindly follows the dictates of his lower nature or self shall not come near the Tree of Life.

"Whilst the protoplasts had not as yet lost their innocence and purity, they heard within themselves the voice divine, the voice out of the Great Silence. Guided and directed by divine wisdom, they walked and lived in the divine light and were not afraid. As soon, however, as they succumbed to temptation, they lapsed into a state of sin, of sorrow and shame and found that though the voice was still audible, they could not endure to hear it; and the sense of sin pervaded and prevailed throughout the world up to the time when Israel stood at the foot of Mount Sinai, purified from all defilement and thus able to become conjoined with the Tree of Life, and partook of its fruits, beholding the celestial glory. They ascended higher and higher in the divine life, and lived in the enjoyment of the Beatific Vision being filled with that interior peace and tranquillity known and experienced only by those who understand the mysteries of the higher and divine life. The Holy One protected them by impressing upon them his divine name, so that the spirit of evil was unable to exercise power and influence over them and thus corrupt them. Thus they lived, pure and protected, until they bowed down and worshipped the golden calf. Then fell they from their high estate and lost the divine protection which was as a cuirasse or coat of mail against the assaults of evil that now again acquired power over them and brought death unto their souls.

"After their fall, scripture informs us, 'and when Aaron and all the children of Israel saw Moses, behold, his face shone radiant with light, and they were afraid to come nigh unto him (Ex. xxxiv-30). Before this, however, it is written, 'and Israel saw the mighty hand of the Lord'; that is, they were able by the purification of the lower nature and mental and spiritual illumination, to attain unto the Beatific Vision and view the splendor and glory of the life on high. And so it is further written, 'and the people saw the thunderings and lightnings, and the sound of the trumpet' (Ex. xx-13). All these glories, however, departed from them after their lapse into sin, so that they could not even endure to behold and regard the luminous face of their intercessor Moses, for, as it is said, 'they were afraid to come nigh into him.'

"Remark, now, what is further stated, 'and the children of Israel stripped themselves of their ornaments by the Mount Horeb' (Ex. xxxiii-6), (Horeb here meaning Sinai). By which is signified, that Israel, after sinning, became divested of their safeguards, the ornaments of purity and integrity, and thus fell under the power of evil. So that, as is stated, 'Moses was compelled to take the tabernacle and set it up away without the camp and called it the Tabernacle of the Congregation' (Ex. xxxiii-7). For what reason?

A FURTHER SYMPOSIUM OF RABBI SIMEON'S STUDENTS

RABBI ELEAZAR and Rabbi Abba differed widely in their opinions on this subject. Rabbi Eleazar maintained that the tabernacle of the congregation (moed) was so called because it was a source of blessing to the children of Israel; that as the day of the new moon is called a feast day symbolizing the decrease of impurity and the increase of purity, so it betokened that the serpent or evil principle had now no power to corrupt and pollute. Rabbi Abba, on the contrary, asserted that it was an indication of evil. At first the sanctuary was simply called the tabernacle, as it is written, "Thine eyes shall see Jerusalem a quiet habitation, a taber-nacle that shall not be taken down, not one of the stakes thereof shall ever be removed (Is. xxxiii-20). From which words we gather that the tabernacle was intended to remain and abide always a source of eternal life to mankind by abolishing death on the soul (or lower nature). But after Israel had sinned, this tabernacle was termed moed, a word denoting a certain or fixed time, as it is written, "I know that thou wilt bring me to death, and to the house (moed) appointed for all living" (Job xxx-23). From that time the tabernacle ceased to be the source of eternal or divine life. Temporal life and blessings were all it could impart. At first it was like the full moon, but after Israel sinned it became like the moon in its fall and therefore from that time was termed by Moses, tabernacle of moed, that is, a temporary erection.

Rabbi Simeon was silently meditating throughout the whole night on the secret doctrine, and Rabbi Jehuda, Rabbi Isaac and Rabbi Jose were seated near him. Said Rabbi Jehuda: "It is written, 'And the children of Israel stripped themselves of their ornaments by the mount Horeb' (Ex. xxxiii-6). Tradition states that Israel after sinning became subject to death and to the power of the evil serpent. How came it then that Joshua died, who had not sinned with Israel, being at the time with Moses on Mount Sinai. Why, therefore was he not exempt from dying?"

Said Rabbi Simeon in reply: "It is written, 'The Lord is just and He loveth righteousness, His countenance doth behold the upright' (Ps. xi-7). These words have already been explained, but there is yet another and more significant exposition of their meaning. Through his justice the Holy One is called just and, knowing that his law is just, mankind directs its way in accordance therewith. Note that the holy One judges every man only according to his deeds. When Adam transgressed by taking of the tree of good and evil, he caused death to appear in the world. His disobedience resulted also in separation from his wife, and the light of the moon became diminished (or, his intellect became darkened). When, however, Israel stood at the foot of Mount Sinai, this defection of the moon's light ceased it shone again in all its former power and brilliance. After sinning by the worship of the golden calf, the moon again lost its light and the evil serpent regained its influence and power in the world. Perceiving that Israel had fallen and lost that purity and innocence that were its protection from the power of the evil one, and that sin would again prevail in the world as in the ease with Adam after his fall, Moses became eager to transfer the tabernacle from amongst the children of Israel and set it up outside and away from the camp. Now if the sin of Adam caused death to enter the world so that no man can escape it, this also was the case with the fall of Israel. Death appeared a second time; so that Joshua though himself pure and unspotted from sin, had along with the rest to succumb to it. With respect to Moses, his death was not due to the sin of Adam but was brought about through the operation of a mysterious power. Tradition confirms this statement which is corroborated by scripture, 'but a young man, son of Nun, who served him, departed not out of the tabernacle' (Ex. xxxiii-11); the explicit signification of which is, that Joshua, though he did not escape physical death, enjoyed that union of the higher and lower natures that enabled him to live the higher and divine life, which the children of Israel through their idolatry and worship of the golden calf had lost and forfeited. Observe also that when Adam fell he lost the protection of the letters of the divine name that the Holy One had impressed upon him, and therewith also the spiritual and divine light in which he had lived, and recognizing this he was overwhelmed with fear and terror, for he perceived himself naked and despoiled of the heavenly glory and bliss he had formerly enjoyed and that he had brought by his disobedience, death, not only upon himself but also upon his posterity throughout all ages. It is written, 'And they sewed fig leaves together and made of them coverings' (Gen. iii. 7). These words have already been discoursed on; what they really signify is that Adam and Eve became attached and subject to the influence of worldly pleasures and sought through them the happiness they had lost, as before stated. By this material or physical enjoyment the stature of

Adam became diminished a hundred cubits and caused a division between the world above and the world below.

"It is further written, 'And He drove out the man' (Gen. iii. 24). Said Rabbi Eleazer. We do not know who drove him out, nor who it was that was driven out, whether the Holy One or not. The words are 'vaigaresh ath' (and he drove out ath). Who was this He? The scripture says 'ha-adam' (the man). After sinning it was Adam who drove out here below who is here called 'ath.' Therefore Scripture first informs us the Lord God drove Adam from out of the garden of Eden, as he had already driven away the 'ath' (the Holy Spirit or Higher Self) when Eden became closed to him, and the path leading to it obliterated or hidden. Scripture, moreover, states, 'and he placed at the east of the garden of Eden, Cherubim and a flaming sword which turned every way to keep the way of the tree of life.' These words allude to angels appointed to chastise the sins and transgressions of man. Numberless are the various forms under which they appear. At times they take on them the male or female human form. Again their aspect is similar to flaming fire, and at other times it is impossible to define or describe their manifestations. Their duty and office is to keep the way of the tree of life and prevent man from acquiring and adding to that occult knowledge which has brought him or resulted in so great misery and misfortune. By a flaming sword is denoted those angels who are charged with casting fire upon the heads of the wicked and wrongdoers. They differ in form and power according to the deeds of those upon whom they inflict penalties for their violation of the great law of right and justice; therefore they are termed in Scripture 'lahat' (the flaming sword), as it is also written, 'For there shall come a day that shall burn as an oven all the proud, and all that do wickedly shall then be as stubble, and the day that cometh shall burn (lihat) them up' (Mal. iv. 1). The word sword also denotes the divine sword or sword of the Lord, as it is written. 'The sword of the Lord is filled with blood'" (Is. xxxiv. 6).

Said Rabbi Jehuda: "The flaming sword denotes all those angels or elementals who tempt and corrupt men through their thoughts, desires and affections so that they fall into sin and forsake the path of righteousness. It is notable that as soon as anyone sins he falls under the power and influence of the evil spirit or elemental that has succeeded in seducing him, and becomes filled with fear and terror and horrid despair, and thus unable to resist and overcome. Solomon was endowed with much wisdom and had acquired a vast amount of occult knowledge, and the Holy One had exalted him to be a king amongst men and to be regarded with awe and reverence by everyone. On his giving way and becoming the slave of desire, he fell under the power of these evil spirits who divested and disrobed him of all his intellectual gifts and endowments, so that he feared and trembled before them and thus became an illustrative example of the misery and unhappiness of those who swerve from the right path by giving way to tempting desires and animal or carnal propensities and inclinations. Through his affections and desires, his passions and emotions, man incurs the greatest danger to himself; only by acquiring power of self-restraint and self-control is he able to achieve self-conquest and thus overcome and successfully resist the power and influence of the tempter, or regulate the currents within himself of the astral fluid or life principle 'coloro che sanno' which by occultists is termed the great serpent. At the moment of death the body becomes by this evil serpent defiled and corruption begins, also they who touch it, as the Scripture saith, 'Whosoever toucheth the dead body of a man, and purifieth not himself by washing of water, defileth the tabernacle of the Lord and that soul shall be cut off from Israel.' (Num. xix. 13.). Observe that every one that retires to sleep upon his bed at night experiences more or less a foretaste of death whilst he sleeps, and night overshadows the world. It is then that the evil spirit is present to defile and corrupt, and therefore on rising, the hands should first of all be washed before touching anything lest it becomes defiled likewise. The greatest care should therefore be exercised at all times in order to avoid and escape from the serpent's impurities. By so doing he will nullify the ill effects accruing therefrom and render himself proof against them. This liability of defilement will not however endure forever, as the day will dawn when the Holy One will cleanse and banish it out of the world, as it is written, 'And I will cause the unclean spirit to pass out of the land.' (Zach. xiii. 2), and, 'he shall swallow up death forever.'" (Is. xxv. 8).

"'And Adam knew Eve, his wife, and she conceived and bare Cain' (Gen. iv. 1) said Rabbi Abba, 'It is written, "Who knoweth the spirit of man that goeth upward and the spirit of a beast that goeth downward to the earth."' (Eccles. iii. 21). As the teachings of the secret doctrine, so these words that have already been dwelt on, have many different meanings, amounting in all to seventy, and all equally good and of great interest and profit to those who are able to grasp and understand them. Observe that when a man walks in the path of truth and light, a pure and holy spirit from on high becomes his interior guide (his Higher Self) educates and makes him receptive of the divine life and its purity, from which he never afterwards is separated. When, however, anyone walks in the way of evil and wrongdoing, he draws to himself those elemental spirits who originate from the left side of the sephirotic tree of life and whose delight is in making him as impure as themselves. Therefore it is written, 'Ye shall not make your souls unclean with them, that ye should be defiled thereby.' (Lev. xi. 43). Observe also that the son of him who is guided by the Holy Spirit in him does it likewise dwell as a friend and guide from his birth to the end of his life, as it is written, 'Be ye holy as I am holy' (Lev. vi. 7). He who is evil and delights in wrongdoing engenders children like unto himself and the end of them will be the same as his own. This is then the meaning of the words, 'Who knoweth the spirit of man who goeth upward and the spirit of a beast that goeth downward.' The Divine who (mi) alone knoweth the souls who incarnate, whether in pure or impure bodies, and therefore whether they will ascend or descend. Adam in himself having become impure before conjugal union with Eve his offspring was therefore impure, but Abel begotten in a state of purity after repentance was consequently pure. Thus we learn why the two brothers, Cain and Abel, were so dissimilar in nature and character."

Said Rabbi Eleazar: "The probable cause of their great dissimilarity of nature arose from coitions of the being termed the serpent, and Adam with Eve who thus brought forth two sons, one of which, Cain, was from an impure, the other, Abel, from a pure progenitor; hence the difference in their lives and actions. As Cain was the issue from the death angel, he killed his brother who issued from the right side of the tree of life. And through him has come all the evil generations of demons and elementals now in the world."

Said Rabbi Jose: "The name of Cain is derived from 'qina' (a nest), showing that he was the nest or origin whence came forth the evil beings before and after making his offering unto the Lord, as it is written, 'And in process of time, it came to pass that Cain brought of the fruits of the ground an offering unto the Lord.'" (Gen. iv. 3).

Said Rabbi Simeon: "What mean the words, 'in process of time' (miqetz yamim)? They denote the being who is termed 'the end of all flesh' or the angel of death to whom it was that Cain brought his offerings, and therefore it is written miqetz yamim, instead of miqetz yemin, signifying the right side. Then also is it written in the book of Daniel, 'But go thou thy way till the end, for thou shalt rest and stand in thy lot in the end of the days.' (Ch. xii. 13). On Daniel hearing the words, 'till the end,' he asked whether they were qetz ha-yamin or qetz-yemin, and the heavenly voice answered: it is 'qetz yemin.' But Cain coming therefore from the qetz yamim, to it he brought offerings and sacrifice, product of that knowledge of the tree of good and evil which had brought so great ruin and misery to his parents."

CHAPTER XXXII.

SAID Rabbi Eleazar: "By these words, 'And Cain brought of the fruits of the ground,' we learn that Cain and Abel offered sacrifices of a character corresponding to their own state and nature. According to the actions or works of a man, so is his offering. It is pure or impure, acceptable or otherwise, as it is written, 'Say unto the righteous, it shall be well with him, for he shall eat of the fruit of his doings, but woe unto the wicked, it shall be ill with him, for he shall eat of the fruit of his doings.' (Is. iii., 10 to 11.) Cain brought the fruits of his doings and met the death angel. Abel brought the firstlings of his flocks and found they were acceptable and pleasing unto God; as it is written, 'And the Lord had respect unto Abel and to his offerings, but unto Cain and his offerings he had no respect,' wherefore the wrath of Cain was aroused and he was greatly incensed and so we read that when they were in the field, he fell upon his brother Abel and slew him. From other words in scripture we infer that a quarrel arose between them respecting Abel's twin sister, which is further confirmed by the traditional rendering of the words, 'And she brought forth again with her brother Abel,' showing that Abel was born with a twin sister. It is written, 'If thou doest well shall thou not he accepted' (Gen. iv., 7). These words have already been explained but there is another signification given of them by Rabbi Abba, thus, 'If thou doest well,' thy soul shall ascend on high and never fall again below (sath). That is, if thou livest according to the dictates of thy Higher Self, thou shalt become united with it; but if not, thou shalt sink lower unto the dust of the earth from which thou hast come forth." Said Rabbi Jose: "This interpretation of the word 'sath' is very good and excellent, but I have heard another interpretation, which is, God said to Cain: 'If thou doest well, the impure spirit will not abide with thee nor cleave unto thee, but if thou doest not well, sin or evil lieth at the door' (ready to overtake thee). By the word 'door' (lepathach) is meant justice or punishment from on high, for the great tribunal of divine justice is designated by this same word, door or gate, as it is written, 'Open unto me the gates of justice' (Ps. cxviii., 19). By 'sin lieth at the door' is meant the impure spirit which if thou fallest into its power, will bring thy soul before the tribunal of divine justice, when it will be hurled to destruction and become dissolved into the original element out of which it has been formed and produced."

Said Rabbi Isaac: "At the time that Cain killed Abel he knew not how to separate or disjoin body and soul, but bit him like a serpent. From that moment he became accursed and wandered about in the world, an outcast shunned and abhorred, until at last repenting of his sin, he became reconciled with the Lord and found a habitation on a lower earth or world."

Said Rabbi Jose: "It was not on a lower, but on our present earth that Cain after his repentance was admitted into human society, as it is written, 'And the Lord set a mark upon Cain'" (Gen. iv., 15).

Said Rabbi Isaac: "From these words we gather that it was from this earth which is called Adamah that Cain was driven, and that it was on the earth called Arqa that he afterwards became a dweller, as it is written, 'And Cain said thou hast driven me this day from the face of Adamah' (earth). After his repentance, however, it was granted him to live on a lower earth (arqa) of whose inhabitants it is written, 'They shall perish from the earth (aqua) and from under these heavens' (Jer. x., 11). It was here that he lived and dwelt as scripture states, 'and dwelt in the land of Nod, on the east of Eden' (Gen. iv., 16). Moreover, when Cain had killed Abel, Adam separated from his wife and cohabitated with two female elementals, and from his intercourse with them was begotten a great and numerous progeny of demons and elementaries who at night time appear in attractive forms and thus give rise to offspring like unto themselves. In scripture, they are termed 'the plagues of the children of men.' Though human in appearance, they are void of hair and of them scripture speaks. 'I will chasten him with the rod of men and with the plagues of the children of men' (Sam. vii., 14), they visit both men and women alike. After a hundred and thirty years he became united again with Eve and brought forth a son and called his name Seth, signifying thereby that as the two letters S and Th are the last of the alphabet, so this son was the ending of the terrible experience through which Eve and Adam had passed and undergone.

Said Rabbi Jehuda: "He was called Seth because he was a reincarnation of Abel, as it is written, 'For God hath appointed me another seed in place of Abel, whom Cain slew' (Gen, iv., 25). Furthermore, we read that Adam begat a son in his own likeness, after his image, and called his name Seth (Gen, v., 3), denoting that the first children of Adam had no resemblance to him either physically or morally. This was the opinion of Rabbi Yeba the aged as given by Rabbi Simeon. The first children brought forth by Eve were begotten by Somoal who appeared to her riding on the back of a serpent, and were therefore not endowed with the human body. If the question be asked: seeing that Abel came from a different side of the tree of life to that of Cain, wherefore had not Cain a human body? The reason was, because neither of them were begotten in a state of absolute purity."

Said Rabbi Jose: "But scripture states that though Adam knew Eve, his wife, and she conceived and brought forth Cain, yet it does not say that Adam begat Cain. Speaking of the birth of Abel it further states, 'She brought forth again his brother Abel.' Therefore, of each of them it is not said that they were begotten after the likeness and image of Adam, as it is expressly said of Seth."

Said Rabbi Simeon: "Adam as stated was separated from his wife a hundred and thirty years, during which time he begat demons and elementals that swarmed throughout the world. Whilst under the influence of the impure spirit he felt no desire to become associated with Eve, but after repenting and overcoming his animal propensities, he became again united to her and then it is said, 'he begat a son in his own likeness.' Observe that when a man begins walking in the wrong and downward path his thoughts and inclinations become impure and carnal, all love of virtue and purity leaves him through the impure elementals he attracts into his aura. Happy and blessed are they who find and walk in the path of light that shineth more and more unto the perfect day, for then are their lives truly clean and real lives and their offspring is like unto them; and of them scripture saith, 'For the upright shall dwell in the land.'" (Prov. ii., 21).

Said Rabbi Hiya: "What signify the words 'And the sister of Tubal Cain was Naamah' (gentleness), and wherefore was this name given her? Was it to indicate that she possessed the power of seducing both human and angelic beings?"

Said Rabbi Isaac: "She overcame Aza and Azael who in scripture are called 'sons of God.'"

Said Rabbi Simeon: "She was the procreatrix of all the demons of Cainite origin, and she it is that along with Lilith afflicts infant children with epileptic diseases."

Said Rabbi Abba to Rabbi Simeon: "Master, you have stated she was so called because she inspired men with carnal desires."

Said Rabbi Simeon: "That is true, for though she excites lust in human beings, yet this does not prevent her from afflicting young children and thus she continues her operations in the world up to the present time."

Said Rabbi Abba: "Seeing that demons and elementals are subject to death, wherefore do Naamah and Lilith continue to exist through the ages?"

Rabbi Simeon replied: "All demons and elementaries do indeed die, but Naamah and Lilith together with Agereth, daughter of Mahlath their offspring, abide in the world until the day that the Holy One will banish and drive all evil and impure spirits out of the world; as it is written, 'And I will cause the unclean spirit to pass out of the land' (Zach. xiii., 2). Woe unto those who are ignorant and therefore unable to avert and ward off the influence of these defiling elemental beings that swarm in their myriads throughout the world. If it were permitted to behold them, we should be amazed and confounded and wonder how the world could continue to exist. Observe that Naamah being the exciter of human concupiscence and carnality, it is obligatory on everyone to practice and perform acts and rites of purification, so that he may become and preserve himself pure and undefiled."

TRADITIONS CONCERNING ADAM

"THIS is the Book of the generations of Adam. In the day that Alhim created man, in the likeness of Alhim made he him." (Gen. v., 1.) Said Rabbi Isaac: "The Holy One showed Adam the forms and features of his descendants that should appear in the world after him, and of the sages and kings who should rule over Israel. He also made known to him, that the life and reign of David would be of short duration. Then said Adam to the Holy One, 'let seventy years of my earthly existence be taken and granted to the life of David.' This request was granted, otherwise Adam's life would have attained to a thousand years. This was the reason that David said: 'For thou, Lord, hast made me glad through thy work; I will triumph in the work of thine hands (Ps. xcii., 5), for thou hast filled me with joy in prolonging the days of my life. 'It was thy own act and wish,' said the Holy One, 'when thou wast incarnated as Adam, the work of my hands and not of flesh and blood.' Amongst the wise men and sages that should appear on the earth, Adam rejoiced greatly on beholding the form of Rabbi Akiba who would become distinguished by his great knowledge of the secret doctrine. On seeing, however, as in a vision, his martyrdom and cruel death, Adam became exceedingly sad and said: 'Thine eyes beheld me ere I was clothed in a body and all things are written in thy book; each day hath its events that shall come to pass, are therein to be found.' Observe that the book of the generations of Adam was that which the Holy One through the angel Rosiel, guardian of the great mysteries and secret doctrine, gave unto Adam whilst yet in the garden of Eden. In it was written all the secret wisdom and knowledge concerning the divine name of seventy-two letters and its esoteric six hundred and seventy mysteries. It also contained the fifteen hundred keys, the knowledge and understanding and use of which had never been imparted to anyone, not even to angels, before it came into the possession of Adam. As he read and studied its pages, angelic beings assembled around him and acquired the knowledge of Hochma, or divine wisdom, and in their delight exclaimed 'Be thou exalted, oh God above the heavens, and let thy glory be above all the earth' (Ps. lvii., 5). Then was it that the holy angel Hadraniel sent one of his subordinates to Adam, saying unto him, 'Adam! Adam! guard thou well and wisely the great and glorious gift entrusted to thee by thy Lord. To none of the angels on high have its secrets ever been revealed and imparted, save to thyself. Be thou therefore discreet and refrain from making them known to others.' Acting on these injunctions Adam zealously and secretly kept this book up to his expulsion from the garden of Eden, studying it and making himself acquainted with its wondrous mysteries. When, however, he disobeyed the commands of his Lord, the volume suddenly disappeared leaving him overwhelmed with grief and most poignant regret, so that he went and immersed himself up to the neck in the river Gihon. On his body becoming covered with unsightly ulcers and sores threatening physical dissolution, the Holy One instructed Raphael to return the book to Adam. After obtaining a full knowledge of its occult teachings, he handed it, when at the point of death, to his son Seth, who in his turn bequeathed it to his posterity, and eventually it came into the possession of Abraham who was able by its secret teachings to attain to higher and more enlightened knowledge of the Divine, as was the case with his predecessor Henoch and enabled him, as it is written, 'to walk with the Alhim,' that is, to converse with them."

MALE AND FEMALE CREATED HE THEM

SAID Rabbi Simeon: "In these words are involved and contained great occult truths, even the greatest and most profound divine mysteries respecting the origin and creation of man, and so beyond human comprehension that they must remain subjects of faith and not of knowledge. Of the creation of the world it is written, 'These are the generations of the heavens and the earth be hibaram (when they were created); but at the creation of man, scripture states, 'God blessed them and called their name Adam, be yom hibaram' (in the day when they were created), From the terms male and female, we gather that every figure that does not bear the form of the male or female, is not in the image and likeness of Adam Kadmon, the primal ideal man of which we have formerly spoken. Observe that in any place of scripture where the male and female are not found united together, the Holy One is said not to dwell or be present with His blessing and the name Adam is only used when such is the case."

Said Rabbi Jehuda: "Since the destruction of the temple, Israel no longer enjoys the blessings that descend from on high daily on the earth. Yea, one may say that they have become lost unto Israel, as it is written, 'The righteous perisheth and no man layeth to heart' (Is. lvii., 1). The word perisheth here denotes the blessings from on high, but which are now of no beneficial effect in the renovation of human nature, for as stated, 'Truth is perished' (Jer. vii., 28); the truth that brings with it light, frees the soul from its downward propensities and informs us whence all blessings descend and come to man, namely, from the Holy One of whom it is written, 'And He blessed them.' It was through Seth that have come forth all the generations of the righteous in the world."

THE ANTEDILUVIANS AND THEIR MAGICAL ARTS

SAID Rabbi Jose: "Adam through disobedience to the divine commandment, lost the knowledge and understanding of the secret doctrine and occult power and meaning of the letters of the alphabet except the two last, namely, the letters Shin (S) and Tau (Th), because though he had sinned yet was not goodness wholly extinguished within him and therefore to express his feeling of gratitude for this concession, he called his son Seth. After his repentance and reconciliation with his Lord, the letters with the knowledge of their mystical meaning and power became known again to him, but in their reverse order thus, Th, S, R, Q, in which they continued up to the day the children of Israel stood at the foot of Mount Sinai, when they became arranged again in their normal order as on the day that the heavens and the earth were created. This redistribution of the alphabetical letters contributed to the permanent welfare and endurance of the world."

Said Rabbi Abba: "When Adam transgressed, the heavens and the earth trembled and wished to become dissolved into their original elements and disappear altogether because the covenant between God and man on which they were founded had become broken, of which it is written, 'If the covenant of day and night had not existed, I would not have made those laws that govern and control the universe.' (Jer. xxxiii., 25.) We know that this covenant was broken by the transgression of Adam as scripture states, 'but they like Adam have transgressed the covenant' (Hos. vi., 7). If the Holy One had not foreseen that Israel on arriving at Mount Sinai would accept the covenant, the very heavens and the earth would have ceased their existence and reverted back into chaos."

Said Rabbi Hezekiah: "The Holy One remitteth and forgives everyone who confesses his sins and wrongdoings. Observe that when the world was created, the Holy One made the covenant upon which it continues to exist. We infer this from the word Brashith which should be written thus, bara, shith: meaning 'He created the foundation' or the covenant, symbolized by the letter Yod (I) in the middle of the word shith which though the smallest of the alphabetical letters, nevertheless represents the covenant through which all blessings come to mankind. When a son was born unto him,

Adam confessed his sin and was forgiven by the Holy One, and therefore he called his name Seth, having the same consonantal letters as Shith without the Yod, symbol of the covenant he had transgressed. Furthermore, the Holy covenant is also symbolized by the letter Beth (B) which became incorporated with S and Th when the children of Israel stood at the foot of Mount Sinai and thus formed the Sabbath (S B Th), of which it is written, 'Wherefore the children of Israel shall keep the sabbath (or covenant) throughout their generations for a perpetual covenant.' It is a sign between me and the children of Israel forever.'" (Ex. xxxi., 16).

Said Rabbi Jose: "The two letters Shin and Tau were then associated and from the time the children of Israel received the covenant at Mount Sinai, they acquired the occult knowledge and understanding of the mystical meaning of all the letters of the alphabet that, with the exception of Shin and Tau, had become lost to mankind."

Said Rabbi Jehuda: "From the birth of Seth to the comin of Israel to Mount Sinai, the mysteries of the letters were gradually unfolded and revealed to the patriarchs, but not fully, as the letters were not in their normal order as at present."

Said Rabbi Eleazar: "In the days of Enos, men were deeply versed in occult knowledge and magical science and the manipulation of natural forces, in which no one was more skilled than he, since the time of Adam whose chief study was on the occult properties of the leaves of the Tree of Knowledge of good and evil. It was Enos that taught and imparted this occult lore to his contemporaries, who in their turn handed it down to the antediluvians, the persistent and perverse opponents of Noah. They boasted that by their magical science they were able to ward off the divine judgments threatening them. Whilst Enos lived, men became initiated into the higher life, as scripture states. 'Then began men to make invocations in the name of Jehovah.'"

Said Rabbi Isaac: "All the just men who lived subsequent to Enos, as Jared, Methusalah and Henoch, did all in their power to restrain the practice of magical arts, but their efforts proved futile and ineffectual; so that the professors of them, proud of their occult knowledge, became rebellious and disobedient to their Lord, saying, 'Who is Shaddai, the almighty, that we should serve him and what profit should we have in praying unto Iam'?' Thus spake they and foolishly imagined that by their occultism and magic they would he able to nullify and turn away the oncoming judgment that was to sweep them wholly out of existence. Beholding their wicked deeds and practices, the Holy One caused the earth to revert back to its former condition and become immersed in water. After the deluge, however, He gave the earth again to mankind, promising, in His mercy, it should never again and in like manner be destroyed. It is written, 'The Lord caused the earth to be covered with the deluge' (Ps. xxix., 10). The word for Lord, here, is Jehovah and not Alhim; the first representing mercy, the other severity and judgment. In the time of Enos, even young children became students and trained in the higher mysteries and knowledge of the secret doctrine."

CHAPTER XXXVI.

SAID Rabbi Jose. "If all this is true, why were they so exceedingly foolish and blind that notwithstanding all their occult science they could not foresee the flood which the Holy One was preparing for their destruction?"

Said Rabbi Isaac: "They knew full well what was about to take place, but in the perversity of their hearts they said: 'We know the angels presiding over the fire and over the water and, by our magical science, will be able to restrain and prevent them from injuring us.' But alas! they were ignorant that the Holy One ruled in the world, that from him cometh judgment and retribution, angels being the executors of his decrees. This they knew not until the day that the deluge appeared, even though the Holy Spirit had preached unto them that 'sinners shall be consumed from off the earth and the wicked shall be no more' (Ps. civ., 35). The Holy One was forbearing and long-suffering towards them during the lives of the just men, Jared, Methusalah and Henoch. After their decease, then judgment quickly overtook these antediluvians and they were cut off in their sins and wrong-doing, as it is written, 'They were destroyed from the earth.'" (Gen. vii., 23.)

OF THE PATRIARCH HENOCH AND THE SIN OF THE ANTEDILUVIANS

SAID Rabbi Jose: "Whilst the king sitteth at his table (bimsibo) my spikenard sendeth forth the smell thereof" (Cant. i., 12). This verse has already been explained, but there is yet another interpretation worth noting. Whenever a man walks with and cleaves unto the Alhim as did Henoch, the Holy One, foreseeing his liability to decline in goodness and uprightness, arranges to take him out of the world whilst the perfume of his good deeds endures. This was the case with Henoch. The words, 'Whilst the king,' refer to the Holy One; 'at his table,' allude to the man who walks and cleaves unto him; whilst the words 'my spikenard sendeth forth the smell thereof, denote the good deeds for which he is taken out of the world and thus escapes and avoids falling into sin. And this is why King Solomon said: 'There are just and upright men who suffer affliction as if they had committed evil deeds and are taken away.' There are also unjust men who live to a good age granted unto them by the Holy One, that they may repent and turn unto him. Henoch was just and walked with the Alhim and he was not, and Alhim took him, for God foresaw that he would ultimately become a transgressor of the law and that this might not be; he was taken from the world before his appointed time. By the words, 'he was not,' is meant that he died whilst he was comparatively young."

Said Rabbi Eleazar: "The Holy One took Henoch away from the evil of the world, into the celestial regions on high, and imparted unto him the secret knowledge of the highest mysteries and of the forty-nine keys necessary for understanding the various combinations of the sacred letters, and which the angels themselves make use of. It is written, 'And God saw that the wickedness of men upon the earth was great and all the imaginations and thoughts of their hearts were only evil continually.' (Gen. vi., 5.)

Said Rabbi Jehuda: "'Thou art not a God that hath pleasure in wickedness, neither shall evil dwell with thee' (Ps. v., 5). Observe that he who gives way to the temper and suffers himself to be led and guided by it, defiles not only himself but also those with whom he comes into personal contact. As already stated, though the wickedness of the antediluvians was great and their evil deeds were many, yet was the Holy One unwilling to destroy them, but long-suffering towards them, notwithstanding, and their shameful propensities and heinous practices, of which it is written 'that they were only evil continually.' Their evil actions are denoted by the word (Ra) (pollution). Of Er, the eldest son of Judah, who was guilty of this sin; it is written that 'he was wicked in the sight of the Lord and the Lord slew him.'" (Gen. xxxviii., 7.)

Said Rabbi Jose: "Is not this sin synonymous with what is termed rashang (wickedness or wrongdoing)? "No," replied Rabbi Jehuda, "for rashang is applied to intentional evil ere it becomes an actuality, but Ra refers to him who defiles himself by the dissipation of his vital powers and thus gives himself up to the unclean spirit called Ra. He who thus renders himself impure will never attain unto the Divine Life nor behold the face of the Shekina, whose disappearance from the world previous to the deluge was owing to the vice termed Ra. Woe unto him who indulges in it, for he will never experience the joy of living in the presence of the Holy One, but will drag on through life as a degraded captive and miserable slave of Ra, the unclean spirit; so true are the words, 'The fear of the Lord leadeth to life, it bringeth peaceful nights free from visits of the impure spirit Ra' (Prov. xix., 23). And therefore it is written, 'Evil (Ra) shall not dwell with thee' (Ps. v., 4). Only the pure in life and thought and deed can say, 'Yea though I walk through the valley of the shadow of death, I will not be afraid of Ra, for thou art with me and causest me to dwell in the house of the Lord forever.'" (Ps. xxiii., 4-6.)

THE DIVINE COMPASSION

SAID Rabbi Jose: "It is written, 'And it repented the Lord that he had made man on the earth and it grieved him at his heart' (Gen. vi., 6). 'Woe unto them that draw iniquity with cords of vanity and sin as it were with a cart-rope' (Is. v., 18). The words, 'that draw iniquity,' refer to those who sin against their "Lord every day and imagine their wrong-doing is of less consequence and worth than a cart-rope. With this class of wrong-doers the Holy One is exceedingly patient and long-suffering, and punishes them not until their misdeeds get beyond endurance. When the Holy One executeth judgment upon sinners in the world, yet is he unwilling they should perish; since notwithstanding their transgression, they are his children, the work of his hands. Though their punishment is inevitable, yet like as a father pitieth his children, so doth he pity them; so great is his love and compassion towards them that even when punishment and suffering overtake the erring and sinful, he is full of compassion and grieved in heart, if we may so express it, like the Persian monarch who sought to deliver Daniel, of whom it is written, 'Then the king went to his palace and passed the night fasting; neither were instruments of music brought before him, and his sleep went from him.'" (Dan. vi., 18.) Said Rabbi Isaac: "The words, 'And it repented the Lord that he had made man on the earth,' have the same meaning as the words, 'And the Lord repented of the evil which he thought to do unto his people.'" (Ex. xxxii., 14.)

Said Rabbi Yusa: "The interpretation of the rabbi is favorable to man, but in the opinion of Rabbi Hezekiah it is otherwise."

Said Rabbi Hiya: "When the Holy One created man to dwell upon the earth, he formed him after the likeness of Adam Kadmon, the heavenly man, when the angels gazed upon him, they exclaimed: 'Thou hast made him almost equal to Alhim and crowned him with glory and honor.' After the transgression and fall of Adam, it is said the Holy One was grieved at heart because it gave occasion for repeating what they had said at his creation, 'What is man that thou shouldst be mindful of him, or the son of man that thou shouldst visit him.'" (Ps vii. 5.)

Said Rabbi Jehuda: "It grieved the Holy One that he must punish man severely and thus appear as acting in contradiction to the greatest of his attributes, (mercy), as it is written. 'And he appointed singers unto the Lord to march in front of the army, praising the beauty of holiness and saying, 'Praise the Lord, for his mercy endureth forever.'" (II. Chron. xx., 21.)

Said Rabbi Isaac: "Why was this song of praise composed like those psalms that begin with the words, Praise the Lord for he is good, was it not because the term 'good' (tob) might not be used when Israel was compelled to destroy people whom the Holy One made and created? When Israel passed through the waters of the Red Sea, the angels on high assembled round the throne of the Holy One and sang praises. Then spake he and said: wherefore sing ye a song of praise, seeing so many, the work of my hands, are drowned in the depths of the sea? So is it when a sinner perishes; the Holy One is grieved at heart, when he is cut off from the face of the earth."

Said Rabbi Abba: "It is of a truth so; for when Adam fell through transgressing the divine commandment, the Holy One said: 'Oh Adam! thou art become dead unto the higher divine life.' At these words, the light of the Sabbath candle became extinguished and Adam was driven out of the garden of Eden. Moreover, the Holy One further said: 'I made thee ascend and placed thee in Eden to offer sacrifices; but seeing thou hast profaned the altar, it is my decree that henceforth thou shalt be a tiller of the ground and die at last--for from it was thou taken, and unto it shall thou return.' Ere, however, this occurred the Holy One had compassion on him and permitted him to live and be buried in the vicinity of Paradise; for Adam had discovered a cave from which emitted a light which he recognized as coming from out of the garden of Eden; and there he, along with his wife, lived and died. Observe that no one goeth out of the world without seeing immediately after death his ancestor Adam, who seeks to know the cause of his decease and what his moral and spiritual state to which he has attained. Then says the deceased one; Woe unto thee, for thou art the cause wherefore I have ceased to live; to which Adam replies: I transgressed but one only of the commandments and suffered therefrom, but what must be thy punishment who hast broken so many by thy misdeeds."

Said Rabbi Hiya: "Adam was seen on different occasions by the patriarchs, to whom he confessed and acknowledged his sin and showed them the place where he had enjoyed the divine light and glory from on high and also where his descendants, the righteous, and those who obeyed the Good Law, through their good deeds now live the diviner life in the garden of the celestial Eden. Then praised they the Lord and said, 'How excellent is thy loving kindness, oh God, wherefore do the children of men put their trust in the shadow of thy wing.'" (Ps. xxxvi., 7.)

CHAPTER XXXIX.

SAID Rabbi Yissa: "Everyone on leaving the world goes into the presence of Adam so that they may learn that not his, but their own sins and wrong-doing have caused their death. Amongst myriads of those that have lived and died, only three have there been whose decease was not owing to sin, but was brought about by the malicious designs of the serpent, namely, Amram, Levi and Benjamin, and also Jesse, who committed no sin worthy of death. Observe that all the antediluvians sinned openly and unblushingly. Rabbi Simeon was once walking in the environs of Tiberias and on beholding men committing pollution, he exclaimed, 'How dare these wretches sin against their Lord so openly and shamefully.' Then went from him a hypnotic or magnetic force that impelled them to cast themselves into the sea and be drowned. Observe also that every species of sin and wrong-doing done openly, causes the Shekina to take its departure from the delinquent and guilty one and cease its abiding with him. This was the case with the dwellers before the deluge and thereby they cut themselves adrift front the Holy One, hence it is written, 'Take away the dross from the silver, then shall it be formed into a vessel; take away the wicked from before the King and his throne shall be established in righteousness.'" (Prov. xxv., 4-5.)

Said Rabbi Eleazar: "It is written, 'And the Lord said my spirit shall not always abide (or dwell) with man, for that he is flesh' (Gen. vi., 3). When the Holy One created the world, he made it after the pattern of the world on high and as long as its inhabitants lived pure and upright lives and caused the divine spirit or life into that part of the world, in which Jacob dwelt afterwards into the land of Israel during the reign of David, whence heavenly blessings and influences gradually extended over the whole earth; and therefore it is written, Praise the Lord for he is good, for his mercy extendeth throughout the world. The word ubed olam (world) has reference to that part of the spheres on high named David, and therefore is written without the letter Van (u), signifying that where the divine influence descends from that celestial region, then blessings are poured down on the world below. But as mankind sinned, the life divine has been taken from the world and only those who strive to attain unto, now enjoy its blessings whilst the unjust are unable to appropriate it for their wicked and magical purposes. The meaning of the words for that he also is flesh (beshagam) is, that, this divine life might not become abused by the serpent and others for their evil purposes, and so kept unsullied and undefiled by contact with the wicked and impure."

"By the word 'flesh,'" said Rabbi Simeon, "is meant the angel of death, whilst the words, 'the days of man shall be a hundred and twenty years,' mean to the thread or silver cord as it is termed, shall be broken that binds body and soul together. It is written, 'There were Nephalim (giants, fallen ones) in the earth in those days.'" (Gen. vi., 4.)

Said Rabbi Jose: "The nephalim here mentioned were the angels Aza and Azael, whom the Holy One hurled from heaven onto the earth. If the question he asked, how could they exist on earth in a state so different to that they enjoyed in heaven?"

Said Rabbi Hiya: "They were of that class of angels of whom scripture says 'and fowl that fly above the earth' (Gen i., 20), and who manifest themselves to mankind, in human form. When descending upon earth they are able to assume various shapes that become materialized and thus visible to mortal eyes. These rebel angels Aza and Azael hurled upon the earth became embodied in material bodies of which they could not after rid themselves. Charmed and overcome with the beauty of the daughters of men, they continue living unto this day, teaching men and initiating them into magical art and science. They begat children who were termed anakim (giants), Giborim (mighty ones). Such were the fallen angels who formerly were called sons of God."

TRADITIONS CONCERNING NOAH

SAID Rabbi Jose: "It is written, 'And the Lord said I will destroy man whom I have created from the face of the earth! (Gen. vi., 7); also, 'My thoughts are not your thoughts and my ways are not your ways saith the Lord' (Is. lv., 8). When anyone seeks to wreak his vengeance upon another, he keeps silent and lets not a word escape his lips lest his enemy learning his intention takes steps to guard and protect himself. The Holy One acts not so, when sending forth his judgments upon the world, but warns it again and again of their coming. He has no fear of being baffled by those whom he is about to chastise, and no one can hide from him nor escapes his decrees. He made known through Noah the judgments he was about to execute upon the antediluvians, but they took no heed and therefore sudden destruction came upon them and they perished from off the face of the earth. Of Noah it is said, 'And he called his name Noah (rest, comfort) saying, this same shall comfort us concerning our work and the toil of our hands, because of the ground which the Lord had cursed' (Gen. v., 29). How was it that his father could give utterance to these words? The explanation is that when the ground had been cursed, Adam said to the Holy One: Ruler and Lord of the universe, how long shall the earth remain cursed?' Said the Holy One: 'Until one be born like unto thyself bearing the sign of the covenant.' In hope and expectation mankind lived on till the birth of Noah, in the anticipation of benefits and blessing they would enjoy during his lifetime. Before the appearance of this patriarch, they were unversed in the science of agriculture and the use of the plough and harrow. Everything was done by hand labor. When Noah attained to manhood, he invented implements for tilling the ground and making it fertile; and so, in the words of Lamech, his father, he became a comforter, a helper unto men, in his work and the toil of their hands, whereby the curse was taken from off the ground, for as at first when sown it brought forth thistle, now it produced corn in abundance, therefore he became known as and called the husbandman."

Said Rabbi Jehuda: "He was called thus for the same reason that the husband of Naomi was called Elimelech (Ruth i., 3). Of Noah it is written also that he was zaddich, just, because by the sacrifices offered up by him, he freed the earth from its curse, concerning which we read that 'the Lord smelled a sweet savour' (Gen. viii., 21); or in other words, was pleased with them and said, 'I will not again curse the ground any more for man's sake.' Such are the reasons why Noah was so called.

Continuing his remarks, Rabbi Jehuda said: "It is written, 'Come and see the works of the Lord who doeth wonders on the earth." (Is. xl., 8.) The words see (hazon) here has the same signification as in the words, 'The Lord has revealed unto me, hazouth qashah, a remarkable prophecy or vision' (Is. xxi., 2), from which we learn this fact, that prophecy is revelation from the Holy One on high to mankind, and also that the word shamuth is usually translated, wonders or marvelous things such as desolation, and yet here it should be read shemoth (names), teaching us that it is God who inspires the naming of everyone's name that corresponds to and is expressive of his or her life and character. Another interpretation is that the word shamoth in the above verse from the Psalms, signifies really 'destructions' for if the world has been created by the divine attribute termed Jehovah it would have been indestructible, but as it is, the work of Alhim (justice) is liable to dissolution and abolishment. It is written, 'Come and see the works of Alhim, that are subject to destructions (shamoth) on the earth.'"

Said Rabbi Hiya: "I cannot agree to this interpretation, seeing that Jehovah and Alhim are alike sacred and names of the Divine Being, and therefore I think in common with several students that shemoth signifies holy names, as by the combination of the divine names, marvellous and wondrous things are done on earth."

Said Rabbi Isaac: "These different interpretations with that of Rabbi Jehuda are all excellent, for if the world was created by the name of 'rakhma,' that is by Jehovah, it is indestructible, if by severity or Alhim, then is everything in it liable to perish; if there were no punishment for evil and wrongdoing, the world and society could not continue to exist. At his birth Noah was named by a term expressive of solace, or comfort, with the idea that he was to be a source of help and consolation to his progenitors and descendants, to the world above and the world below, to this world and the world to come. This was not however the case with respect to his relations with the Divine Being, for on reversing the letters of his name, Noah became Khen, meaning grace, and so it is written, 'But Noah found grace in the sight of the Lord.' (Gen. VI. 8.) The name of Judah's eldest son Er, when reversed becomes Ra (evil) and is an anagram expressive of his natural character, therefore scripture describes him as 'wicked before the Lord.' When Noah came into the world and grew up to manhood, beholding the perverse lives of men sinning against the holy One, he retreated from amongst them and devoted himself to the worship of his Lord, and thus escaped from the general pollution. If it be asked what was the subject of his studies whilst in retreat? It was the Book of Adam that had been handed down till at last it came into the possession of Henoch; and from it Noah learned how essential and necessary it was to offer sacrifices unto his Lord. From this book he also learned that the world had been created by Hochma, (the sephiroth wisdom) and that it was owing to sacrifices it still existed; for without them or were they not made, neither angels above nor man below would be able to exist.

CHAPTER XLI.

RABBI SIMEON was walking one day in the country accompanied by Rabbi Eleazar, his son and his students, Rabbi Jose and Hiya. As they wended on their way, Eleazar said to his father: "That this our walk may be profitable, instruct us further, we pray thee, in the secret doctrine."

Then spake Rabbi Simeon and said: "It is written, When he that is a fool goeth on his way, his heart faileth him and he saith to everyone that he is a fool' (Eccles. X. 39). When a man desires that his ways may be agreeable to the Holy One and before going on a journey he ought first of all to seek counsel from his Lord (higher self) and repeat the traveler's prayer, as saith the scripture, 'The upright shall walk before him and follow him on his way' (Ps. LXXXV. 13). That is, the Divine Shekina will never forsake us on our pilgrimage through life. But he who lives without faith in his Lord is as the fool whose heart or courage when on his way faileth him. The occult meaning of the word heart (leb) is the Holy One, who never accompanies a fool on his way nor grants him the aid and assistance he needs, because by his infidelity and indifference to the teachings of the good law, his heart faileth him, or in other words, the Divine Presence goeth not with him and he becomes known to others as a fool, for whenever he hears others speaking and discussing together on divine things, he derides and despises them. It is related of such an one, after pondering over the mark of the covenant, that every son of Israel bears on him, he affirmed it was a mere rite and no sure sign either of true religion or of faith in the Divine Being. When the venerable Rabbi Yebba heard these words he directed his looks and gaze upon the heretic, who gradually shrivelled up into a lifeless mass of skin and bone. As however it is our desire to be blessed with divine help and guidance whilst on our way, we will endeavor to give expression to a few teachings out of the secret doctrine. It is written, 'Teach me thy way oh Lord, I will walk in thy truth, unite my heart to fear thy name' (Ps. LXXXVI, 11). The interior signification of these words is difficult to understand, yet they inculcate that all things are in the hand or power of God except the purity or impurity of our lives and deeds. What David meant by them was, open my eyes that I may understand thy secret mysteries, then shall I be assured I am walking in the true path of light, swerving therefrom neither to the right or left; 'Unite my heart to thee,' then shalt thou become my strength and portion forever and it shall be filled with the fear of thee and thy Holy name. Observe that everyone who reveres the Holy One, in the proportion of his reverence, makes himself recipient of the higher life and daily approximating to it becomes eventually united with the Divine. On the other hand, he who is lacking in reverence and faith in the divine, makes himself unworthy and unfitted for entering into the joys of the world to come. We read that the path of the upright is as a shining light that shineth more and more unto the perfect day (Prov. IV. 18). Blessed are the upright both in this world and the world to come for the Holy One, blessed be he! takes delight and joys in their progress and ascension towards the higher life. The light here spoken of, is the light that the Holy One created at the beginning of the world and reserved for those who by their obedience to the good law, become united to their higher self and so are qualified to enter into its enjoyments in the world to come. But of the worldly minded and selfish it is written, 'The way of the wicked and unjust, is as darkness--they know not at what they stumble' (Prov. IV. 19). If the question arise, know they not why they stumble and fall? scripture informs us, it is because their paths are tortuous and serpentine, their irrational lives are spent in the indulgence of sensual desires and unredeemed with few if any generous deeds of self-sacrifice or consideration for the welfare and happiness of others, and thus they live on never realizing that for all these things they shall be brought into judgment and stand self-convicted and self-condemned at the bar of their own conscience, filled with unavailing regrets and crying, 'Woe unto us that we never gave heed nor opened our hearts whilst in the world for the entrance and reception of truth, woe unto us!' Note, that for their good deeds, the Holy One will grant unto the upright and unselfish, abundance of light and enjoyment in the region on high which eye hath not seen, nor hath it entered into the heart to conceive of (Is. LXIV. 3), the celestial sphere of the Beatific Vision. Happy the lot of the just and pure in both worlds, for of them scripture affirms, the righteous, the unselfish shall inherit the earth forever; (Is. LX. 21), they shall praise thy name, and the upright shall dwell in thy presence (Ps. CXL. 12). Blessed be the Divine Being forevermore, Amen and Amen."

It is written, "These are the generations of Noah" (Gen. vi. 9). The students of Rabbi Simeon were assembled together and meditating upon the secret doctrine. Then spoke Rabbi Hiya and said: "Thy people also shall be all righteous, they shall inherit the laud forever, the branch of my planting, the work of my hands, that I may be glorified" (Is. lx. 21). Blessed is Israel who delights in the study of the secret doctrine, the knowledge of the mysteries of which qualifies than to live the higher life of the world to come. Observe that every Israelite or initiate in the mysteries never fails to attain unto it, inasmuch as he obeys the good law of the universe, and therefore it is written of him, "Had I not made my covenant with day and night, I should not have prescribed the laws that govern the heavens and the earth" (Jer. xxxiii. 25). True Israelites are moreover called zaddikim (righteous) on account of the purity of their lives, symbolized and distinguished by the mark or sign of the covenant (circumcision). Whence do we infer this fact? From the example of Joseph who was termed a Zaddik or just one, because of his purity of life and observance of the covenant.

Said Rabbi Eleazer: "Wherever in scripture the word 'Aleh' (these) occurs there is an antithesis of some kind between what precedes and what follows it. For instance, in (Gen. ii. 10) it is said, 'and a river went out of Eden to water the garden and from thence it was parted and became into four heads.' This said river that went out of Eden and entered into paradise, brought into it waters of celestial origin which gave life to the plants and flowers which grew therein and which only ceased on the completion of creation when, as it is written, 'God rested from all his work that he created and made.' Herein consists the mystery of the word aleh, occurring in the verse, 'These are the generations of Noah,' marking an antithesis between the generation of Noah and those preceding him, namely, the generations of Adam, or in other words, comes between the manifestation and development of life on the celestial and earthly planes of existence. Noah symbolized humanity beginning its earth career and for this reason is said to be 'aish ha-adamah,' the earthly man (Gen. ix., 20). The biblical account of Noah and the deluge contains a deep mystery that explains why it was necessary that Noah should enter the ark. It was in order to keep seed (human race) alive upon the face of all the earth (Gen, vii., 3). If so, of what then was the ark a symbol? The ark of the covenant (the good law) by which celestial or Adamic humanity was kept and preserved and without which it could not have entered upon its mundane career of existence and progression; that is, without the continuance of the good law in the world, the higher self could not have operated in the progressive development of the lower self, which therefore would have perished and reverted back to its pre-evolutionary or elemental state. Ere present humanity began evoluting on the earth, the Holy One entered into a covenant with the Higher Self, as it is written, 'But with thee I will establish my covenant and thou shalt come into the ark' (Gen. vii., 8). Scripture states that Noah was a just man (Gen. vi., 9) because a type of the ideal man Adam Kadmon, who is described as 'the righteous or just,' and also the foundation of the world (Prov. x., 25). Both alike have the same appellation of 'just,' the one in the celestial world, the other in the terrestrial world. This occult mystery is contained in the words 'Noah walked with Alhim' (Gen. vi., 8); that is to say, that Noah and Alhim were never disjoined or separated, one being the reflection of the other on the earth plane, and therefore it is written, 'Noah found grace in the eyes of the Lord' (Gen. vi., 8). Noah, moreover, is said to have been 'a just man and perfect in his generations' (bedorothav). The word 'perfect' (thamin) here denotes that he was born circumcised, and was also the source of perfection not only to his generation but also to his future posterity. This being so, it appears that Noah from the time of creation was predestined to enter and be incorporated within the ark, and also that previous to this event, humanity was not in a perfect state or condition, and only after his abode in the ark is it written, 'and of them was the earth overspread' (Gen. ix., 19). The word 'overspread' (naphzali) here has the same meaning 'ipared' (divided itself), as in Gen. ii., 10 'and a river went out of Eden to water the garden and from thence it was parted, that is, became divided into four heads.' In the work of creation it was at the moment of this dividing that the fertilizing and fructifying principle from on high entered into the world and made the earth fruitful as it does on the celestial plane, and therefore scripture states that 'aleh,' this principle of life, descended into Noah in order that through him the human race might appear and be perpetuated on the earth plane."

After Rabbi Eleazar had ceased speaking, Rabbi Abba went and embraced him, saying: "Oh lion! that breaketh rocks and dasheth them to pieces. Truly hast thou exposited the occult signification of the ark."

Rabbi Eleazar, continuing his discourse, said furthermore: "It is written, 'And he called his name Noah, saying this shalt comfort us concerning the work and toil of our hands' (Gen. v., 29). Here the word 'ath' is found before 'shemo' (his name). That is not so in the words 'And he called him Jacob.' What is the reason of this commission? Noah and Jacob symbolize two different divine principles of operation. Thus in vision Isaiah says, 'I saw the (ath) Lord' (Is. vi., 1), the prophet using 'ath' to intimate that he beheld both the Schekina and the Lord together. So is it also found with the name of Noah, teaching us that he was named by the Holy One and Schekina together, whilst Jacob, another patriarch symbolizing a lower state of existence, received his name from the Holy One only."

"These are the generations of Noah," said Rabbi Jehuda, 'A good man is gracious and lendeth (to the poor); he will guide his affairs with prudence' (Ps. cxii., 5). The term 'good man' designates the Holy One, and therefore is it written, 'The Lord is good to all (Ps. cxlv., 9). 'The Lord is a man of war,' for he alone giveth light and nourishment to this lower world and guideth it with judgment, as it is said, 'Righteousness and equity are the foundation of thy throne' (Ps. lxxxix., 14). Furthermore, the Just One or the ideal man is also designated as 'a good man,' and so it is written, 'Say unto the Just One that he is good, for he shall gather the fruit of his labors' (Is. iii., 10)."

Said Rabbi Jose: "This verse refers to Noah, as it is expressly said of him 'Noah was a just man.'"

Said Rabbi Isaac: "I think the words are an eulogy of the Sabbath, in the honor of which the Psalmist begins his praise of it by the word 'good.' It is good to praise the Lord (Ps. xciii., 2)."

CHAPTER XLII.

SAID Rabbi Hiya, after listening to these comments of his fellow students: "These different expositions really amount to one and the same meaning. The generations of Noah signify the present human race in the world, the offspring and work of the Holy One."

Said Rabbi Simeon: "When the Holy One arrays himself, it is in the ornaments from both the celestial and terrestrial worlds, from the former with that heavenly light on high that no human being can approach unto; from the latter with the souls of the righteous who the more they approximate themselves to this divine light the more receptive and filled with it do they become, so that through them it expands in all directions and the world like a cistern or ocean is filled with it. It is written, 'Drink water out of thy cistern (meborecha) and running waters out of thy well' (beareche) (Prov. v., 15). Why does scripture use these two terms cistern and well, beginning with bar (cistern) and ending with bear (well or fount). Because the one contains; the other produces or sends forth water, and scripture wishes to teach us that the cistern will eventually become a well. Like a poverty stricken and poor man, the souls of the righteous or just are possessed of nothing in themselves, and are as a cistern into which water is poured. Every worldly minded and unjust man bears on him the mark of the letter D (daleth meaning poor) and is like a cistern without water. But the souls of the just become founts or wells sending forth water in all directions. Who operates and produces this change? It is he, the source and origin of celestial light, who causes it to now into human souls on the earth plane as we have stated before. Another signification of these words is, that they apply to David, whom scripture makes to say, 'Who (mi) will give me to drink water of the cistern in Bethlehem?' The term 'running water' also designates Abraham, 'out of' (bethokh) Jacob and 'thy well' Isaac who is called a 'fount of springing or living water' (Gen. xxvi., 9). In this same verse is contained the holy and profound mystery of the patriarchs, amongst whom King David is included. The desire of union between the opposite sexes is only excited when the female becomes receptive and filled with the female spirit or principle which, becoming conjoined with the male principle from on high, causes fertility. So is it with the synod or congregation of Israel (or the pure and initiated in the secret doctrine). It experiences a desire after the Holy One only when it becomes filled with the spirit of righteousness and then is made fruitful in goodness and then union with the Divine is a source of the greatest joy and delight, that has been thus expressed by a writer. 'The Holy One then comes forth and takes delight in the company of the souls of just men made perfect.' Observe that the children of the garden of Eden, or the Edenic race of beings, became human only after Noah, the Just One, had entered the ark, or in other words had become incorporated. Until that happened, they were invisible and unmanifested as humanity which would never have been able to exist as at present on the earth plane unless Noah had entered the ark (of incarnation) and given birth and origin to offspring, subjected to the laws of evolution and development that generate alike both in the celestial and terrestrial worlds by which it was rendered competent to multiply and replenish the earth. Such is the occult meaning of the oracular words 'Drink waters out of thy cistern and running waters or streams out of thy well.'"

"And the earth also was corrupt before God" (Alhim) (Gen. vi., 11). Said Rabbi Jehuda, "Scripture states that the earth was also corrupt and then adds, 'before the Alhim.' Why so? It was in order to show the men of that generation then existent on the earth lived in violation both of natural and moral law,--that their wickedness was flagrant and open before man and God."

Said Rabbi Jose: "I think otherwise. The words signify, that men committed crimes secretly and known only to Alhim and that only by their enormity and heinousness did they manifest to everyone. The words 'these are the generations of Noah' apply equally to mankind who before the advent of Noah lived in open wickedness and to his posterity whose sin was in secret."

Said Rabbi Abba: "From the time of Adam's transgression of the divine commands all his descendents were called sons or children of Adam, not as a term of honor, but as a characteristic of birth from an ancestor who by his disobedience had broken the divine law. When Noah appeared in the world, men were termed the sons of Noah, an honorable distinction, as being the offspring of him who preserved the human race from extinction and not of Adam whose sin caused it to disappear by bringing death into the world to every soul."

Said Rabbi Jose in objection to this statement: "If this were really true, wherefore is it written 'And the Lord came down to see the city and the tower which the children of Adam builded' (Gen. xi., 5), the sons or children of Adam and not of Noah and who were living after the time of the deluge.'"

Said Rabbi Abba in reply: "Through his disobedience it would have been better for Adam had he not been created, as all who like him become transgressors of the law are denominated 'sons of Adam,' not because deriving their birth from him but as being transgressors as he was, and such were the builders of the tower of Babel. Now may we gather why scripture uses the word Aleh (these are the generations) to distinguish the difference existing between the Adamic and Noachic races of mankind. The generations of Noah were now no longer termed the sons of Adam, but the sons of Noah who introduced into and brought them forth out of the ark in order to re-people the world. Adam did not bring forth children or sons out of the garden of Eden, for had he done so they would have been immortal or extra human. Then also would not the light of the moon have become diminished and the work of creation would have endured everlastingly. Even the highest angels themselves would not have equalled man in the endowment of celestial light, beauty of form and wisdom as it is written, 'In the image of Alhim created He him' (Gen. 1. 27). But the children of Adam, begotten after his expulsion from the garden of Eden, were both mortal and unworthy."

Said Rabbi Hezekiah: "How was it possible for Adam to beget offspring in the garden of Eden, as it is certain, the tempter would have had no power over him and he would have remained childless in the world, even as Israel if they had not sinned by worshipping the golden calf, would have remained unique as a race and would not have given birth to another generation?" Said Rabbi Abba in reply: "My contention is this. If Adam had not sinned he would not have engendered and begotten offspring under the influence of the tempter (sexual desire), but of the Holy Spirit (the Higher Self). After the fall, his offspring begotten under the influence of animal sexual propensities, were mortal, not being pure and unalloyed in their origin and constitution but compounded of the animal and spiritual. If however he had not fallen and remained in the garden of Eden, he would have begot offspring entirely spiritual and who in their constitution would have been as pure and immortal as the angels and other celestial beings.

The children born after his expulsion from Eden enjoyed only a temporary and ephemeral existence up to the appearance of Noah who, after entering the ark (of incarnation) and by his righteous living becoming united with his Higher Self, was then able to produce offspring that eventually spread themselves throughout all parts of the earth, leaving behind a posterity that will survive to the end of the world.

Said Rabbi Hiya: "It is written, 'And God saw their works, that they turned from their evil way' (Jonah III. 10). Observe, when men become upright and obey the dictates of the good law, the earth itself changes and acquires a virtue to administer to the enjoyment and happiness of mankind, as then the Schekina or that divine something termed life that operates in all organic and inorganic creatures and by its attractive power binds together the mundane and heavenly sphere, the harmony between which, results in peace and joy. On the contrary, when sin and wrongdoing prevail, this divine life and influence is banished from the earth, which becomes itself infected and desolate and infertile through the evil influence that then pervades it. But if Israel sins, which God forbid, scripture states that then Alhim quits the earth and ascends into heaven (Ps. LXII 6) and also gives the reason thereof, 'because they have prepared a net for my feet. My soul is bowed down through their iniquity; which words are expressive of a degree of wickedness similar to that of the antediluvians. If it be asked, do they apply equally to Jerusalem? Doth the Schekina forsake it when men become corrupted? for we have been taught that it is under the special care and protection of the Holy One who has chosen it for his habitation, so that no other spirit or celestial chief reigns and rules in the land of Israel. Notwithstanding this, we affirm that it comes to pass that an evil spirit or influence visits it and corrupts the dwellers therein. How know we this? From King David of whom it is written, 'And David beheld the angel of the Lord standing between' the earth and the heaven having a drawn sword in his hand stretched over Jerusalem' (I. Chron. XXI. 16), owing to the land of Israel having become corrupted by evil."

CHAPTER XLIII.

SAID Rabbi Eleazar: "What David beheld at that awful moment was not an angel but a manifestation of the Holy One. The scripture uses the words 'The Angel of the Lord' as a metaphoric appellation of the Divine Being, as did also Jacob when blessing Ephraim and Manasseh saying, 'The Angel which redeemed me from all evil, bless the lads.' And furthermore, in Exodus XIV. 19. The Almighty is referred to and designated as 'The Angel of the Lord that went before the camps of Israel removed and went behind them.' Whether Israel acts uprightly or not, the Holy One is still its ruler and governor in order that it may not become subject to other nations, and that its good works may put them to shame. It may however be said, yet it is written, 'The adversary hath spread out his hand upon her pleasant things, for she hath seen the heathen entered into her sanctuary' (Lam. I. 10). If the Holy One governs Israel as stated, how was it that the heathen entered her sanctuary and destroyed it? Scripture itself gives the reason, as it is written, 'Thou hast done all these things (Jer. XIX. 22). The Lord hath done that which he hath devised. He hath fulfilled what he proposed in days of yore (Lam. II. 19). From these words we conclude and affirm that notwithstanding the occurrence of all these calamities, the Holy One is still ruler of Israel and that only by his permission could they have happened. Observe, scripture states, 'And Alhim looked upon the earth, and behold, it was corrupt,' because the Schekina had deserted it, as we have said. Moreover it is stated, 'And God saw their works that they turned from their evil way' (Ion. III. 14). The cry of the earth is always ascending heavenwards and desirous of union with the celestial world, enrobes itself with raiments of beauty and splendor, as doth a maiden expecting the arrival of her lover. When its children are upright and virtuous, they become its ornaments. Far otherwise was it when the deluge came, for then they were vile and depraved and corrupted, so that the earth blushing with shame at their deeds of wickedness hid itself, as doth an unfaithful wife from her husband. When, however, they became brazen, openly lewd, obscene and sensual, then like an immodest courtesan casting aside her veil, it also became unclean and corrupted, as it is written 'The earth is defiled by the inhabitants thereof, because they have transgressed the laws, changed the ordinance, broken the everlasting covenant' (Is. XXIV. 5).

Then corruption both moral and physical prevailed throughout the world, for all flesh had corrupted it's way upon the earth."

Rabbi Eleazer was once on a visit to Rabbi Jose the son of Rabbi Simeon and grandson of Lakunya, who on beholding him spread a sumptuous couch on the floor in order to recline and rest himself. After engaging a while in silent meditation, his grandfather said: "Have you ever heard your father explain the meaning of the words, 'The Lord hath done that which he had devised. He hath fulfilled his word that he had commanded in the days of old?'"

Said Rabbi Eleazar: "Initiated students have interpreted them thus, the words 'fulfilled his word' (bitza emratho) signify that God hath rent his purple robe of glory and light with which he had arrayed himself from the beginning of creation, and contributed to the beauty and perfection of his sanctuary."

Then asked his grandfather again: "Does a king think or devise punishment before his son has acted wickedly?"

To this Rabbi Eleazar replied; "A certain king possessed a most costly and precious vase. Fearing the loss of it, he caused it to be continually placed before him. At length his son came to visit him and on a dispute arising between them, the king in a moment of anger seized hold of the vase and dashed it to pieces on the ground. Such is the signification of the words; 'The Lord hath done what he had devised.' Observe, from the day the sanctuary was finished and completed, the Lord regarded it with continuous joy and delight, yet fearing that Israel would act wickedly, he determined it should be destroyed. Whilst Israel kept the good law and lived in obedience to its dictates, purely and uprightly, there was the sanctuary the glory of God on the earth, but when Israel fell with idolatry and forsook his worship it was destroyed. At its destruction then only did the Holy One feel grief at the punishment of the guilty. On all other occasions it is a source of delight to him when the wicked through their misdeeds are swept out of the world, as it is written, 'When the wicked perish there is shouting.' (Prov. XI. 10). If, however, it be objected, we are taught that the Holy One never rejoices at the punishment of the evildoer observe that punishment is twofold in its character. There is the punishment of those who, despite the admonitions and long-suffering of God, continue in their wickedness. The suffering of these causes joy to the Holy

One. There is also the punishment of those whose perversity in crime has not attained its climax. Far from being a source of joy to him, their suffering causes the Holy One to sorrow and grieve over them. There are wretches who are afflicted before their wickedness has reached its culmination, as it is written, 'For the iniquity of the Amorites is not yet full' (Gen. XV. 16). If, again, it be asked, wherefore God chastises sometimes those whose iniquity is not full? We answer, evildoers whose bad deeds injure only themselves are punished only when the measure of their iniquity is filled, whilst the unrighteous who attach themselves to Israel with the object of afflicting and injuring it are punished before their evil intentions are realized. It is the chastisement of this class of evildoers that causes grief to the Holy One. Amongst such were the Egyptians that were drowned in the Red Sea, and the enemies of Israel in the time of Jehoshaphat It is written: 'For yet seven days, and I will cause it to rain upon the earth, forty days and forty nights, and every living substance that I have made will I destroy from off the face of the earth'" (Gen. VII. 4).

Said Rabbi Jehuda: "Wherefore this limit of forty days and nights? It was because this number is always found in connection with the infliction of punishment, as it is written, 'Forty stripes he may give him and not exceed' (Deuter. XXV. 3). This number is fixed to correspond with the four cardinal quarters of the world, each of which is divided into ten parts or degrees as man was created to correspond with them in a manner, for the commission of crime he must not he beaten with more than forty stripes. For a like reason, this number forty was equally necessary in the punishment of the world."

Rabbi Isaac was sitting in presence of Rabbi Simeon, and in course of conversation asked the question: "What is the real meaning of the words, 'And the earth was corrupt before the Alhim.' Though man commit crime how can it affect the earth and make it corrupt?" Rabbi Simeon replied: "Scripture informs us that the earth and all flesh upon it had together become corrupt. There is found another and similar expression or statement, 'And the land is defiled and therefore I do visit the iniquity thereof upon it.' Now, if it be said, though men sinned, how could their crimes cause the earth to be corrupt, so that along with them it is subject to punishment? Observe that the sins of mankind that corrupt it are effaceable by repentance except that of self-defilement; and so scripture states, 'Though thou wash thee with nitre and take thee much soap, yet thine iniquity is marked before me saith the Lord God' (Jer. II. 22); and again, 'For thou art not a God that hath pleasure in wickedness, neither shall evil dwell with thee' (Ps. V. 5). Only by extraordinary penitence can this heinous sin be expiated, respecting which it is written, 'And Er the elder son of Judah was wicked before the Lord, and the Lord slew him'" (Gen. XXXVIII. 7), which verse has already been commented upon.

Again Rabbi Isaac questioned Rabbi Simeon: "Wherefore did God punish the antediluvians by a deluge of water rather than by fire or some other scourge?"

Rabbi Simeon replied: "Therein is involved a deep mystery. In indulging in the heinous sin of self pollution man impeded and prevented the union of the waters above with the waters below, or in other words, the male and female principles, and as therefore punished by a watery element; so that in their case the punishment fit the crime. Scripture states, 'All the foundations of the great deep were broken up and the windows of heaven were opened.' (Gen. VII. 4). The fountains of the great deep refer to the waters below, and the windows of heaven to the waters above."

Rabbi Hiya and Rabbi Jehuda when traveling, passed near some great and lofty mountains, in the gorges and fissures of which they observed bleached skeletons of the remains of men who had perished in the deluge. They measured two hundred feet as they extended on the rocks. Overcome with astonishment, they said: "Now we comprehend what the masters have told us, why the antediluvians feared not the divine punishment, as it is written. 'Therefore they say unto God, depart from us for we desire not the knowledge of thy ways (Job XXI. 14).' But their haughtiness and pride of strength availed them nothing, for they perished, swept off the face of the earth by the waters of the deluge." "'And Noah begat three sons, Shem, Ham and Japhet'", (Gen. VI. 10), said Rabbi Hiya to Rabbi Jehuda, "Come and I will make known unto thee what I have learned as to the occult meaning and sense of these words. The life of Noah was similar to a man entering into a cavern, from which after a certain time, come forth two or three sons, each of them different in character, habit and temperament, one being upright, one unjust, whilst the third is void of any special trait of disposition. The same peculiarity and distinction between individuals obtain alike in the three worlds. Observe when the soul descends from the celestial sphere or plane in heaven it becomes as it were entangled in mountain ravines, and meeting with its lower intellectual self, they take on the animal bodily life, and thus blended form one individual."

Said Rabbi Jehuda, "The mind and the lower nature depend the one on the other, but the spirit (the higher or real self) is independent of both of them. They are located or inhere in the physical organization, but not it, which as yet has never been discovered or seen by any individual. When a man leads a pure life, his higher self is present and aids him in his endeavors, and by its purifying and enlightening influence enables him to attain to and enter into the enjoyment of the higher life of peace and bliss unspeakable. If, however he is careless and unwilling to live the higher life, then though he may become intellectual, he can never become pure and one with the Divine. Furthermore, whose lives impurely depraves his nature, and by ignoring the dictates and admonitions of the spirit within him renders himself more and more receptive of and swayed by objects of sense in following the bent of his animal appetites and inclinations."

It is written, "And God said unto Noah, 'the end of all flesh is come before me'" (Gen. VI. 12). Said Rabbi Jehuda: "David says, 'make me to know mine end and the measure of my days, what it is, that I may know how frail I am.' From these words addressed unto the Holy One, we learn that there are two ends, one on the right hand, the other on the left, which man must choose to walk in during his life on earth. Of that on the right it is written, 'Go thou thy way until the end be, for thou shalt rest and stand in thy lot at the end of thy days' (Dan. XII. 13). Of that on the left it is said, 'He setteth an end to darkness and searcheth out all perfection, the stones of darkness and the shadow of death. He considereth the depth of all things.' (Job XXVIII. 3.). When by affliction and suffering the stones buried in darkness become manifested and the shadow of death hovers over, then the end of darkness becomes visible, or in other words, the angel of death or the serpent. Thus 'the end of all flesh' has the same meaning as the words 'the end of darkness,' that is, the death angel or the serpent. 'He considereth the depth of all things' refers to the same being who, when judgment falls upon the world, constitutes himself the satan or accurser of mankind and strives to disparage and blacken the characters of all creatures. With reference to the end on the right, the Holy One said to Daniel, 'Go thy way till the end come, for thou shalt rest.' Thereupon Daniel turned and said, 'In which world shall my rest be, in this or the world to come?' 'In this world,' replied the Holy One, "where rest is necessary, 'as it is written, 'He who walks in the right way shall rest in his bed' (Is. LVII. 2). Then asked Daniel again of the Holy One, 'Shall I be of the number of those who will rise again at the end of the world?' The Holy One replied 'Thou, shalt rise.' Said Daniel then 'I know that amongst these who shall rise, there will be upright and just men who during their lives on earth walked in the path of truth, and others there will be who have done wickedly, but as yet I know not amongst which I shall rise again.' Said the Holy One, 'In thy lot or state in which thou diest.' Again Daniel spake and said, "Thou sayest unto me, 'Go thou thy way to the end (lekh lecetz). There is an end on the right and an end on the left, which of these meanest thou?'" 'The end on the right,' answered the Holy One. David also said unto the Lord, 'Make me to know my end,' and found no rest until he knew which it would be, and it was said unto him, 'Sit thou on my right hand.' Observe, the Holy One also spake unto Noah, 'The end of all flesh has come before me.' What does the word 'end' here mean? It is that which causes the faces of all creatures to become pale and darkened. Hence we learn that the worldly minded and impious attract to themselves this end or state that causes the hue and complexion of their visages to become dark and gloomy. This unknown something or terror called 'the end' does not seize hold of anyone except by permission from on high. When God spake to Noah, it was present before him, waiting for his word of authority to seize hold of the antediluvians, and then he added, 'I will destroy them with the earth,' at the same time saying unto Noah 'Make thee an ark of gopher wood,' in order to protect himself and ward off the attack of the death angel that he may have no power over him. Observe, we have heard that when death invades a city or enters into the world abroad, a man should not walk in the public streets and thoroughfares if he wishes to avoid the death angel, who then has the power to afflict and destroy anyone whom he meets and encounters. Therefore, was it the Holy One said unto Noah, 'Thou must conceal thyself within the ark and so avoid meeting the destroying angel and thus be secure from his lethal power.' If it be said, there was no such being existing at the time of the deluge whose waters caused the destruction of the human race, observe that no judgment has ever overwhelmed the world but what this malefic angel has been present to inflict it. At the time of the Flood, he was present in the water which was an instrument used by him, and so God warned Noah and counselled him to avoid his presence by building and entering into the ark. But if it be furthermore asked, what advantage could accrue to the patriarch by so doing? How could that prevent the entrance into it of the destroyer? Our reply is, that he has no power over anyone so long as he keeps himself out of his sight. We gather this from what happened to the Egyptians, since God commanded, 'Let none of you go out of the door of his house until the morning.' (Ex. XII. 22). What was the reason of this prohibition? That he might avoid meeting the destroying angel who had the power of inflicting death. Therefore was Noah admonished to include and hide himself in the ark and thus escape destruction."

Rabbi Hiya and Rabbi Jose, whilst traveling in Armenia, and passing by some great and lofty mountains, observed in them vast gorges and deep ravines resulting from the action of the waters of the deluge. Said Rabbi Hiya. "These have existed from the time of the flood and, by the will of the Holy One, will endure unto the end of the world as tokens or reminders of the great wickedness of the antediluvians, even as it is his will that by their good deeds, the memory of the righteous should abide before him and never be effaced. And even with those who delight not in his service, their evil works are transmitted and become manifested throughout all generations, as it is written, 'Though thou wash thyself with nitre and take thee much soap, yet thine iniquity is marked before me, saith the Lord God'" (Jer. II. 22).

Said Rabbi Jose "We read, 'Lift up thy voice, Oh daughter of Gallim, cause it to be heard unto Laish, Oh! poor Anathoth' (Is. X. 30). These words already explained apply really to the congregation of Israel. The daughter of Gallim besides designating the daughter of Abraham our father, refers also to Israel who in another part of scripture is termed 'a closed fountain:' The term 'Gallim' also signifies rivers, which all flow towards the garden they fill and irrigate, as it is written, 'Thy plants are an orchard of pomegranates with pleasant fruits' (Cant. IV. 13), cause it to be heard at Laish has the same meaning as 'the lion (laich) perisheth from lack of prey' (Job. IV. 12). Laish denotes the male and laishah the female. Wherefore so, is it because scripture states, 'The lion is strongest amongst beasts and fearless of any it meets' (Prov. XXX. 30) or 'The lion is dead through lack of prey.' The true interpretation is in the word laish, an occult term of that mundane virtue which emanating from on high manifests itself on the earth plane. When the affluents of the celestial virtue cease descending and are no longer transformed into the lower mundane power, 'laish' then takes the name of 'laishah'; that is, it manifests itself as female. The words 'aniah anathoth (oh, poor anathoth) signify the same as those (in Jer. I. 1), namely 'Jeremiah, son of Hilhiah, of the priests who lived in poverty (ba-anathoth), and also those I Kings II. 26'. And unto Abiathiar, the priest, said the king, 'get thee to Anathoth, or, rather, live thou in poverty in thine own fields; the signification of which words is as follows: During the life of David

Abiathar lived in wealth and opulence, but after David's decease Solomon condemned him to live in poverty on his own laud or property."

CHAPTER XLIV.

SAID Rabbi Hiya "Since the day that Adam transgressed the command of God, the world became affiliated with poverty until the advent of Noah, who, through the sacrifice he offered up, caused it to regain its normal fertility. "

Said Rabbi Jose, "the earth recovered its fertility, but did not become freed from the infection of the serpent until Israel stood at the foot of Mount Sinai and was united with the Tree of Life. And if they had not broken the law; there would have been no death in the world, Israel having become purified. When they sinned through their idolatry of the calf, the first tables of the law that freed it from the power and influence of the serpent or 'the end of all flesh' were broken. When the Levites rose up to slaughter and kill, the Israelites engaged in idolatrous worship the serpent who is the same as the destroying angel, placed himself at their head, but was unable to inflict any injury on them, as they were protected by certain amulets that made then impervious to his attacks. And only when God said unto Moses, 'Put off thy ornaments from thee' was the serpent able to smite them as it is written, 'And the children of Israel stripped themselves of their ornaments by Mount Horeb' (Ex. XXXIII. 5). Why is the word here used vaithnatzelon (they were despoiled) and not vainatzelon (stripped off). It is in order to show that the Israelites deprived and despoiled of the protecting ornaments (amulets or pentacles) they had affixed on themselves at Mount Sinai when receiving the law, fell under the influence of the serpent who had now the power to afflict them."

Said Rabbi Hiya: "Why, if Noah was just and upright, did not death disappear out of the world? It was because it was not altogether purified and freed from the infection of the serpent. Moreover, the antediluvians had lost all faith and belief in the existence of the Holy One and were really atheists and given up to the worship and service of the evil one, who after the deluge caused men to sin in a similar manner to those who lived before it, for the holy law that constitutes the Tree of Life was not revealed on earth by the Holy One until Israel stood at the foot of Mount Sinai. Noah was, therefore, unable to suppress death in the world, but rather, after his exit from the ark contributed to its continuance and perpetuity therein, as it is written, 'and he drank of the wine and was drunken; and he lay naked in his tent'" (Gan. IX. 21).

KABBALISTIC EXPLANATION OF THE FEAST OF TABERNACLES AND THE LOULAB

AS Rabbi Hiya and Rabbi Jose travelled onwards, they beheld a stranger approaching them whom they judged by his appearance, to be an Israelite. After saluting him they asked "Who art thou?" "I am," he replied, "a resident of the village of Ramin and as the feast of Tabernacles is coming on I have been specially deputed to prepare the Loulab and am therefore on may way to cut down palm branches and prepare them according to ancient and legal custom. After walking a little together, the stranger turning to them said, "Do you know why the Loulab must consist of four different objects in order to secure the blessing of rain upon the earth?" "With Students of the Secret Doctrine," they answered, "it has often been a subject of much discussion, but if you know anything that will further enlighten us, we pray you to impart it unto us."

Then spoke again the stranger and said, "The village in which I live, though small and in an obscure locality, is distinguished by the residence of students of the Secret Doctrine and also of a master, Rabbi Isaac, son of Jose of Melrozaba, who daily gives discourses and lessons on occult subjects from which we always gather knowledge new and most interesting. Once when conversing with him, he stated that during the Feast of Tabernacles the Israelites are exalted and pre-eminent above all other people and nations of the world and therefore we carry the Loulab in hand as a trophy of victory over them, inasmuch as only from Israel, do the great chiefs of idolatrous nations receive and participate in the blessings that descend from heaven. These chiefs or governing angels are called in scripture "hamayim hazzedonim" (the proud waters) as it is written 'Then had the proud waters gone over our soul. Blessed be the Lord who hath not given us as a prey to their teeth.' (Ps. CXXI V. 5.) The four components of the Loulab (the palm, willow, myrtle and citron) correspond to the four letters of the sacred name I H V H by which Israel is exalted above all other nations and to whom is owing the descent of water to serve as libations upon the altar of sacrifice. From the beginning of the Feast of Tabernacles to Cippur or day of expiation, the holy One sits and judges the world, during which period, the Serpent no longer appears before Him as man's accuser, being attracted to the goat that is offered to him and therefore heedless of anything of a sacred character. So is it with him when a goat is offered to him at the time of new moon. For this reason, the children of Israel pray then the Holy One to grant them remission and forgiveness of their sins."

THE OCCULTISM OF SACRIFICES

THERE is yet another subject the knowledge of which is only imparted to those who are conversant with the teachings and wisdom of the Secret Doctrine. From all others I am prohibited and forbidden to discourse thereon. "What may that be?" asked Rabbi Jose. "I cannot," said the stranger, divulge it unless I am assured of your fitness to receive it." Travelling on together in silence, he turned to them and said: "When the moon approaches the sun, the Holy One by his power revives the North and attracts it to himself to himself in love; whilst the South revives itself. When the influences of these two combine and blend together; then occurs the conjunction of the two luminaries. When the sun rises in the east it attracts the influences of these two cardinal quarters and reflects them upon the moon at full. The approximation and conjunction of the sun and moon are analogous to that of the male and female. The law of attraction prevails throughout the universe, in the world above as in the world below and is expressed in the aphorism--"as above so below." As the right side of the sephirotic tree stands for love, the attractive principle, so does the left stand for rigour or the principle of repulsion personified by the serpent from whom emanate all impurity and corruption and death. It draws and attracts all who are receptive of its evil influence.

Now when the North is not revived by the Holy One, the moon becomes drawn to the left side and in order to prevent this, Israel is obliged to sacrifice a goat in which the serpent delighted, lets go his hold of that luminary that then begins to shine and daily increase in light and splendour. Thus on the day of atonement when the serpent or Evil One is engaged with the goat offered unto it, the moon freed from its evil influence undertakes to defend and protect Israel as a mother watches over the safety and welfare of her child. Then it is that the Holy One grants his blessings with remission and pardon of sins. During the Feast of Tabernacles the influence of the right side of the Sephirotic tree so attracts the moon that she attains its fulness and heavenly blessings are showered upon the tutelary guardians of pagan nations on earth in order to preclude them from imagining they have any right to share in those that are reserved and allotted to Israel. During its rise and fall the visible disk of the moon symbolises those blessings that are bestowed upon Israel, but the obscured part, those of idolatrous nations. When the moon however is at the full, Israel receives and profits from the full tide of blessings from heaven and therefore it is written "On the eighth day there shall be an "abzereth" amongst you (Num. XXVIII. 15) the word abzereth here meaning as the Targum translates it "a reunion" in order that the divine in all their fulness and extent may descend upon Israel as a whole. On this day, Israel prays to the Holy One for the blessing of rain not only for themselves but also all other nations. This feast peculiar to Israel is referred to in the words of scripture "My beloved is mine and I am his" or its attendant blessings are shared in by no other nation; in the dispensing of which the Holy One is like unto a King who invites his friends to a banquet on a certain day. After reflection, the monarch says to himself, "I wish to enjoy myself with the company of my friends but in sending invitations to my governors, and chiefs and rulers of provinces I am afraid these will be so numerous as to interfere with and lessen my enjoyment." What did the King do? He first regaled his official guests with the usual meats and vegetables, and after their departure well filled and satisfied, he sat down at the table laden with the best and most delicious viands and after his friends had feasted thereon, he further added to their pleasure by granting the requests they made unto him and so the banquet passed off pleasantly and without any exhibition of ill-feeling or discontent. In a similar manner the Holy One acts with Israel and therefore scripture saith, "on the eighth day shall be your abzereth (coming together) that is, for the reception of blessings to be participated in only by yourselves." Amongst the requisites used during the Feast of Tabernacles, were the palm and the citron. During every day of the feast, Jews with a citron in their left hand and in their right a bundle of branches viz.: one of the palm tree and two of the willow and myrtle, pass around the altar exclaiming seven times, in memory of the conquest of Jericho and hence called the Great Hosanna. In preparing the Loulab, the stem of the branches was covered over with palm leaves. If it was dry or withered, crooked or split in the least, it was considered worthless. It must be fresh and green, smooth and without burr or blemish. It was encircled with sprigs of willow and myrtle each of which must have three leaves otherwise the Loulab was Posoul.

Then said Rabbi Hiya and Rabbi Jose to the stranger, "This; has indeed been a most pleasant and interesting journey; blessed are they who delight to study the Secret Doctrine." Then embracing him, Rabbi Jose exclaimed, "Surely thou art of the number of those referred to in Scripture "And all thy children shall be taught of the Lord and great shall be the abundance of their peace" (Ps. LIV. 14). Proceeding on their way, they at last sat down and rested themselves.

A VEXATA QUESTIO IN BIBLICAL PHILOLOGY

THE stranger began speaking again. "Know you," said he, "why the sacred name I. H. V. H. is found mentioned in the verse, "Then Jehovah rained upon Sodom and Gomorrah brimstone and fire from heaven" (Gen. XIX. 24) instead of the divine name Alhim which is exclusively used in connection with the account of the deluge? Listen to the explanation handed down by tradition through the masters of the Secret Doctrine. Wherever the name Jehovah is found in Scripture it designates the Holy One sitting and presiding over the members of his executive tribunal of justice. But when Alhim is used, it refers to his tribunal only. At the destruction of these two cities involving but a small part of the world, Jehovah acted along with his judicial executive whilst at the deluge when the whole world perished only the members of it were concerned in carrying out the divine decrees. If it is objected, that the whole world of human beings was not destroyed, inasmuch as Noah and his family were preserved from perishing, what differentiates the punishment of the deluge from that inflicted upon Sodom and Gomorrah. Our reply is, that Noah by his entry and inclusion in the ark became sequestered from mankind as a whole which was destroyed by the operation of the Alhim, whilst the overthrow of the cities of the plain was accomplished openly by Jehovah in concert with His celestial tribunal.

The mystery of this difference is referred to in the words "the Lord was seated at the time of the flood" (Ps. XXIX. 10). What does the word yeshab (was seated) really mean? but that He was alone and by himself at the time the deluge occurred; which interpretation unless corroborated by other texts in scripture, we would not have dared to apply to the Divine Being and therefore conclude that the Holy One was not conjoined with the members of his justiciary tribunal, the Alhim in the destruction of the world by the deluge. That this view is correct is further proved by the use of the word yasheb in Lev. XIII, 46. "He shall dwell alone (yasheb) without the camp shall be his habitation." Thus it was that Noah hidden in the ark, escaped the general destruction and after divine justice had been appeased, we read that then the Alhim remembered or thought of Noah (Gen. VIII. 1). From these remarks we infer that the Holy One punishes sometimes openly and sometimes in secret, openly when acting with and through the Alhim whose jurisdiction extends over and throughout the world--secretly when sitting in that celestial sphere whence descends all the blessings of heaven. Knowing this we can understand why the precious goods a man hides are sources of blessings, whilst those that are visible and perceived by all excite envy and covetousness through the influence of the demon known as Ra-ain (evil eye)." [1]

As the stranger ceased speaking Rabbi Jose was delighted and exclaimed, "blessed are we students of Rabbi Simeon through whose teachings and instruction we have been able to understand and comprehend what has just been imparted to us. Truly this stranger has been divinely directed and sent to instruct us in the Secret Doctrine concerning truths and teachings the most ennobling and sublime." On reaching the dwelling of Rabbi Simeon they related to him all that the stranger has said unto them whereon after listening to them he replied, "well and truly hath the stranger spoken."

---

[1] This opinion is frequently expressed in the Talmud: see Tract Baba Bathra fol. 6.

KABBALISTIC EXPLANATION OF THE GOAT AZAZEL

RABBI Eleazar whilst sitting in presence of his father Rabbi Simeon, spake and said, "the demon called 'the end of all flesh' doth it take pleasure and receive any advantage from the sacrifices of Israel or not?"

Whereupon Rabbi Simeon replied "Yea truly, both heaven above and earth below are benefited. Observe that priests (cohanim) Levites and Israel are collectively termed Adam when imbued with the same holy will and desire to, offer up a sacrifice either of a sheep, an ox or any other animal. Before so doing, however, they must make confession and expiate their sins of word, though and deed, for then only are sacrifices of any avail and become charged with the sins confessed as was the case with the Azazel or scapegoat driven forth into the wilderness bearing the sins of the congregation of Israel, as it is written--'and Aaron shall lay both his hands upon the head of the goat and confess over it all the iniquities of the children of Israel and all their transgressions, putting them upon the head of the goat and shall send him away by the hand of a fit man into the wilderness.'" (Lev. XVI. 21). It is the same with other sacrifices. When placed upon the altar they become charged with the good deeds and thoughts, as also of the sins and evil thoughts of the sacrificer, each of them ascending to its own appropriate place on high and distinguished as emanations from a man's higher self and denominated Adam or from his animal or lower nature and called "behemoth" (beastly). This distinction is referred to in scripture, "Thou savest both man (adam) and beast." (Ps. XXXVI. 6). Offerings of unleavened cakes and all other comestibles, are for attracting the Holy Spirit and inducing it to operate through the service of the priest, the chanting of Levites and the prayers of the worshippers. In the oil and wheat of such offerings, none of the expeditive angels of retribution can participate so that they are unable to acid to the severity of their afflicting judgments, being attracted for the time being by the offerings of animals. This is why sacrifices of both kinds take place at one and the same time, in accordance with the injunctions of the Secret Doctrine that gratitude and thankfulness the true elements of every oblation and sacrifice may ascend on high pure and sincere before the Almighty and thus obtain responsive blessings.

RABBI SIMEON'S REFLECTIONS ON THE SUPREME AND ITS UNION WITH HUMAN SOULS

SAID Rabbi Simeon, during prayer, I raise my hands on high as a token and expression of the gratitude of my will nature that goeth up to the almighty supreme Being whose essence is Will infinite and beyond all human comprehension. He is the great Beginning, the mystery of all mysteries. All created things in the universe are but emanations from Him who is the height of height that neither man nor angel can approach unto, nor hath ever seen or can see its origin and source. In vain the mind of man attempts to fly towards the omnipotent Will Being of which it is a fraction infinitesimal and infinitely small. Vain are all efforts to grasp and comprehend Thought Supreme and eternal, as we sink confounded, overwhelmed with feelings of awe ineffable. Yet though the height Divine remains eternally invisible to human vision, it manifests its presence and operates within the minutes and hours chiefly within the soul of man with whose natural light it blends whenever its aspirations and thoughts tend towards and are centered on the great source of all being and creation, the primal light that enlighteneth every man that cometh into the world. Between the enlightened human soul and the great Beginning are nine palaces or grades of evolutionary development two Kabbalah are designated Sephiroth whose culmination is Kether or The Crown. These grades, palaces or sephiroth call them as we may, are not entities but modes or stages of ascent towards union with the Divine Will and their respective lights are but the luminous reflection of the Divine Thought. Though nine in number, they are really one in this sense, they are derivations of the great Thought without which they could not exist and can never be but imperfect and obscure representations of the Divine Entity that must remain always unknown in its sublimity and transcendency beyond all human comprehension. Through these palaces the enlightened soul enters by continuous aspirations and thus they become the intermediaries to it between the known and unknown, between the comprehensible and the incomprehensible. Within them are hidden all the great spiritual mysteries and realities that to humanity as at present must remain objects of faith rather than of reason and intellectual perception. Only by the enlightened soul can they become cognised in its gradual ascension through them on its way to the great and transcendent Being termed The Eternal, The Everlasting One. But this cannot be effected only as it becomes receptive of and imbued with the light and splendor of the Sephiroth Binah (Doctrine Intelligence) by which it is brought into union with the Divine and enters into the enjoyment of the Beatific Vision. From these observations we are better able to understand and penetrate into the meaning and mysteries of sacrifices in general which as mere rites and ceremonies have no intrinsic efficacy. Only when they are the expression of the soul, gradually becoming purified and enlightened by and through its higher self are they a means of spiritual ascension in the divine life which is the true light of mankind assimilating and bringing it into closer relationship with the divine, Eternal I Am in whose presence there is fulness of joy and at whose right hand there are pleasures forevermore.

CHAPTER L.

THIS union and harmony between the finite and the infinite, God and man is the highest and deepest of mysteries, the mystery of all ages since the creation of the world. Happy are they in this world and the world to come who have attained unto a knowledge of it. Observe furthermore that the destroying angel known as "the end of all flesh" derives benefit and pleasure from acts of charity in this sense, that as such acts and deeds of charity and gratitude are a source of joy to the angels on high, so the material part of sacrifices symbolising the element of the impurity and imperfection of human nature becomes a source of strength and enjoyment to the inferior orders of spirits and this being the case, the Holy Spirit Israel's Watcher that neither slumbers nor sleeps, provides against their troubling her children and preventing their good deeds from becoming perfect and freed from impure thoughts.

At the rising of the moon in the early part of each month a goat is offered up as a supplementary sacrifice which the demon delighting in, cease for the time being from troubling Israel who is thus able to make its offerings in peace that bring them into closer relationship with their Lord and King. As a he-goat is what demons delight in, so is Israel the delight and choice of the Holy One as stated in scripture "for the Lord hath chosen Jacob unto himself and Israel for his peculiar treasure" (Ps. CXXXV. 4). Still further, "the end of all flesh" joys only in what is carnal and when he acquires power and influence over any one, it is over his animal or lower nature and not over his higher self. This is spiritual and celestial in origin, that is earthly in its production. So is it with the two elements or parts in a sacrifice; like goeth to like, the material part remaineth below, take spiritual part ascendeth on high. When any one lives the higher and diviner life, there is a continual sacrifice, that in a measure atones for the sins of humanity in general, whereas the life of an iniquitous man is of no benefit or advantage whatever to the world or it is blemished with sin and wrong doing and therefore it is written, "Whatsoever hath a blemish ye shall not offer, for it will not be acceptable" (Lev. XXII. 20). From what has been said we can understand and gather the true meaning of sacrifice and how the lives of good men subserve to the benefit and salvation of humanity.

THE OCCULT MEANING OF THE SIX HUNDRED YEARS OF NOAH'S LIFE

REFERRING again to the words "And Alhim said unto Noah, the end of all flesh is before me," Rabbi Simeon spake and said: "These words mean that the destroying angel presented himself before the Holy One, demanding power and authority to mark for destruction the race of the antediluvians. We further read, 'And behold! I will destroy them with the earth' (Gen. VI. 13). make thee an ark of gopher wood wherein entering thou mayst be preserved, and he may have no power over thee. And Noah did according to all that Alhim commanded him, "and in the six hundredth year of Noah's life, in the second month, the seventeenth day of the month, the same day were all the fountains of the great deep broken up and the windows of heaven were opened" (Gen. VII. 11). These words imply that only in that year of his earth life and incarnation, did Noah attain unto human perfection and by thus becoming a just man and perfect, was able to escape the doom impending over the wicked generation in which he lived, whose iniquity had then reached its climax. When Noah had attained unto this age, then the forbearance and long suffering of the Holy One ended and the destruction so long deferred overwhelmed the world and the race of the antediluvians was suddenly swept out of existence from off the face of the earth. Note the words, 'Behold I (ani) even I (hinneni) do bring a flood of waters upon the earth.' Wherefore the repetition of the personal pronoun, the one being the synonym of the other? It is because wherever in scripture Ani (I) is found it is used to designate God and having the same relation to Him as the soul has to the body. Thus it is written, 'I (ani) will make my covenant with thee' (Gen. xvii. 4), implying that God sometime or other will manifest himself and make himself known to mankind. Again, why is it written, 'Ath hammabbul mayin' (the deluge of waters), because thereby to show by the word 'ath' that in addition to the waters of the deluge, Alhim sent the angel of death to destroy the world and gave him authority to accomplish it by the element of water. We know also from tradition that the words 'I (ani) am the Lord' have the same meaning as, I am faithful in my promises of recompense to the righteous, as also in my denunciations of punishment on the wicked in the world to come, and all are made under the name of Ani. The additional words 'to destroy all flesh' also imply that the death angel is the real destroyer of the world and is alluded to as such in (Ex. xii. 23). 'And He will not suffer the destroyer to come into your houses to smite you.' That is to say, that the destroyer, who in the account of the deluge is designated 'the end of all flesh' shall have no power over you, nor authority to afflict and injure you. All this occult teaching in the secret doctrine respecting the deluge was imparted to me by Rabbi Issac."

ADAM SITTING AT THE GATE OF THE GARDEN OF EDEN

ON another occasion Rabbi Simeon spake and said: "It is written, 'I said, I shall not see the Lord even the Lord in the land of the living; I shall behold man no more with the inhabitants of the world' (Ps. xxxviii. 11). How great the number of those who are ignorant and take no interest in the secret doctrine. They expend their strength and energy in the acquisition of worldly knowledge, oblivious altogether of that true wisdom which is both spiritual and divine. When a man departs out of earth life, he has to account for every act and deed committed in it and meets many with whom he has been acquainted and held intercourse in the world. Eventually he beholds Adam seated at the Garden of Eden rejoicing over those who have faithfully observed and kept the divine commandments. Surrounding him are the righteous who were wise and avoided walking in the way that leads down to Gehenna and found the path of light. Such are termed by scripture 'inhabitants of the world' hadel, not haded. The inhabitants of this latter are mouselike in their habits of heaping up riches and know not who shall enjoy them; but the just and upright are termed dwellers of hadel, which word signifies to shun and avoid, because they have learned to shun the way to death and found entrance into the Garden of Eden. Another interpretation is this: by 'the inhabitants of the world' (hadel) is signified those who through repentance, ceased to do evil and learned to do well, as did Adam who was afterwards appointed leader into Eden of all repentant souls, and thus termed inhabitants of hadel, and therefore is it written, 'that I may know what I lack (hadel)' (Ps. xxxix. 5), Note the words, 'I shall not see Jah.' 'Who then is able to see him?' the other part of the verse explains, 'Jah in the land of the living.' When souls encircled with an aura of light, the result of righteous living, ascend on high to the sphere especially prepared for those who have attained unto the higher life, they are then able to gaze into the Zohar, the luminous mirror, or in other words the beatific vision whose splendor and brightness are reflections from the highest heavenly sphere, since a soul clothed in any other raiment than this light would be unable to behold and endure its intense vibrations. For even as souls in their progress and development on earth life and clothed and girded with an aura, so in the world on high, they become encircled with one brighter and still more luminous, by which they are able to contemplate the transcendent light coming down out of the lightest of the heavenly spheres known as 'the land of the living.' It was this aura of the higher life encircling him that Moses was able to behold what he did, as it is written, 'And Moses went into the midst of the cloud (as it seemed to human vision) and ascended the mount' (Ex. xxiv. 15). That is, he became clothed with an aura of divine light, in order to gaze into the luminous mirror, or beatific vision, similar to that which time just or perfected human beings' on their entrance into the higher heavenly spheres are clothed, of which the aura surrounding them during earth life is only a faint shadow and reflection. We now understand why the word Jah in the verse just cited is found repeated. 'I shall not see Jah in the land of the living,' were uttered by Hezekiah and mean that he feared and had no hope of ever experiencing the joy and delight of gazing upon the splendor of the light emanating from 'the land of the living,' through his dying childless, and therefore he said also, 'I shall not see Adam sitting at the gate of the Garden of Eden on high.' But why should he be afraid of this? because Isaiah the prophet had said unto him, 'Thou shalt die, thou shalt not live,' that is, thou shalt not live in the world to come as thou shalt die childless; for whoever leaves and quits the world without offspring is not admitted into the garden of the celestial Eden and is therefore altogether precluded from contemplating the glory and splendor of its light. If therefore Hezekiah with all the inherited merits of his forefathers, besides being an upright and just person, feared lest by dying childless, he should fail to attain unto the beatific vision, or enter into 'the land of the living,' so ought he be alarmed who, lacking ancestral merit and virtues, transgresses divine laws. The aura surrounding the just and perfected in the world to come who have lived the higher and diviner life is known and designated by initiates of the secret doctrine as 'The Master's Robe.' Happy they who wear it, for it is on their account the Holy One has reserved and put by unnumbered joys in the world to come, as it is written, 'For from the beginning of the world, men have not heard nor perceived by the ears, neither have seen, Oh God beside thee, what thou hast prepared for him that putteth his trust in Thee.'" (Ps. lxiv. 4.)

REMARKS ON THE DESTROYING ANGEL AND THE ANTEDILUVIANS

"'Behold I even I will bring a flood of waters upon the earth,'" said Rabbi Jehuda. "These words have reference to the waters of strife (Meribah), when the children of Israel murmured against the Lord and caused his holiness to appear amongst them. But was this act of insubordination and murmuring against God the only occurrence in the history of the children of Israel, that scripture should thus characterize it? The fact is, it is recorded as the occasion Israel afforded to the executors of divine justice of overcoming and afflicting them. For there are waters sweet and bitter, waters clear and turbid, waters of peace and waters of strife, to which scripture alludes as waters of Meribah where the children of Israel strove with the Lord: that is, they attracted to themselves the impure, unclean spirit that defiled them (vayiqqadesh bam) (Num. xx. 13).

In objecting against this exposition, Rabbi Hezekiah said: "If your interpretation was correct, the word vayiqadshou (they were deified) would have been used by scripture. The true meaning of the words is I think as follows: 'He whom the children of Israel should have worshipped and adored became degraded by them, if I may so express it. They became so obdurate and wilfully irrational both in mind and heart that the sense of the Divine presence with them became lost and extinguished, as doth the light of the moon at its fall. Therefore as the word vayiqadesh used by scripture should not be translated in its best sense of being sanctified; so the words, 'Behold I even I do bring a flood of waters,' should be understood as meaning, 'I will send unto them the impure and destroying angel by whom they have allowed themselves to become defiled.'"

Said Rabbi Jose: "Woe unto those who are unwilling to repent of their evil ways and deeds before the Holy One during their life on earth, for if, continuing unrepentant, at the close of it, they become cast into that outer darkness, where their torment ceaseth not and there shall be wailing and gnashing of teeth. Observe that by the open persistence of the antediluvians in their heinous and flagitious iniquity they were condemned and punished by the Holy One in a remarkable and open manner.

Said Rabbi Isaac: "Even when a man sins in secret, the Holy One is long suffering, and if he repents, has mercy upon and forgives him. On the contrary, if he continues in his evil and secret deeds, they become at last revealed and manifested and he is punished openly. Of this ordeal of the 'mey hammarim' (bitter waters) is an instance. It was so with the antediluvians, and how were they punished? They were exterminated from the face of the earth. The fountains of the great deep became opened and poured forth rain and mighty volumes of boiling water, so that their fleshless skeletons only remained to show they had once lived and had totally perished from off the face of the earth."

Said Rabbi Isaac: "The words 'and they were destroyed from the earth' (Gen. vii. 23), have the same meaning as 'let them be blotted out of the book of the living' (Ps. lxix. 28). Thus by the use of the word mahha (blotted out, destroyed off) in these two passages of scripture we are taught that the names of the wicked and evil doers are expunged out of the book of life--that they will never use again and appear in the day of judgment.

KABBALISTIC REMARKS ON THE COVENANT OR UNION OF THE HIGHER AND LOWER SELF

SAID Rabbi Eleazar: "It is written, 'But with thee will I establish my covenant' (Gen. vi. 18): as the continuity of the covenant or good law on earth is the same as in the higher spheres, we infer from these words that when men become just and upright in this world they contribute to the stability of the good law in both worlds.

Said Rabbi Simeon: "The words just cited have an occult meaning. The love of the male for the female is based upon jealous desire. Observe, when there is a just man in the world, or one whose higher and lower self have become harmonized and unified, the divine spirit or Shekinah is ever with him and abides in him, causing a feeling of affectionate attachment towards the Holy One to arise similar to that between the male and female. Therefore the words, 'I will establish my covenant with thee' may be rendered thus, 'Because of the union between thy higher and lower natures giving rise to a yet diviner life, I will abide with thee forever. I will never leave nor forsake thee. Come thou therefore into the ark into which no one unless he is just can enter.'"

Said Rabbi Eleazar: "As long as this covenant or union remains intact and undisturbed between himself and the Holy One, nothing can injure or afflict him. It was so with Noah who keeping the covenant was preserved along with his children, whilst the wickedness of the antediluvians caused them to perish from off the face of the earth."

Rabbi Jehuda whilst on a visit to Rabbi Simeon entered into a discussion with him as to the meaning of the words 'And Elijah repaired (vayerape) the altar of the Lord that was broken down' (I Kings xviii. 30). "What," said he, "is the occult meaning of this word vayerape, which literally signifies to heal."

In answer to this Rabbi Simeon remarked: "Note that in the days of the prophet Elijah all Israel had forsaken the worship of the Holy One and transgressed against his covenant made with their forefathers, to such an extent that it had become altogether forgotten and sunk into oblivion. Seeing and recognizing this, Elijah brought it back to their remembrance and thus restored it and made known again to them the everlasting covenant, and therefore it is written, 'And Elijah took twelve stones according to the number of the tribes of the sons of Jacob;' implying by this that it was by the occult virtue of the number twelve that the altar of the Lord was erected as aforetime; and then we read further, 'Unto whom the word of the Lord came saying, "Israel shall be thy name."' Why is this name of Israel here mentioned? Truly because when Israel attaches itself and adheres to the good law, it is so called; but when they forsake it, they are termed the children of Israel, or sons of Jacob. This is therefore why the word vayerape is written, because Elijah causes the covenant to become a subject of faith with the children of Israel and thus healed the breach between them and the Holy One and restored love and affection between them. Observe further that Phinehas, filled with zeal, inflicted punishment on Zimri and thus helped to reestablish the covenant, and so it is written of him, 'Behold, I give unto him my covenant of peace' (Num. xxv. 12). Now it is certain that Phinehas had in no way violated the covenant and needed not this gift. The real meaning is that he prevented it from becoming regarded as obsolete, a thing of no avail and therefore not worth consideration. For so doing he secured the blessing of the 'Covenant of Peace' the occult signification of which is, the mysterious Word, the Mediator between the two worlds, the celestial and terrestrial, and so it is added, 'And he shall have it and his seed after him, even the covenant of an everlasting priesthood, because he was zealous for his God and made an atonement for the children of Israel.'" (Num. xxv. 13.)

Said Rabbi Simeon: "There is no greater transgression in the sight of the Holy One than the breaking of the covenant, as it is written, 'and I will bring a sword upon you that shall avenge the breaking of my covenant.'" (Lev. xxvi. 25.) Note that the sin of the antediluvians reached its climax by the practice of self pollution, so that the earth itself became corrupted and defiled thereby (va thishaheth) before God, and for this reason he said, 'I will destroy them with the earth (mashitham).' There are, however, some who affirm that the measure of their iniquity became full when ignoring all moral right and justice; and might with them becoming right they broke the laws of heaven and earth, of God and humanity, and reaped their karma, the executors of which never fail to avenge the wrongdoing of those who infringe the Good Law."

VARIOUS KABBALISTIC EXPOSITIONS OF BIBLICAL TEXTS

SAID Rabbi Simeon: "We read, 'And God said unto Noah, enter thou and all thy house into the ark.' Wherefore in the narrative of the deluge is the divine name of Alhim used throughout, except in this particular passage in which the sacred name I H V H is found. The explana-tion is this. It is not in accordance with the rules and custom of good society for a wife to receive a guest into her home without the consent and permission of her husband, so Noah though desirous to enter into the ark, it was first of all necessary that the husband of the ark, designated here by the Holy Name, representing divine goodness, should give Noah authority and permission to do so, and not before this did he enter the ark; and it is added, 'For thee have I seen righteous before me in this generation,' from which words we infer that no one should ever be received as a guest in a house whose character is blemished and has a stain upon it."

Said Rabbi Jehuda: "We find written in scripture, Ps. xxiv. 1, 'A psalm of David. The earth is the Lord's and the fulness thereof, the world and they dwell therein.' We know from tradition that wherever the name David occurs in the psalms, that it was composed by him himself, but whenever it precedes a psalm it was composed and written by the aid of the Holy Spirit's influence. The words, 'The earth is the Lord's and the fulness thereof' refer to the land of Israel which is called the Holy Land, whilst 'the fulness thereof' signifies the Schekina, as it is written 'for the glory of the Lord filled the houses of God.' (1 Kings v. 11) Why in this passage is the word mla (full) in place of mile (filled). Thereby is meant that the Schekina was as the light of the moon at its full. The Schekina is full of heavenly blessings as a treasure house is with jewels and gold so long as it remains and abides in the land of Israel which belongs unto the Lord. According to another exposition these words refer to heaven on high wherein the Lord delights to dwell, but 'the fulness (oumloah) thereof' are the souls of the righteous filled with the principle of justice, the divine attribute that sustains the universe. Should it however be said, 'Is the earth sustained only by a single pillar?' observe what is written. 'For He lath founded it upon the seas (yammim) and established it upon the floods or rivers (recharoth).' He here refers to the Holy One, of whom it is written, 'It is He that hath made us.' (Ps. c. 3). 'For He looketh to the ends of the earth and seeth under the whole heavens' (Job xxviii. 24). These words also designate the seven pillars or columns upon which the world stands and when these columns fill the earth then, as scripture states, the earth is said to be full; that is, when the number of the just increases, the earth becomes fertile and fruitful. When however they are outnumbered by the wicked then as it is written, 'The waters fail from the sea, and the flood decayeth and drieth up' (Job xiv. 11). 'The waters fail from the sea' signify the Holy land watered by rivers of life from on high, but the 'stream (naahr) decayeth and drieth up' refer to the column of justice and righteousness repaired in the Holy Land in order to enlighten it and have the same meaning as the words, 'The righteous perisheth and no man layeth it to heart.'" (Is. lvii. 1.)

THE DIVINE LEHAEROT ON EZECHIEL'S VISIONS

SAID Rabbi Hezekiah: "The title of one of the Psalms is thus, 'A psalm of David Maschil' (for understanding), 'Blessed is he whose transgres-sion is lifted up and whose sin is covered' (Ps. XXXII. 1). This verse has already been commented on. There is however an occult meaning in the word maschil (understanding), and, having reference to divine wisdom, it requires explanation. We learn from tradition that King David in composing his hymns and songs of praise to the Holy One, made use of ten different meters (one of which is termed ("maschil") corresponding to the various progressive states in the divine life symbolized by the ten sephiroth of the tree of life. In order to attain to these, David prepared and disciplined himself, that he might become receptive of their respective states of inspiration and spiritual enlightenment and thus be able to compose his psalms. The meaning of the words, 'blessed is he whose transgression is raised on high' is this, when the Holy One places in the scales of his balance a man's merits and demerits it sometimes happens that the scale in which his sins are placed rises, being overbalanced by the scale containing his good deeds. Such is the meaning of these words. Happy they! whose transgression is forgiven, that is,--when the scale in which it is placed, ascends. The words 'whose sin is covered' refer to those whose sins the Holy One, when his judgments are abroad in the world, covers and hides from the view of the destroying angel, as was the case with Noah whom he saved from experiencing the effects and consequences of the sin that was prevalent in the world through the fall of Adam. As long as sin and wrong-doing subsist on earth, man suffers, because not in his normal and primal sate of innocency. He trembles and flees from before wild and savage animals, no longer subject to his will and control. When Noah came forth out of the ark, the world had become cleansed and purified and humanity entered on a new era of existence and therefore it is written, 'And Alhim blessed him and his sons and said unto them, be fruitful and multiply and replenish the earth.'"

Said Rabbi Simeon: "Though in these words no mention or reference is made to his wife and his sons; wives, yet are they included in, the term 'vaathem' (and ye), as also in the word 'ath' before the name of Noah which includes both males and females, both being subjects and recipients of divine benedictions. Then was it the Holy One gave unto them the seven precepts to be observed as rules of life until Israel should stand before Mount Sinai and receive the full law."

THE MYSTERY OF THE BOW IN THE CLOUD

"It is written, and Alhim said, This is the token of the covenant which I make between me and you and every living creation that is with you for perpetual generations, I do set (nathati) my bow in the cloud! (Gen. IX. 12. 13). The word 'nathati' here refers to the past, as the bow from the days of Adam had always been witnessed in the clouds. In his further comments on these words Rabbi Simeon said: 'In the vision of Ezechiel we read, "And above the firmament that was over their heads, was the likeness of a throne, as the appearance of a sapphire stone" (Ez. I. 21). Preceding these words, scripture states, 'I heard the noise of their wings, like the noise of great waters, as the voice of Shaddai (Almighty), the voice of speech as the noise of a host, when they stood they let down their wings.' We have here given a description of the four celestial cherubic beings by whom the firmament is supported. They were all joined together by their wings which covered their forms. When they extended their wings, they uttered in far resounding tones hymns of praise to the glory of God, that reverberated throughout the universe incessantly. The burthen of their song was, 'The Lord hath made known his salvation, his righteousness hath he openly shewed in the sight of the heathen' (Ps. XCVIII. 2). It is also stated that when they moved, there was heard a sound as of a great host on the march, like that of the celestial angelic host when their legions with united voice, utter their hymns of praise to the Holy One, saying, 'Holy, holy, holy is the Lord of Hosts, all the earth is full of his glory' (Is. VI. 3). As the four cherubic angels of the heavenly chariot turn to the four quarters of the world, their cry is still the same, 'Holy! holy! holy!' Above them is the glittering firmament, whose cardinal quarters reflect the image of each of their forms when turned towards them, as also the colors peculiar to each of them. They are the forms of a lion, an ox, an eagle and a man. In three of these, the human countenance is so prominent, that the lion resembles a lion man and so with the two others, that are termed the eagle man, the ox man, and thus as scripture states, 'They four had the face of a man.' As the firmament was above them it not only reflected their forms but also the colors peculiar to each of them and that correspond to the four letters of the sacred name I. H. V. H. and visible to man, as green, red, white and blue, and which when refracted form twelve different shades and hues, and therefore it is stated, 'as the appearance of the bow that is in the cloud, in the day of rain, so was the appearance of the likeness of the glory of the Lord' (Ez. I. 28). This then is the mystical meaning of the words, 'I do set my bow in the cloud.' The term 'my bow' has the same signification as that which was said of Joseph. 'This bow abode in strength, and the arms of his hands were made strong by the hands of the mighty God of Jacob, from thence is the shepherd, the stone of Israel' (Gen. XLIX. 24). As Joseph was a just man, it is said of him, 'He placed his bow in God', that is the covenant, symbolizing equally the bow and the Only Just One, these two signifying both one and the same thing. Noah being also a just man, the covenant made with him was symbolized by the bow and the arms of his hands were made strong (vayapozow). This word refers to the light proceeding from the bow of the covenant which is the source of joy and happiness to all the world and of which it is written, 'More to be desired is it than gold, yet than much fine gold, sweeter also than honey and the honey comb' (Ps. XIX. 10). This light was the cause of Joseph's mental and spiritual illumination, and therefore is he known as and termed, 'Joseph the upright!' It is termed the bow of the covenant, as the ray in the how though refracted in three others is one way, so is the celestial light reflected downward by the firmament supported by the four cherubic forms of the heavenly or divine chariot. Therefore is it forbidden to gaze at the rainbow that appears in the heaven because thereby the Schekina of which it is an image is profaned. As the great archangels standing in presence of the Holy One bow their heads, not daring to regard the divine majesty, so on the appearance of the bow in the heavens ought we to bend ourselves with feelings of reverence and worship of the Divine Being. When it appears, the earth feels assured that the lost harmony between the celestial and terrestrial worlds has been restored. We have already observed that it consists of a ray of light composed of three other rays blended and conjoined as one, forming a mystery only dimly perceptible to initiates of the hidden wisdom. It is further added, 'and above the firmament that was over their heads was the likeness of a throne as of the appearance of a sapphire stone' (Ez. I. 26). This stone is the central point (shethiya) of the whole world and is the basis of the Holy of Holies in the sanctuary at Jerusalem. This foundation stone is the sacred celestial throne placed above the four cherubic beings whose forms are engraved on the four sides of the heavenly or divine chariot and symbolized the traditional law. 'And upon the throne was the likeness as the appearance of a man upon it,' symbolizes of the written law. Hence we conclude it is to be observed and regarded as higher and superior to the traditional. This throne being the foundation stone, Jacob who is the image of the man beheld in vision by the prophetic seer Ezechiel, placed his head upon it ere he went to sleep in Bethel.

RABBI JEHUDA'S DISCUSSION WITH THE MERCHANT, ON JACOB'S PILLAR

RABBI JEHUDA, whilst staying at an inn in the town of Masheya, rose up at midnight in order to meditate and study the secret doctrine. In the same apartment there happened to be sleeping a Jewish merchant who had come thither to dispose of two bales of wearing apparel. Said Rabbi Jehuda: "It is written, 'and this stone which I have set for a pillar shall be God's house (Beth Alhim).' The stone here mentioned is the foundation stone at the center of the world, and also on it the sanctuary was built."

The merchant on bearing these words raised himself from his Led. and said: "What you have just observed is an impossibility, for this foundation stone existed before the creation of the world and the origin of it. Now the words, 'And this stone which I have set up for a pillar, shall be God's house' refer distinctly to the particular stone that Jacob then set up, and to none other. More than this, it is said, 'And took the stone that he had put for his pillow and set it up for a pillar.' But Jacob was then in Bethel; how could this stone therefore be one and the same with that at Jerusalem on which the sanctuary was built!"

Without taking any notice of the merchant's remarks and question, Rabbi Jehuda, proceeded: "It is written said he, 'Prepare to meet thy God, oh Israel' (Amos IV. 12) 'Take heed and hearken, oh Israel' (Deuter. XXVII. 9), teaching us that the study of the secret doctrine claims and demands from those who engage therein, both a thoughtful mind and a reverent spirit."

On hearing these words, the merchant instantly arose and putting on his garments sat down by the side of Rabbi Jehuda and said: "Blessed are the righteous who study and meditate on the secret doctrine, day and night." Said Rabbi Jehuda: "Whilst thou finishest dressing thyself, repeat to me the objections to which thou hast given utterance, that we may calmly, thoughtfully and reverently discuss them. Because so, I rose from my bed to engage in its study with earnestness and attention. We are taught that the Schekina associates with anyone who is an earnest student of truth even though he be alone and far remote from his fellows. Knowing this, how could I remain in bed while sensing the presence of the divine Schekina, and knowing also that the Holy One walks in the garden of the celestial Eden with the righteous who listen attentively to the words and meditations of those who rise at midnight and devote themselves to the study of the law until the dawn of day. Repeat now I pray thee thy objections and questions."

Said the merchant: "My question was this, How can you truly affirm that the foundation stone at the center of the world and forming the base of the sanctuary at Jerusalem was one and the same as that which Jacob used as a pillow and afterwards set it up as a pillar and poured oil on the top of it. He was at Bethel and the foundation stone was in Jerusalem, so that your affirmation respecting it was an inexactitude.

THE SYMBOLISM OF THE FOUNDATION STONE

SAID Rabbi Jehuda: "During the night that Jacob slept at Bethel, there was a marvelous replication of the earth's surface so that the foundation stone under the sanctuary in Jerusalem occupied the place where Jacob was, in order that he might rest his head upon it. This explains how it was that the stone was under him. Ah! replied the merchant, but scripture explicitly states that Jacob took the stone that he put for his pillow and set it up for a pillar and said, 'This stone which I have set up for a pillar shall be Bethel.' There is here nothing to warrant your assertion that it was the foundation stone on which the world and the Holy of Holies are based.

Then said Rabbi Jehuda, "If you can give any other explanation of the words, I pray you to give it."

Said the merchant, "It is written, 'As for me I will behold thy face in righteousness, I shall be satisfied when I awake with thy likeness' (Ps. XVII. 15). All the love and desire of David was concentrated on this foundation stone, which is justice or righteousness, and speaks of it as 'The stone which the builders rejected has become the headstone of the corner' (Ps. CXVIII. 22). When David desired to contemplate and behold the glory of his Lord, he first took this stone and possessed himself of it, after which he was able and qualified to enter into the sanctuary; for everyone who earnestly desires to come into the presence of his Lord, it is impossible to do so unless he possesses this stone, as it is written, 'with this (bezoth) shall Aaron come into the holy place' (Lev. XVI. 3). David was therefore congratulating himself when he said, 'As for me, I will behold thy face with justice,' of which the foundation stone was a symbol, and which he so ardently desired to possess. Observe, Abraham instituted the morning prayer and made known the goodness and benignity of his Lord, so that the matutinal hour became regarded as most suitable for addressing vows to the Divine Being, and it is written, 'And Abraham rose up early in the morning' (Gen. XXII. 3). Evening prayer, 'minhah,' was established by Isaac who taught the world that justice exists, and also that there is a judge by whom it is administered. Jacob originated nightly prayer, that had never been uttered and addressed to heaven by anyone anterior to him, and therefore in a moment of self-commendation said, 'This stone which I have set up as a pillar.' What is the real signification of this word pillar (matzebah)? It refers to the foundation stone of the universe, namely, justice that had been thrown down by the wickedness of mankind. It was Jacob who raised it again and his pouring of oil on the top of it denotes that he, more than any other, contributed in re-erecting it and causing its existence to become regarded as a reality.

Rabbi Jehuda, as the merchant ceased speaking, rose and embracing him said: 'How is it, that possessed of such knowledge of the secret doctrine, thou art engaged in worldly pursuits to the neglect of things appertaining to the higher and diviner life?"

Said the merchant: "It is through necessity. I have two sons attending school for whose maintenance and education I have to provide in order that they may become inculcated in the secret and hidden wisdom." Again the merchant spake and said: "We read, 'and Solomon sat upon the throne of David his father and his kingdom was established greatly' (I. Kings II. 12). How great the encomium of Solomon as expressed in these words, implying that he set up the foundation stone (shethiya) on which he erected the sanctuary in Jerusalem and thereby established his kingdom greatly, as it is stated. We read, 'And the bow shall be in the cloud and I will look upon it, that I may remember the everlasting covenant' (Gen. IX. 16), from which we gather that the bow gives rise to feelings of delight to the Holy One. No man in whom the divine light is not reflected, can ever enter into the presence of his Lord. The words 'And I will look upon it' (urithiha) have the same occult meaning as, 'The Lord said unto him, go through the midst of the city, through the midst of Jerusalem and mark the letter Th (thau) upon the foreheads of the men who sigh,' (Ez. IX. 3) from which we learn that God looks upon the face of every man to observe if this than is impressed thereon and if so he remembers the everlasting covenant. Another exposition of these words is, that they refer to the holy sign impressed on the human form.

Said Rabbi Jehuda: "All you have said, is quite correct. The origin of the bow visible in the heavens involves a profound mystery. When Israel returns out of captivity, the bow that then will be visible, will be as radiant and beautiful as a bride, adorned for her husband on her marriage day."

"Listen," said the merchant, "to the words of my father, addressed to me just before his death, 'Never expect to behold the banner of Messiah until the bow appears in the heavens, flashing forth rays and colors of light so transcendently glorious and splendid, that the sheen of it will lighten up the whole world. When this happens then look for Messiah. We learn this from the esoteric meaning of the words, 'I will look upon the bow and remember the everlasting covenant.' At present it appears in colors, faint and lustreless and only as an object to remind us that the Holy One will never again destroy mankind by a deluge of waters. When however the advent of Messiah occurs, it will appear radiant in all its beauty and splendor and God will then remember Israel and raise them out of the dust, as it is written, 'And they shall serve the Lord and David, their king, whom I will raise up unto them.' (Jer. XXX. 9), 'And in that day I will raise up the tabernacle of David that is fallen' (Amos IX. 11), that is, in the day that the resplendent bow appears in the heavens, God will look upon it and remember his covenant, so that David, becoming reincarnated, shall appear again and reign in Israel.' This is what my father declared and his belief is confirmed by the words, 'For as in the days of Noah, so have I done unto thee and as I have sworn that the waters of Noah should go no more over the earth, so have I sworn that I will not be wroth with thee nor reproach thee.'" (Is. LIV. 8).

RABBI SIMEON ON MYSTERIES AND THE HIGHER LIFE

"AND the sons of Noah that went forth of the ark were Shem, Ham and Japhet" (Gen. IX. 18). Said Rabbi Eleazer: Why are these names only mentioned? Had Noah other sons who did not go with him on his exit from the ark?

In reply Rabbi Abba said: "Noah had other children than the three mentioned in scripture, who likewise had children of their own, and the reason this is not explicitly stated is, that grandchildren are in scripture classed and referred to as sons."

Said Rabbi Simeon: "Had I been incarnated and lived on earth at the time when the Holy One entrusted the Book of Mysteries containing the secret doctrine to Enoch and Adam, I would have strongly urged that the contents of it should never be divulged save to those who by their upright and unselfish lives had rendered themselves worthy to receive and understand them; for such only are able to appreciate their value and importance that distinguish it from all other books. The truly wise in this world are they who attain to a comprehension and understanding of its esoteric teachings that under the veil of symbols, emblems, allegories and enigmas, are concealed from esoteric students whose thoughts and labors are concentrated and directed merely towards what is phenomenal and ephemeral. Known only to sages and initiates are the grand mysteries of the hidden wisdom, the knowledge of which they never impart to the 'profanum vulgum' and use only in ministering to the welfare of humanity. Of these great mysteries, one of the most abstruse and profound is contained in the above cited verse of scripture. When the divine life or in other words, the consciousness of the Divine, the cause of all cause, the life of all life, the pleroma of all joy and happiness rises and dawns within the human soul or man's lower nature, like the great orb of day sending forth its effulgent rays of light and warmth, it diffuses within it and makes itself recognized by a feeling, a sensation of enjoyment and delight greater than that which rich and generous wine causes the heart of man to pulsate with an ecstasy of delight not to be expressed. This effluence of the divine life is intermediate between the joy and pleasure that reaches and flows into human nature from the celestial and terrestrial planes of existence. There are within us two souls or natures, the higher and the lower, blended and united together by the mysterious Augoides, that corresponds to the upper triad of Sephiroth in the decenary of the human constitution. These three souls, or rather natures, manifest themselves in their differing modes and direction, the Higher Self attaching itself and approximating towards its superior principle produces three offspring, symbolized by Noah's sons, Shem, Ham and Japhet, who came forth from the ark; Shem corresponding to the principle on the right of the Sephirotic tree, Ham to that on the left, whilst Japhet is the medium of connection that like the color of purple is a combination and a reflection of the other two. Ham was the father of Canaan. He symbolizes the lower or animal nature of man susceptive of all material and gross influences that trend to the excitation of animal instincts, desires and passions. He was also the father of him who caused the world along with himself to be cursed and the human face to become blanched and pale through sorrow and suffering; therefore it is not stated of Shem or Japhet that they were the father of this or that one. This is also wherefore it is written, 'And Abram passed through the land,' (Gen. XII. 9) neither abode in it because the patriarchs through their merits and works had not purified it, neither had Israel made known the sacred name so that it was still suffering under the primal curse pronounced upon the earth and the serpent, 'Cursed he the ground because of thee, cursed art thou above all the beasts of the field.' And of the land of Canaan it is written, cursed is Canaan, a servant of servants, shall he be unto his brothers. Furthermore we read, 'These are the three sons of Noah, Shem, Ham and Japhet, and of them was the whole earth overspread' (Gen. IX. 19). These words also include within them a great mystery of the heavenly or superior colors, teaching us that though refracted throughout the universe, the divine glory remains ever the same both in heaven above and on earth below."

SYMBOLISM OF THE COLORS OF THE BOW IN THE CLOUD

SAID Rabbi Eleazar: The three primal colors become differentiated into many shades and hues and, as such, are symbols of the divine life and its numerous descending grades of holiness that merge and blend imperceptibly into the evil, just as the animal glides into the vegetable rendering it difficult and almost impossible to distinguish where the one ends and the other begins. The colors of the rainbow have each of them twenty-seven different shades and similarly the principle of holiness has the same number of descending gradations until it disappears into that which is unholy and sinful, indiscernible to the ordinary observer, but clearly perceived and distinctly cognized by those who have become recipients of divine wisdom. Blessed is the lot of the upright in heart, to whom the Holy One delights to impart it and entrust to them its secret teachings. It is of them the psalmist speaks, 'The secret of the Lord is with them that fear him and he will shew them his covenant' (Is. XXV. 1). Greatly obligatory upon everyone is it to meditate upon the glory of his creator, who hears and attends to the prayers of all such as worship and serve him in sincerity of heart, for then blessings are showered upon them from on high with increasing knowledge of the Holy One who glories in his servants, of whom it is written, 'Thou art my servant, oh Israel in whom I will he glorified.'" (Is. XLIX. 3).

THE MYSTERY OF THE CURSING OF CANAAN BY NOAH

"And Noah began to he a husbandman and he planted a vineyard" (Gen. IX. 20). In their comments on these words, Rabbi Jehuda and Rabbi Jose greatly differed, the one affirming that Noah planted a vine taken from the garden of Eden, the other maintaining that he had plucked it by its roots before entering the ark and now planted it in suitable soil, after which it brought forth grades, the juice of which after expressing, he drank and became intoxicated therewith.

Said Rabbi Simeon: In this verse is included a fragment of the hidden wisdom. When Noah, desirous of investigating into the cause of man's fall from his primal state of holy innocence not with the intention of imitating it but of healing the sin of the world, he soon realized his inability to achieve his object. He then pressed the juice of the vine in order to ascertain the natural properties of it, or in other words, he speculated deeply upon the nature of the Divine Being. His intellectual faculties soon became exhausted and he was as one puzzled and drunken with thought, and therefore we read 'He drank of the wine and was drunken and lay uncovered in his tent' (Gen. IX. 21), that is, on lifting only a corner of the veil that hides divine mysteries from human gaze and catching a glimpse of what is never revealed and imparted save only to the enlightened and pure in heart, he became mentally stupefied, confused and overwhelmed with the sublimity and grandeur of the noumenal world so transcendently beyond all human cognition and comprehension. This occurred as stated in his own tent (bethok oholoh) the latter word of which written with a final H, which is a feminine pronominal suffix giving it the same meaning as in the verse. 'Remove thy way from her (mesleyah) and come not nigh the door of her house (bethah) (Prov. V. 8), from which we learn that the words 'within his tent' refer mystically to the tent of the wine, or more explicitly still, to divine mysteries. Furthermore we know from tradition that the sin of the sons of Aaron was that of intoxication, arising not from the indulgence in wine and strong drink, for how was it possible that anyone should bring them intoxicants to drink within the sanctuary even were they so void of all shame as to desire them. Truly their inebriety was not owing to drinking wine but from the abuse of the mystical knowledge of which we have just spoken and of which scripture states metaphorically, 'They offered strange fire (ash zarah) before the Lord which he commanded them not' (Lev. X. 1). The words 'strange fire' have here the same significance as, 'That they may keep thee from the strange woman (ashah zarah), from the stranger that flattereth with her words' (Prov. VII. 5). This then was the kind of drunkenness indulged in by Noah as stated and he drank of the wine and was drunken and he was 'uncovered in his tent.' This fatuous act of spiritual inebriation enabled his son Ham, the father of Canaan, to acquire certain esoteric knowledge and occult powers as we have before explained, that endowed and invested him with a potency to exercise sway and domination over others, for knowing that Noah was a just and perfect man and that his holiness arose from his chastity, he wickedly deprived him as tradition informs us of his virile power by the infliction of eunichism. Through this heinous indignity committed upon him it was that Noah said, 'Cursed be Canaan, a servant of servants shall he be unto his brethren,' as aforetime it had been said to the serpent, 'Cursed art thou above all the beasts of the field.' Eventually at the end of the ages, the erring, the sinful and guilty will be saved and become children of the light, but not Canaan whose irreversible doom is absolute and certain perdition and final extinction a fact not unknown to those initiated in the teachings of the secret doctrine. It is written, 'I acknowledge my transgression and my sin is ever before me' (Ps. LI. 5). How cautious and ever watchful should every man be, that he sin not before the Holy One, lest Cain-like he become branded with a mark that can only be effaced after long years of protracted penance and suffering as stated in scripture, 'For though thou wash thyself with nitre and take thee much soap, yet is thine iniquity marked before me saith the Lord God' (Jer. II. 22). Observe that when a man transgresses for the first time before the holy One, his fault is distinguished on high by a mark which, after a second repetition of it, becomes more visible and noticed, but on his further and continuous persistency in evil doing, it abides on him and remains ineffaceable, as it is written, 'Thou shalt he soiled with thy iniquity before me.' Note further that when David had sinned in acquiring Bathsheba for his wife, he became exceedingly afraid that the mark upon him would abide forever. The prophet wishing to comfort him said unto him, 'the Lord hath put away thy sin, thou shalt not die' (II. Sam. XII. 13) meaning that the mark on high had become effaced."

REMARKS ON PREDESTINATION

SAID Rabbi Abba: It has been handed down by tradition that Bathsheba was predestined from the creation of the world to become the wife of David. If so, how was it that the Holy One permitted before becoming so that she should be the spouse of Uriah the Hittite?"

Said Rabbi Simeon in reply: "The ways and designs of the Holy One are such that even when a woman is predestined to be the wife of a certain individual, he does not debar her from marrying before meeting and becoming acquainted with him who is fore-ordained to he her husband. When this occurs, the first husband disappears in order that she may become united with her future partner in life. God could prevent the first marriage by causing the death of one who wished to marry a woman destined to become the bride of another man, but it is neither the will nor the pleasure of the Holy One that anyone should die before the time fixed for his departure out of earth life. Such was the mystery in connection with Uriah and Bathsheba before she became the wife of David. Ponder well and meditate upon this exposition, and you will become convinced of its correctness. It may be asked why was the Holy Land given in patrimony to the Canaanite before the advent of the Israelites, but on reflection over what I have just stated, you will find the explanation by following the same line of exposition I have followed in respect to the marriage of David with Bathsheba. Notwithstanding David's confession and penitence, the consequences of his sins and especially those in connection with his marriage with Uriah's wife and the remembrance of them were always with him, nor was he even able to divest and rid himself of the fear that they would be visited upon him in times of danger and suffering. In the words 'My sin is ever before me' there is an occult allusion to the horned new moon, symbol of the impurity existent in the world that would only disappear on the advent of Solomon, when it would again attain its full, and the earth give forth a sweet perfume and Israel live in peace and security, as it is written, 'Israel shall dwell safely every man under his own vine and fig tree.' Notwithstanding this, the evidences and remains of the sins of former times were not altogether effaced and obliterated in the reign of Solomon, but will continue to exist until the coming of Messiah into the world at the time appointed, as it is written, 'And I will cause the unclean spirit to pass out of the land.'" (Zach. XIII. 2).

CHAPTER LXIV.

IT is written of Nimrod, "And he was a mighty hunter before the Lord' (Gen. X. 9). He acquired authority and renown by wearing the primoge-nital robes and garments of Adam and was able thus to corrupt the minds and habits of mankind in his days.

Said Rabbi Eleazer: "Nimrod first led men into error and caused them to fall into idolatry. Having possessed himself of the habiliments of his ancestor Adam, he usurped rule and authority over his fellows who submissively yielding to his tyranny made him the object of their worship and adoration. Why was he called Nimrod? Because he rebelled [1] against the Lord, the most high King of Heaven, and brought about a revolt in both worlds, the celestial and terrestrial. Becoming regarded as an universal sovereign and succeeding in wielding; the minds of mankind, he induced then to cease and discontinue their allegiance to their Lord and creator."

Said Rabbi Simeon: "Initiates of the secret doctrine recognize in the expression 'Adam's habiliments,' a very deep and occult mystery, the explanation of which is never divulged or imparted save to advanced students of the Hidden Wisdom."

---

[1] "to rebel" = מרד; Nimrod = נמרד--JBH.

THE THAUMATURGICAL ERECTION OF SOLOMON'S TEMPLE

"It is written, 'And the whole earth was of one language and of one speech' (Gen. XI. 1). Said Rabbi Simeon, 'Scripture relates of Solomon's temple, it was built of stones made ready before brought to the house so that the sound of hammer, nor axe, nor of any tool of iron was heard whilst it was building' (1 King VI. 7). What is the meaning of the words, 'whilst it was building?' From the form of expression, we might infer it was in some marvelous and wonderful manner self-builded. Were not Solomon and his artizans the builders of it? Ere replying to these questions let us give the mystical meaning of the words, 'And thou shalt make a candlestick of pure gold, of beaten work shall the candlestick be made' (Ex. XXV. 31). Now since the candlestick was to be made of beaten gold, and scripture distinctly states, it was 'self-made' (yerechah) how could this possibly be? Our answer is, it was done by the operation of an unknown and invisible force or power, in other words by a miraculous agency. When the artisans of Solomon wished to begin their labors, he instructed them to do work to which they had never been accustomed and of which they were wholly ignorant, so that it was only through the blessing of the Holy One, with wisdom and power from on high directing their hands, that they were able to begin and complete the structure of the holy temple, and therefore it was as scripture states, "and the house when it was being self-built" (vehabeth behibbanothou) through divine power and influence operating in the minds or wills and hands of the artisans who worked according to a plan or a certain method, from which they never deviated until the temple was finished and completed. It is also said, it was made of stone ready prepared (shelemah) (which against the general rule is written without the yod)[1]. This strange marvel is further confirmed by the word next following, massang (brought or conducted thither) indicating that the artisans engaged in the construction of the house simply used or made passes with their hauls and the work was accomplished though they understood not, nor comprehended the mystery of its modus operandi. It was further stated, 'There was neither hammer, nor axe nor any tool of

---

[1] shelemah = שלימה, without the Yod = שלמה = Solomon--JBH.

iron used in the house while it was building itself.' No wonder therefore is it that whilst wielding, controlling and manipulating such a mysterious and occult power and agent they observed the strictest silence and refrained from the use of tool and implement in the erection of the sacred temple. How deep and occult are the mysteries of the secret doctrine and few are there who have any notion or idea and knowledge of them. When the Holy One wishes to manifest his glory and power to humanity, he causes to descend from a part of the universe termed the 'thought sphere,' whose locus is unknown, save to himself, and pass through the bodily organ known as the 'larynx,' the mysterious breath of life which is designated in scripture and described as 'the living God,' 'the only true God and King eternal.'"

THE MYSTERY OF THE LOGOS

THE three primordial elements of nature are fire, air and water. Really they are one in use and substance and are able to change the one into the other. It is the same with Thought and Speech and Logos, they are one and the same in themselves. Their seeming duality arises from the different aspects in which they are observed and cognized. That Jacob might become a perfect man it was necessary that the Divine Being should manifest himself to him by the Word or Logos, even as a man in order to make known his thoughts and ideas to another is obliged to clothe them with words in order that the sound produced by the motion of his lips may make them known to his listener, otherwise they would remain unknown and he incommunicable, so in order that the sanctuary of God might exist upon earth, it needed manifestation by means of a Word or Logos, through which it might communicate and speak to mankind. Scripture therefore states, whilst the house was building itself, and not whilst it was building, alluding mystically to the manner of divine manifestation by the Logos in the world. The mystery of the erection of the temple is hinted at in the words, 'Go forth ye daughters of Zion and behold King Solomon with the crown wherewith his mother crowned him on the day of his espousals' (Cant. III. 11). Respecting the stones used in building the sanctuary, it is said of them they were 'prepared' (massang) which also signifies 'carried or transported thither or taken from one place to another.' As thought existing in the Sphere of Mind becomes transformed into vocal speech by descending into the larynx, the ultimate stage for its manifestation in its downward flight from on high, so is it with the Divine Word or Logos and its silent entrance in the mind and soul of man, descending from on high through inferior degrees and states or worlds of being, each working and operating in harmony with it under the control of the great supreme ruler and architect of the universe, and each obedient to the law of evolution for the accomplishment of its destiny, unification with the Divine. Slowly and in silence, the innumerable majestic worlds careering in their orbits throughout the boundless realms of space under the dominance and guidance of an almighty principle of unity, are progressing and approximating to one Divine center, so that unified and conjoined in harmony, they may form an universal temple wherein all souls may worship and serve the one true God, the Almighty Father, the great All, and within all who then shall reign forever and ever and to his Kingdom there shall be no end.

THE IDOLATRY OF THE POSTDILUVIANS

IT is written, "And the earth was of one language and had the same words" (Gen. XI. 1) and it is further added "And as they, these words, went from the east" (miqqedem). This word here signifies he who is the Alpha or Premier of the world. It is also said, "They found a plain or valley in the land of Shinar, and they dwelt there." As soon as they separated themselves from this premier, unity of thought and mind amongst them was no longer possible, and they became dispersed and scattered abroad in all parts of the earth. If in opposition to these remarks, anyone should refer to the words of scripture 'And a river went out of Eden to water the Garden and from thence it was divided and became into four heads,' (Gen. II. 10) in order to show that even in association and close proximity with the Divine Presence, divine separation occur and therefore it was nothing extraordinary that this deflection and revolt from the Premier of the world should take place, just as it was with the river of Eden that it should become parted into four heads. In reply we admit that it was not impossi-ble it should do so after but not before its exit from the garden, so with respect to mankind after the deluge, so long as they remained united together they were attached to the worship of God, the premier of the world. They had one in common, one language, one faith, one mode of worshipping the Divine Being, binding them together in an universal Brotherhood that prevailed amongst them. But declining in divine knowledge and reverence, they gradually veered away from allegiance to their great Premier (miqqedem) until at length they found a plain in the land of Shinar, or in other words, they became ignorant of God their creator and devoid of all knowledge of the higher and diviner life. Scripture relates of Nimrod, 'The beginning of his Kingdom was Babel' from which we gather, it was he who first seduced the postdiluvians from the worship and service of the true god, and introducing confusion and disunion amongst them, he eventually succeeded in usurping rule and sovereignty over them and led them to a plain in the land of Shinar, by which is meant, that from that time men forsook the worship of the Divine and began to live in defiance of his law, then degenerated and gave themselves wholly up to the pursuit of and indulged in worldly pleasures and enjoyments, worship-ping the creature rather than their creator who is blessed forever. It is further related, 'And they said, go to, let us build us a city and a tower whose head may reach into heaven and let us make us a name (shem)' (Gen. XI. 4).

THE TOWER OF BABEL

SAID Rabbi Hiya: It is written, 'The wicked are like the troubled sea' (nigrash) (Is. LVII. 20). Is there then a troubled sea? Truly so, for when it exceedeth its boundaries, it becomes 'nigrash' and bursting its barriers, as a man intoxicated with wine, rolling and staggering and unable to keep himself erect, and scripture further adds, of the sea when in this troubled state, 'It cannot rest; and its waters cast up mire and dirt,' meaning that whilst it is calm, the mud concealed in its depths remains undisturbed but the moment its surface begins to be ruffled and agitated by tempestuous winds and storms it is ejected, similarly with a man who as long as he is devoted to the service of his Lord, his lower nature or self is calla and peaceful, its animal propensities repressed and restrained, but as soon as his relation with his divine higher self becomes disturbed and broken, like a drunkard, he begins to reel and stagger, and give utterance to the depraved feelings and emotions that have lain dormant within him, and in proportion as he babbles forth his obscure and filthy gibberish, so does his profanity increase, for it is the reflection of his impure animal self that then becomes manifested. Observe the words, 'And they said, go to, let us build us a city and tower whose top shall reach into heaven.' The term "habah" (go to) whenever used in scripture is always found in connection with some thing or project unrealizable by those who conceived it. Their blind impulse to build such a city and tower arose only from a wicked and foolish desire that animated and prompted them to live in open revolt against the Holy One."

Said Rabbi Abba: "They were the subjects of a horrible and demoniacal infatuation in that they impiously wished to abandon the worship of their Lord for that of Satan or the serpent to whom they rendered homage and glory. The words, 'go to, let us build us a city and tower,' have a deeply occult meaning and contain a mystery most profound. Remark that when the Postdiluvians arrived at the plain in the land of Shinar (a strange kingdom or domain) and had become acquainted with and accommodated themselves to its natural advantages coming from its proximity to the sea, they said amongst themselves, it will be best for us to settle down and dwell here, for with little trouble and at once we can indulge in those sensual pleasures and delights that are the charm of life, making it worth the living. But why worship heavenward and what advantage will accrue to us in so doing. Here let us build us a temple and make a deity of ourselves. Come and let us make a shem (name, a synonym for God, or a Divine Being) whom we can adore and have him always in our midst as a center of attraction, and thus avoid becoming dispersed abroad on the face of the earth."

A COMPARISON BETWEEN NOAH AND MOSES

SAID Rabbi Jehuda: "Whilst the antediluvians were living, the Holy One looked down up the hearth and beheld no one able to save them from being destroyed. If it be asked, was there not Noah? the question is of no force, since Noah had not that abundance of personal merit to save them; it only sufficed to save himself and for repeopling the world. Therefore it is written of him, 'For thee only have I seen righteous before me in this generation' (Gen. VII, 1); that is, compared with the rest of his contemporaries, he was the only one who lived uprightly."

Said Rabbi Jose: "The words 'in this generation' far from diminishing the merits of Noah, rather exalt and increase them. The meaning of scripture is, that they were not comparative with respect to others, but intrinsic and would have made him distinguished had he lived in any other age, even if it had been in that of Moses. If Noah with his righteousness was unable to save the world, it was because there were not ten righteous men to be found to effect this. We infer this from the request of Abraham, whilst ruin was still impending over and threatening the destruction of Sodom and Gomorrah. 'Let not the Lord be angry and I will speak yet but this once: peradventure ten should be found there; and he said, I will not destroy it for ten's sake' (Gen. XVIII, 32). Now in the time of Noah, including himself with his sons and their wives, there were not to be found ten such men as he, in that generation, otherwise it would have been spared for their sake and escaped destruction."

Said Rabbi Eleazor to Rabbi Simeon, his father: "Tradition informs us that when the sins and iniquities of unrighteous men abound in the world and attain their climax, and divine justice is ready to overtake and destroy them, the just and upright should plead on their behalf, for they alone are able to expiate the guilt of their fellowmen."

Said Rabbi Simeon in reply: "We have learned that when Noah came forth out of the ark, the Holy One desired he should repeople the earth. The judgment of the antediluvians was unable to fall upon and affect him, as he was concealed in the ark and so escaped the eye of the destroying angel.

Observe it is written, 'Seek after righteousness, seek after meekness, it may be, ye shall be hid in the day of the Lord's anger' (Zeph. II, 3). This was done by Noah, and by entering into the ark he was hid in the day of the Lord's anger and so escaped the power of the accusing angel. This passage of scripture has reference to a great mystery known and understood only by the highest initiates and adepts; that is, the thaumaturgic power of the twenty-two letters of the celestial alphabet wielded by angels in destroying and exterminating the wicked. Therefore it is that scripture states, 'they were destroyed from the earth' (va-imchon). Remark now the difference that distinguished Moses from all other men. At the time the Holy One said unto him, 'Now let me alone that my wrath may wax hot against them and that I may consume them and I will make of thee a great nation' (Ex. XXXII, 10). Moses without a moment's hesitation replied, 'Shall I give up and forsake Israel for my own personal exaltation and advantage? If so, will not worldly people say that I was a traitor and sacrificed them because of my ambitious and selfish desire of becoming ruler and chief of a great nation, like unto Noah who when the Holy One said unto him, 'Behold, I, even I, do bring a flood of waters upon the earth to destroy all flesh, wherein is the breath of life from under heaven and everything that is on the earth shall die, but with thee will I establish my covenant and thou shalt come into the ark, thou and thy sons and thy wife and thy sons' wives with thee' (Gen. VI, 17-18). Far from entreating God for his fellowmen, not to destroy them, Noah thought only of his own safety and that of his own family, and, owing to this neglect on his part, the waters of the deluge bear his name; for so it is written, 'For I have sworn that the waters of Noah should no more go over the earth' (Is. LIV, 9). But Moses thought thus: If the people of Israel is destroyed, it will be said I acted selfishly in that I refrained from interceding on their behalf and allowed them to perish for the sake of personal gratification and ambition to become the head of a great nation. No, it is better for me to die and by my death save Israel from perishing; and so it is written, 'and Moses besought the Lord, his God, and said, Lord, why doth thy wrath wax hot against thy people' (Ex. XXXII, 11). He prayed for mercy and it was granted to him, and thus was Israel saved."

Said Rabbi Isaac: "How could Moses in his entreaty with the Lord on behalf of Israel say, why doth thy wrath wax hot against thy people? The Israelites had worshipped an idol as God, had just informed him and become idolators as other nations, for they had made them a molten calf and bowed in worship to it and sacrificed unto it and said, 'These be thy gods, oh Israel, which have brought thee out of the land of Egypt.' Yet after such heinous iniquity and forgetful ingratitude, Moses could say, 'Let not thy wrath wax hot against thy people.' What was his reason in so doing? In reply we say, whoever takes upon him the office of a mediator and intercessor is bound to exterminate the delinquency of the offender before the injured one, and magnify it in the sight of the guilty one. Thus acted Moses who spoke as though the iniquity of the Israelites was of little account, yet did he not fail to upbraid them severely, and said unto them, 'Ye have sinned a great sin' (Ex. XXXII, 30). Yet ceased he not pleading for them, and even offered his own life for their forgiveness and preservation, as it is written, 'If thou wilt forgive their sins, and if not, blot me I pray thee out of thy book which thou hast written. It was after the utterance of this prayer, the Holy One pardoned the Israelites and repented of the evil which he thought to do unto his people. Not so did Noah act, but prayed only for his own salvation and made no effort to save the world; so that when divine judgment afflicts it, the cry of the Holy Spirit is heard far unto the world when no Moses is found to intercede for it. But it is written, 'He remembered the days of old, of Moses and his people. Where is he that brought them up out of the sea with the shepherd of his flock? Where is he that put his holy spirit within him' (Is. LXIII, 11). These words allude to Moses, especially to his earnest intercession; so that the Lord said, 'Wherefore criest thou unto me? Speak unto the children of Israel that they go forward' (Ex. XIV, 15), and thus they were saved at the Red Sea through his prayer, so that they went into the midst of the sea upon the dry ground and the waters became as a wall unto them on their right and on their left.' It was also through Moses that the Schekina descended and made its abode in their midst and, therefore, on account of his constant care and solicitude for their welfare, are they described as 'the people of Moses.'"

Said Rabbi Jehuda: "Though Noah was a just man, yet was his righteousness not such as to prevail with the Holy One to forgive the sin of the antediluvians. Observe that Moses never trusted in or made mention of his own merit, but of that of the patriarchs, and in this had a great advantage over Noah."

Said Rabbi Isaac: "Notwithstanding Noah could not avail himself of the merits of the patriarchs, he should have prayed for his fellowmen when God said unto him, 'I will establish my covenant with thee,' and the prayer of thanksgiving he offered after coming out of the ark, he ought to have made before the deluge, and pleaded for the preservation of the world."

Said Rabbi Jehuda: "In defence of Noah, how could he offer sacrifice on behalf of the antediluvians when they were continually committing outrageous and heinous offenses against the Holy One. It is true he saw the awful judgment impending over mankind that was about to destroy them off the earth on account of their exceeding wickedness, and feared lest he himself might be overwhelmed by it."

Said Rabbi Isaac: "Always whenever the wicked increase in the world, it is the righteous found amongst them who are the first to suffer, as it is written, (and begin at my sanctuary) (Ez. IX, 6) (mimiqdashe). Now this word should not be translated and read at my sanctuary, but rather by those who sanctify me (miniqdashi). But why was it that Noah escaped the impending destruction? Because it was destined, through him, the earth should be repeopled, inasmuch as he alone was found just amongst his fellowmen. Furthermore his preservation was owing to his earnest exhortations and continuous preaching to them, notwithstanding they persistently refused to listen to him or to regard his predictions of coming evil. It is therefore to him the words of scripture apply, nevertheless if thou warn the righteous man that he sin not and he doth not sin, he shall surely live because he is warned, also thou hast delivered thy soul. (Ez. III. 21). From which words we may gather that whoever warns sinners, saves himself even though they give no heed unto him. He has performed his duty, and if they perish, it is owing to their perverse refusal to take advice."

WHY THE ANIMAL WAS DESTROYED BY THE DELUGE

RABBI Jose, whilst on a visit to Rabbi Simeon, asked this question: "What impelled the Holy One to Destroy, along with sinners, the beasts of the field and the fowl of the air? Were they alike responsible for the vast wickedness of the antediluvians?"

Said Rabbi Simeon: "It was because, as we read, And God looked upon the earth and behold it was corrupt; for all flesh had corrupted his way, upon the earth (Gen. VI. 12); implying that the animal creation also had forsaken its natural habits and desires after its own species resulting in the production of monstrous and abnormal forms. This was mainly owing to man's corruption and transgression against natural laws, and therefore the Holy One said, Through following and indulging in your lustful inclinations and passions you seek to derange and destroy the order of nature, I will destroy from off the face of the earth all living creatures and will purify the world by water, as at the beginning of creation; and, after that, will repeople it with a new progeny both of men and animals, better than what now exists.' It is written, 'Noah with his sons and his wife and his sons' wives entered into the ark, because of the waters of the flood.'" (Gen. VII. 7).

Said Rabbi Hiya: "We read, 'Can anyone hide himself in a secret place, that I shall not see him, saith the Lord. Do I not fill heaven and earth (Jer. XXIII. 24). How great the number of those who foolishly refrain from meditation on the law and the words of their Lord, imagining they can conceal their sins and wrong doing from his all-seeing eye, and say unto themselves, who will see and know what we do? Of such it is written, 'Woe unto them that seek deep to hide their counsel from the Lord, and their works are in the dark, and they say, Who seeth us and who knoweth us?' (Is. XXIX. 15). To them may be applied the following parable. A certain king built a large palace with subterraneous passages and chambers. Eventually his attendants rebelled against him. He then ordered his guards to seize and imprison them. In order to escape punishment, the rebels went and hid themselves in the secret underground chambers. On hearing of this, the king said, 'Do they think to hide from me who planned and built the palace and therefore am fully acquainted with all its secret hiding places?' To those who seek to hide their sins and misdeeds, God says, 'It is I who have built the secret places; it is I who concealed light and darkness, and you imagine you can hide from me.' Observe when anyone commits sins secretly, the divine law of karma will cause them to become revealed and manifested to the world. But if he repents and desires to atone for them, the Holy One hides him in a manner that the avenging and destroying angle is unable to behold and afflict him. Therefore it is the opinion of Rabbi Simeon that one who has the evil eye, that is, who is naturally envious and jealous in disposition, is biased by the spirit of evil, and, in the sphere wherein he moves, becomes himself a power of evil to others and should be avoided, in order to escape injury from him. For the sake of self-preservation it therefore behoves everyone to shun by the exercise of caution the deadly glances of the destroying angel. Speaking of Balaam, the scripture states, 'And Balaam the son of Beor hath said, and the man whose eye was closed hath said' (Num. XXIV. 3). Now Balaam possessed the evil eye and whenever he directed on anyone his looks, on him the destroying angel alighted. And knowing this, he turned his gaze upon Israel in order to afflict and destroy them. But note what is said. 'And Balaam lifted up his eyes.' It is not written eyes, but 'his eye,' and he beheld Israel abiding in their tents according to their tribes.' As he looked, he detected the presence of the Schekina in their midst, overshadowing and protecting them, so that the glance of his evil eye proved powerless and ineffectual to afflict and injure them. Then he exclaimed, 'How can I prevail against them, seeing that the Holy Spirit their protector is watching over and guarding them against all evil, for he coucheth and lays down as a lion and as a great lion, who shall stir him up?' (Num. XXIV. 9) or, in other words, who shall cause the Shekina to depart from the midst of Israel so that I may attack them with the power of my evil eye? It was in a similar manner the Holy One wished to protect Noah and hide him from the power of the destroying angel's evil glances to afflict him, and so commanded him to enter and conceal himself within the ark and thus escape from the onrushing waters of the deluge."

Said Rabbi Jose: "Noah saw the angel of death approaching and therefore went into the ark in which he was concealed for a period of twelve months, respecting which there is a difference of opinion between Rabbi Isaac and Rabbi Jehuda, one affirming that this term is the fixed duration of the punishment of the wicked, the other that it was necessary for Noah to pass through the twelve degrees or stages of righteousness ere he could become a just and perfect man."

Said Rabbi Jehuda: "The punishment of the wicked endures six months by water and six months by fire. The punishment of the antediluvians was by water, why therefore did it endure twelve months?"

Said Rabbi Jose: "The punishment of the guilty in Gehenna is effected both by water and fire; that is to say, first by the descent upon them of waters cold as ice, for a period of six months, and of boiling waters for a like period and that rise from below, and is the chastisement by fire, as has been handed down by tradition. It was therefore essential that Noah should remain in the ark for twelve months to avoid the glances of the death angel who was then unable to afflict him when it floated upon the face of the waters, as scripture states, 'And it was lifted up above the earth.' Woe unto evil doers who will never rise again and appear at the day of judgment. They become blotted out of existence, as it is written, 'Thou hast blotted out their names forever'; (Ps. IX. 6) words spoken of those who perish everlastingly in the primordial fire. 'And the waters bare up the ark and it was lift up above the earth.'" (Gen. VII. 17). The actual punishment lasted only forty days upon the earth, as scripture states, 'And the flood was forty days upon the earth,' the remainder of the year serving for the complete effacement of the antediluvians from off the face of the earth.

Said Rabbi Abba: It is written, 'Be thou exalted, oh God, above the heavens, and let thy glory be above all the earth' (Ps. LVII. 11). Woe unto the wicked and unrighteous who daily insult their Lord and by their misdeeds repulse the schekina from them and cause it to forsake and depart from the world. In this verse the Schekina is called Alhim. Observe the words of scripture, 'And the waters bare up the ark'; that is to say, the deeds of sinful men repel the Schekina, of whom the ark is a symbol. When this happens, the earth is left without a defender and protector against impending judgments and affliction that assail it from all sides. Only after they have run their course and the wicked have been destroyed, does it return again into this lower world."

Here Rabbi Jose asked the question: "If this be so, why has not the Schekina returned again to the land of Israel after the dispersion of faithless and sinful Jews?

Rabbi Abba replied: "Because there are found in it no longer any just and righteous men. Wherever the just are, there is the Schekina abiding and dwelling amongst them, even though they leave their native land and emigrate to a foreign country. Of all the sins that tend to drive the Schekina from the world, self-defilement is the most heinous, as was already remarked, and he who is guilty of it will never behold the face of the Schekina, and never ascend into the heavenly palace, but will become as scripture states, 'destroyed from the face of the earth,' and that completely, so the Holy One shall raise the dead.

THE GILGAL OR REVOLUTION ANIMARUM

"Observe when the Holy One shall raise the dead he will form bodies for them similar to what they were incarnated in during their earthly existence, whether they lived in a foreign country or in the Holy Land; for in every body there exists a mysterious bone, like unto a seed hidden in the earth, and by it the body will be formed anew at the day of resurrection. It will be to it, what leaven is to bread and by it the Holy One will reconstitute the whole body, but only those who are raised again out of the Holy land, as it is written, 'Prophesy and say unto them, thus saith the Lord God, behold oh my people, I will open your graves and cause you to come up out of your graves and bring you into the land of Israel' (Ez. XXXVII. 12). At the time of the resurrection their bodies reformed and renewed will revolve under the earth and appear in the Holy Land in order that they may be incarnated again by their souls, scripture states, "And I will put my spirit in you and ye shall live and I shall place you in your own land." Thus will all bodies be reanimated by their souls, excepting those who have defiled themselves and corrupted the earth by the sin of self-pollution, for of them is written as of the antediluvians, 'They were destroyed from off the face of the earth.' Though amongst the doctors and sages of ancient times there have been great disputes and differences of opinion respecting the exact meaning of the word va-imahou (and they were destroyed or effaced from), yet by its use, it is certain that scripture teaches such sinners shall never rise again, the elements composing their lower selves being dissolved and consumed in the primal fire out of which they were first evolved, equivalent to being effaced and blotted out of the book of life."

Rabbi Simeon, in replying to these observations of Rabbi Abba, said: "It is certain that the antediluvians will have no part in the life to come, as it is written of them, 'they were destroyed from the earth'; this word here signifying the future life, as in the words 'they shall inherit the earth forever' (Is. LX. 21). And even if they do appear at the judgment day, it is written of them, 'and many of those that sleep in the dust of the earth, shall awake, some to everlasting life and some to everlasting shame and punishment' (Dan. XII. 2). The difference of opinion that exists arises from the question whether or not the unjust will ever rise again in the judgment day. On all points the initiates of the Secret Doctrine are in perfect accord."

AND EVERY LIVING SUBSTANCE WAS DESTROYED WHICH WAS UPON THE FACE OF THE GROUND. GEN. VII. 23

SAID Rabbi Abba: "The word 'ath' preceding 'col hayqoun' (every living substance) includes in the deluge also the celestial chiefs and rulers under whose jurisdiction the earth was placed at that time, for when the Holy One punishes mankind he first chastises their spiritual rulers and then those over whom they ruled, as it is written, 'In that day shall the Lord punish the host of the high ones that are on high, the kings of the earth upon the earth' (Is. XXIV. 21). But how can these angel chiefs be destroyed? Are they consumed in the primordial fire, as is written, 'For the Lord they God is a consuming fire and by that element, angel rulers are destroyed as those under their rule were destroyed by water, and thus it was that every living substance upon the ground was exterminated therefrom; that is, the cattle and creeping things and the fowl of the heaven, all were destroyed from the earth and Noah only remained along with those in the ark." Said Rabbi Jose: "Even Noah himself did not wholly escape injury, for it has been said that he was crippled by the bite of a lion. 'And God remembered Noah and every living thing and all the cattle with him in the ark.'"

Said Rabbi Hiya: "A prudent man forseeth the evil and hideth himself' (Prov. XXII. 3). These words refer to Noah who entered the ark and hid himself therein, seeing the oncoming of the waters and the destroying angel."

Said Rabbi Jose: "They refer to the man who when death rages in the world hideth himself and goes not forth that he may not be seen by the destroying angel who has then the power of afflicting and destroying whom he beholds, and so in the second part of this verse it is added, 'but the simple pass on and are punished.' By the word along (abron) scripture teaches that the simple pass along before the exterminating angle and suffer. This word also signifies to transgress, and we are taught the simple break the commands of their lord and consequently are punished, My second part of the verse is also applied to the contemporaries of Noah who if he had not hid himself in the ark would have perished along with them in the waters of the flood, but was saved by his obedience to the divine commands, and therefore it came to pass, as it is written, 'and God remembered Noah.'"

Said Rabbi Simeon: Whilst divine judgments operate in the world, the word zacar (remember) is never found used in scripture only after punishment and judgments have been accomplished and the world has been broken and the destroying angel reigns rampant, and not until he has executed his mission, does the world revert to its normal state, and therefore it is written, 'and God remembered Noah.' The word remember is here applied to Noah as being a just and perfect man. It is written, 'Thou rulest the raging of the sea, when the waves thereof arise thou stillest them' (Ps. LXXXIX. 9). When the waves of the sea arise mountains high and its depths are upheaved, the Holy One unseen sends forth his word by which the angry billows are assuaged and the fury of the waters is restrained and calmed. Jonah was cast into the tempestuous sea and a fish was prepared to swallow him. How was it he continued to exist and retain consciousness? It was because the Holy One rules and governs the powers of evil that proceed from his left and excite and cause storms and tempests. When however the good powers come forth from his right and, descending upon the waters, meet those from the left, then the billows rage as beasts hungering after prey. Then it is that the Holy One stilleth them and causes them to return to their place. Another interpretation of the word 'stillest,' (the-shabhem) giving the literal sense is, 'thou praisest them,' because the tempestuous billows are a manifestation of the desire on the part of the evil forces, to come into contact, and union with the good ones proceeding from the right, and hence we infer from this passage of scripture that a man is worthy of praise when, desirous of the knowledge of divine mysteries, he engages and addicts himself to the study of them. He is worthy of commendation even if, through lack of intellectual and natural abilities, success does not crown his endeavours.

Said Rabbi Jehuda, whilst in the ark, Noah became apprehensive lest the Holy One had forgotten him, but after the judgment on the antediluvians was completed and they had been swept off the face of the earth, then is it written, 'And God remembered Noah.'"

Said Rabbi Eleazar: "Observe, when the world was undergoing punishment, it was better for man that his name should not be mentioned before the presence of the Holy One on high, as then his sins and misdeeds would have been remembered and given rise to examination into them. What ground have we for making such a statement? From the case of the Shunamite woman. It was on New Year's day, when God sits and judges the world, that Elisha was staying in her house. And he said unto her wishest thou that I should speak unto the king for thee, that is, the Holy One who called a King, the King of righteousness, the Holy King. And she said, I dwell amongst mine own people; meaning, I wish not to be remembered or spoken of to the Holy One save as one and along with those with whom I live, so that our deeds and acts may not be judged and examined separately but collectively together. This she said because when the actions of a whole people are adjudicated upon, those of an individual are less remarked and manifest and therefore avoid censure and disapprobation. Observe, that whilst judgment was being executed on the world, there was no remembrance of Noah. When however it was accomplished, then the Lord remembered him. Another interpretation of these words is, they have one and the same meaning as the words 'I have remembered my covenant'" (Ex. VI. 5).

WHAT TWO RABBIS LEARNED FROM A YOUTH

SAID Rabbi Hezekiah to Rabbi Jose, whom he met when travelling from Cappadocia to Hyda and who had expressed surprise at his journeying alone and without any companion with whom to converse, contrary to the usual custom: "I am accompanied by a youth whom I expect to join me presently."

Said Rabbi Jose: "I am still more astonished to find you travelling with a youth who must be wholly unable to converse with you on matters relating to the secret doctrine. To do so, as you are aware is not discreet nor prudent."

"What thou sayest is quite true, replied Rabbi Hezekiah." At that moment the youth joined them.

Said Rabbi Jose: "Where residest thou, my child?"

He replied, at Hyda. This learned man informed me he was traveling thither and it afforded me great pleasure to accompany him thither.

Then Rabbi Jose asked the question: Hast thou any knowledge of the secret doctrine and its teachings?"

"What I know, replied the youth, I have learned from my father, who taught me the meaning of sacrifices, and I have often listened attentively to lessons he gave to my brother."

Then said Rabbi Jose: "Impart to us what thou hast heard and the knowledge thou hast acquired."

The youth spoke and said: "It is written, 'and Noah built an altar unto the Lord, and took of every clean beast and of every clean fowl and offered them a burnt offering on the altar (Gen. VIII. 20). The altar here mentioned was that on which Adam himself had formerly sacrificed. But why offered he a burnt offering instead of a sacrifice? Because it is that a burnt offering is offered only as expiation of sins committed in thought. This was the case with Noah, for he had said within himself, the Holy One having executed judgment on the world and exterminated all mankind, saving myself, from off the earth, I fear he has forgotten me, so that I shall perish with no hope of reward in the world to come. In imagining this, Noah sinned and therefore in expiation, as soon as he came forth out of the ark, he built an altar and offered a burnt offering unto the Lord. Why did he build it when that whereon Adam had sacrificed yet existed? The reply is that by the action of the deluge everything had been destroyed or overthrown, it was necessary for Noah to rerear it again. It is stated he offered burnt offerings (oloth), which word though in the singular is pronounced in the plural; the mystical reason of which is this. It is written, 'The burnt offering or sacrifice is a woman, a female (asheh), a sweet savour unto the Lord' (Lev. I. 17). Now an animal offered as a burnt offering must always be a male, as it is written, 'Let him offer male without blemish' (Lev. I. 17), and also, 'He shall bring a male without blemish.' Wherefore does scripture state, the burnt offering is a female (asheh) which literally designates offerings to be consumed by fire which if this was the true meaning, the word should have been written ash without the final H. The fact is, a burnt offering has for its object the union of the male with the female principle, between which there should never be any separation, and though the word asheh is translated 'consumed' yet, according to tradition, it has a mystical meaning not generally known. It was necessary for Noah to offer up a burnt offering as he represented the male principle which the Holy One joined and united with the ark, a symbol of the female. The offering Noah made was therefore a symbol of this union of these two principles, and this is the reason why the burnt offering (olah) is called asheh (female). Scripture further states, 'And the Lord smelled a sweet savour,' and Asheh is also called so. Respecting this 'asheh' we have been taught that the smoke and flame are so united and conjoined that the one is never without the other; as it is written, 'and Mount Sinai was altogether on a smoke because the Lord descended upon it in fire' (Ex. XIX. 18). Observe that fire, being an element of rare subtlety, is in itself invisible like heat to the naked eye and continues so until, its vibrations becoming increased and intensified, it comes forth from the body or substance in which it lies concealed and then manifests itself. When this occurs, its existence is only detected and recognized by smoke proceeding from the body in which it lies latent, as breath exhaled from the nostrils is indicative of the fire latent in the body; and so scripture states, 'They shall put incense in thy nostrils' (Deuter XXXIII. 10), because fire returns to its place of origin and the nostrils sensing its odour give rise to thoughts, feelings and desires, becoming, as it is written, 'A sweet savour, 'nihoah,' a something that allays wrath, calms anger and restores peace; and when the fire and smoke are unified, joy becomes universal, the fire appears with greater brilliancy, and God smells a 'sweet savour' as though he breathed in and absorbed all into himself.

As the youth ceased speaking, Rabbi Jose embraced him and said: "What a treasury of knowledge thou possessest, and we knew it not. We will return and go with you further." And so they journeyed together.

Said Rabbi Hezekiah: "May the Schekina go with us, for we have enjoyed the privilege of acquiring knowledge of mysteries, of which we were wholly ignorant." Taking then the youth by the hand they entreated him to recite verses and texts of scripture, the interpretation of which he had learned from his father.

Yielding to their request the youth said: "It is written, 'He shall kiss me with the kisses of his mouth' (Cant. I. 2). These words refer to the heavenly desire that cometh not from the fire of the nostrils but from the mouth, for when the lips meet and touch, love is engendered and felt as a fire enlightening the face, whilst the eyes become suffused with joy and delight; and, therefore, it is further added, 'for thy love is better than wine,' meaning the wine which makes the heart pulsate with joy and the features glow with delight and the eyes of those who drink thereof to glisten with rapture, altogether different from the intoxicant that excites quarrels, sours the visage, making it appear dull and heavy. The wine spoken of in this verse is good. It brightens the countenance, brings a mystic light into the eves, excites love and desire and fills the hearts of all who drink it with feelings of inexpressible joy and ecstasy and is symbolized by the libations of the words, 'thy love is better than wine.' For, according to the aphorism, 'As above, so below,' there is a joint conformity between the two worlds, when desire is excited in the one, so is it in the other. They may be compared to two lighted candles, when that above is extinguished, the flame of that below mounting up in the smoke of the burnt offering enkindles it again."

Said Rabbi Hezekiah: "It is truly so, for the two worlds are blended and dependent the one on the other, and it was owing to the disharmony between them when the temple at Jerusalem was destroyed that blessings from heaven have not descended and prevailed throughout the world."

Said Rabbi Jose: "Because the source of all blessings is dried up, maledictions and afflictions are so widely rampant and Israel no longer dwells on the earth discharging duties necessary to keep the candles burning and so obtain and enjoy those heavenly benedictions, from the lack of which the earth no longer exists in her primal and normal state of peace and happiness."

Said Rabbi Hezekiah: "It is written, 'And the Lord said in his heart, I will not again curse the ground any more for man's sake' (Gen. VIII. 21). What do these words mean?"

Said Rabbi Jose: "I have heard Rabbi Simeon say, 'When fire from heaven is intense and comes into contact with matter, it produces a thick smoke that is exceedingly harmful to the world; and the more its heat falls on mankind the more injurious it is to them, on account of the smoke sent forth by which they are suffocated and destroyed. But, when it is moderate and not in excess, it is no longer a destructive agent.' The meaning of the words to asiph (will not again) is, 'I will not augment the heat that I send unto the world below and which on coming into contact with the matter of the earth gives rise to smoke that is deleterious and destructive to life.'"

The youth again spoke and said: "I have heard that when God said unto Adam, 'Cursed is the ground for thy sake,' the evil spirit then obtained power to rule over the earth and also to destroy and afflict mankind dwelling thereon. But from the day that Noah offered a burnt offering and the Holy One smelled 'a sweet savour,' the earth became endowed with the power of freeing itself from the yoke of the serpent and of purifying itself from the infection with which it was tainted; and for this reason it is that Israelites offer burnt offerings to the Holy One, in order to enlighten the face of the earth." Said Rabbi Hezekiah: "That is true, but the earth did not become wholly purified until the Israelites arrived and stood at the foot of Mount Sinai."

Said Rabbi Jose: "The Holy One diminished the light of the moon and gave the serpent power to rule over the earth because of the sin of Adam, through which all creatures on it became cursed and remained so, up to the sacrifice offered by Noah. The moon, however, still retains its horned limbs, except when sacrifices were offered up, and Israel became an inhabitant of the earth."

Said Rabbi Jose to the youth: "What is your name?" He replied: "Abba (father)."

"May you," said Rabbi Jose, "become a father in everything--in wisdom as in years--and may it be said of thee, 'Thy father and thy mother shall be glad, and she that bare thee shall rejoice'" (Prov. XXIII. 25).

Said Rabbi Hezekiah: "The Holy One is arranging and planning to drive the death angel out of the world, for it is written, 'And I will cause the unclean spirit to pass out of the world,' (Zach. XIII. 2) 'and death also shall be swallowed up forever, and the Lord God shall wipe away tears from all eyes and take away from the earth the shame of his people, for the Lord hath spoken it.' The day will surely dawn when the Holy One will cause the moon to shine as the sun and, though at present bedimmed by the serpent and shorn of its radiancy, it shall regain its former light, as saith the scripture, 'And the light of the moon shall be like that of the sun, and the light of the sun sevenfold as the light of seven days' (Is. XXX. 26). That is, as the light which the Holy One hid at the conclusion of the seven days of creation for the enjoyment of the righteous."

"And God blessed Noah and his sons and said, be fruitful and multiply and replenish the earth."

CHAPTER LXXIV.

SAID Rabbi Abba: "'The blessing of the Lord maketh rich' (Prov. X. 22). The blessing of the Lord is the Schekina who rules over the blessings that come to mankind, To the words of this verse in scripture is added, 'And he added no sorrow with it.' Now the term atzeb (sorrow) is here used because it alludes to the mystery expressed in the words, 'cursed be the ground for thy sake, in sorrow (beitzabon) shalt thou eat of it all the days of thy life.' The utzeb here designates that sense of the divine wrath and displeasure that causes the face of man to lose all traits of joy and to become pallid with fear and alarm. In addressing these words to Adam God wished to say that henceforth man would not partake of spiritual food and nourishment freed from and unsurrounded by evil spirits, whose object would be to prevent his reception of heavenly and divine benedictions pure and unalloyed with sorrow and regret. This is why scripture states that he, the Divine Being, will not add (yosiph) sorrow (atzeb) with his blessings, thus expressing the same mystery as in the words, 'I will not again (aseph) curse the ground for man's sake.' Scripture further states, 'And the fear of you and the dread of you shall be upon every beast of the earth, and upon every fowl of the air, upon all that moveth on the earth and upon all the fishes of the sea,' meaning, 'From this day henceforth you shall be endowed with a human form, of which man by his wickedness had become divided.' After Adam's transgression, the human countenance became so changed that it lost all resemblance of Alhim in whose image he had been created, so that man, instead of inspiring animals with fear of him, lived in fear of them. As they gazed upon him before his fall, they recognized the marks of his divine origin and stood in awe before him, but, after the loss of his innocency, they regarded him only as a creature like unto themselves. Observe that all men living the higher and divine life and observing obediently the commandments of their Lord, exhibit in their countenances the imprint of the divine, before which all creatures on beholding it tremble and fear. But immediately that men begin to transgress the good law it fades and becomes obscured, that animals are no longer restrained through fear of attacking them. The world after the deluge became renewed and purified, and God in blessing men restored to them the lost power of ruling over the animal creation and over the fish of the sea, as it is written, 'And upon all the fishes of the sea into your hand are they delivered' (Gen. IX. 2)."

Said Rabbi Hiya: "These words signify that the Holy One, as at the creation of man, said unto him, Have dominion over the fish of the sea, and over the fowl of the air, and over every living thing that moveth upon the earth' (Gen. I. 28), so at the reinstoration of mankind after the deluge endowed him again with the power of ruling over all animals and living creatures."

COMPARISON BETWEEN ADAM AND THE POSTDILUVIANS

IT is written, "And the Lord came down to see the city and the tower which the children of men builded" (Gen. XI. 8). This is one of the ten manifestations and descents of the Schekina in the world. If it be asked what need was there for descending on this occasion, seeing that the erection of the city must have been well known on high? we reply, it was to pass and execute judgment upon the presumption of these Postdiluvians. The word "liroth" (to see) is sometimes taken in this sense as in the words, "The Lord look upon you and judge" (Ex. V. 20). The esoteric meaning of the words "to see the city and the tower" is this. It was not with the object of seeing them but the men who were engaged in their erection. When the Holy One is about to execute judgments upon men for their evil deeds, he begins with those who are first and foremost in wrongdoing, and afterwards, turns attention to their ignorant and misguided followers. But why are these builders of Babel here mentioned and referred to not as men, but as the children of Adam? It was because they acted similarly to our first ancestor who revolted against his Lord and caused death to enter into the world. Even so did they denounce allegiance to the rule of the Lord and by their audacious and presumptuous project thought to scale the heights and invade the domain of heaven itself.

RABBI SIMEON ON THE CLOSING OF THE SANCTUARY

SAID Rabbi Simeon: "We read, thus saith the Lord God. The gate of the inner court that looketh toward the east, (quadim), shall be shut the six working days, but on the Sabbath, it shall be opened and on the day of the new moon it shall be opened' (Ez. XLVI. 1.). These words have a hidden meaning which should be made known, in order to comprehend and better understand the true signification of what has formed the subject of our discussion. In the first place, let us inquire why it was enjoined that the sanctuary should be closed during the six working days and opened only the Sabbath and the first of the month? It was in order to guard against the entry of the profane, so that they might not abuse what was sacred and holy, and therefore the gate of the sanctuary was opened only on the Sabbath and the day of the new moon when its light became blended with that of the sun. Observe that during the six working days, the lower world seeks to obtain and draw nourishment from the higher world. It is also during these days that the accuser or spirit of evil, save in the land of Israel, is rampant in the world. At the time of the sabbath and new moon, he is compelled to withdraw his presence and recede into his own dark realm as long as the gate of the sanctuary remains open. Then is it the world rejoices on being freed from the power and influence of the evil one. If it be asked: Is he the only one that rules and operates during the week days? we reply, that before the elementals begin their work in the world, the Holy One beholds and looks down upon it, but only during the sabbath and the time of new moon does he provide for its sustenance that comes through the sanctuary, all of whose gates are then opened and peace prevails in both worlds. Remark that it is said, 'and the Lord came down to see (liroth) the city. . . .' that is, divesting himself of a part of his glory, he manifested himself in a visible form in order that, after viewing the city and tower they were building, he might confound their audacious plans and disperse them throughout the world."

THE OBJECT OF BUILDING THE TOWER OF BABEL

WHILST sitting one day in the presence of Rabbi Simeon, this question was asked by Rabbi Isaac: "What impelled these Postdiluvians to be so foolish as to revolt against the Holy One, and how did they become actuated with the idea of building a tower whose top should reach unto heaven?"

Said Rabbi Simeon: "We learn from tradition that by the words, 'and it came to pass as they journeyed from the east' (miquidem) scripture informs us that they quitted the highlands for the plains, the land of Israel, in order to fix their habitation in Babel. 'Here,' said they, 'we can live and dwell, come let us make to ourselves a name, or in other words, let us worship and adore the god of this world, and by so doing acquire and enjoy his favor and help; so that when catastrophes and calamities occur, we shall have here a sure refuge and means of escape from their baneful and destructive effects. Here is abundance of food, and we may reap plentiful harvests which in the past have cost us so great toil and labor. Nay, more, let us make a tower reaching up to heaven, so that we may mount and wage war in the domain of the Premier himself, and thus prevent him from again overwhelming and destroying mankind with a deluge, as in the past.' It is written, 'And the Lord said the people is one and they have all one language and this they begin to do, and now nothing will be restrained from them which they have imagined to do' (Gen. XI. 6). The meaning of which words this is. In the celestial world when all its spheres are harmonious, power is the result. So is it in the world of mankind when all minds become imbued and swayed by unity of thought and feeling. Whatever enterprise or project is undertaken, it is bound to succeed and be accomplished whether its object be good or evil. To nullify their impious intention and purpose of waging war against it was essential that this unity of design should be broken and their plans be thwarted and, therefore, as stated, 'The Lord scattered these builders of Babel and dispersed them abroad upon the face of the earth. And that they might be compelled to cease the building of their city, he confounded their language so that they were unable to understand each other's thoughts and respond to them. Before this the holy language was universally spoken.

THE PRIMEVAL LANGUAGE AND THE BOOK OF ADAM

"Its chief characteristic was, it enabled everyone to express himself clearly and unmistakably in terms exactly corresponding to his thoughts, wishes and intentions, otherwise they were not understood and comprehended by the heavenly powers. Thus it came to pass that, by confusion of their speech, their power resulting from union of will and purpose was destroyed and nullified. Note that words of the holy language are understood by celestial beings who, when hearing them are impelled to assist and help those who utter them, otherwise they pay no heed or regard to them. This now occurred to the builders of Babel who, on ceasing to speak the holy tongue, lost power and ability to carry out and execute their design and therefore left off building the city. It is written, 'Blessed be the name of the Lord forever and ever, for wisdom and might are his' (Dan. II. 20), for they come from and are only with God.' Man being naturally too weak and powerless to possess, has corrupted the divine wisdom which the Holy One imparted and made known to the world and also using it for selfish ends and purposes and presuming on the knowledge of it, has dared to rebel and revolt against their lord. This secret hidden wisdom was revealed at first and imparted to Adam who by it became instructed in its secret doctrine respecting the celestial spheres and their guarding angels. Though endowed with all this profound knowledge, he allowed himself to be influenced and deceived by the tempter so that the fount of this divine wisdom and treasury of knowledge became closed to him. After his repentance, it was again opened to him, but only partially so. In the book that bears his name, he has transmitted this divine wisdom to his successors who, after acquiring a knowledge of it, provoked the wrath of the Holy One against them by their abuse of it for selfish purposes. Its mysteries were taught by the Holy One to Noah who at first did the will of God, but alas! as scripture records of him, he drank of the wine, that is, of the secret wisdom, and was drunken and lay uncovered within his tent, a full explanation of which words we have already given. Afterwards it was imparted to Abraham who in the service of the Lord used it with great advantage to himself, but he begat Ishmael, who vexed the Holy One. So also was it with Isaac who begat Esau. Jacob married two sisters. To Moses was this secret wisdom imparted; and of him it is written, 'Who is faithful in all mine house' (Num. XII. 7), for he manifested his faithfulness in that he never ceased making it the great study of his life. King Solomon became entrusted with it; and of him it is written, 'The proverbs of Solomon, son of David, King of Israel,' and also the prophetic visions of a man who had God with him and was thus able to do all things. Said Solomon himself, since God is with me and hath given this wisdom unto me, whatever seemeth good unto me, I can do. But of him scripture relates, 'And the Lord raised up the adversary unto Solomon' (I. Kings XI. 14). Observe, it was owing to their abuse of true wisdom that the builders of Babel foolishly and rashly revolted against the Holy One, and after striving to execute their evil project became scattered over the face of the earth and lost entirely all knowledge of the mysteries of the secret wisdom. The time will, however, come, when it will be revealed and made known to the world by the Holy One, and he will then become the sole object of man's worship and adoration, as it is written, 'And I will put my spirit within you and cause you to walk in my statutes, and ye shall keep my judgments and do them' (Ez. XXXVI. 27); or in other words, I will not impart my wisdom to man as aforetime that so they might avoid falling, but slowly and gradually they may learn it by meditation, and thus by assimilation walk uprightly and keep my commandments."

ON WORDS AND THE PHILOSOPHY OF SOUND

RABBI Jose and Rabbi Hiya whilst going together on a journey began conversing on the secret doctrine. The chief subject of their discourse were the words, "For the Lord thy God walketh in the midst of thy camp to deliver thee and to give up thine enemies before thee, therefore shall thy camp be holy that he see no unclean thing in thee and turn away from thee" (Deuter. XXIII. 10). Why is the word mithalekh (walketh) here used instead of 'mihalekh'?

Said Rabbi Jose: "These words have the same signification as 'And they heard the voice of the Lord God walking (mithhalekh) in the garden in the cool of the day' (Gen. III. 8). In them is expressed the mystery of the tree of whose fruit Adam ate. 'Mithhalekh' denotes the female and 'mihalekh' the male. It was the same divine Being which marched or walked before the children of Israel whilst travelling through the wilderness; as it is written, 'And the Lord went before them by day . . .' (Ex. XIII. 21), and is the same divine Schekina that walketh before a man when he goeth forth, as scripture states, 'The Just One shall go before him and shall set him in the way of his steps' (Ps. LXXXV. 13) in order to deliver him from all peril and from all his enemies. That this may be so, it is essential that a man keep himself pure and his camp holy; by which is implied bodily purity, as through it, his body, he is influenced and tempted by the world and the Evil One. It is further added, 'that there be no unclean thing (ervath dabar) in thee'; which, literally translated, signifies foul words and obscene language. By this expression scripture teaches us that not only should we preserve our bodies pure, but also see to it that our words and speech be clean and free from obscenity, which, of all things, is an abomination to the Holy One. And therefore scripture warns us, 'lest he turn away from thee,' for the Schekina abides not with a man of unclean lips."

Ere ceasing to speak, Rabbi Jose said: "Since we are journeying together, let our discourse be on subjects relative to the secret doctrine so that the Holy Spirit of truth may be and abide with us."

Said Rabbi Hiya: "It is written, 'And the Lord said, behold! the people is one and they have all one language, and this they begin to do--and now nothing will be restrained from them which they have imagined to do!' Previous to these words it is said, 'And it came to pass as they journeyed from the east' (miqqedem); meaning their defection from the worship and service of the Premier of the world, 'they found a plain or valley in the land of Shinar.' Wherefore is the term 'found' here used instead of 'they came to'? The esoteric explanation is, they found the Book of Hidden Wisdom that had once been in the possession of the Antediluvians, and by a prolonged study had acquired a thorough knowledge of its many and deep mysteries, so that they became emboldened to rise in revolt against the Holy One, imagining that by the pronunciation of certain mystic and occult sounds, words and verses, success would attend them and crown their mad enterprise. But note what is written, 'The people are one and they have all one language; that is, they were one in mind and thought and spoke one, the holy, language. Perceiving this, the Lord knew well that nothing could hinder or prevent them from realising their object, except by confounding their speech and thus rendering them insensible to the vibrating tones of mystic words and phrases they had learned from the Book of Adam. And so they became disunited and scattered over the face of the earth. Had this not occurred their union of will and purpose, together with the knowledge they had acquired of manipulating the occult forces of nature, would have empowered them to achieve and accomplish their bold project, as it is written 'Nothing would have restrained them from doing what they imagined to do'. Had they been obedient and made themselves amenable to the good law, and applied their knowledge for the development of the divine life within them and the subjugation of their lower natures, the history of mankind instead of being a record of moral retrogression and spiritual declension, would have been a chronicle of progress and ascension in the path of light that is now only to be found through suffering and crucifixion of self. The world, instead of being as at present, an Inferno, would long ago have become an Elysium. Its children would have become all sons of light, living together in unity, with one faith, one hope, one God, the Father of light, the All and in All, with whom is no variableness nor shadow of turning or change."

Said Rabbi Jose: "From the account of these builders of Babel, we conclude that union is strength, for as long as they were of one heart and mind, not even divine justice could have prevented them from accomplishing their purpose, and which was only frustrated because, as it is written, 'And the Lord scattered them upon the face of the earth.'"

Said Rabbi Hiya: "From this account of Babel and its builders we also learn something of the great power and might of words or speech, that on the external manifestations of thought and mind, without which there could have been no creation; for, as it is written, 'by the word of the Lord, the heavens were made.' The science of words and sounds since the dispersion of mankind is a lost science, but not irretrievably so. In the ages to come it will be recovered, and heaven and earth, men and angels joined in unity and living in harmony, nations, kindreds and tribes of man now scattered abroad throughout the world, will again be one people and have all one language and the knowledge of the Lord shall cover the earth as the waters cover the seas. The holy language, lost and forgotten, will be spoken again in all its purity, and the prophecy in scripture become realised. 'For then will I turn to the people a pure language, that they may all call upon the name of the Lord, to serve him with one consent' (Zeph. III. 9) 'And the Lord shall be king over all the earth; in that day shall there be one Lord, and his name One' (Zech. XIV. 9). Blessed be the name of the Lord forever and ever. Amen."

SECTION LEKH LEKHA OR THE CALL OF ABRAM

NOW the Lord said unto Abram: 'Get thee out of thy country and from thy kindred, and from they father's house, unto a land that I will shew thee'." (Gen. XII, 1.)

At a meeting of Rabbi Simeon's students, for meditation on the esoteric meaning of this passage in scripture, Rabbi Abba said: "It is written, 'Hearken unto me, ye stout-hearted that are far from righteousness.' (Is. XLVI. 12.) By the phrase 'stout-hearted' is meant those hardened souls who, though acquainted with and having some knowledge of the secret doctrine, yet manifest no inclination nor desire to adapt their lives to its teachings and principles and walk in accordance with the precepts of the good law, and are therefore said to be 'far from righteousness'."

Said Rabbi Hezekiah: "The meaning of these words is, that they are altogether void of the divine life and so do not enjoy inward peace of conscience, as it is written, 'There is no peace unto the wicked.' (Is. XLV III. 22.) Observe, it was Abraham's desire to live the higher life, and to him may he justly applied the words, "Thou hast loved righteousness and hated wickedness, therefore Alhim, thy Alhim, hath anointed thee with the oil of gladness above thy fellows.' (Ps. XLI. 8.) For this reason it is further written, 'Thou, seed of Abraham, my friend.' (Is. XLI. 8.) Wherefore does the Holy One style Abraham 'my friends?' It was because he loved righteousness, for of all who lived in his day and generation he alone was faithful, upright and obedient to the divine law."

Said Rabbi Jose: "It is written, 'How amiable are thy tabernacles; oh Lord of Hosts.' (Ps. LVIII. 1.) How incumbent upon us it is to study the works of the Holy One, for our knowledge of them is only small and limited. Men know not upon what the world is founded and how it is sustained and upheld. Still less do they know anything of its creation or the composition of fire and water that, blending together, become solidified under the action of the Holy Spirit, which, when it is withdrawn, they revert back to chaos, and attraction between their individual atoms then ceases, as it is written, 'It is he who shaketh the earth out of her place and the pillars thereof tremble.'

(Job IX. 6.) Everything in the universe is founded on and governed by law, and so long as there are students found engaged in its study, so will the world endure. Observe at the hour of midnight when the Holy One enters the garden of Eden on high, to converse with the righteous, all the trees of it rejoice and chant forth praises to the glory of his name, as it is written, 'Then shall the trees of the wood sing out at the presence of the Lord because he cometh to judge the earth.' (Chron. XVI. 33.) When is heard a great voice from on high saying, 'Who hath ears, let him hear, who hath eyes let him behold, and who hath a heart to understand, let him listen and attend to the words and teachings of the spirits of all spirits respecting the tour quarters of parts of the world.'

1. The One Absolute, above all	= The sublime Kether, spirit of all spirits.
2. One is below	= The nephesh or soul.
3. One is between two	= The ruach between the soul and spirit.
4. Two beget a third	= The Neshama.
5. Three become one	= The individual
6. One emits rays of color.	= Divine light and life.
7. Six on one side and six on the other	= The visible and invisible world.
8. Six rise into twelve	= The spiritual zodiac in man.
9. Twelve produce twenty-two	= twenty-two letters, the signatures of all created things.
10. Six are included in ten	= Sephiroth.
11. Ten are included in One	= The ten sephiroth, emanations of the Absolute.

"Woe unto those who sleep, who know not, and do not desire to learn what will happen them when in the presence of the great judge they will have to account for their deeds. When the body is defiled, the soul departing out of it flees to the pure atmosphere on high and goes hither and thither, but the gates of heaven remain unopened to it. Like chaff by the wind, or a stone from out a sling so it becomes cast about. Woe unto those who care nought for and live indifferent to the joys on high that are the recompense of the just, for they fall into the power of Duma and descend into a hell out of which they will never again come forth. It is of them scripture saith, 'As a cloud that is consumed and vanished away, so is he who goeth down into Sheol. He shall come up no more.' (Job VII. 9.)

"As the voice ceased uttering these words a light flashed forth from the north, illumining the whole world and falling on the wings of the cock caused it to crow at midnight. At that time no one rises from his couch save those lovers of truth whose chief delight is in the study of the secret doctrine. Then the Holy One, surrounded by souls of the just made perfect, in the garden of Eden listens and attends to the voices of truth-seekers, as it is written, 'Thou that dwellest in the gardens, the companions hearken to thy voice; cause one to hear'." (Cant. VIII. 13.)

INTERLOCUTORY EXPLANATIONS

"Get thee out of thy country." (Gen. XII. 1.) "In the preceding chapter it is stated that Haran died in the lifetime of his father Terah, by which words is indicated that up to that time no man had ever died before the decease of his parent. When Abraham was cast into a fiery furnace in Chaldea, Haran was present at the time. As the men of Chaldea beheld the deliverance of Abraham by the Holy One, they seized hold of Haran and in their rage cast him into it, in presence of Terah, his father. As it becomes the general opinion that the Divine Being alone had saved Abraham, many went unto him and said: "We see thou art a believer in the Holy One, the ruler of the world, instruct our children in the way.' Therefore it was said, 'The princes of the people become joined with the God of Abraham.' (Ps. XLVII. 9.)

"Observe the words, 'And Terah took Abraham, his son, and Lot the son of Haran, his son's son, and Sara, his daughter-in-law, his son Abraham's wife, and they went forth with them from Ur of the Chaldees.' Terah being the leader, it is therefore written, 'They went with them and not with him.' The fact is that both Terah and Lot went forth with Abraham and Sara, who were the chief parties that the Holy One wished to save and deliver out of the power of the wicked Chaldeans. As soon as Terah beheld the wonderful deliverance of Abraham out of the fiery furnace, he adopted his faith and became a believer in the one true God, and therefore in saying, 'They went forth with them,' scripture intends to convey that both Terah and Lot became converts to the faith and religion of Abraham and Sara. So, after going forth from Chaldea, it is added, 'to go into the land of Canaan'; that is to say, that as soon as they had fixed their minds to go to Canaan, it was as though they were really there. From this we may infer that from the moment anyone decides to live the life divine, he is aided and assisted by the powers on high. That this is so, may be gathered from the fact that it is only after scripture tells us that Abraham and his brethren decided to leave their native country, we learn that the Lord said unto him, 'Get thee out of thy country.' Observe nothing is ever effected above unless there first be an impulse or effort from below. The reason of this may be illustrated by the different colored parts of the flame of a candle blending together, as has been already described. It is essential that the dark or lower part project itself upward ere the white flame can appear above it. This is why it is written, 'Keep thou not silent; hold thou not thy peace.' (Ps. LXXXIII. 2.) A prayer unto Alhim not to keep back or strain the white ray of heavenly light from descending upon the earth beneath; and furthermore it is written, 'I have set watchmen upon thy walls, oh Jerusalem, which, shall never hold their peace, neither day nor night; ye that make mention of the Lord keep not silence and give him no rest until he establish and till he make Jerusalem a praise in the earth.' (Is. LXII. 6-7.) From these words we learn that heavenly gifts and blessings descend only when by acts and deeds we qualify ourselves for their reception. Observe that it is distinctly stated, Terah and all his family quitted Ur of the Chaldees, and that then the divine command was given to Abraham, 'get thee out of thy country,' when he had already done so and was on his way to the land of Canaan. How is this invasion of the real facts to be explained?" Said Rabbi Eleazar: "By the order, 'Get thee out of thy country.' God intimated that it was better for Abraham and to his interest that he should do so, as his future safety depended upon his immediate departure from amongst his enemies."

ABRAHAM'S FIRST STUDIES IN OCCULTISM

"The esoteric meaning of the words, 'Get thee out of thy country,' is this: the Holy One endowed Abraham with the spirit of wisdom by which he attained to a knowledge of the names and powers of the spiritual chiefs and rulers over the different nations of the world. When, however, he began to study in order to find the locality of the center of the earth, he soon recognized he was not in possession of the knowledge that would enable him to discover the name of the chief that ruled over it. On further pursuing his studies and investigations, he concluded that Palestine was the real center, and, that being so, its chief must be superior to all other celestial powers and potentates. Anxious, therefore, to continue his studies, he at once determined to migrate thither; and therefore it is stated, 'They went forth with them from Ur of the Chaldees to go into the land of Canaan.' On arriving in Haran, he set about investigating wherefore Palestine was superior to all other parts of the world, but failed to arrive at any certain and definite conclusion. Entering on a more profound study, by means of mathematical calculations and combinations of the geometrical symbols and signatures of the spiritual rulers of the various nations in the world, and also by his science of the courses and influences of the stars and planetary bodies, Abraham at last acquired an extensive knowledge of their grandeur and mystic powers, as also of the hierarchies ruling in the universe. All his knowledge and science, however, was unable to enlighten and instruct him as to the nature and essence of the Supreme Being to whom all creatures owe their existence and upon whose care and providence they depend for their food and sustenance. When the Holy One observed his great yearning and pursuit after divine knowledge, he appeared unto him and said unto him, 'lekh lekha, (get thee out of thy country), or, in order words, study to know thyself and look within thyself and cease investigation on the moral influences pervading other lands;--'from thy kindred,' cease from thy astrological studies on rules for predicting the future by the positions of planets in the different constellations of the zodiac and determining the influence resulting from their conjunctions with one another, over the birth and life of human beings. 'From thy father's house,'--change the manner of living under which thou hast been brought up at home,--renouncing astrological science and henceforth placing no faith in it. Observe it was after departing from Ur of the Chaldees and whilst Abraham was dwelling in Haran that the divine command was given him to 'get thee out of thy country,' and therefore the exposition just given of these words is the only feasible explanation that can be given for their position in the text of holy scripture. It is further added, 'and go to a land I will show thee.' By the word 'arekha' (I will shew thee) is implied that Abraham was to cease all his transcendental studies and investigations on the divine nature and essence, which, being beyond the limits of all human intelligence must of necessity remain unrecognizable and an insoluble mystery. 'And I will make of thee a great nation and will bless thee and will make thy nation great and thou shalt be a blessing.' There is here a correspondence between these four blessings and the four commands given to Abraham that may be grouped together, thus: 1. 'Lekh lekha,' (I will make of thee a great nation.) 2. 'Get thee out and I will bless thee.' 3. 'From out of thy country,'--'and make thy name great.' 4. 'And from thy father's house'--'and thou shalt he a blessing.'"

Said Rabbi Simeon: "These four promises correspond to the four feet or pedestals of the heavenly throne and as the blessings signified by them were to be enjoyed by Abraham, it was indicated to him that all nations should draw their spiritual nourishment and sustenance through him. Therefore it is written, 'I will bless them that bless thee and curse him that curseth thee, and in thee shall all nations of the earth be blessed'."

Rabbi Eleazar was one day sitting before Rabbi Simeon, his father, along with Rabbi Jehuda, Rabbi Isaac and Rabbi Hezekiah.

"Wherefore," asked Rabbi Eleazar, "is it written, 'And God said to Abraham, 'Get thee out of thy country' instead of 'get ye out?' in the plural, since all the members of his family went out with him at the same time? Though Terah was an idolator, God could have given him a like command in case he repented of his idol worship, as we know the Holy One accepts such and regards them with favor. That Terah had renounced his early faith is shown clearly from his going forth with Abraham from Ur of the Chaldees, when as yet the Lord had not commanded the Patriarch to do so. Why was, therefore, the order given only to Abraham?"

Said Rabbi Simeon in reply: "If you imagine that it was through renunciation of his former faith Terah left the land of his birth, you are mistaken. It was to escape from his fellow-countrymen who sought to kill him. When they observed the miraculous deliverance of Abraham out of the fiery furnace, they said to Terah, 'Thou has deceived us by thy worship of images.' On hearing this, Terah departed to Haran, where he lived and died. This is, therefore, why the order was given only to Abraham, and so he departed, as it is written, 'According as the Lord had spoken unto him, and Lot went with him,' no reference being made to Terah because he was already deceased. Furthermore, it is written, 'And from the wicked their light is withdrawn and the high arm shall be broken.' (Job XXXVIII. 15.) These words refer to Nimrod, founder of Babel and the men of his generation, from whom Abraham, who was their light, was withdrawn; and so it is not said 'the light,' but 'their light' which was with them was withdrawn and withholder. 'The high arm' signifies Nimrod himself, who held all his fellows and contemporaries under his tyrannical rule. The command of 'Get thee out of thy country' may, therefore, be paraphrased thus, 'Get thee away hence for thine own future safety, that thou and thy family and kinsmen and companions may enjoy the light divine.' Furthermore, it is said, 'That now they see not the bright light which is in the clouds, but the wind passeth and they are dispersed.' (Job XXXVII. 21.) What the esoteric meaning of these words is, may be illustrated from the great event in Abraham's life, namely, his departure from out of his native land in which as long as he continued to live, but he was unable to attain to the light of the divine or higher life, that from amongst his countrymen had been withdrawn and continued so, until the wind passed and dissipated the clouds that concealed and hid it, and resulted in Terah and his family eventually renouncing idolatry and becoming monotheists. That this was what occurred may be gathered from the form of expression, 'the souls they had gotten in Haran'; that is, who had changed their former faith, as also from the words of scripture, referring implicitly to Terah, 'And thou shalt go to thy fathers in peace; thou shalt be buried in a good happy old age'." (Gen. XV. 18.)

Said Rabbi Eleazar: "We read, 'So Abraham departed as the Lord had spoken unto him.' (Gen. XII. 4.) Observe it is not said 'he went forth (ayatza),' but 'he departed (vayelekh); for he had previous to this forsaken his country and was then dwelling in Haran. It is stated, 'And Lot went with him,' that he might follow Abraham as a guide, but as the future proved, to little or no effect. Happy are they who study assiduously the commandments of the Holy One, that they may walk in his ways and fear him and the day of judgment, when each one will have to give in his account of the deeds and acts of his life, as it is written, 'By what a man writes, shall his deeds be known to all.' (Job XXXVII. 7.) The esoteric meaning of which words is, that at the moment of death, when the soul is about to leave the body, things previously unseen and uncognized become visible. Ere the separation of the soul from the body takes place, three celestial messengers appear who take account of the number of years each one has lived, and of all the deeds he has committed in earth life. After its correctness is acknowledged, it is signed and sealed by his own hand and so, as scripture states, 'By what is written and admitted, he shall be judged in the world to come for his misdeeds, whether committed in youth or old age, whether recent or in days gone by, all will be made known when the account is handed in.' Observe how callous and hardened, wrongdoers become in their nature and character as they pass through earth-life and continue so to the end of it. Wherefore truly blessed is he who has learned to conform his ways according to the good law and lived in obedience to its dictates and admonitions. How perverse in their ways! how self-conceited and self-opinionated are evil doers; how unmindful and regardless are they of the exemplary lives of good and noble men who spare not themselves to raise and elevate them on to the plane of a higher life and never cease their efforts, notwithstanding the many rebuffs and checks they have to endure, for well they know and realize that upon themselves lies the burdensome task to save and rescue humanity from destruction and ruin. If the wicked therefore perish, it is through their own acts and deeds. They reap what they sow, as did Gehazi, the servant of Elisha, and also Lot, who, whilst associated with Abraham, refrained from mingling with evil-doers. As soon, however, as he dissociated himself from the patriarch and went on his own way, scripture states, 'And Lot chose him all the plain of Jordan' and after visiting and dwelling in various cities, took up his residence amongst the inhabitants of Sodom, of whom it is related, 'the men of Sodom were wicked, and sinners before the Lord exceedingly.' (Gen. XIII. 13.).

Said Rabbi Abba, when Rabbi Eleazar had ceased speaking: "The explanation of the difficulty attending the call of Abraham to leave his native country is quite satisfactory and I agree wholly with the remarks you have made thereon, but how do you explain the words at the end of the verse, 'And Abraham was seventy and four years old when he departed out of Haran.' Did the divine call come to Abraham whilst sojourning there or whilst living in Ur of the Chaldees?"

Said Rabbi Eleazar in reply: "The words of scripture you have just quoted refer to Abraham's departure from Haran and not from his native land, which took place many years previous to his receiving the divine command.

And Abraham took Sara his wife.' Why is the word 'took' (va yecakh), here used instead of 'led (mashakh)?' Because it is intended to convey that it was by persuasion and not by compulsion, he induced Sara to go with him; for under any circumstance it ill becomes a man to force his wife to emigrate to a foreign land without her free consent. As in the case of Moses, who 'took' Aaron, and also 'took' the Levites, so with Abraham it is written, 'he took Sara, his wife, an Lot, his brother's son'; that is, seeing the dangers threatening them from the perverse manner of the people among whom they were living, he persuaded them so that they willingly consented to go along with him into the land of Canaan. If it be asked what led Abraham to take Lot along with him? It was because by divine prevision he foresaw that through Lot's descendants King David would be born into the world. It is further related, 'And all the souls that they (Abraham and Sara) had gotten in Haran,' meaning all those whom they had influenced to renounce idolatry and become worshippers of the one and only true God."

Said Rabbi Abba: "If what you say is true, there must then have been a great number of adherents and believers who followed and accompanied Abraham and Sara. Was this the case?"

Said Rabbi Eleazar: "Certainly it was, and all those who went forth with them were called 'the people of the God of Abraham.' It was owing to the great number of them that he was able to pass through the land as stated without any feeling of fear or dread."

Said Rabbi Abba: "If scripture had said 'And the souls they had made (asou) in Haran,' your remarks would be quite correct, but the actual words are 'with the souls (ve-eth hanephesh).' I think the meaning intended is, that Abraham acquired and was credited with the merits of those whom he had induced to change their faith when in Haran, for whoever leads erring ones into the path of truth, to him is attributed, and rightly so, the merits of all those whom he has succeeded in converting from the error of their ways; and this was the case with Abraham."

ABRAHAM'S INITIATION INTO THE LESSER MYSTERIES

SAID Rabbi Simeon: Wherefore on first revealing himself to Abraham did the Holy One say unto him, 'Lekh lekha, (Get thee out) when as yet he had not spoken a word to him? It was that by the numerical value of the letters of these words he might indicate that when he was a hundred years old [1], a son should be born unto him. Observe: everything the Holy One does on earth, is wrought by a mysterious wisdom and beyond all human comprehension. Abraham at the time of his call was far from being perfect in his relationship to the Holy One, and knowledge of divine science; and, in these words first spoken unto him, allusion is made to the true path and manner of spiritual ascension by which the soul of man is able to become harmonized and assimilated with the Divine Being, and this Abraham could not attain unto previous to his entry into the land of Canaan.

King David experienced the same difficulty ere he could become qualified to rule. In connection with him it is written, 'And it came to pass after this, that David enquired of the Lord, saying, 'Shall I go up to any of the cities of Judah?' And the Lord said unto him, 'Go up,' and David said 'Whither shall I go up?' And He said, 'unto Hebron.' As soon as Saul was dead, the kingdom became David's by right, why, therefore, was he not at once invested with sovereignty over Israel? By understanding the occult signification of the words of scripture just quoted, the reason why may be discerned. David could not merit and qualify himself for the assumption of royalty and pre-eminence until he had attained to the same degree of spiritual life and esoteric science as that of the patriarch Abraham, who lay buried in Hebron. Only by the merit of perfection (telera in the mysteries) could he become invested with kingly authority. To attain unto this, he was obliged to live and abide seven years in Hebron in order to qualify himself for the sovereignty over Israel, similar to Abraham, who was unable to come into direct covenant with the Holy One until he had entered into the land of Canaan.

---

[1] the numerical value of לך לך = 50 + 50 = 100.--JBH

"Note now what is written, 'And Abraham passed through the land (va-yaaabor)' rather than he marched or journeyed, indicating the mystery of the Holy Name, the Shemhamphorash of seventy-two letters, the almost infinite combinations of which form the signatures impressed upon every living created being and thing. It is also the synthesis of all other divine names. The same word (yaabor) is used when it is stated, 'And the Lord passed before him (Moses) and proclaimed, 'The Lord, the Lord God be merciful and zealous, long suffering and abundant in goodness and truth.' (Ex. XXXIV. 6), in which verse is contained the Divine Name implicitly and the seventy-two letters of which it is composed. In the book of Rabbi Yessa, the Aged, it is stated that the word (va yaabor) in the verse, 'And Abraham passed through the land' is also in the words, 'And I will make all my goodness pass (aaber) before thee' (Ex. XXXIII. 19), and is intended to convey that the holiness of Palestine proceeds and originates from on high. Concerning Abraham's journey to Canaan it is further added, 'unto the place of Sichem, unto the plain of Moreh;' that is, from the impure to the pure part of the Holy Land. 'And the Canaanite was yet in the land.' These words confirm what has already been stated, and refer to the evil spirit which after being cursed, brought maledictions into the world, as it is written, 'Cursed be Canaan, a servant of servants shall he be unto his brethren.' 'Cursed art thou above all cattle and above every beast of the field.'

It was whilst the world was under the rule of the wicke one and had become depraved, that Abraham beginning to live the higher life, God, as we read, appeared unto him as He had never before revealed himself to any human being, as the one supreme power and sovereign of the world. On learning this great truth, until then unknown, Abraham, as scripture states, 'builded an altar unto the Lord who appeared unto him,' for the first time causing him to feel assured that the one true God and Lord of the universe had manifested and made known his existence unto him. 'And he removed from thence unto a mountain (ha-harah)' or the mountain of the 'He,' where were found all kinds of plants, or in more explicit terms, where existed a community or sodality composed of various classes and grades of neophytes (sometimes called plants or little ones). 'And he pitched his tent (oholoh),' having Bethel on the west and Hai on the east. The word 'oholoh (tent)' is here spelled with a superfluous H, by which is meant Kaballistically that entering on a course of initiation into the mysteries of the higher life, he pitched his tent on the sacred mount of the 'He' and lived there in accordance with the occult teachings imparted unto him. As soon as he knew that the Holy One was ruler of the world, he built an altar. In fact, he built two, the first when the Lord revealed himself unto him, the other when he had attained the science of the 'Hidden Wisdom' and having passed through the various grades, became a full initiate. This we gather from the esoteric meaning of the words, 'And Abraham journeyed, going on still towards the south,' until he reached adeptship, symbolically described as the Holy Land, after taking the solemn oath and obligation of silence and obedience. After this, scripture states, 'there was a famine in the land'; that is, 'through laxity of life and non-observance of the good law, a decline in moral and spiritual life occurred to such an extent that it is further stated, 'for the famine was grievous in the land.'

ABRAHAM'S DESCENT INTO EGYPT FOR INITIATION INTO THE HIGHER MYSTERIES

"On observing this general depravation of manners and modes of living, it is written, 'And Abraham went down into Egypt to sojourn there.' Here the question may arise, what was the reason and object of his going down into Egypt? It was because at that time Egypt was a great center of learning, of Theosophy and the science of the Divine Mysteries, and therefore referred to in scripture as 'the garden of the Lord like the land of Egypt.' In it, as in the garden of Eden, of which it is stated, 'From the right of it went forth a river called Pison that encompassed the whole land of Havilah, where there is gold,' flowed a great mystical river of divine knowledge, very precious and unobtainable elsewhere. Abraham having entered into the garden of Eden and become an adept in the secret doctrine, desirous of passing through all its grades on two the higher mysteries in order to become 'teloios' or perfect, went down into Egypt where there was gold, or the Hidden Wisdom."

Said Rabbi Eleazar: "It is written, 'And it came to pass that when he was come near to enter into Egypt.' Why is the word 'higrib (come near)' found here instead of 'carab' the Hiphil and not the Kal form of expression. The explanation is, that as the same word 'hicrib' is used when the Israelites were before the Red Sea, it is said, 'And Pharaoh drew near' (Ex. XIV. 10), and so were excited to fuller dependence on God for deliverance, so was it with Abraham on his nearing Egypt, where he was soon to come into contact and intercourse with men whose bad actions arising from their ignorance of the worship of the true God; it made him feel a greater need of the divine life and power to preserve him from the evils of idolatry then prevailing there."

CHAPTER LXXXV.

SAID Rabbi Jehuda: "Observe that as Abraham went down into Egypt without the divine permission, he caused his descendants to suffer four hundred years of bondage. He should first have obtained this and all would have gone well. From the first night of his entrance into Egypt, he had to suffer on account of Sara, his wife, as it is stated, 'And he said unto Sarah his wife, behold now I know that thou art a fair woman to look upon.' Did he not before know this; that she was such, and if so, why did he use the word 'now.' It was because up to then the conjugal life of Abraham had been so pure and chaste that he had not gazed upon and beheld her face to face. It was only on approaching Egypt, Sara raised her veil, when her beauty became manifested to Abraham. Another explanation is, that during the fatigue and wearisomeness of a long journey the human body becomes shrunken and enfeebled, but with Sara it was not so, for she had retained her beauty of feature and form without the slightest change or diminution. Observing this, Abraham used the word quoted. A third and most likely reason is what has been traditionally stated, that Abraham then beheld the Shekina or divine glory and presence about her that so affected him with a feeling of joy and delight that he exclaimed, 'I see that thou art fair to look upon.' Knowing also the manners and customs then prevailing in Egypt, he considered how to avoid the taking of Sara from him and therefore said unto her, 'Say I pray thee that thou art my sister.' This word sister (achath) has a two-fold meaning, one literal, the other allegorical or mystical, as in the verse, say unto Wisdom, thou art my sister.' (Prov. VII. 4.) By Wisdom is here meant the Schekina, who is also called sometimes a sister. In inducing Sara to say thus, Abraham was guilty of causing her to prevaricate and utter a falsehood, as the Schekina was really with her, and becomes as a sister to every human soul that enters on the divine and higher life, It is further added, 'that it may be well with me for thy sake, and my soul shall live because of thee.' These words were addressed by Abraham to the divine glory, their meaning being, 'that the Holy One may through thee do good unto me and my soul preserved and saved' as it is only through the grace of the Holy Spirit that a man on quitting earth life is accounted worthy of everlasting life."

Said Rabbi Yessa: "Though Abraham knew of the luxurious manners and unchastity of the Egyptians, yet he was not afraid of taking his wife thither, because the Schekina was with her and therefore he felt no apprehension of the future."

Said Rabbi Jehuda: "'And the Egyptians beheld the woman that she was very fair.' Abraham had concealed his wife in a coffer, which when opened by the Egyptian excise officers there flashed forth a light as bright as that of the sun, and therefore it is said, 'she was very fair.' What they really beheld was a form other than that of Sara that remained visible after they had brought her out of the coffer. This explains the somewhat pleonastic and similar expressions: 'the Egyptians beheld the woman that she was very fair,' and 'the princes also of Pharaoh saw and commended her before Pharaoh,' because, as tradition asserts, they beheld the Schekina abiding with Sara."

Said Rabbi Isaac, "Woe unto the evil minded and unbelieving souls! who know nothing, nor care to understand the doings and acts of the Holy One, therefore they perceive not that every event that takes place in the world is arranged and ordered aforehand by him who sees the beginning and the end of all things ere they come to pass, as it is written, 'Declaring the end from the beginning and from ancient times the things that are not yet done.' (Is. XLVI. 10.) Observe, if Sara had not been brought before Pharaoh, he would not have been visited with great plagues, similar to those that afflicted the Egyptians in after years. In both cases the same term 'gedolim (great)', is applied to them. 'And the Lord plagued Pharaoh and his household with great plagues (negaaim gedolim) and the Lord shewed signs and wonders great (gedolim) and sore upon Egypt, upon Pharaoh, and upon all his household.' (Deuter. VI. 22.) From the use of the term 'great' we may infer that the plagues inflicted upon Pharaoh in the time of Abraham were the same in number if not in character as those in the time of Moses, and in both instances were done during night time." Said Rabbi Isaac: "It is written, 'But thou, oh Lord, art a shield for me, my glory and the lifter up of my head.' (Ps. III. 4.) David said these words unto the Lord, 'Even though all men should stand up against me, I will not fear, for thou art my protector (a shield before me)'. Remark here the use of the word 'a shield (magen).' David at one time said unto the Holy One, 'Ruler of the world, wherefore is it no form or prayer of benediction is found ending with my name like that of Abraham which the children of Israel address to heaven, and concluding with 'Blessed be thou, oh Lord, protector of Abraham.' To which the Holy One replied, 'Abraham by enduring great protracted trials, proved himself faithful and perfect.' Then said David, 'If this be the reason examine me, oh Lord, and prove me and try my reins and my heart.' (Ps. XXVI. 2.) After his sin in connection with Bathsheba, David remembered these words he had said unto the Holy One and exclaimed, 'Thou hast proved my heart, thou hast visited me in the night without finding--oh, that I had never spoken! I said try me and thou hast proved me; try my reins and my heart as by fire, and thou hast done so and found me not as I wished or ought to be. Better if I had kept silent and not demanded to be tested and tried.' Yet, notwithstanding David's weakness and frailty there is now a prayer of benediction concluding with, 'Blessed art thou, oh Lord, protector of David.' This is why he said, 'Thou, oh Lord, art my protector (magen), my glory and the lifter up of my head' which he appraised more than his jewelled crown and kingly sceptre."

KABBALISTIC COSMOLOGY

IT is written, "And Pharaoh commanded his men concerning him and they sent him away and his wife and all that he had." Note that the Holy One is the protector of the upright that they may not fall under the power of evil and suffer injury from men of the world. Thus he delivered and saved Abraham and his wife. The Schekina remained with Sarah during the whole night. Each time that Pharaoh approached her, an angel obeying the commands of Sara struck him. Abraham, however, trusted in his Lord and rested assured that He would suffer no one to do her violence and had no apprehension of any evil befalling her, as it is written, "the righteous are bold as a lion" (Prov. XXVIII) and in the hour of trial and danger, remains steadfast and faithful and trustful in the Holy One.

Said Rabbi Isaac: "Abraham went down into Egypt without first obtaining permission from the Holy One, who, however, did not forbid or prevent him going thither, as He knew that after the trial of his faith and steadfasteness the world would have no occasion to say that though God had sent Abraham into Egypt, he did not preserve and save him from enduring trouble on account of Sarah. It is further stated, 'The righteous shall flourish like the palm tree; he shall grow like a cedar in Lebanon' (Ps. XCII, 12). What does this comparison mean? This, that as the palm owing to pruning takes a long time ere it begins to bud and bear fruit, so when a righteous man departs out of the world, a long time elapses before a similar one appears and takes his place. This comparison may be further extended, for as the male palm must be planted near a female of its own species in order that fructification may take place, so is it with the upright, who are always joined and linked with an upright wife, as was the case with Abraham and Sarah. 'As a cedar in Lebanon.' As the cedar tree rises higher than all other trees that grow beneath its branches, even so the righteous in their moral spiritual life exceed all others, to whom they are a protection. The world subsists and endures only by the presence in it of the righteous, as it is written, 'The righteous are the foundation of the world' (Prov. X.25) and by the Just One was it brought into existence.

Said Rabbi Jehuda: Are we not taught that it is based upon seven columns, as it is written, 'Wisdom hath built her house, she hath hewn out her seven pillars' (Prov. IX. 1)."

Said Rabbi Jose: "That is very true, for the Just One upholds the seven pillars that sustain the world. He it is that waters it and nourishes it and to him the scripture refers, 'Say unto the Righteous One, it is good, for they shall eat of the fruits of their doings' (Is. III. 10), and also 'The Lord is good to all and his tender mercies are over all his works'." (Ps. CXLV.)

Said Rabbi Isaac: "The words, 'And a river went forth out of Eden to water the garden' refer to the pillar on which the world stands. It is the river that watereth the garden of Eden and causeth fruits to abound that nourish and sustain the world, that also establish the secret doctrine and bring forth the souls of the just who are the fruits of the works of the Holy One, and because they are such, they arise each night and ascend on high, and at midnight the Holy One rules the garden of Eden to delight himself in their midst. It may be asked, whose souls are they?"

Said Rabbi Jose: "With all the souls of the just, whether yet living in the world below or those residing in the heavenly mansions in the world on high, He rejoices with all of them. Observe, the world above must first receive an impulse from the world below and when the soul of a just man ascends into the celestial regions it becomes garbed with a halo of light transcendently bright, which observing, the Holy One is pleased, for such a soul is the fruit of the divine operation within. For this reason such souls are called 'Israelites,' holy children, sons of God, as it is written, 'Ye are children of the Lord your God' (Deuter. XIV. 1)."

Said Rabbi Jose: "How does the Holy One delight in souls living yet in the world?"

Said Rabbi Jose in reply: "At midnight, all truth-loving and seeking souls arise and engage in the study of the secret doctrine, and hymns of worship. It has already been stated, that the Holy One and all the souls of just men made perfect residing in the garden of Eden on high, delight to listen to their voices of praise and observe the blessings that accrue to such on the day that follows after their nocturnal studies, as it is written, 'The Lord will command his loving kindness in the daytime and in the night I will sing' (Ps. XLII. 9). All worship at this time is therefore true and perfect worship.

Observe when the Holy One caused the first born in Egypt to be smitten, the children of Israel were safely enclosed within their houses chanting and singing praises unto him throughout the night. King David used to rise at midnight, for it cannot be imagined or supposed that he sang praises and composed psalms in bed. He therefore said, 'At midnight I will arise to give thanks unto thee' (Ps. CXIX. 62). For this reason his kingdom will abide and he will reign even when King Musiah comes, who, his tradition states, will be called by his name whether David be yet alive or dead at the time of his coming, in expectation of which he always rose at midnight and sang, 'Awake up my glory, awake psaltery and harp, I myself will awake early' (Ps. LXII. 8). Observe that during the night Sarah was in Pharaoh's house, the angels on high sang praises and worshipped the Holy One who commanded (them to go and afflict the great ones in Egypt, and him I intend visiting in the future, as it is written, 'And the Lord plagued Pharaoh with great plagues.' After this it is stated, And Pharaoh called Abraham.' How did he come to know that he was the husband of Sarah? It was through a dream, as was the case with Abimelech, to whom the Lord spake and said, 'Now, therefore, restore the man his wife, for he is a prophet'." (Gen. XX. 7.)

Said Rabbi Isaac: 'We read, 'The Lord plagued with great plagues Pharaoh and his household, because of Sarah, Abraham's wife.' Pharaoh, when the plagues first struck him, heard a voice saying, 'Because of Sarah, Abraham's wife.' Though God spoke the same words to Pharaoh as to Abimelech, yet he learned from what was uttered, who Sarah was, and therefore, as scripture states, 'And Pharaoh called Abraham, and commanded his people concerning him, 'in order that no injury should be done unto him.' And they sent him away, and his wife, and all that he had; that is, they led him to the boundary or frontier of Egypt. The Holy One said unto Pharaoh, 'Thou wilt in likewise deal with Abraham's descendants'."

Said Rabbi Abba, "Why was Abraham subjected to suc a disagreeable and unpleasant incident, and why did the Holy One suffer it to befall him? It was in order that the names of Abraham and Sarah might become magnified and known throughout the world, and especially amongst the Egyptians, who at that time were regarded as magicians par excellence, yet were they inferior to Abraham, as it is stated, 'And Abraham went up (va-iaal) out of Egypt' or ascended higher in Egypt. In what direction? In or towards the south, or in other words, the higher and diviner mysteries."

Said Rabbi Simeon: "In the words, 'Abraham went down into Egypt,' and 'Abraham went up in Egypt,' is contained an occult reference to the mysteries of the Hidden Wisdom, for though Abraham descended into Egypt to be initiated into the occult science of that country, yet he suffered himself not to be seduced and deluded thereby, but remained faithful and steadfast in the faith and worship of his divine lord and master. In this he was unlike Adam, who, notwithstanding the divine command, allowed himself to be deceived by the serpent, and thus caused death to enter into the world. Neither followed he the example of Noah, who succumbed to evil as it is written, 'And he drank of the wine and was drunken and he was uncovered in his tent' (oholoh) this word with a final meaning, Noah appeared naked in the tent of the Schekina. With Abraham it was otherwise, as it is written, 'And he ascended in Egypt.' That is, after learning the occultism or secret meaning of evil, he turned from it and abused not occult science for sensuous gratification and purposes, owing to the Hidden Wisdom he had previously acquired. It is stated that Abraham in ascending from Egypt went into the south (hanegebah), alluding to the high degree in the knowledge of the mysteries he had attained before his descent into Egypt. If Abraham had not gone down thither and been put to the test, he could not have manifested his faithfulness to the Holy One. Also, his descendants, unless they had been tried and disciplined in Egypt, would never have come forth distinguished as the only nation that the Holy One chose for his own portion. Also, if the Holy Land had not been inhabited by the Canaanites previous to the entry of the children of Israel into it, it would not have been the land under the rule and governance of the Holy One. In all these instances the same occult principle and purpose prevailed."

KABBALISTIC PHILOSOPHY OF THE SOUL

RABBI SIMEON, when on a journey accompanied by Rabbi Eleazar, his son, Rabbi Abba and Rabbi Jehuda, said: "How astonishing it is that men give so little consideration to the study of the secret doctrine and the precepts of the good law. It is written, 'My soul delights in thee during the night, yea, my spirit within me seeks thee early' (Is. XXVII. 9). Though these words have been commented upon, we will give a further interpretation of their meaning. When a man retires to rest at night, his nephesh or soul leaves the body and ascends on high. If it be said so do all souls, it is not so, for not all ascend and behold the face of the king. When the soul leaves the body, its connection with the body remains intact, by means of what is termed the silver cord or magnetic tie. In its ascent it passes through hosts of elementals, until it arrives and reaches the region of light and purity. If found undefiled and untarnished by any immoral or unjust act and deed transacted during the previous day, it mounts still higher. If, on the contrary, it bears the least mark or stain of evil, these elementary spirits gather around it, deterring its ascent with pleasing delusions of future happiness or with visions of delight that are never realized and fulfilled. In this state of false and deceitful dreaming, it remains during the night until it returns and, re-entering its body, becomes awake. Blessed are the righteous to whom the Holy One reveals his secret things by vision or dream so that they are forewarned and preserved from coming and incumbent judgments and calamities. But woe unto those wrong and evil doers who corrupt themselves both in body and soul.

"Note that when the pure and undefiled retire to rest, their souls ascending through all the intervening different hosts and degrees of elementary spirits, direct their course towards the region of pure spirits, impelled and guided thither by their own interior impulses and, ere the day dawns, they enter into loving intercourse and converse with kindred souls, and, in company with them, behold the glory of the celestial King and visit his splendid temples. He who has attained to this stage and state of spiritual development in the higher and diviner life, will find an everlasting portion in the world to come, and also that his soul becomes an ark to his real self and spirit ego and which, when unified and blended in one, the perfected being proceeds on its eternal ascent towards the Holy One, for from the divine has it, the spirit ego comes forth, and unto the divine will it return at length. This is then what the psalmist meant,--'My soul longeth after thee in the night,' that is, desires to ascend to its source and will suffer nothing to divert it from its course.

"The word nephesh (soul) designates the lower self in the time of sleep, whilst the term 'ruach' is applied to it in its state of wakefulness and activity on the earth plane. The nephesh and ruach proceed from one and the same origin, being only productions of one principle, the spirit or higher self. So, then, as man is a; microcosm, a copy or paradigm of the universe, he is in his constitution a reflection of the divine nature, the Supreme Wisdom. The nephesh and ruach are the two angles at the base of a triangle and with that of the apex form a whole or perfect figure. When the neshama, the spiritual ego or higher self, prevails and rules within a man, he becomes holy and divine, because he then begins to conform himself to the image or likeness of the Holy One. The nephesh is the lower part of the individuality and its personal manifestation is the outward material body. Without the one, the other could not exist. As the body is to the nephesh so is this nephesh to the ruach. The ruach is superior to the nephesh and is referred to in the words, 'Until the ruach (translated spirit) be poured upon us from on high'. (Is. XXXII. 15). The lower self, consisting of nephesh and ruach, is susceptible of the influence of the neshama acting upon it. Thus there is a logical and intimate connection and relation between these three parts of every individuality, forming a scale of ascension from the nephesh to the neshama, whose nature and existence, its present connection with the soul and its own future state and destiny, is a most profound mystery. Though beyond human comprehension, through and by meditation thereon, we can rightly infer that all the grades of existence between the lowest and highest, between man and the zoophyte on the one hand and between man and archangel on the other, though infinite in number, are but terms in the infinite series of organic and inorganic life, the integration and summation of which is the Divine Himself, the life of all lives, the fount of all being.

"Note that the nephesh joined to the outward body has the same relation to it as the lowest part of the flame of a candle has to the wick from which it is never separable and could not exist on or manifest itself apart from it and form a basis or substratum to the higher and brighter part of the flame to which the wick and the dark or lower part of the flame give rise. Above all of them imperceptible to human vision there exists a higher and brighter flame than its lower components, giving forth a clear and perfect light. The same or similar relation exists between the component parts of every individual being, the highest of which and invisible to human eye, is the neshama or divine part of man's nature and constitution, and so when the nephesh, ruach and neshama are in harmonic relation with each other, a man becomes holy through the divine life that then flows into him, and qualifies him for the reception and perception of divine mysteries, as it is written, 'He makes known through the righteous that are on the earth, all that we wish to know of him' (Ps. XVI. 3).

"When Abraham entered the Holy land, the Holy One manifested himself unto him, as it is stated, 'And the Lord appeared unto Abraham.' This was his first initiation in the divine mysteries, the beginning of his ascension in the divine lfe, and therefore he built an altar as a symbol of the degree he had attained unto, after which he journeyed, going still towards the south, by which is signified, that passing through the various grades of initiation, he attained to that of ruach, adeptship, and subsequently to that of the neshama, symbolized by the hexagon, that indicates the harmony and union of the higher and lower self with the Divine. This attained unto, he built another altar corresponding thereto. This union with the Divine is the mystery of all mysteries; but ere Abraham could attain unto this high degree of spiritual life and knowledge, it was necessary to subject him to trial and probation, and therefore it was that he went down into Egypt; that is, he had to intermingle and come into personal contact and intercourse with the sinful world, its seductions and charms, its allurements and enticements to sensual indulgence, against which Abraham resisted, suffering himself not to be deluded and beguiled, thereby standing firm and steadfast and impervious to all assaults, proved himself faithful to the great principles and dictates of the divine life to which he had attained; and then, as stated, 'He ascended up out of Egypt toward the south, or in other words, he came out of his ordeal and period of probation purified and inwardly illuminated, to become regarded as a guide and paradigm to all other souls who are wearily climbing their way upwards on the steep and lofty spiral of the divine life. It is further added, 'And Abraham was very rich in cattle, in silver and in gold.' 'Very rich' signifies the east, cattle the west, silver the south, gold the north, the four quarters of the world, symbolizing totality of divine knowledge and wisdom."

When Rabbi Simeon ceased his discourse, Rabbi Eleazar, along with the other students, saluted him with feelings of the deepest respect and reverence, and Rabbi Abba, deeply moved, spake and said: "When thou leavest us where shall we find another master such as thou who will teach and indoctrinate us into the esoteric meaning of the secret doctrine? Blessed are they whose privilege it is to listen to the teachings and instruction that proceed from thy lips."

ABRAHAM'S INITIATORY PROBATION

AGAIN Rabbi Simeon spake and said: "Observe further what is written, 'And he went on his journeys' (Gen. XII. 3), signifying that after the termination of his trials and probation he lived the perfect life. By the term journeys (masaav) is implied the various ulterior stages through which Abraham had to pass ere arriving at perfection. There had been a descent from the time the Lord first appeared unto him; that is, a putting off or a ridding himself of affections and propensities and attachments of the lower self to the sensual and phenomenal, resulting in purification of the soul which, when attained, prepared and enabled him to commence ascending onward and upward through the various states and stages of the divine life after coming out of Egypt; that is after his probation. It is stated, 'He went on his journeys from the south even into Bethel, the place where he had pitched his tent at the beginning'; he progressed and advanced in the divine life so that by the mental and spiritual illumina-tion which he ultimately attained, he became fully initiated into the comprehension and understanding of the mysteries of the Hidden Wisdom and graduated to that degree termed 'teleiaor,' perfection, when it is written, 'And there Abraham called on the name of the Lord' (Gen. XIII. 4) and became a just man made perfect. Blessed are they who attain unto this degree of righteousness, for they become invested with an aureole of light and are jewels in the crown of the Holy One. Blessed are they in this world and in the world to come. Of these it is written, 'The path of the just is as the shining light that shineth more and more unto the perfect day' (Prov. IV. 18)." As Rabbi Simeon ceased speaking, they came to a shady grove where they all sat down to rest themselves. After a while Rabbi Simeon began speaking again.

"It is written," said he, "'O turn thou unto me and have mercy upon me' (Ps. LXXXVI. 16). Though these words have been commented on, they possess an esoteric meaning that has not as yet been given forth. They are occult words. What caused David to give expression to them? David was longing and desiring to reach unto that state in the divine life which would be as a crown unto him; therefore, he said, 'Give thy strength unto thy servant.' That is, the power that descends into the soul when it becomes receptive of the divine; as it is written, 'he shall give strength unto his king' (I Sam. II.

10), alluding to King Messiah, 'and save the son of thy handmaid.' Why did he designate himself as 'the son of thy handmaid' and not as the son of his father, Jesse? Because when a man enters on the higher and diviner life he becomes as one born again of the Schekina or Holy Spirit, through whom as through a mother all supplications and prayers are made and offered. Tradition states that David in this petition makes reference to King Messiah.

THE ESOTERIC EXPLANATION OF LOT'S PARTING FROM ABRAHAM

"It is further stated of Abraham that there was a strife between the herdsmen of Abraham's cattle and the herdsmen of Lot's cattle. The word strife (riv) is here written with a yod (i), by which is indicated that Lot wished to return and relapse into his former state of idolatry and mingle in intercourse with the people of the land, as it is written, 'And the Canaanites and the Perizzites dwelled then in the land.' We are further confirmed in this inference by the words, 'and, Lot journeyed east' (miqqedem), or rather, 'from the east,' the word 'qedem,' as previously expounded, meaning the worship of God, and, giving way to the inclinations and propensities of his lower nature, went and dwelt among the inhabitants of the land in order to enjoy the delights and pleasures of a sensual and worldly life. Observing this tendency in Lot, Abraham inwardly grieving thereon, said unto him, 'Let there be no strife, I pray thee, between thee and me; let us separate, for I perceive there can be no unanimity of faith and worship between us. Thy heart goes out after and is fixed upon the phenomenal and sensual, mine after the one eternal and true God and Lord of the universe.'

"Then it came to pass that they parted, Abraham unwilling to be associated with his kinsman in a life which he knew would prove a calamity to both of them because of the sure and unavoidable doom of everyone who ignores and disregards the divine life and refuses to obey the precepts of the Good Law. Of this, Jehosephat in allying himself with the wicked Ahab was a remarkable example. But for divine goodness, he would have been slain along with his sinful companion, but perceiving his danger ere it was too late, it is written, 'He cried unto God and He helped him'; so that he escaped with his life, whilst the King of Israel, the wicked Ahab, smitten and wounded, died ere the sun went down. This was the reason Abraham was unwilling to continue his intercourse with Lot, who chose all the plain of Jordan, preferring to indulge in the gay pleasures and obscenities of Sodom and Gomorrah rather than live, following the divine light that had begun to dawn within him, which would, as it did with Abraham, have led him safely through and enabled him to avoid and escape the dangers and resist and overcome the temptations that beset the path of every individual on his pilgrimage through earth-life. 'And Abraham dwelled in the land of Canaan,' to progress and go from faith to faith and to attain the higher knowledge of the hidden wisdom, but Lot dwelled in the cities of the plain, gravitating slowly and gradually toward Sodom, where he fired his tent at last to become engulfed in a world of vice from out which no human means could have entreated and saved him from the fearful and terrible doom that awaited those amongst whom he took up his abode. For as it is written, 'They were wicked and sinners before the Lord exceedingly.' Thus Abraham and Lot parted in peace, each of them going his own way and living their own lives, the one of the higher and divine, the other of the worldly and lower self. Blessed the lot of those who choose that better part that shall never be taken from them and whose delight is in the study of the Secret Doctrine, its teachings and principles, and their joy is in the consciousness of the divine presence. They are the true children of Israel, of whom it is written, 'He that cleave unto the Lord your God are alive, every one of you this day' (Deut. 1V.4)."

REMARKS ON THE SCHEKINA

SAID Rabbi Abba: "It is written, 'But Jonah rose up to flee unto Tarshish from the presence of the Lord' (John I. 3). Woe unto him who thinks to hide himself from the Holy One, of whom it is said, 'Can anyone hide himself in secret places, that I shall not see him; do I hot fill heaven and earth, saith the Lord' (Jer. XXIII. 24). Knowing this, how came Jonah to flee and go down to Tarshish thinking he could hide from the All-seeing? The explanation lies in the esoteric meaning of the words, 'My dove (Ionathi) is in the clefts of the rock, in the secret receptacles on the stairs' (Cant. II. 14). 'My dove' here signifies the congregation of Israel; 'in the clefts of the rock' refers to Jerusalem, elevated above all parts of the world as a rock is above the plain; 'in the secret recesses on the stairs' denote that part of the temple called the Holy of Holies, the heart or center of the world; for there is the Schekina concealed from view like a faithful and virtuous wife who never quits the abode of her husband, as it is written, 'Thy wife shall be as a fruitful vine in the recesses of thy house' (Ps. CXXVIII. 3).

"Such was the congregation of Israel when living happy and blessed in the Holy Land with the Schekina in their midst. After her captivity and exile, the Holy Spirit departed and took up its residence amongst other nations and peoples who abound in plenty and peace. Observe, at the time Jonah dwelt in the Holy Land, everything went right, right worship and service prevailed throughout and thus Israel was the only people in the world that could cause the earth to be blessed and fruitful, owing to the divine presence in their midst. For this reason idolatrous nations dared not attack Israel and were unable to gain domination over it as at present, because all the world received through Israel their needful supplies of food and sustenance.

"If it be objected that kings ruled and dominated Israel up to the destruction of the first temple, note that during its existence and as long as Israel polluted not the Holy Land, other nations had no power over it. When, however, by their sins and idolatrous practices, they drove away the Schekina, thus compelling it to seek another residence, they lost their protection and shield against foreign nations who were thus able to conquer and subdue them, through their foolish offering and burning of incense to other strange gods. Whilst Israel dwelt in the Holy Land and was faithful and true in its worship of the Holy One, the Schekina as a virtuous woman, in her own house remained with them and never left them and was the great inspirer of all the distinguished prophets who lived during the existence of the first temple. Jonah fled out of the Holy Land because he had not become endowed with the gift of prophecy and therefore was unwilling to become a servant and messenger of the Holy One. If it be said that the Schekina manifested itself to Israel when in Babylon, which is far away from the Holy Land, our reply is, the Scripture states, 'The word of the Lord came expressly (hayo, haya) with Ezeckiel the priest, son of Ruzi in the land of the Chaldeans by the river Chebar' (Ez. I. 3). By the repetition here of the word haya (was) is indicated that from the time that the temple was erected in Jerusalem, the word of the Lord or the Schekina did not manifest itself elsewhere save in the Holy of Holies. 'By the river Chebar,' it is intended to convey that it had previously appeared in that locality before the building of the temple, as it is written, 'And a river went out of Eden to water the garden and from thence it was parted and became into four heads, one of which was the river Chebar,' by which the Schekina occasionally appeared there, but only in times of Israel's need and distress. Therefore it was that Jonah fled out of the Holy Land to avoid its manifestation to himself; and the sailors, we are informed, knew this, for he had told them.

"Observe that as the Schekina appears only at a time when it is needed, and in a suitable place, so it manifests itself only to persons qualified by some special or peculiar gift to receive its communications. From the moment the desire arose in the heart of Lot to return to his former worldly state of living, the Holy Spirit departed from Abraham, but immediately returned to him when Lot had separated and betaken himself from his intercourse with Abraham, and thus it is written, 'The Lord said unto Abraham after Lot had separated from him . . ." Observe when Abraham learned of Lot's apostasy in the faith and worship of the Holy One, he greatly feared, and said to himself, is it because of my intercourse and relation with Lot that the divine life and light within me has become bedimmed and obscured? After the separation of the two kinsmen had occurred it is stated, 'God said to Abraham: Lift up now thine eyes and look for the place where thou now art.' These words meaning that by separation from Lot he had returned to his former state of spiritual illumination and inward assurance of the actuality and certainty of the divine presence with him, and therefore the Lord further added, 'Northward and southward, eastward and westward,' referring to his previous journeyings, and then gave him to understand that he would be a shield unto him and that his presence henceforth should always abide with him, and added further, 'All the land that thou seest, to thee will I give it and to thy seed forever.' The words, 'which thou seest,' in their esoteric meaning, refer to the higher degrees of the divine life that had been manifested unto him, when, as it is stated, 'He built an altar unto the Lord who appeared unto him.' This degree includes and is the synthesis of all other degrees and therefore it was said unto him, 'all the land which thou seest.'

RABBI ELEAZAR AND RABBI HEZEKIAH, AND THEIR NOCTURNAL STUDIES

RABBI Eleazar was once staying at a wayside inn in Lud, where he met with Rabbi Hezekiah. At midnight, as was his custom, he arose to meditate on the Secret Doctrine. His fellow student did the same.

Said Rabbi Eleazar: "An inn affords good opportunities to students for meeting together. It is written, 'As the apple tree amongst the trees of the forest, so is my beloved among the children of men. I sat me down under his shadow with great delight and his fruit was sweet to my taste' (Cant. II. 3). The esoteric meaning of these words is this: The apple tree that is distinguished by its color from all other trees in the woods refers to the Holy One, the most desired of all beings. Therefore it is said, 'I sat me down under his shadow,' that is, under the divine and not of any other inferior celestial ruler. 'His shadow,' since when? From the time that Abraham appeared in the world, of whom it is written, 'Abraham my friend' (Is. XL. 8). The words, 'and his fruit was sweet to my taste,' refer to Isaac, who was holy fruit. Another interpretation of 'I sat me down under his shadow with great delight' is that they refer to Jacob, as it is written, 'These are the children of Jacob,' whilst 'his fruit was sweet to my taste' denote Joseph, whose children were the quintessence of the descendants of Jacob, and because of this were called by the name of Ephraim, as it is stated, 'Ephraim my dear son' (Jer. XXXI. 20). Also Abraham may be likened unto the apple tree among the trees of the wood, for his pure life was as a sweet perfume. By his faith and obedience to the Holy One he far excelled others both in the world on high as those in the world below, and thus became distinguished as Abraham the Unique, to whom no man that has ever rested in the world is to be compared."

Said Rabbi Hezekiah: "Do not the words, 'The souls that they had gotten in Haran,' indicate that they were individuals who had attained the true faith, the same as Abraham?"

Said Rabbi Eleazar: "They certainly refer to those who were converts to Abraham's faith, yet they never attained unto his excellency in the divine life."

Rabbi Eleazar here for some moments remained silent, and then said: "It has just been said unto me that Abraham was not termed 'Unique' until after the birth of Isaac and Jacob, when all these three patriarchs became conjoined and regarded as the fathers of the faithful."

Said Rabbi Hezekiah: "What has been said unto you is perfectly true. Whilst the 'apple tree among the trees of the wood,' and also 'my beloved among the children of men,' together with 'under his shadow,' all refer to the Holy One; the words 'I sat me down with great delight' signify the time when the Divine Presence was manifested on Mount Sinai and Israel received the Secret Doctrine and said, 'All that the Lord hath said, we will do and obey' (Ex. XXIV. 7). 'And his fruit was sweet to my taste' signify the Secret Doctrine, as it is written, 'Sweeter than honey and the honeycomb' (Ps. XIX. 11). Another interpretation has reference to the souls of the righteous, who are all the fruit of the works of the Holy One and dwell with him on high. Observe that all souls in the world are the fruit of his work before they become incarnated, and form one grand aggregate which, after descending into the earth life, become separated and differentiated into male and female forms that eventually become united. Observe that the desire of the female towards the male induces in it a similar and corresponding feeling resulting in marriage. This reunion is brought about and accomplished by the Holy One alone, and not by any celestial chief or ruler. Blessed is the man whose life is pure and who walks in the path of truth, for their soul becomes united with soul as they existed before incarnation. He whose life is a pure and spiritual life is the perfect man, of whom it is written, 'His fruit is sweet to my taste.' or he is not only blessed himself, but is a blessing to the world and we are able to conclude, therefore, that weal or woe, happiness or unhappiness, are the results of our own acts, words and deeds."

Said Rabbi Hezekiah to Rabbi Eleazar: "Listen to what has been said to me. It is written, 'From me is thy fruit found' (Hes. XIV. 8). This is what the Holy One said to the congregation of Israel, 'thy fruit,' and not 'my fruit,' meaning that as through the united desires of the male and female fruit is born, or a soul is born, so it is with the union of the congregation of Israel with the Holy One. They become united to them by the tie of holy and pure love resulting in holy fruit, as marriage does in the production of offspring."

RABBI JOSE ON THE SEVEN HEAVENS OR FIRMAMENTS

SAID Rabbi Jose: "It is written, 'And it came to pass, in the days of Amrafel King of Shinar' (Gen. XIV. 1). In the prophecy of Isaiah we read, 'Who (mi) raised up the Just One from the east and called him to follow after him' (Is. XLI. 2). This verse has already been the subject of comment to the neophytes, being replete with the mystery of the hidden wisdom that teaches that the Holy One created seven firmaments or heavens above, wherein to manifest his glory, all of them being based and founded on principles beyond human comprehension, which therefore remain subjects of faith and not of knowledge. The highest of these heavens is altogether invisible and rules all those below it, and is therefore called mi (who), as it is written, 'From the womb of Mi came forth the ice' (Job XXXVII. 28). The lowest of these firmaments or heavens is void of light and non-luminous; and, because so, it is attached to those above it to receive it from them. It is distinguished from them by the letters 'y' and 'm' and called yam (the sea), and such it really is to the highest heavens termed Mi (the same letters changed in their order). All the higher firmaments pour their light into it, as rivers discharge their waters into the sea, so that this lower heaven produces fruit, fish, after their species. David refers to it in the words, 'The great and wide sea wherein are things creeping innumerable, both small and great beasts' (Ps. CIV. 25). 'Who raised up or called the Just One to come from the east' alludes to Abraham, and 'to follow him' refer to this lower heaven that forms, as just stated, a sea to the higher heavens above it. It is further added, 'and cast down nations before him.' To whom are these words to be applied? To the lower heaven, also that avenges the oppressed and causes their enemies to fall and be destroyed. In speaking of it David said, 'Thou hast given me the necks of my enemies and destroyed them that hate me' (Ps. XVIII. 40). The above words refer also to Abraham, whose enemies the Holy One caused to be destroyed. Again it is further added, 'and made him rule over kings,' that is, those celestial chiefs that are set over nations as rulers, and protectors who are chastised at the same time that the nation or peoples under their control are afflicted with divine judgments. 'He pursued after and passed safely' refer to Abraham, who pursued his enemies without harm or suffering to himself, for the Holy One destroyed them from before him and 'he passed safely,' or rather, 'peace went before' (yaabor shalom), leaving no traces behind; that is, the Holy One who is sometimes called 'Peace,' intimating that either concealed and hidden by a cloud, or carried in a chariot, Abraham passed through the land instead of marching through it on foot. Now scripture states it was no angel or divine messenger, but the Holy One who went before him; 'with his feet,' that is, with angels that are subordinate to him; as it is written, 'And his feet shall stand in that day,' etc. (Zach. XIV. 4). According to another interpretation of the words, 'Mi (who), raised up or brought the just One from the east,' it is affirmed that after creation of the world the Holy One determined to bring Abraham into it, that he might serve him and become a progenitor of Jacob and the twelve tribes of Israel, who, like their forefathers, were servants of the Holy One. The esoteric meaning of these words, therefore, is that he called Abraham, the just One, out of the east to serve him and do his will, as it is stated, 'Get thee out and all the people that follow thee' (that are at thy feet) (Ex. XI. 8). A further exposition is that the words refer to the east, where the light first dawns and illuminates the south and is pressed by Mi heir (who raised), whilst by 'called the Just One to follow him' have reference to the west. The mystic meaning of the whole verse is that the West will eventually be able to subdue all other nations receiving accessions of power and numbers from the East, in the world."

Said Rabbi Jehuda: "Who has called the Just One to come from the east' refer certainly to Abraham, for from observing the rising of the sun in the east he obtained the first true conception of the Holy One and reasoned then within himself, 'This sun is the king who created me.' He therefore bent in adoration before it and worshipped it all that day. Then, however, the sun set and the moon arose and began to shine. 'This truly,' said he, 'is the deity and rules over the sun whom I have been worshipping all the day, whose light and splendor have faded and given way to that of the moon who now rules supreme.' He thereupon worshipped it all through the night. In the morning he observed the moon disappear and the sun arising again from the east, and said to himself, 'Surely above those kings there is some other and higher power that rules and governs and commands their obedience.' Then the Holy One, seeing the desire of Abraham for divine knowledge rising within him, manifested himself unto him and spake unto him as it is written. He called the just One to follow him; that is, he made himself, both by sight and speech, known unto Abraham."

KABBALISTIC REMARKS ON MARRIAGE

SAID Rabbi Eleazar: "It is written, 'What shall we do for wives for them that remain?' (Jud. XXI. 7), and further it is added, 'Therefore they commanded the children of Benjamin saying, go and lie in wait in the vineyards and catch you every man his wife, and see and behold if the daughters of Shiloh come out to dance in dances; then come ye out of the vineyards, and catch you every man his wife of the daughters of Shiloh.' This incident in connection with the tribe of Benjamin shows how a man may and can become the husband of one who is the sister soul of another, and how as tradition teaches us, betrothment may take place during a feast through fear lest another may pray to obtain the betrothed herself. On further reflection you will discover and understand the mystery or secret law that governs marriage, which is similar to that which operates when a man marries and dying leaves no offspring. When that happens, his widow is bound to espouse her late husband's brother. If she brings forth a son, he is animated with the soul of his defunct father who incarnates a second time within him. This son finds no wife who is his sympneumata because this animates his own mother. Therefore, esoteric students declare that it is permissible to celebrate betrothals during feast days, lest another, by his ardent prayers addressed to heaven, may obtain her who is about to become betrothed, as it is possible by such means to obtain a wife whose soul is the sister or twin of another man."

Said Rabbi Jehuda: "Truly the subject of marriage must be of the greatest anxiety to the Holy One. Blessed is the lot of Israel who enjoys the secret doctrine that teaches them His Holy way, as also the secrets and mysteries attending them. It is written, 'The law of the Lord is perfect converting the soul' (Ps. XIX. 7). Blessed is he who studies in it and rules his life thereby, for then he acquires length of days and learns the secret of life, as it is written, 'For length of days and long life and peace shall it add to thee.'" (Prov. III. 2).

ON THE STUDY OF THE SECRET DOCTRINE

SAID Rabbi Jose: "We read, 'And Abraham was ninety-nine years old' (Gen. XVII. 1), and also, 'Thy people are all righteous, they shall inherit the land forever' (Is. LX. 21). Blessed is Israel above every other people, for the Holy One calleth them righteous. We learn by tradition that there are a hundred and twenty-eight thousand winged messengers who fly throughout the world, listening to the cry of sorrow and the voice of joy or pain and suffering, proceeding from man and beast and bird, all of which with their prayers are gathered and borne by these angelic beings up before their lord, who judges accordingly as intimated by the words, 'Because a bird of the air shall carry the voice and that which hath wings shall tell the matter' (Eccles. X. 20). When are the judgments resulting from these voices and cries and prayers executed and carried out?"

Said Rabbi Hiya: "When a man falls asleep, his nechama or higher self leaves him and, ascending on high, gives account of his deeds and acts and words; therefore is it written, 'Keep the doors of thy mouth even from her who sleepeth near thee' (Mich. VII. 5), alluding to the soul of man."

Said Rabbi Jehuda: "Every deed, act or word a man speaks or does, the higher self or 'neshama' has to give an account of it. It was the teaching of Rabbi Eleazar, that ere the evening begins with the setting of the sun, the angels or mighty ones of the signs of the zodiac, close the gates of its constellations that have been open during the day. Then the voice of a herald cries aloud: Assemble and gather yourselves together! As they ascend in silence on high, those who gather up the world cries and prayers descend and go on their mission through the world. When the moon begins to shed her light upon the earth, these winged messengers sound their trumpets in unison and give forth a sound as the shout of great joy. They blow them again when a plaintive sound is heard and then presently myriads of angelic beings begin chanting hymns and praises before their Lord and Master, after which the judgment of the world commences. Then it is when we sleep, our higher selves quit us and give in their account of us and by the grace and goodness of the Holy One are ordered to return and come back again to us, even when we have done and said things we ought not to have done. After midnight when the cock crows and birds begin to waken up, a wind from the northwest commences to blow, which is met by a current from the south. Then it is that the Holy One delights himself in the souls of the just in the garden of the heavenly Eden. Happy and blessed is he whose delight is to rise and study and meditate on the Secret Doctrine, for then the Holy One with all the souls of the just made perfect, listen and attend to his voice, as it is written, 'Thou who dwellest in the gardens, thy companions listen to thy voice, cause me to hear it' (Cant. VIII. 13). More than this, the Holy One surrounds him who rises at midnight for study with an aura of light (chesed) to keep and protect him whilst on earth, so that angels above and below become his guardians, as it is written, The Lord will command his loving kindness in the day time and in the night season, his song shall be with me' (Ps. XLII. 9)."

Said Rabbi Hezekiah: "Everyone who, rising at midnight, studies and meditates on the secret doctrine enjoys a lasting (thader) portion in the world to come."

"What," said Rabbi Jose, "does the word 'thader' mean?" Said Rabbi Hezekiah: "Hear what I have been taught. Every midnight when the Holy One enters the garden of Eden, all its plants (the souls of the Just) are then refreshed by the water of the river Qedumim, known as the beautiful stream" (nahaladanim) that flows through the universe, and he who studies the secret doctrine at midnight comes into relationship and communion with the souls of the just made perfect on high, and finds himself refreshed and strengthened for as soon as they hear his voice, they are filled with great delight and impart to him the water of life by which they are themselves refreshed and which continually flows forth from under the throne of God on high. This being so, is the reason why he who studies at midnight the secret doctrine is sure of a lasting (thader) supply each night from the water of the river of life.

RABBI ABBA'S VISIT AND WHAT OCCURRED

RABBI Abba of the town of Tiberias went on a visit to his father-in-law, accompanied by his son, Rabbi Jacob, to attend a meeting of novitiates of the Hidden Wisdom. On arriving at the village of Tarsha, they decided to stay there for the night. The keeper of the inn, when Rabbi Abba asked him whether there was a "Tarnagula" on the house (a cockbird) replied, why do you ask such a question? In order, said Rabbi Abba, that at time of midnight I may not fail to rise and engage in the study of the secret doctrine. Let that not trouble you, rejoined the inn-keeper, for we have an alarum in the house that never fails to strike and ring at the hour of midnight. It was the invention of an old man who used to stay here. He was an esoteric student and most punctual he was in rising at midnight to study.

Said Rabbi Abba: "Blessed be the Merciful One who guided us hither."

When midnight arrived, the clepsydra or alarum sounded and was heard throughout the house and awakened Rabbi Abba and his son who, on rising, heard the inn-keeper, seated on the threshold of the door, saying to his two sons: "It is written, 'At midnight I will rise and give thanks unto thee because of thy righteous judgments' (Ps. CXIX. 62). Why did David say 'midnight' (khatzoth lailah) instead of 'at midnight' (bekhatzoth lailah) I will rise, etc. It was because that by this word (midnight) he denotes and distinguishes the Holy One Himself."

Then spake the two sons and said: "Did David really call upon and address Him thus?"

"Truly he did," replied their father, for at the exact hour of midnight the Holy One enters the garden of Eden to enjoy intercourse with the souls of the righteous." Said Rabbi Abba to his son, Rabbi Jacob: "If we go and join them in their study, the presence of the Schekina will most certainly be with us." They went and sat with their host and said, repeat the words you have just spoken, for they are excellent. Who was your teacher?"

He replied: "The old man that formerly stayed here. He also told me that during three hours before midnight angels, deputed to take record of the deeds of men that judgment might be pronounced upon them, fly through the world and return at the exact moment when the Holy One enters the garden of Eden. All the judgments that befall men and the sentences decreed in the world above thus become operative. Where do we learn this? From the history of Abraham, of whom it is written, 'And he separated the night for them' (Gen. XIV. 15), and also from what is said regarding the plague of the Egyptians, 'And it came to pass that at midnight, the Lord smote all the first born in the land of Egypt' (Ex. XII. 29). In many other places of scripture the old man taught me the esoteric meaning of the word midnight, of which David himself was well aware, and knew that his royalty and sovereignty depended on "Midnight" and therefore he rose at that time and composed psalms and called the Holy One by this term, in order as he says, 'to praise thee for thy righteous judgments' which descend from on high at the division of day and night. David knowing that his occupancy of the throne depended upon the divine 'Midnight,' he rose as we have just said to sing praises and give thanks to the King of Kings."

Said Rabbi Abba, as the host ceased speaking: "True are the words thou hast spoken and blessed he the Lord who has directed our steps and guided us hither." He then embraced him and said: "Observe that night is the time of judgment everywhere, as we have learned from Rabbi Simeon."

One of the inn-keeper's sons here asked the question: "If," said he, to his father, "what you have learned is true, why did David say, 'In the middle of the night?'"

The father replied: "Because, as we have stated, at that time the rule and sovereignty of the Holy One makes itself felt by everyone."

Said the son: "There is another explanation which has been imparted to me."

Said Rabbi Abba: "Speak, my boy, and give it forth as I think the Voice of the Silence has spoken unto thee."

The boy spake and said: "Night is the time when judgments are decreed and determined upon, and during night they are executed in all places above and below. Why David used the term 'middle' was because the night is divided into two periods; the first of judgment, the other of mercy that causes the faces of all to become radiant with feelings of joy and delight."

Said Rabbi Abba, placing his hands on the head of the boy and blessing him, "I have always thought that wisdom was only to be found with those worthy of receiving it, now I see that in the life time of Rabbi Simeon, children are able to become possessors of heavenly wisdom and light. Blessed art thou, Rabbi Simeon. Woe to the world when thou goest hence." Until daybreak they continued their studies of the Secret Doctrine.

A FEAST OF THE CIRCUMCISION

SAID Rabbi Abba: "Scripture states, 'All thy people are righteous.' These words have been explained by the students initiates. Why are thy people called righteous? Were all the children of Israel upright and just? Were there not amongst them sinners and transgressors against the commandments of the law? Certainly there were. But let us learn from tradition what it teaches us respecting the esoteric meaning of these words. Blessed the lot of Israel who offer up sacrifices. The will of the Holy One is that they should sacrifice their sons to him on the eighth day after birth, from which time and after they become recipients of the good part that will never be taken from them, as it is written, 'The righteous One is the foundation of the world' (Troy. X. 25). When the rite of the covenant is duly performed, children enter into the blessing of the Holy One and are then accounted just and righteous, and therefore it is written of them, 'They shall inherit the land forever,' and also, 'Open unto me the gates of the righteous (zadecq) one that I may enter in; and further, 'This is the gate of the Lord, and the righteous shall enter therein' Ps. CXVIII. 20). Those who are circumcised are therefore termed righteous, and as we read, 'They shall inherit the land forever, the branch of my planting' (Is. LX. 21), which the Holy One has planted in the garden of Eden. Now the earth below is one of these plants, and therefore the children of Israel have a good part in the world to come and, as just stated, shall inherit the land forever. The esoteric meaning of the word "forever" has already been explained. The letter He (H) is not found in the name of Abraham until after his circumcision, when from Abram it was changed to Abraham. Then it was that the Schekina became attached to and abode with him, and therefore it is written, 'These are the generations of the heavens and the earth when they were created.' Now from tradition we are informed that the word 'behibaram' (when they were created) should be read, 'behe baram' (by or through Abraham). It may be objected, how can it be said the heavens and the earth were created by Abraham, who corresponds to the Sephir Hesed (mercy) on the Tree of Life, since we know also from tradition that the word 'belubaram' signifies that the heavens and the earth were created by the Schekina, of which the letter H is the symbol? Our reply is that these two traditions are not really contradictory to each other, but refer and amount to the same thing."

Said Rabbi Jacob to his father, Rabbi Abba: "The letter H in 'behibaram' is found written smaller in size than the other letters composing the word, but in the word halayehorah, which is found beginning the verse, 'Do ye thus requite the Lord, oh foolish people and unwise' (Deuter. XXXII. 6), it is written larger than the other letters in the Pentateuch. What is the reason of this difference between the two H's?"

Said Rabbi Abba: "The first H denotes that degree of divine life within the soul or lower self, that corresponds in signification with the sabbatical year that symbolizes it; the second larger H, that heavenly state of which the Jubilee is the symbol. Now, though the moon is at one time new and at another full, yet it is always one and the same notwithstanding its various phases, so is it with the mysterious Schekina that is distinguished by the smaller or larger letter H. Blessed is the lot of Israel in whom the Holy One delights more than any of her nation or people. As a token of his covenant with them, they perform the rite of circumcision, which whoever bears it shall never enter into Gehenna, for if he lives a chaste life, he will never be overcome by temptation nor break the vow taken in the name of the heavenly king. When a parent arranges and prepares for his son to enter into the covenant of circumcision, the Holy One summons all his celestial angels and says, 'Observe the child I have created in the world.' Then the prophet Elijah immediately descends at the time of the ceremony and takes the seat that has been placed apart for him and which the father is bound by law to declare at the same time, 'This seat is for Elijah the prophet.' Otherwise, the prophet refrains from taking it and forthwith ascends and testifies before the Holy One of what has occurred. Observe that at first the scriptures state, 'And the Lord came unto him and said, 'What doest thou here, Elijah?' And Elijah answered and said, 'I have been very zealous for the Lord God of hosts, because the children of Israel have forsaken thy covenant a,' (1 Kings XIX. 9-10). Then said God unto him, 'I swear by thy life that wherever and whenever my children shall practice and obey my covenant, there shalt thou be present and thy mouth which now testifies that the children of Israel have forsaken my covenant, shall also testify when they keep it.' We are also taught by tradition that Elijah was punished for making himself the accuser of God's children."

Thus they continued their studies in the secret doctrine until the day began to dawn, when Rabbi Abba and his son prepared to go their journey. Then spake the inn-keeper and said: "Ere you leave us, finish your remarks on the subject on which you have discoursed." On asking him what subject he meant, he answered: "Tomorrow you will behold and come into the presence of the Master who will be present here. It is the earnest desire and wish of my wife that you stay with us, as our son who has just been born unto us will be circumcised tomorrow."

Said Rabbi Abba: "The wish is a command, and we shall rejoice in seeing the Schekina and will postpone our departure." They stayed until the following night, when there was a gathering of all the friends of the host, who spent the time in the study of the secret doctrine, and no one slept that night.

CHAPTER XCVII.

"I WOULD like," said the host, "each one of you to give forth, according as he is able, some new idea or thought relative to the secret doctrine."

Then spake one of the guests and said: "It is written, 'Praise ye the Lord, for the avenging (biproa peraoth) of Israel when the people willingly offered themselves' (Jud. V. 2). Wherefore did Deborah and Barak begin this song with these words? We learn from tradition that the world stands and is established only on the divine covenant. As long as Israel continues to obey and conform to it by the rite of circumcision it will abide stable, but if it should, be which God forbid, that Israel neglect their duty and ignore the covenant, then the blessings accruing from the observance of it will cease coming into the world. Observe, no other nation or people will ever rule over Israel so long as it abides true and faithful to the covenant. What mean these words, 'Faithful to the covenant?' They indicate that when the command respecting the rite attached to the covenant is ignored, or in other words, when the worship of God is forsaken as was the case in the time of Deborah, as it is written, 'And the children of Israel did evil in the sight of the Lord and served Baalim and He delivered them into the hands of Sisera' (Jud. IV. 2); the meaning of these words is that they forsook God; that is, they neglected to perform the initiatory rite attached to the covenant which their forefathers, the patriarchs, had inaugurated and performed. When Deborah, however, appeared, she brought them to a sense of their infidelity towards God, so that they willingly and of their own accord (behithnadeb) returned to the observance of the law respecting the 'persia'[1] and found that obedience brought them blessings, together with overthrow and defeat of their enemies. We also learn from tradition that the Holy One said unto Joshua, 'The children of Israel are impure, they have ceased obeying the law respecting 'persia' and so have not entered into the covenant, and thou wishest to lead them into the holy land and overthrow their enemies, go and circumcise the children of Israel again.' And not until they had conformed to this injunction were they able to enter the Promised Land and conquer their foes. The same thing occurred when

---

[1] פרהסיא, from פרס, to declare openly--JBH.

Deborah appeared; and when by obedience they returned to the path of duty, victory attended their arms and blessings were again showered upon them and the world. This is why it is written, 'biproa peraoth' and by obeying the law respecting it willingly and of their own accord, they were able to say, 'barcou Iehovah,' praise for the renewal of his blessings."

Said another guest: "It is written, 'And it came to pass as Moses was journeying, the Lord met him in the inn and sought to kill him' (Ex. IV. 24). The question may here b asked, kill whom? Moses or his son. Moses most certainly, for the Holy One had said unto him: 'Thou art going to bring forth Israel out of Egypt and vanquish a great king and ruler, yet thou forgettest and neglectest to circumcise thy own son.' For this gross neglect on his part, he sought to kill him. Now we learn from tradition that the archangel Gabriel descended at this moment, enveloped in flaming fire to consume Moses and a serpent leaped out of it to destroy him. But why a serpent? The Holy One had said to Moses: 'Thou intendest to go and kill a mighty and powerful despot (pharaoh) and hast not circumcised thy son.' Then made he a sign to the serpent to kill him. At that moment Zepporah, his wife, appeared and, taking the boy, performed the rite at once, when the serpent let go his hold on Moses, as it is written, 'Then Zepporah took a sharp stone (tzour) and circumcised the son' (Ex. IV. 25). What does the word 'tzour' here denote? A remedy, an antidote, which was the rite of circumcision, to the performance of which she was impelled by an inner inspiration of the Holy Spirit, and thus saved the life of her husband."

Then spake another guest and said: "It is written, 'And Joseph said unto his brethren, come near me, I pray you' (Gen. XLV. 4); and they came near. Wherefore spake Joseph thus, as his brethren were already near him? It was because when he said unto them, 'I am Joseph your brother' they became filled with amaze and astonishment, seeing him head ruler of Egypt. Then said Joseph: "This is the cause of my elevation to the high position I occupy," and manifested the sign of the covenant he bore upon him. From this we infer that success and prosperity in life accrue sooner or later to everyone who observes the rite of the covenant and keeps himself pure and chaste. We are confirmed in this by the example of Boaz, concerning whom we read, 'As the Lord liveth, lie down until the morning' (Ruth III. 13). The tempter wished to lead Boaz into sin; but faithful and true to his oath, he resisted the temptation and thus kept pure the sign of the covenant. Therefore, he was honored in giving birth to those whose offspring became kings and rulers over all other kings, and also of becoming the ancestral progenitor of King Messiah who is called by the name of the Holy One.

Another guest spake and said: "It is written, 'Though a host should encamp against me, my heart shall not fear, though war should rise against me, in this (bezoth) will I be confident' (Ps. XXVII. 3). The word "bezoth" here denotes the sign of the covenant a man bears here below as on high, and this is why David said, 'In this will I be confident.' It is written, 'Zoth is the sign of the covenant' (Gen. IX. 12). 'Zoth is my covenant.' These zoths refer to one and the same sign of the divine life. We learn from tradition that ze, male, and zoth, female, are one and never separate. If it be said, then everyone, whether bearing the mark of the covenant or not, enjoys the blessings of it. Why should not everyone, as well as David, say the same words? But David was united with and enjoyed the presence of the Schekina, of which he was an image by virtue of the royal crown or diadem he wore. Observe, it was owing to his failure in preserving zoth in all its purity, that the kingdom was taken from him for a period, as tradition states. This zoth is impressed on the celestial kingdom as on Jerusalem the Holy City. When David by his sin in connection with Bathsheba transgressed against it, a voice from on high called unto him and said, 'Thou shalt reap the fruit of thy deeds. Thou shalt be ejected out of Jerusalem and the kingdom shall be taker from thee.' We learn this from the words of scripture, 'Behold, I will raise up evil against thee out of thine own house' (2 Sam. XII. II). Thus was David punished for breaking the covenant by his unchastity; and, as it was with him, so will it be with all others who likewise transgress against it."

Another guest spake and said: "It is written, 'Unless the Lord had been my help, my son would have dwelt in silence (duma)' (Ps. XCIV. 17). Through what are the children of Israel blessed that they descend not into Gehenna and come under the power of the angel Duma like other idolatrous nations' Because, as tradition informs us, when a man leaves the world, hosts of angels, the executors of justice, approach him, but on perceiving the sacred sign or token of the covenant he bears on him, they leave him and trouble not to deliver him unto the hands of Duma who sentences men to descend into Gehenna, the fate and doom of all those who are delivered into his power. The man who by chastity preserves himself pure, fears no judgment for he is united with the name of the Holy One. David failed to do this and in consequence lost his kingdom and was driven out of Jerusalem and feared greatly that the avenging angels would consign him into the hands of Duma, which would have meant for him eternal death (the annihilation of the soul through absolute separation from the higher self). This fear and terror abode with him until Nathan, the prophet, announced unto him the good news, 'The Lord hath taken away thy sin so thou shalt not die.' Then was it that David said, 'If the Lord had not been my help, my soul would have dwelt in hell.'"

Another guest spake and said: "'If I shall find favor in the eyes of the Lord, he will bring me again and make me to see his sign (otho) and his tabernacle' (2 Sam. XV. 25). Who can see the Holy One? Tradition states that when judgment was decreed and passed upon David, he knew it was owing to his sin in violating the sign of the covenant, for punishment attends everyone who transgresses against it and observes not its obligatory duties, which, if not performed, no one is accounted just, if he keep not himself pure and chaste in deed and thought. Knowing this, David prayed, 'If I find favor in the eyes of the Lord, he will answer me and make me to see his sign (otho) and tabernacle,' or as these words may be paraphrased, God grant me to see his holy token, for I tremble and fear because I have lost mine. What is meant by 'the token of God?' It denotes the sovereignty of Israel and Jerusalem. Nov he who lives unchastely forfeits the mark or token of God, that is the divine life in the soul."

Another guest spake and said: "It is written, 'And in my flesh shall I see my God, Eloha' (Job XIX. 26). What is meant by this expression, 'in my flesh'? Why said he not, rather, 'in myself'? If he really said 'in my flesh,' what did he mean? Job here alludes to the flesh which scriptures mentions, 'The holy flesh they have soiled' (yaabrou) (Jer. XI. 15), and also, 'My covenant shall be in your flesh for an everlasting covenant' (Gen. XVII. 13). We are taught whenever a man bears this token on him, he sees the Holy One himself, and when this occurs it is through the unification of the lower and higher selves, resulting in the Beatific Vision. If, however, he does not preserve purity of thought and act, scriptures states, this union ceases and becomes broken, and the soul or lower self perishes, going back and becoming resolved into its original elements out of which it has been prepared and built up, like as the material body returns to the dust out of which it has been formed; and therefore it is written, 'They lose the breath divine (minishmath Eloha).' The divine Schekina never separates from one who by his pure life and faithful obedience observed the good law, or covenant. If it be asked, when does the holy Spirit or divine life manifest itself in a man? it is when the union we have just mentioned is effected. It is the true, the divine, marriage when they twain become one flesh. From tradition we learn why the letters V and H are placed together in their alphabetical order. Vau being the symbol of the male and He that of the female principle, which are united and operate in combination with each other, as husband and wife, and from one becoming invested with a nimbus or covering of divine light that emanates from the male principle and known in scripture as grace (chesed), as it is written, 'The goodness (chesed) of God endureth continually' (Ps. LII. 1). This ray of divine light comes through the Sephira "supreme Wisdom" and penetrates the male principle, which is communicated to the female. Another tradition states that the name Aloha is separable into, al, V and H, al designating the light of wisdom, V the male principle and H the female principle, and their totality form Aloha. The holy soul or higher self, as it has been stated, is in intimate relationship with the nephesh or soul only so long as it keep itself pure and preserve intact the holy covenant, and therefore it is written, 'In my flesh shall I see God' (Aloha) (Job XIX. 26). A pure life, a pure soul, are reciprocal and convertible terms and never separated. Happy the lot of those who, attached to the Holy One, live the divine life, both in this world and the world to come. Of them it is written, 'Ye who have become joined unto the Lord your God are alive everyone of you this day' (Deuter. IV. 2). For theirs is the one true and divine life that they live."

After the guest had ceased speaking, Rabbi Abba addressed them thus: "How is it," said he, "that so mentally and spiritually enlightened, you are content to reside and live in such an obscure place, and are so versed in the teachings of the secret doctrine?"

They answered and said: "When the young birds leave their nests they know not whither to go, as it is written, 'As a bird wandereth from its nest so is a man that wandereth from his place' (Prov. XXVII. 9). Now this place is our nest and is suitably adapted for study of the secret doctrine. During the first part of the night we sleep. The other part we devote to study. When daybreak begins, the refreshing morning breezes and the light of the sun so invigorates us that we apply ourselves with renewed energy to meditation, and readily assimilate, digest and understand the teachings that come into our minds. A great calamity once happened in this place and a great many of illustrious and learned teachers perished, and which they might have escaped but for their neglect in the study of the secret doctrine. Made wise from their example and fate, we study assiduously by day and night, preferring to remain here because its situation is highly favorable and helpful to a student of life. He who leaves it would be as foolish as he who takes away his own life."

On hearing these words, Rabbi Abba raised his hands and blessed them. They were all sitting together and when day began to dawn, it was said to the young people who were there, "Go out and see if it is daybreak, and if it be so, then let each one address something to our excellent and esteemed guest, Rabbi Abba, and some remarks on the secret doctrine."

CHAPTER XCVIII.

THEY went out of the house and found the sun had already risen above the horizon. Then said one of them: "Today fire will descend from on high." Said another: "It will descend upon this house and envelope someone in flames." A third said: "It will be one who is in our midst and well on in years."

"God forbid that this should happen," exclaimed Rabbi Abba, who was exceedingly troubled, so that he was unable to speak. After a few moments, he became composed and said: "I perceive heaven is communicating to the earth and predicting through these children, events that will occur during the day."

The predictions proved true, respecting Rabbi Abba, for the joy he felt in the study of the secret doctrine was so great that his countenance and head became irradiated with a nimbus of light. All that day, the guest remained in the house and none went out of it. It was surrounded with something similar to a thin cloud of mist, and the friends assembled there experienced a sense of inward joy and delight so intense as that which was felt by the children of Israel when they received the law at Mount Sinai. So intent and absorbed were the guests in their meditations that when their meeting ended, they knew not whether it was day or night.

Then Rabbi Abba spake and said: "Whilst we are all present, let each one direct and concentrate his thoughts and speak on the subject of 'Wisdom,' that our host may be blessed and profited now that he is about to celebrate the feast of the circumcision."

Then stood up one of the guests and said: "It is written, 'Blessed is the man whom thou choosest and causest to approach unto thee, that he may dwell in thy courts. We shall be satisfied with the goodness of thy house, thy holy tabernacle' (Ps. LXV. 5). Observe in this verse the sequence of the words, court, house, tabernacle, in an ascending grade from the lower to the higher. To dwell in thy courts, is to dwell in Jerusalem and be accounted holy, as it is written, 'He that remaineth in Jerusalem shall be called holy'

(Is. IV. 3), and also, 'We shall be satisfied with the goodness of thy house.: 'Through wisdom a house is builded and by understanding it is established' (Prov. XXIV. 3). By the word wisdom, allusion is made to the occult words, 'And a river went forth out of Eden to water the garden.' 'Thy holy tabernacle,' then, is the higher and supreme degree of divine life, for the term "hecal" (tabernacle) is the same as he-cal (there is everything), the tabernacle being the perfection and union of all things. The beginning of the verse confirms this interpretation. 'Happy is the man whom thou choosest that he may dwell in thy courts.' He who offers as a sacrifice to the Holy One his own son by causing him to undergo the rite of circumcision, becomes a friend and servant of the Holy One and enables him to dwell also in the house and tabernacle or the secret place of the Most High. The word "hatzerekha" (thy courts) is here found in the plural and includes house and tabernacle. It is for this reason that true men and faithful servants of the covenant, when the rite was performed, were accustomed to recite this verse in the following way, one of the assistants repeated the words, 'blessed is he whom thou choosest to approach unto thee.' Another said, 'we shall be satisfied with the goodness of thy house.'

Then followed the benediction pronounced by the child' father: "Blessed be thou, Lord and Master of the universe who hast sanctified us and commanded us to bring this child unto the covenant of Abraham our father." The witnesses then say, 'God grant that as you have caused thy child to enter into the covenant, so may thou also initiate him into the secret doctrine respecting marriage and good works.' We know from tradition that a man ought first of all to pray for mercies to be extended to himself and then to others, as it is written, 'Make atonement for himself and for his household and for all the congregation of Israel' (Lev. XVI. 17). We think this a precept that should be always followed."

Said Rabbi Abba: "Truly and rightly so, and he who neglects and ignores it excludes himself and enters not into the ten canopies or pavilions which the Holy One has prepared for the righteous in the world to come and for all who obey this injunction. For this reason the words of this verse are ten in number, corresponding each of them to one of these pavilions. Blessed is your lot in this world and the world to come, for the secret doctrine is written in your hearts as though you had been in bodily form at Mount Sinai when the law was given forth to the children of Israel.

Said another guest: "It is written, 'An altar of earth shalt thou make unto me and sacrifice thereon thy burnt offerings and thy peace offerings' (Ex. XX. 24). We are taught that everyone who brings his child as a sacrifice, or in other words, causes him to be circumcised, makes an offering the greatest and most acceptable that can be rendered to the Holy One, and also the altar he makes is the most perfect that can be possibly made. Therefore, at the performance of this rite it is necessary that there be an altar consisting of a vase filled with earth, into which is cast the prepuce, this being accounted by the Holy One as an offering equally as agreeable and acceptable to him as the sacrifice of sheep and oxen, and therefore it is further written, 'Where I record my name, I will come unto thee and will bless thee.' What do the words, 'where I record my name' signify? They allude to the sign of the covenant, as it is written, 'The secret or mystery of the Lord is with them that fear him, and he will show them his covenant' (Ps. XXV. 14). Further it is added, 'If thou wilt make me an altar of stone, thou shalt build it of unhewn stones, for if thou lift up thy tool upon it, thou hast polluted it' (Ex. XX. 25). These words refer to heathen converts to Judaism who are generally stiff-necked and hard of heart, and therefore termed an altar of stone. 'Thou shalt built it of unhewn stones' signify those who have the desire to serve and worship the Holy One, who enjoins that no gentile convert should undergo the rite of the covenant until he has renounced his former religion and parted with his hardness of heart, as his conversion would prove vain and of no good effect. He would be like unto a stone, carved and polished outside but interiorly is still rough and hard. The real meaning then of these words is, unless the heart is softened by entering into the covenant, it is of no benefit whatever, either to them who take part in the ceremony or bear the sign on them. Happy is he who in this pleases the Holy One by this offering of his son unto him, for he will rejoice daily, as it is written, 'But let them rejoice, all they who put their trust in thee, let hem shout for joy because thou dwellest with them, let them also that love thy name be joyful in thee'" (Ps. V. 11).

Said another guest: "It is written, 'And Abraham was ninety and nine years old and the Lord appeared unto him, and said unto him, I am the Almighty God, walk thou before me and be thou perfect' (Gen. XVII. 1). This verse needs critical examination, as it abounds with several difficulties that require explanation. It may be asked, had not the Holy One appeared unto Abraham before attaining unto this age, which might be inferred from the words of this verse. In previous accounts of the divine manifestations no mention whatever is made of Abraham's age. It is simply said, 'the Lord said unto Abraham * * *.' Another difficult question is, how was it that before Abraham had reached this age, scripture nowhere states that the Lord appeared unto him? It was because that up to that time he was uncircumcised, and it was only after he had performed the rite the Holy One revealed himself in a way and manner he had never done before, and therefore scripture states, 'And the Lord appeared unto him.' But why did the Lord appear and manifest himself to Abraham on this particular occasion? Because he wished to make known unto him the relation existing between the sign of the covenant and that most sublime degree of elevation in the divine life, termed the "Holy Crown." Moreover, the Holy One intended that from Abraham should proceed a people and nation wholly sanctified unto himself; it was essential that he himself should first become such, which did not occur until he had attained to the age of ninety-nine years. Another reason why scripture states this age of Abraham is, that until he had attained thereunto, his years were not reckoned or taken any account of and only began to be so when he became circumcised at this advanced age. When the Lord appeared unto him and said, 'I am the Almighty God' (El Shaddai). Why up to this time had he not appeared unto him and announced himself by this name? Respecting this question tradition informs us that at the creation of the world, he made higher and lower spheres, some of the latter of which were void of holiness and spiritual life, such as the world of elementals who are able to influence those in this earth who are uncircumcised and who become impressed with their mark, the letters S and D denoting they are soiled and subject to the influence of the evil one. But as soon as men are circumcised, they become freed from the influence of the elementals and live under the wings or protection of the Schekina. It is then that the Yod (I), symbol of the sign of the Covenant, becomes impressed upon them and they bear on them the full-divine name Shaddai (S D I). When this occurred in the case of Abraham, then, as stated, the Lord appeared unto him and said unto him, 'I am the Almighty God,' (El Shaddai) 'walk thou before me and be thou perfect' (thanaim), which word signifies full and complete. In other words, he said, until now the mark thou hast borne is incomplete, being composed only of the letters S and D. Circumcise now thyself, then wilt thou bear my full and complete name of Shaddai, for whoever bears it is blessed, as it is written, 'And God Almighty (Al Shaddai) bless thee' (Gen. XXVIII. 3). It is from him that all blessings come. He it is who rules the inferior worlds that tremble and fear before him, so that they are unable to exercise any influence over those who bear on them the full sign of the covenant who will never descend or fall into Gehenna, as it is written, 'Thy people also shall be all righteous'" (Is. LX. 21).

A FEAST OF CIRCUMCISION (CONTINUED)

WHAT is truly so, but what tradition teaches us respecting this, is, when the yod (I) is united with teeth (H) they form a celestial river, as it is written, "And a river went out of Eden to water the garden.' Let no one, however, object and say, 'when they are united,' as though it was something impossible and absurd; for they most certainly become so, and after this manner scripture uses the expression 'ben horin,' and such also is the meaning of the words, 'blessed the land whose king is a "ben horin," and whose princes eat in due season (with delight and thankfulness).' The preceding verse runs thus, 'Woe to the land whose king is a child,' referred to the world below, for we learn by tradition that all lands inhabited by idolatrous nations and people are under the rule of great chiefs who themselves are governed and controlled by one to whom scripture refers, as saying, 'I was a child, and now am old, yet have I not seen the righteous forsaken' (Ps. XXXVII. 25). These are the words of the prince of this world, who terms himself a child (naar). 'Woe unto the world when it is sustained and ruled by him. When Israel is in captivity and exile, then is he as one who derives his food and nourishment from a foreign land not his own.' 'Whose princes eat in due season' for they eat only in the morning and evening, when tradition informs us judgment prevails in the world, at the rising and setting of the sun, by whose worship gentile idolators offend and excite the anger of the Holy One. The evils and afflictions that befall the world are therefore owing to the prevalent sway and rule over the earth of the evil one, who is here termed a child (naar). Blessed are all ye that are present on this occasion, for ye are fellow citizens with the saints and children of the Holy King and are nourished not with worldly food, but with the bread of heaven; and of you it is written, 'ye are all joined unto the Lord and are found alive unto this day'." (Deuter. IV. 4.)

Then spake and said Rabbi Abba, at the close of the ceremony: "It is written, 'now will I sing to my well beloved, a song of my beloved touching his vineyard. My beloved hath a vineyard in a very fruitful hill (qeren ben shamen) and he fenced it and gathered out the stones thereof and planted it with the choicest vines' (Is. V. 1). These words have a deeply esoteric meaning and therefore demand most thoughtful consideration on account of the difficulties arising in the exposition of them. The first is why is the word song (sherath) here found instead of the term (reproof). Why also is it said, 'to my well beloved,' (lebidi) instead of 'to my friend?' Again, what is the meaning of the expression 'my well beloved had a vineyard in a very fruitful hill' or, as it should be rendered, a vineyard in Qeren ben Shamen? We have studied long the secret doctrine and have failed to find any mention of a place or locality so called.

"Many and various excellent explanations have been given by esoteric students who have interpreted this verse, as follows: 'I will sing to my well beloved,' refer to the patriarch Isaac, called and known as "well beloved" before his entry into earth life, because he was greatly beloved by the Holy One and was not born until after Abraham had entered into the divine covenant and attained to that degree of initiation in divine life and science symbolized by the letter A, indicative of full adeptship. This degree was also imparted to Sarah, and is typified by this letter being added to her name and that of Abram. The addition of this letter may be further elucidated and explained thus: A is the symbol of the female principle; this being so, it may be asked, why was it added to the name of Abram instead of the letter Yod (I), the symbol of the male principle. The explanation involves a great mystery. Abraham attained to the highest degree of initiation, symbolized as we have just stated by the first letter in the divine name, I H V H, that has its polarity in the last or lower letter (H). The first being symbol of the male, the last, of the female. It is written, 'and he said unto them,' 'so (Coh) shall thy seed be,' referring to the multiplication of his posterity who should attain to the same degree of divine life and science as himself. Hence it is that every gentile that enters into the Covenant is called ger zedek (a true proselyte) and becomes a son or child of Abraham. Therefore, said God unto him, 'so shall thy seed be,' or in other words, all gentiles who enter into the Covenant shall be of thee and called by thy name.

"This, then, was why the letter H was added to the name ' Abram. Had Sarah only attained this H or degree, the posterity of Abram would then have been only children of the lower degree of divine life and knowledge or merely proselytes, here designated by the name of Coh. Owing, however, to the addition of the higher H symbolizing the divine life, to Abram, and the lower H to the name of Sara, it became possible to engender and bring forth offspring who would be able to attain to the same degree of initiation in divine life as their ancestors, Abraham and Sarah. The union of the two H's produced the yod or I, the first letter in the name of Isaac (yitzchak) emblem of the male principle, which from the time of his birth, began to increase upon the earth; that is to say, from the time of the birth of Isaac, men began to be born and come into the world who lived the higher and diviner life, and therefore it is written, 'for in Isaac shall thy seed be called' (Gen. XXI. 12). Isaac in his turn begat offspring susceptible of attaining to the life symbolized by the higher H, as it is written, 'thou wilt perform the truth to Jacob' (Mich. VII. 20), and Jacob was the highest manifestation of what it does and can accomplish in man, If, however, it be objected: was not this exhibited more so in the life of Abraham than on any of his posterity, as it is stated of him, 'thou gayest grace to Abraham?' (Micha-ibid); in reply we say that Abraham exercised mercy to men. It was, however, Isaac who contributed most to the sanctification of humanity, for Abraham was far advanced in life, being ninety and nine years old when he entered into covenant with the Holy One, the mystical meaning of which is known to and understood by students of the secret doctrine and its occult teachings.

CHAPTER C.

AT the birth of Isaac, justice became united to mercy; these divine attributes, symbolized by the patriarchs Isaac and Abraham, became blended in the person of Jacob, their offspring; and, therefore, it is written, 'Thou art my servant, oh Israel, in which I will be glorified' (Is. XLIX. 3).

"Notwithstanding what has just been stated, we can divine why scriptures uses the word song (sherath), and 'I will sing to my well beloved.' These words refer to Isaac, who was so called before his birth in the world. Another interpretation applies them to Abraham, as it is written, 'What doth my beloved in my house' (Jer. XI. 15). Now it is true, Abraham acquired by merit what his posterity afterwards inherited and enjoyed. The words 'the song of my beloved for his vineyard,' refer to the Holy One who is called 'beloved,' as it is written, 'My beloved (dodi) is white and ruddy (Cant. V.10). We observe the terms ledidi (well beloved) and dodi (my beloved or friend) are joined together, and from their union of the male and female principle comes forth a vineyard planted in Qeren ben Shamen, which appellation, indicates its origin and nature. Qeren has here the same meaning as in the words, 'And it shall come to pass when they make a long blast with the Qeren Hayyabel (the horn of Jubilee)' (Josh. VI. 5). Thus the vineyard has for its origin the Jubilee or the deliverance, and this horn or trumpet of deliverance is associated with the male principle, termed here ('Ben Shamen,' which has the same meaning as the term 'ben horin' (son of nobles) (Eccles. X. 7). It also means 'son of the oil,' because of the source whence the oil flows, for supplying all the heavenly lamps whose light becomes more intense in proportion to its abundance. Furthermore, at the coronation of kings, this oil is poured into a horn, called the horn of Jubilee, and for this reason no one is crowned except he is first anointed with oil from this horn. On account of this the reign of David was of long duration.

"It is further added, 'And he fenced it (vajatzqchou) with a fence like a ring on the finger.' The words, 'and gathered out the stones thereof,' denote that he separated it and so arranged that it should not be under the rule and government of the spiritual chiefs that hold authority over idolatrous nations; and, having freed and delivered it from evil demoniacal influences and force, he chose this vineyard for his own possession, as it is written, 'He chose his people for his portion, and took Jacob for his inheritance' (Deuter. XXXII. 9). 'And he planted it with the choicest vine.' 'Which words have the same meaning as the verse, 'I have planted thee a choice (soreq) vine, wholly (couloh) a right seed' (Jer. II. 21). The word couloh is here written with a final H, symbol of the grade on the divine life to which Abraham attained and then gave rise to offspring to whom was imparted divine truth which made them righteous. The words, 'Thus (coh) shall thy seed be,' have the same esoteric meaning. Blessed is the lot of Israel who possess such a holy inheritance.

"The second part of the verse is, 'And he built a tower in the midst of it.' What is here the mystical meaning of the word tower? It is the same as that of the words, 'The name of the Lord is a strong tower, the righteous runneth, into it and is safe' (Prov. XVIII. 9). It is further added, 'and also made a wine-press therein,' referring to the gate of the Just, as it is written, 'Open unto me the gates of righteousness' (Ps. CXVIII. 19). How know we that at the time of circumcision every Israelite enters into the tower of the Just and the gates of righteousness? Or how know we that whoever offers his son as a sacrifice, that is, causes him to undergo the rite of the covenant, initiates him into the mystery of the sacred name on which heaven and earth are both founded? We are assured of it from the words, 'Thus saith the Lord, if my covenant had not been made with day and night, I should not have prescribed the laws that govern heaven and earth' (Jer. XXXIII. 25). Blessed is the master of this house, who by his obedience to the law and rite of the covenant has enjoyed the presence of the Holy One this day. Blessed also are we who have been present on this occasion as witnesses of it. To this child, I shall apply the words of scripture, 'Everyone that is called by my name, I have created him for my glory. I have formed him, yea, I have made him' (Is. XLIII. 3), and also the verse, 'And all thy children shall be taught of the Lord, and great shall be the peace of thy children' (Is. LIV. 13).